Framing Iberia

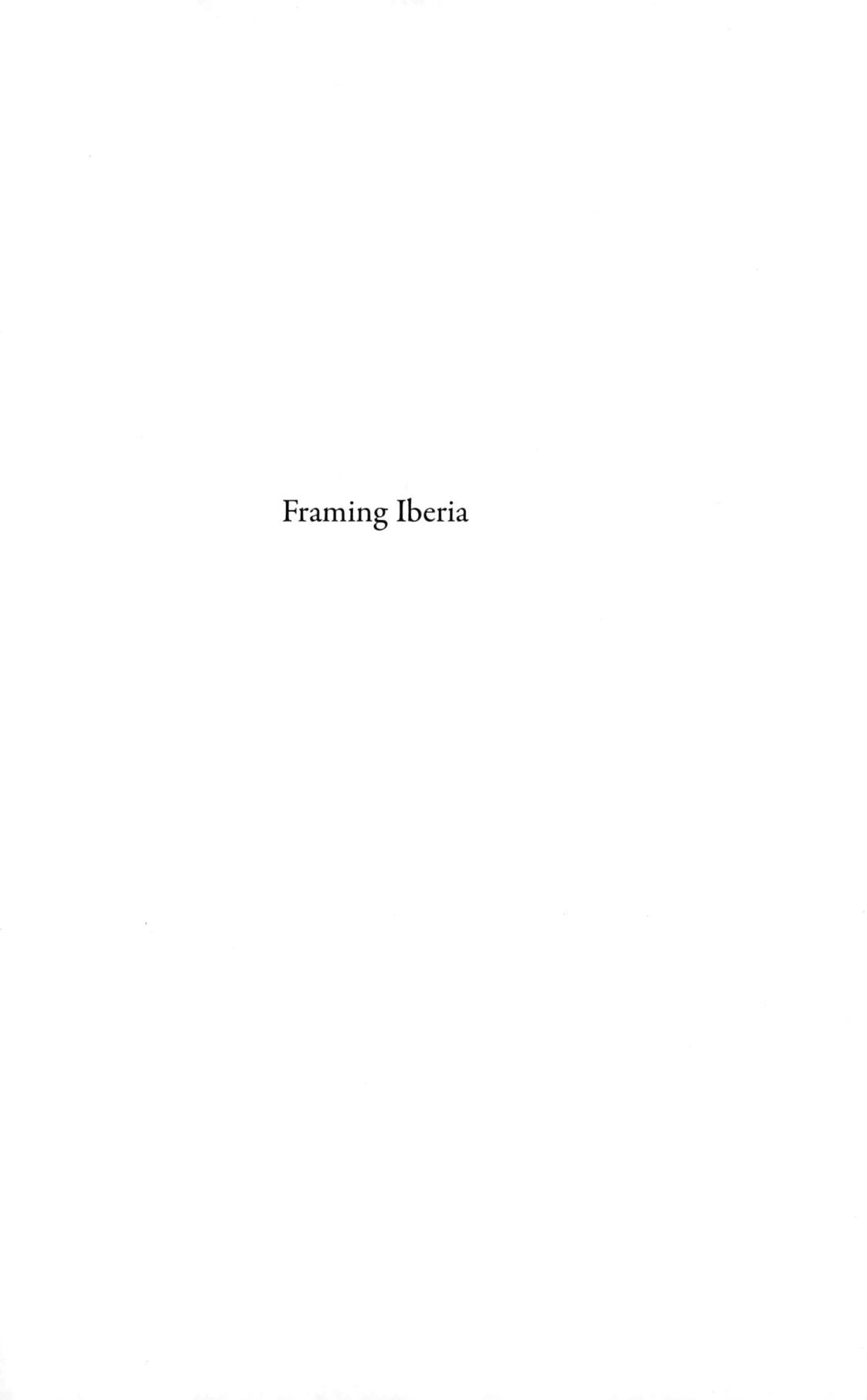

The Medieval and Early Modern Iberian World

Editors

Larry J. Simon (Western Michigan University)
Gerard Wiegers (Radboud University Nijmegen)
Arie Schippers (University of Amsterdam)
Donna M. Rogers (Dalhousie University)
Isidro J. Rivera (University of Kansas)

VOLUME 33

Framing Iberia

Maqāmāt and Frametale Narratives in Medieval Spain

by

David A. Wacks

BRILL

LEIDEN • BOSTON
2007

Cover Illustration: Door of the Great Mosque of Córdoba
©Photograph by Gregory Hutcheson (2006)

This book is printed on acid-free paper.

ISSN 1569-1934
ISBN 978 90 04 15828 3

PRINTED IN THE NETHERLANDS

For Katharine

CONTENTS

ACKNOWLEDGEMENTS

When I was a young boy in Hebrew school, the teacher gave me a blue notebook that opened from left to right (the "wrong" way), in which we would practice writing the letters of the Hebrew alphabet. On the cover was a portrait of Maimonides, a stern, authoritative-looking guy with a long but tastefully formed beard wearing a turban. This portrait, and the force of Hebrew learning and tradition it represented to an eight-year-old boy, was possibly my first encounter with medieval Iberian culture. Thus I was taught (if not explicitly) that Spain was a place of great Jewish learning whose eminent figures were role models and intellectual heroes.

Eventually I learned that Spain was also a modern country, with a modern national language—Spanish, that was promising to become the second national language of the United States. Some years before demographers began to predict the imminent Hispanization of the US, my father encouraged me to study Spanish, in the hopes that it would give me some advantage in what he imagined to be the hispanophone future of our country. Having studied Hebrew as a child, I found Spanish somewhat easier to digest and in any event quite to my liking. A period of study in Madrid as an undergraduate confirmed this, but also opened my eyes to the intriguing question of Spain's medieval past. Here, I thought, was a country that very obviously possessed a rich, multicultural and multireligious past. Yet Spaniards seemed to me to be very alienated from any part of their past that they viewed as "Semitic," that is, having to do with Islam, Judaism, Arabic, Hebrew, or practically any aspect of what we might call Andalusī or Sephardic culture.

In my first teaching job out of college, I taught English as a Second Language in a now-defunct public junior high school on Manhattan's Lower East Side, where I experienced an intense sort of North American *convivencia*. The school's students were divided between Spanish-speaking Catholics from the Dominican Republic and Muslims from Bangladesh (there was also a single student from Poland), and the faculty were largely US-born Jews or Latinos from either the US or Latin America. Watching these groups interact in a real-life, intensely urban setting, I began to reflect back on my impressions of Spain's vanished multiculturalism and what life must have been like in the Castile-León of Don Juan Manuel and Juan Ruiz. These authors lived in a society that in some ways resembled the US urban jumble of ethnic and religious groups brought together by a common vernacular—English, and the daily realities of sharing space and resources. The combination of these three visions of medieval Iberia, the Sephardic Maimonides of Hebrew school, the contemporary specter of modern Spain's multicultural past, and the very immediate experience of gritty Lower Manhattan *convivencia*, combined to propel me into a career as a student of medieval Iberian culture, especially in its Arabic, Hebrew, Latin, and Romance literary traditions, that so far has been a blast.

I would like to begin my acknowledgements, then, by recognizing those who helped to plant the seeds of what would grow to become an obsession, and serendipitously, a career. Thanks to my teachers at the religious school at Temple Emunah in Lexington, Massachusetts, where I first encountered Maimonides' stern visage. Thanks to my instructors, and in particular Prof. Francisco Bustos, at the Universidad Complutense, where I studied in 1989–1990, and to my students and fellow teachers at the Marta Valle Junior High School (JHS #25), NYC Board of Education District 1, where I worked in 1991–1992.

As this book began life as my doctoral dissertation, I would like to thank Prof. Charles Faulhaber (UC Berkeley), who directed my dissertation, and Profs. James Monroe, Ignacio Navarrete (UC Berkeley), and Sam Armistead (UC Davis), who supported the project as readers. All of them provided indispensable input, painstaking edits, and support both intellectual and moral. Several colleagues were good enough to read preliminary drafts of individual chapters and provide very useful suggestions, including Shamma Boyarin (UC Berkeley), and Professors John Dagenais (UC Los Angeles), Vincent Barletta (U Colorado), Ivonne del Valle (U Michigan), Judith Dishon (Bar Ilan U), Luis Girón Negrón (Harvard U), Michelle Hamilton (UC Irvine), Gregory Hutcheson (U Louisville), Sharon Kinoshita (UC Santa Cruz), John Tolan (U Nantes), and Tania Triana (U Oregon). In addition, I would like to thank my senior medievalist colleagues at the University of Oregon, Professors Barbara Altmann, Regina Psaki, Judith Baskin, Warren Ginsberg, and James Earl, all of whom have been extremely helpful and generous with their time and suggestions while I worked on this project. Thanks also to the staff, faculty, and students of the Department of Romance Languages and Literatures at the University of Oregon for their collegiality, sharp insights, and moral support.

Completion of this project has been made possible by financial support from a number of sources. From Fall 2003 through Spring 2005 I worked on it while teaching in the Department of Romance Languages and Literatures at the University of Oregon. The College of Arts and Sciences of the University of Oregon provided me with a Summer Research Award in 2005, during which time I was able to revise two chapters. In the fall of 2005 I was the recipient of a Faculty Research Fellowship at the Oregon Humanities Center, where I revised the remaining chapters. A Starr Fellowship in Judaica at the Harvard Center for Jewish Studies during Spring 2006 provided me with the time necessary to prepare the manuscript for submission to the publisher. I would also like to thank the Dean's Office of the College of Arts and Sciences at the University of Oregon and the Oregon Humanities Center, both of whom contributed funds to pay for copyediting expenses. Their generous support has been key in bringing this project to completion.

All translations that appear in this study are mine unless otherwise indicated. Hebrew words are transliterated using a modified form of the conventions used by the *Jewish Studies Quarterly*. Arabic words are transliterated using a modified form of the conventions used by the *Encyclopedia of Islam*. In Arabic and Hebrew proper names I have suppressed diacritics if the name in question is commonly known (i.e., Ibn Rushd and not Ibn Rušd, Baghdad and not Baġdād), but maintained them in the case of more obscure figures and places (al-Saraqusṭī and not al-Saraqusti).

TRANSLITERATION OF ARABIC

أ	a	غ	ġ
ب	b	ف	f
ت	t	ق	q
ث	ṯ	ك	k
ح	ḥ	ل	l
ج	j	م	m
خ	kh	ن	n
د	d	ه	h
ذ	ḏ	و	u (vowel), w (semivowel)
ر	r	ى	à
ز	z	ي	ī (vowel), y (semivowel)
س	s	َ	a
ش	š	ُ	u
ص	ṣ	ِ	i
ض	ḍ	ّ	doubled consonant
ط	ṭ	ء	ʾ
ظ	ẓ	ة	suppressed after ´
ع	ʿ		

TRANSLITERATION OF HEBREW

א	ʾ	פּ	p
ב	v	צ	ts
בּ	b	ק	q
ג	g	ר	r
ד	d	שׁ	š
ה	h	שׂ	s
ו	v	ת	t
ז	z	◌ְ	-
ח	ḥ	◌ִ	i
ט	ṭ	◌ִי	ī
י	y	◌ֵ	e
כ	kh	◌ֶ	e
כּ	k	◌ַ	a
ל	l	אֲ, אָ	ā
מ	m	◌ָ	a
נ	n	◌ֹ	o
ס	s	◌ֻ	ū
ע	ʿ	וּ	ū
פ	f		

INTRODUCTION

This book is the story of how medieval Iberians tell stories in writing. It is a story as yet untold, except in more narrowly focused studies of short narrative in Catalan, Castilian, Hebrew, Arabic, and Latin. Because authors native to medieval Iberia wrote collections of stories and tales in all of these languages, it made sense to me to try to include texts from all of these linguistic traditions in constructing a narrative of a medieval Iberian tradition of narrative collections including frametales[1] and *maqāmāt*.

Each of the authors studied here engages in their literary practice from a different perspective, according to the changing political, social, linguistic, religious, and literary circumstances of medieval Iberian life, but all of these circumstances converge at one point or another. The resulting tradition of frametales and *maqāmāt* is unique to the Iberian Peninsula during the late Middle Ages, and here serves as a literary lens through which to consider the fascinating and very complex cultural history of medieval Iberia.

What name do we attach to the resulting narrative culture? The familiar metaphors—melting pot, hybrid, cross-pollination—seem insufficient. Fraught as they are with the weight of usage and context, none of these alone can encapsulate a literary practice that spans four hundred years, three religions, several languages, and an untold number of individual life experiences. Any term you care to think of is problematic, its referent hopelessly afield from the historical realities[2] of medieval Iberia. Without dallying too long in the groves of deconstruction and semantics, I would like to take a solemn moment to acknowledge my shortcomings on this question of nomenclature. What follows is a short glossary of terms that I use in this study. I have adapted some from contemporary post-colonial critical thought, though a full accounting of the origins and uses of these terms falls outside the scope of the present study. Most I will revisit in the subsequent chapters; others I submit to the reader as points of departure for the engagement of

---

[1] I use the word 'frametale' without hyphens intentionally, though historically it has been either written as two separate words 'frame tale', or hyphenated 'frame-tale'. As it is a natural progression in English word formation for compound words to begin as two separate words, then become hyphenated, then finally merge into a single word, I am simply doing my part for progress as has been defined by historical linguists.

[2] I use this term with a nod to Américo Castro's *La realidad histórica de España*.

post-modern (and post-colonial) critical discourse with medieval Iberian cultural history.

- *Multicultural*: a term predicated on the existence of a participatory democracy in which all racial, ethnic, linguistic, religious, and cultural groups are entitled to access to, and representation in, public discourse and political power. It has a strong association with questions of primary and secondary school curricula in the United Kingdom, Australia, and the US. Here I use it to refer to the simple fact of coexistence (without consideration of power dynamic) of members of different religious, ethnic, or linguistic communities of practice.
- *Medieval Iberia*: the lands of the Iberian Peninsula, during the Middle Ages.[3] While I will not attempt an authoritative definition of the Middle Ages, the period under consideration in this study is approximately 711–1492 CE.[4]
- *Spain*: the lands that now constitute the modern nation state.
- *Spanish*: subject of the united kingdoms of Castile-León and Aragón, beginning with the fall of Granada and Expulsion of the Jews in 1492.
- *Sefarad*: the Hebrew word for the Iberian Peninsula, referring to medieval Iberia as experienced by its Jewish communities. It is still used by Sephardic Jews (the descendents of the Jews expelled from Spain) to refer to their ancestral homeland.
- *al-Andalus*: The Arabic word for the Iberian Peninsula, referring to the lands of the Iberian Peninsula ruled by Muslim monarchs. To this day it is used in the Arab world with this same meaning.
- *Andalusī*: An adjective describing the inhabitants and culture of al-Andalus (and not modern day Andalusia).
- *Reconquest*: The traditional and ideologically burdened term to describe the centuries-long struggle between Christian and Muslim polities on the Iberian Peninsula. In its broadest sense it can be said to extend from 711 to 1492. I deal with the problematics of this term in chapters 1 and 3, relative to my discussions of Petrus Alfonsi and the Castilian translation of *Kalīla wa-Dimna*. In its stead I use the term (mouthful though it may be) "Christian conquest of al-Andalus."

[3] On the question of the construction of "Iberia" in the context of twentieth-century Spanish political and social change, see the very thorough article of Sáez-Arance.

[4] For clarity's sake, throughout the rest of this study I will refer to dates using the Gregorian calendar years without a suffix, except for dates in the years before the Common Era (BCE).

- *Acculturation*: A term coined by the anthropologist Melville Herskovits to describe how the cultural practices of dominant groups are adopted by minority groups.[5] The term has recently come under some fire for not being critical (enough) of the power dynamic that obtains between, for example, colonizing and subaltern groups. Here I would like it to refer to the learning of a cultural practice from one community of practice by another, or perhaps to the redefinition of a community of practice by the introduction of new members formerly considered outsiders.
- *Hybridity*: A term borrowed by cultural studies relatively recently from biology, where it refers to the (often sterile) offspring of the male of one species and the female of another. In the study of human culture, it generally refers to anything "abstractly heterogeneous in origin or composition" (Stross 254). Contemporary cultural critics have objected to its use to describe human cultural practice and identity because it infers the genetic superiority of one parent over another.[6] Homi Bhaba sees hybridity as a dynamic, emergent phenomenon, in constant reaction to historical circumstances.[7] In Hispanic studies, it has been most famously adapted by the Argentine critic Nestor García Canclini.[8]
- *Colonial*: While the circumstances of medieval Iberian colonialism differ significantly from early modern and modern colonialisms, here it refers to the conquest, settlement, and administration of formerly Muslim lands of the Iberian Peninsula by Christian Iberians.
- *Transculturation*: A term coined by anthropologist Fernando Ortiz in his study of Cuban culture. Ortiz builds on the ideas of acculturation and the biological metaphor of hybridity, acknowledging that the 'child' of the two parent cultures, while possessing characteristics of both parents, has a unique genetic signature, personality, and experience (260). In this, Ortiz anticipates contemporary post-colonial thinkers by stressing the emergent quality of transculturation.

---

[5] Writing in 1938, Herskovits rejected as purely subjective the binary acculturation-assimilation, by which the former assumed an equal power balance between the two groups in contact and the latter assumed an imbalance (9).

[6] This assumption has been criticized (among others) by Easthope (341).

[7] "The social articulation of difference, from the minority perspective, is a complex, ongoing negotiation that seeks to authorize cultural hybridities that emerge in moments of historical transformation" (2). For an overview of the reception of the term in contemporary critical thought, see Mabardi.

[8] García Canclini prefers hybridization because it is not racial (*mestizaje*), religious (syncretism), or limited to the "combination of traditional symbolic movements" (2).

- *Frontier/Border*: The former tends to evoke the popular cowboys and Indians and Alamo narratives and official histories that still dominate public discourse about the US Western frontier during the nineteenth century. In Spanish, especially when referring to medieval Iberia, *fronterizo* refers to people or cultural practices (such as historical ballads) that are products of the frontier zone between al-Andalus and Christian Iberia. In contemporary US cultural thought, 'border' refers to the people or cultural practices native to the US/Mexico borderlands.[9] Because 'border' is (as yet) so historically specific,[10] I use the term 'frontier' (as both adjective and noun) instead. In order to maintain some critical distance from the traditional Spanish sense of *fronterizo*, I use the term 'frontier' with an awareness of the power dynamic that obtained in the Andalusī-Christian Iberian contact zone.

I define these terms with the understanding (as befits a good post-modern subject) that they are ultimately insufficient to the task at hand and that a certain leap of faith is necessary in order to be able to proceed. The texts that are the subject of this study are all products of very different authors writing in very different cultural moments. What unites them is a common geography—the Iberian Peninsula—and a dynamic unity of narrative practice that gains a critical density in Iberia between the 12th and 15th centuries. That is, they have in common both stories and ways of telling stories that are in constant flux.

Throughout these chapters, I have used various terms to try to describe these moments and interactions. I admit that the word 'multicultural' (as per my comments above), with its roots in the identity politics of the post-modern, post-Commonwealth Anglophone world, may not be the ideal term to describe medieval Iberian society. It is useful, however, in that it attempts to avoid privileging one linguistic or cultural tradition over another. This is not to say—by any stretch of the imagination—that the authors of these texts all enjoyed a perfect political and social equality irrespective of their individual religion or literary language. Let me be perfectly clear: to be a Christian or a Jew in al-Andalus or a Jew or Muslim in Christian Iberia was to be a subaltern, a minority, a less-enfranchised member of society. Hebrew

---

[9] On border culture and critical thought, see Paredes, Anzaldúa, Arteaga, Michaelsen and Johnson, Saldívar, and Martinez.

[10] Walter Mignolo has already loosed 'border' from its historical moorings (pun intended, *con perdón*) along the US/Mexican border and applied it to global cultural dynamics (250–66).

was not accorded the same prestige in the Christian and Muslim communities as it was in the Jewish, and so forth for Arabic, Latin, and the various Romance dialects. The rosy *convivencia* envisioned by Américo Castro has long been deconstructed. Christians, Jews, and Muslims had to share space, resources, languages, and at times a common vernacular culture, but that is as far as it goes. There were bitter political struggles and bloody military confrontation between Christian and Muslim, but also among Christians and among Muslims. There were productive alliances between the three groups as well, in various combinations. The historian Brian Catlos has recently introduced a second model, that of *conveniencia*, by which individuals are defined not first by religion, but by occupation, hometown, family, or sex. To this I would add a third way of understanding the cultural jumble of medieval Iberia: one of *contravivencia*, an agonistic yet productive symbiotic relationship in which each participant is a *sine qua non* in the construction of the other's identity and cultural formation. This coexistence—however one chooses to conceptualize it—of Muslims, Jews, and Christians is one of the most salient features of medieval Iberian culture and is reflected in many forms of cultural practice, one of which is the tradition of frametale and *maqāma* literature that is the object of this study.

The frametale is a type of prose narrative fiction in which a series of unrelated tales or episodes is narrated by characters in an overarching story that provides a context and a pretense for the narration of the tales. The best known frametale is probably the Arabic *Thousand and One Nights*,[11] in which Shahrazād evades execution by narrating a new tale each night to King Shahryār. In European literature its most famous examples are Chaucer's *Canterbury Tales* (ca. 1400), in which a group of pilgrims stave off the boredom of the road by telling each other stories, and Boccaccio's *Decameron* (ca. 1350), in which young courtiers fleeing the Black Death take turns narrating stories on a given theme over ten days. The genre has traveled widely, adapting itself to extremely diverse environments and cultural realities. It has produced classics in several literary traditions and was an important step in the development of the novel. While a number of texts, such as Don Juan Manuel's *El Conde Lucanor* (Castilian, 1340) and Isaac ibn Sahūla's *Mešal haqadmonī* (Hebrew, ca. 1281), written in a variety of languages in medieval Iberia have been described as frametales, to this date there has been no comprehensive study of the medieval Iberian frametale

[11] First known in Europe through the French translation of Jean Antoine Gallard (ca. 1710).

as a unified tradition comprised of texts written in Arabic, Hebrew, Latin, and Romance. This study proposes to open the question of such a tradition and to reframe [pun intended] the study of these texts as a unified, multilingual tradition.

The medieval Iberian frametale tradition was cultivated in a culture defined by centuries of close, sustained contact between Muslims, Jews, and Christians. The idea that the formation of Spanish culture was heavily influenced by a prolonged and intimate contact with the Islamic and Arabic culture of al-Andalus has long been a point of contention between literary scholars and historians.[12] As early as the end of the nineteenth century, Spanish Arabist Julián Ribera y Tarragó argued that such influence is the logical and obvious result of the *convivencia*:

> no en valde hemos vivido siete siglos en vecindad continua con los musulmanes, formándose nuestra nación al influjo constante de su trato, en la época de nuestra infancia, es decir, en aquella edad en que los instintos de la imitación aparecen más desarrollados. (5)
>
> (not in vain have we lived in continuous proximity with Muslims for seven centuries, forming our nation under the constant influence of dealing with them, in the era of our infancy, that is, in the age in which the instinct of imitation appears most developed.)

Angus Mackay supports Ribera's assertion that influence logically follows contact and that the 12th and 13th centuries in Castile were characterized by an informal, mutual acculturation between religious groups.[13] Américo Castro (*Realidad, España*) demonstrated how cultural contact with Islam affected the development of nearly every mode of Spanish cultural expression, including language, literature, social institutions, and religion.

The specific mechanisms of this acculturation have been studied by Thomas Glick, who applied Kroeber's theory of 'stimulus diffusion' to Medieval Spain. Glick, reacting to and building upon Castro's ideas of 'imitative' and 'reactive' cultural formation (Glick and Pi-Sunyer 9) maintains that power balance is the key concept in understanding the dynamics of acculturation and that the primary motivation for acculturation is the approximation of

---

[12] The most visible participants in this debate were Américo Castro (*Realidad, España*) and Claudio Sánchez Albornoz. More recently, scholars such as Menocal (*Arabic, Shards, Ornament*), Catlos ("Cristians" and "Contexto"), Ray, and Robinson and Rouhi have updated and nuanced the discussion. For more on this debate, see chapter 3, note 42.

[13] "La mezcla de cristianos, mozárabes, mudéjares y judíos refleja de una manera obvia que una aculturación informal debió de producirse principalmente durante los siglos XII y XIII" (Mackay 102).

the cultural practices of a minority group to those of a dominant one. This drive stems from the most basic human instinct of self-preservation: one's access to resources, and therefore one's chances of flourishing, increases in direct proportion to the degree of one's affiliation with or participation in the social and political institutions where power is concentrated. Since conversion to Islam (especially prior to the thirteenth century) was one of the chief avenues of acculturation, we can posit a direct link between levels of conversion and levels of acculturation. According to Bulliet, the highest rate of Christian acculturation to Islam occurred during the years of Muslim hegemony, up until the Christian conquest of Toledo in 1085.[14] After this date, the balance of power on the Iberian Peninsula began to tilt in the direction of the Christians, and Christian conversion to Islam dropped off sharply. Thus, during the years between 711 and 1085, conversion to Islam was one of the chief modes of acculturation. According to the treatment of *ahl al-ḍimma*, or the protected minorities under Islam, conversion was encouraged by financial and social advantages, but not imposed institutionally (Glick and Pi-Sunyer 1–5). If a Jew or Christian chose to continue to practice his religion of birth, he was subject to a tax, the *jizya* (Qur'ān 9:29). Other social and economic restrictions applied as well.[15] Therefore, there were clear economic benefits to conversion. Either way, the Islamic polity benefited: if minorities chose not to convert, the government collected a tax; if they converted, they collected new Muslims (EI, "*Dhimma*").

According to Glick, the fourteenth century witnessed an increasing intolerance and resistance to Muslim and Jewish cultural influences[16] in Christian Iberia (*Islamic* 294). This rigidity is what begins to characterize Christian society some years after the appearance of Juan Manuel's *El Conde Lucanor* and Juan Ruiz's *El Libro de buen amor*. Glick argues that evidence of acculturation during this period is inversely proportionate to the level of

[14] The rate of conversion to Islam rises dramatically from the eighth century until the middle of the thirteenth, when it drops to almost zero. By the Battle of Navas de Tolosa in 1212, the popularity of Muslim names plateaus completely (Bulliet 117–18). It bears noting that and Lapidus has sharply criticized this thesis, and the methodology with which he arrived at it, as a "tissue of assumptions... stretched too far for any historically reliable conclusions" (187), while Norris considers the merit of Bulliet's approach as "very debatable" (163).

[15] For example, the right to marry a Muslim woman, own a Muslim slave, or in some cases, wear fine cloth and travel on horseback, all of which had been (at one time or another, and at least *de jure*) forbidden to members of *ahl al-ḍimma* (*Encyclopedia of Islam* = *EI*, "Dhimma").

[16] The question of 'semitic influence' has been dealt with admirably by Robinson and Rouhi, who deconstruct the very categories by which scholars of medieval Iberia have tended to classify the cultural production of Christian Iberia.

prestige of the mode of production. He explains that "of all the processes of acculturation non-formal cultural diffusion is perhaps the most important" (*Islamic* 152). This complicates the study of acculturation in literature and especially in folk tradition, since the less formal (or prestigious) the text, the less likely it is to have survived in a form useful to textual scholarship.[17] Even manuscripts written by Christians in Castilian are in relatively short supply in comparison with analogous works in French or Italian (Deyermond, *Perdida* 18). However, this poverty pales in comparison to the scarcity of medieval Iberian Arabic, Hebrew, and Aljamiado manuscripts, many of which were either hidden inside walls and beneath floorboards to avoid the scrutiny of the Inquisition, whose agents burned untold numbers of manuscripts in Hebrew and Arabic characters. In an extreme example, one cache of *aljamiado* manuscripts (Romance texts written in Arabic script) that managed to survive centuries of Inquisition was discovered in 1884 by a local priest in Almonacid de la Sierra (Aragón) who came across a group of children burning the manuscripts in a "childish bonfire" for entertainment's sake.[18] Much of this story, therefore, must be read in what is *not* said, or rather in what has been said or written but not preserved. The lost translation, the performance never transcribed, the text not copied, the manuscript still buried under the floorboards or plastered inside a wall, and the texts and traditions that the tens of thousands of Muslim and Jewish exiles took with them into the Andalusī and Sephardic diasporas.

Given that most of the evidence for popular tradition is culled from manuscript texts and that the manuscript tradition of Spain is quite poor in comparison to the rest of Romance Europe, the pool of potential evidence of popular material is shallow indeed. Any study of hybridity (acculturation, transculturation, etc.) in medieval Iberian literature based solely upon traditional philological analysis of manuscripts is doomed to present a fragmentary vision of medieval Iberian literary practice. The gaze of the Romance philologist is not sufficient to this particular task. This study begs a different approach, one that takes into account types of evidence not found in manuscript.[19]

---

[17] To wit, while Jewish writers such as Maimonides (twelfth century) and Shelomo Bonafed (late 14th–early 15th centuries) make reference to the Romance language compositions of Jewish poets (Monroe, "Maimonides" 20; Millás Vallicrosa, "Review" 242), very few such texts have survived, most likely due to the relatively low prestige and ignorance of Romance as a literary language in Jewish society outside of the Iberian Peninsula.

[18] This is told by Pablo Gil, Julián Ribera, and Mariano Sánchez in the introduction to their anthology of *aljamiado* texts from the same collection (Gil y Gil et al. vii, cited in Barletta 69).

[19] Examples include evidence from contemporary oral tradition, the plastic arts, and anecdotal information from medieval authors.

Architecture, for example, offers ample, well-preserved evidence of such hybridity, as stone buildings are generally more durable than parchment manuscripts or oral performances of tales. For example, the cathedrals of Aragon raised during the thirteenth century were built with techniques imported from beyond the Pyrenees and do not exhibit many features of what has been described as the *mudéjar* style. The parish churches, however, were built with local materials and methods, those of *mudéjar* artisans native to Aragon (MacKay 103; Hilgarth, *Kingdoms* 197–204).[20] Likewise, the Latin literature of the period can be said to exhibit little to no "Andalusī" influence, with a few possible exceptions.[21] However, the vernacular literature of the period, and in particular the frametale, provides abundant evidence of influence resulting from contact with Andalusī culture, owing primarily to an influx of translations from Hebrew and Arabic texts and secondarily to authors' contact with Jewish and Muslim culture in their own environments.[22]

This culture of synthesis and adaptation is not unique to Christian Spain, but rather is inherited from the Muslim leaders of al-Andalus. Again, the architectural evidence is the most reliable. It was common practice to appropriate cathedrals and recast them as mosques. The best known example of this type of conversion is the cathedral at Cordova, which was converted into a mosque in the second half of the eighth century (Lévi-Provençal 340–41). This type of monument conversion is an unequivocal sign of political shift in the region, a palpable manifestation of the changing times. Such synthesis was crucial in the expansion of Islam, as Muhammad's army of peninsular Arabs came into contact with the many cultures of the lands they conquered. Américo Castro has argued that Christian Iberians inherited

---

[20] The question of Andalusī "influence" is highly problematic, in that it is difficult to point to any given aesthetic trait and call it "Islamic" or "Christian." For an overview of *mudéjar* art and architecture see Borrás Gualis et al. (*El arte mudéjar*). For the creation of meaning from specific design elements in Islamic art and architecture, see Grabar (*Mediation*) and Robinson ("Mudéjar").

[21] For example, the Latin translations of Arabic scientific texts carried out under the direction of Archbishop Raymond of Toledo during the second half of the twelfth century (González Palencia, *Arzobispo*; Burnett "Arabic," "Institutional," and "Translating"; Jacquart), the thirteenth-century translation of *Kalīla wa-Dimna* by Johannes of Capua (*EI*, "*Kalīla wa-Dimna*"), and the early twelfth-century *Disciplina Clericalis* of Petrus Alfonsi (Tolan, *Petrus Alfonsi*; Alvárez). See also chapter 1, notes 25 and 26.

[22] For example, the translation of *Calila e Dimna* and *Sendebar* from Arabic in the mid-thirteenth century, the adaptation of the frametale genre by Don Juan Manuel in *El Conde Lucanor* and by Juan Ruiz in the *Libro de buen amor* (see chapter 3). While these texts do not constitute a large percentage of the literary output of the period, their influence in the modern study of Castilian literature has been significant, as both *El Conde Lucanor* and the *Libro de buen amor* are routinely taught in Spanish secondary schools and as part of introductory courses on medieval Spanish literature in universities in the US and abroad.

this capacity for synthesis from Islam (*España* 213), but in the final analysis, *every* cultural practice is emergent and in constant dialogue with neighboring practices. Medieval Iberia, if such a place existed, was hardly unique as a cultural crossroads in recorded human history; it simply happens to be the object of the current study.

If medieval Iberian culture is distinguished by such synthesis and interplay, the frametale is perhaps the limiting example of the cultural complexity of the peninsula during the thirteenth and fourteenth centuries, a milieu to which words like "plurality" and "multicultural," with all the contemporary baggage they bear, must be used only tentatively and with the caveat that they are a point of departure for further discussion. The extreme scarcity of source material (relative to those available to students of contemporary cultures) makes understanding this complexity even more difficult.

Just as Iberian Romance (and in particular Castilian) culture has long been viewed as somehow different from that of its Romance neighbors north of the Pyrenees, the Hebrew and Arabic literature written by medieval Iberian authors has likewise been recognized by Hebraists and Arabists as belonging to a uniquely Iberian literary culture, one that still conjures up images of wealth, cultural achievement, and literary refinement.[23] The geographic specificity and cultural conditions that obtained in medieval Iberia—the close proximity and exchange between Muslims, Jews and Christians, during both Muslim and Christian rule—gave rise to an Iberian-ness, a sense of local identity that was felt equally by residents of the Iberian Peninsula regardless of their religious, linguistic, or political affiliations. Though scholars of Spanish, Hebrew, and Arabic literatures historically have studied authors such as Juan Ruiz, Judah al-Ḥarīzī and al-Saraqusṭī in isolation from one another, all authors are participants in the multicultural practice of the medieval Iberian frametale and *maqāma*. By this I do not mean that all cultural production during the 13th and 14th centuries in the territories of Castile and León was reflective in equal parts of what we might now consider Jewish, Christian, and Muslim aesthetic sensibilities (if we can even assert that such sensibili-

[23] This aura of prestige is attributed even to the (self-identified) twentieth-century descendents of the Andalusīs, who are considered more "European" and enjoy a higher level of social prestige than their compatriots of "African" origin. According to Abbou (writing in French in 1953), the Andalusīs have lighter, finer complexions than their southern neighbors, and many have family names thought to be derived from Spanish, such as Loubariz (Alvarez), Mulin (Molina), Bargach (Vargas), Carrakchou (Carrasaco), etc. (76 and 80–81). This lingering prestige is reflected in marketing practices in the contemporary Arab world, where al-Andalus gives its name, to name only two of many such examples, to a luxury shopping mall in Riyadh and a brand of zaʿtar (a spice) made in Jordan.

ties existed in distinguishable categories). Rather, I mean that the culture of this land during this time was not experienced by medieval Iberians in terms of the disciplinary categories constructed by the modern university. Consequently, studying it in terms of such categories may not bring us to any meaningful understanding of the people, culture, and aesthetic expression of medieval Iberia.

Such was the society that gave us the medieval Iberian frametale, which in turn exercised a powerful influence on the medieval literatures of Western Europe. Boccaccio's *Decameron*, Chaucer's *Canterbury Tales*, and the French translation of the *Thousand and One Nights* have been highly influential, important examples of episodic prose narrative for writers who would later produce the first modern novels. The frametale structure, with its pretense of storytelling, offers insight into the authors' narrative culture, the ways in which they participated in and experienced short tales, anecdotes, fables, and stories. The frametale (as I shall discuss in chapter 2) occupies a space between oral traditional narrative and public literary reading. It encodes the socially situated act of storytelling (or the performance of a story) and the interaction between storyteller and audience, within a textual medium. However, the meaning of such performances depends on the community in which they take place, and written medium of the frametale gives these encoded performances a textual fixity and portability. This literary mobility changes the relationship of the encoded performances to the community in which they are performed and received; once encoded into the frametale text, such performances are less dependent on a specific community for their meaning, yet the community of each encoder (author) leaves its mark on the encoded performance. As the frametale crosses cultural boundaries and gains popularity and authority in different linguistic, religious, and cultural communities, it serves to transmit the narrative aesthetics, techniques, and sensibilities across communities of practice, and in doing so redefines the boundaries between them.

In this process, the storytelling acts portrayed in frametales and *maqāmāt* acquire different meanings. For example, in the Sanskrit *Panchatantra*, animals are represented as telling stories to each other in the Aesopic manner. In Hinduism, the doctrine of metempsychosis (the transmigration of souls) holds that a human soul can be reincarnated as an animal. Therefore, the idea that an animal could conceive of a narrative (much less communicate it through spoken language) is not out of the question. However, when the *Panchatantra* is translated into Pahlavi and then into Arabic (by a Muslim) to become *Kalīla wa-Dimna*, the idea that a human soul could transmigrate to an animal's body becomes blasphemous in the Muslim context, and the phenomenon of the talking animal must be understood differently, or simply ignored. Similarly, notions of fiction and the literary representation of reality differ among religious groups. These attitudes both exercise influence upon a frametale translated from another culture and in turn are changed by the frametale genre, which brings its own narratology to bear upon the culture by which it is adopted. In short, the frametale is a catalyst for literary innovation that produced some of the most celebrated and widely studied and taught Castilian texts of the Middle Ages, including Juan Manuel's *Conde Lucanor* and Juan Ruiz's *Libro de buen amor* (1343).

The literary practice of the frametale in medieval Iberia dates to at least the tenth century. Ibn al-Muqaffaʿ translated *Kalīla wa-Dimna* into Arabic around 750, and the work was well known in Andalusī literary circles. At the beginning of the twelfth century, the Aragonese *converso* Petrus Alfonsi wrote the *Disciplina clericalis*, a collection of stories in Latin culled from the Arabic and Aesopic traditions as a dialogue between teacher and student. Later in the same century, al-Saraquṣṭī (d. 1160) wrote his Arabic *maqāmāt* in Cordova in imitation of those of the famous Eastern author al-Ḥarīrī (b. 1054). At the beginning of the thirteenth, Judah al-Ḥarīzī wrote his *Taḥkemonī* in an attempt to legitimize the *maqāma* genre for Hebrew audiences. The *maqāma* underwent a good deal of innovation in Hebrew at the hands of Ibn Zabāra (*Sefer Šaʿašūʿīm*) and Ibn Shabbetay (*Minḥat Yehudah, soneh hanašīm*), both of whom lived in Christian Iberia during the early thirteenth century. Around the same time, the Arabic *Sindibād* (known in Latin translation as the *Seven Sages of Rome*) served as the basis for the Hebrew frametale *Mišlei Sendabar*. In 1251, *Kalīla wa-Dimna* was translated into Castilian, followed by the Castilian translation of *Sendebar* in 1253. Ibn Sahūla's Hebrew frametale *Mešal haqadmonī* ('Fable of the Ancient One') appears around 1281. These are followed by the Castilian classics *Conde Lucanor* of Don Juan Manuel (1340) and *Libro de buen amor* (1343) of Juan Ruiz, and finally by the Valencian *Llibre de les dones* or *Spill* of Jaume Roig (ca. 1450). This list, although incomplete, illustrates the scope and diversity of the medieval Iberian frametale tradition, one expressed in several languages over approximately four hundred years. Therefore, the *Conde Lucanor* and the *Libro de buen amor*, long considered as classics of Castilian literature, are also part of a broader tradition of medieval Iberian frametale narrative that began when the first copies of Ibn al-Muqaffaʿ's *Kalīla wa-Dimna* circulated in al-Andalus, possibly in the eighth or ninth century. *Kalīla wa-Dimna* is studied as a classic of Arabic literature (Bonebakker), Judah al-Ḥarīzī is considered one of the fathers of modern Hebrew literature; yet all of these authors have yet to be studied together in the context of a unified tradition of medieval Iberian frametales.

How to form a vision of a cohesive frametale tradition despite such temporal and cultural distance? Our aim is not to prove that Juan Ruiz read Ibn Zabara or that Don Juan Manuel's audience would have been familiar with *Calila e Dimna*, much less the Arabic original. Rather, I see medieval Iberia as home to a literary polysystem[24] that fostered various types of literary production, transmission, and reception (writing, reading, copying, listening, discussion, etc.) that was meaningfully interconnected at various points. In short, I maintain that the *Conde Lucanor*, the *Libro de buen amor*, and the *Spill* were not products grown in a Romanic hothouse, but rather are representative of a medieval Iberian culture and literary tradition that cannot be contained or adequately addressed by Romance studies alone. These texts are examples of Castilian and Valencian language production in a system that was the site of literary activity in several languages, Latin, Romance, Hebrew, and Arabic.

An examination of the social contexts of our authors reveals a good deal of bi- and multilingualism, di- and polyglossia, conversion, and other types of crossings and syntheses. Petrus Alfonsi was born a Jew and received an education in Hebrew and Arabic. His conversion to Christianity and extensive travel throughout Christian Europe is a documented source of diffusion of much Arabic and Hebrew learning. Al-Saraqusṭī was born in Zaragoza in Aragon (as his name indicates) but migrated south to al-Andalus after his hometown was captured by Alfonso the Battler of Aragon in 1148. Judah al-Ḥarīzī, on the contrary, was of a generation of Castilian and Aragonese Jews whose families had fled north from religious persecution at the hands of the Almohads in al-Andalus in the 1140s. Alfonso X, patron of the Castilian translation of *Calila e Dimna*, ruled over Seville and Cordova, Andalusī cultural centers that had been conquered by his father, Fernando III. Juan Ruiz lived and studied in a Toledo that was host to a great deal of Arabic and Hebrew literary activity in the early 1300s. Don Juan Manuel counted among his allies several Muslim monarchs and as *Adelantado* (Governor) of the frontier of Murcia, carried out many diplomatic missions in the Kingdom of Granada. At home, his most trusted advisor was a Jew, Don Salamón. While the political boundaries on the Iberian Peninsula were subject to the fortunes of war, political power was only one factor that defined a medieval

[24] The literary polysystem is discussed in depth in chapter 2.

Iberian literary practice characterized by its linguistic and cultural flexibility. The frametale is the genre most characteristic of this practice.

With chapter 1, I begin my story of the medieval Iberian frametale with a book by Petrus Alfonsi, a man who was raised an Andalusī Jew but converted to Christianity in midlife. His collection of tales and fables, the *Disciplina clericalis*, introduced Latin audiences to the frametale genre, to a new way of telling stories in writing. Petrus Alfonsi was a product of a frontier culture, a person who was able to capitalize on the drastic political and cultural changes taking place in the frontier society of twelfth-century Aragon. By positioning himself as a transcultural author, he refashioned himself from Andalusī Jewish scholar into Christian international intellectual star.

In chapter 2, "Storytelling and Performance in Medieval Iberian Frametale and Maqāma," I examine the literary representation of storytelling events or performances by Arabic and Hebrew authors as shaped by their individual interpretations of Muslim and Jewish traditions regarding textual transmission, performance, and fictionality. The explicit performance (in which characters are portrayed in the act of narrating a tale) characteristic of *Kalīla wa-Dimna* and *Calila e Dimna* is representative of a homiletic sensibility, as befits its origin as tales collected by Buddhist priests for use in sermons. In al-Saraqusṭī's *maqāmāt*, the characters' performance is implicit. That is, they are simply mentioned as having narrated an anecdote, but are not portrayed narrating it. This implicit performance draws on the tradition of oral transmission of Islamic *ḥadīṯ* (traditions of Muhammad). Within the episodes themselves, these same characters—whose own performances are indicated in the text only telegraphically—narrate literary descriptions of the performances of rogue street preachers, a theme common to Arabic literature from Eastern authors of the ʿAbbāsid era (ninth-tenth century). Jewish authors writing in Hebrew later adapt these ways of representing performance in accordance with their own religious and literary tradition. All of these performativities commingle in the medieval Iberian frametale tradition, which gives us the *Conde Lucanor* and the *Libro de buen amor*.

In chapter 3, "Translating the Frame," I discuss the importance of the translation of *Calila e Dimna* into Castilian from Arabic in 1251, commissioned by the Infante Alfonso (soon to be Alfonso X). The translation of *Calila e Dimna* occurs within the context of the establishment of Castilian as a language of literary production and as part of an ambitious royal project of linguistic prestige-building. I examine the political importance of the rise of Castilian and the impact on early literary Castilian of Alfonso's translation initiative. Despite its origins in the Muslim- and Arabic-dominant literary system of al-Andalus, there are no significant barriers to the reception of *Calila e Dimna* by Christian, Castilian audiences. The secular nature of the tales and pragmatic didactic voice of the author set the stage for a common community of reception that included both Arabic and Castilian audiences. As the first work of prose narrative fiction in Castilian, *Calia e Dimna* was an important model for Don Juan Manuel's *Conde Lucanor*.

In chapter 4, "Reconquest Ideology and Andalusī Narrative Practice," I examine Don Juan Manuel's use of Andalusī narrative practice in the context of the Christian conquests of al-Andalus as a colonial enterprise. While his position of *Adelantado* (Governor) of the frontier of Murcia with Granada demands a certain adherence to official narratives of Reconquest, Juan Manuel demonstrates a great deal of admiration for and affiliation with Andalusī cultural practice. He was, in fact, an avid participant in Andalusī oral narrative practice, both in his choice of genre (the frametale) and in his use of Andalusī historical anecdotes and tales. These two seemingly contradictory tendencies, opposition to Islam and affiliation with Andalusī culture, are characteristic of the colonial frontier culture of medieval Castile.

Chapter 5, "The *Libro de buen amor* and the Medieval Iberian *Maqāma*," situates the *Libro de buen amor* in the tradition of the Hispano-Hebraic *maqāmāt*, in particular the *Sefer Šaʿăšūʿīm* of Ibn Zabāra. Arguing that Juan Ruiz was familiar with Ibn Zabāra's work, I cite historical and literary evidence that places educated Jews in contact with high-ranking Christian monarchs and nobles. Juan Ruiz's familiarity with certain aspects of Jewish custom and religious practice also supports the idea that his understanding of Iberian Jewish culture went beyond the stereotyping and clichés more common to the Christian Iberian literature of his time and suggests that his experience in Toledo during the early 1300s placed him in significant contact with Jewish intellectuals. Finally, the figure of the unstable or unreliable narrator found in the *Libro de buen amor* is part of the Iberian *maqāma* tradition including such authors as al-Saraqusṭī, al-Ḥarīzī, and Ibn Zabāra.

Finally, chapter 6, "Jaume Roig's *Spill*: A Misogynist *maqāma* from Bourgeois Valencia," is a reading of the idiosyncratic Valencian poet as a stepping stone halfway between the medieval Iberian *maqāma* and the Spanish picaresque novel. Roig wrote during a difficult time of social change that was punctuated by an explosion of bourgeois wealth, literary experimentation by authors rejecting the values of traditional poetry, and ethnic tensions that periodically overflowed into violence. His misogynist rant, which bears striking similarities to Hebrew *maqāmāt* written in Christian Iberia, is the last medieval Romance language witness to the Iberian *maqāma* tradition.

CHAPTER ONE

WRITING ACROSS THE FRONTIER

The first chapter of the story of the frametale in medieval Iberia is about a man who lived his life on the Andalusī-Christian Iberian frontier. Petrus Alfonsi, born in one of the cities of al-Andalus toward the close of the eleventh century, was raised and grew to adulthood as an Andalusī Jew. After the Christian conquest of Huesca he converted to Christianity and parlayed his Andalusī education in *adab* and Arabic science into a career as an intellectual luminary in Latin Europe. Although Petrus Alfonsi produced numerous works in Latin on a wide range of subjects both scientific and religious,[1] this chapter will focus on the two for which he is best known, the *Disciplina Clericalis* (= *DC*),[2] and the *Dialogus Contra Judaeos* (= *Dialogus*).[3] The former is a collection of fables and tales drawn from Arabic and Hebrew sources that was widely copied and today exists in over 70 manuscripts. It introduced European audiences to new stories and to new ways of telling them, and by virtue of its international popularity, exercised significant influence on the development of early European vernacular prose fiction.[4]

---

[1] Among those scientific works attributed to Petrus Alfonsi are a Latin version of the astronomical tables of al-Khwārizmī. For a full discussion of his works and those attributed to him, see Burnett ("Works") and Millás Vallicrosa ("Works"; "Aportación").

[2] For a list of all the extant manuscripts containing complete and partial versions of the *Disciplina clericalis*, see Tolan (*Petrus* 199–204). For a bibliography of pre-1899 editions and translations, see Chauvin (9: 1–44). The authoritative critical edition is that of Hilka and Söderhjelm. See also the edition of Migne, the English edition/translation by Hermes and Quarrie, the English translation by Jones and Keller, the German edition/translation by Hermes, and the two Spanish edition/translations by González Palencia and Lacarra. I cite the original from Hilka and Söderhjelm's edition and the English from Quarrie's translation. References to titles of *exempla* and sections are to those of Quarrie's translation of the edition of Hilka and Söderhjelm.

[3] The *Dialogus* is extant in 79 manuscripts dating from the twelfth to the fifteenth centuries. It first appeared in print in 1536 in Cologne, which edition was reproduced in Migne's *Patrologia Latina*. The best modern edition is that of Klaus-Peter Miethe, originally found in his doctoral dissertation but reproduced and accompanied by Ducay's Spanish translation in 1996. On the *Dialogus*, see Tolan (*Petrus* 182–98; "Diálogos"; "Pedro Alfonso"), Lacarra (*Pedro Alfonso* 22–26), and Alvárez ("Petrus Alfonsi" 284–86). All citations are from the 1996 edition of Miethe. English translations are my own, following the Spanish of Ducay.

[4] González Palencia includes a lengthy list of works that bear signs of the influence of the *DC*, including quite well-known texts such as Boccaccio's *Decameron*, Chaucer's *Canterbury Tales*, the *Fables* of Odo of Cheriton, the French *Fabliaux*, Juan Manuel's *Conde Lucanor*,

Although it is a bit of a cliché to write of Petrus Alfonsi as a man who bridged two cultures, or a sort of intellectual Prometheus who facilitated the medieval Iberian *translatio studii*, the transfer of Arab learning to Christian Europe, one cannot deny that it is true. Petrus Alfonsi indeed introduced a Latin readership to a great amount of material previously available only in Arabic and Hebrew. This is noteworthy and important for students of medieval Iberia. However, in the rush to talk and think about the history of great ideas and great books it is easy to overlook the role of experience of the human beings who nurture, develop, translate, and disseminate these ideas and books. The cultural crossings, hybridity, and synthesis that characterize medieval Iberian literature are the result not only of cooperation and collaboration (*convivencia*), but also of war, conquest, colonization, and intolerance (*contravivencia*). Petrus Alfonsi's reputation as a literary innovator who was able to bridge Arabic and Latin learning came at the cost of a lifetime of difficult experiences. Along the road that eventually led him to intellectual stardom in Latin Western Europe lay significant obstacles. Whether he was a native of Aragon who saw his homeland invaded and conquered or whether he was one of the many Jewish refugees from Almoravid al-Andalus who migrated north to Christian kingdoms, he made what must have been a painful decision to embrace a colonial religion and culture. It is fitting that we read his work with this experience in mind.

The inner conflict engendered in Petrus Alfonsi by his experience as a member of the colonized élite comes through most clearly in his *Dialogus*, a religious polemical dialogue in which Petrus Alfonsi, arguing with Moshé, his own former, Jewish self, strives to prove the truth of Christianity with Andalusī rationalist argumentation, using the Hebrew Bible and Talmud as authoritative sources. While there is a good deal of scholarship regarding the *DC* and the *Dialogus* as regards their textual traditions and the impact on later European authors, there is no study that considers Petrus Alfonsi's colonial, *converso* experience as primary in understanding both of these texts.[5]

The historical circumstances in which Petrus Alfonsi lived were essentially colonial: his homeland was conquered by a people who imposed a new

---

the *Lais* of Marie de France, Juan Ruiz's *Libro de buen amor*, and the *Novelle* of Giovanni Sercambi ("Introduction" xxiv–xxxiii). On the influence of the *DC* on Boccaccio's *Decameron*, see Avalle-Arce. On the *DC* and Chaucer's *Canterbury Tales*, see P. Brown (187).

[5] One notable exception is the section of Hermes' introductory study titled "The Jewish Experience," although he mostly deals with the idea that Petrus Alfonsi carries on a tradition of Jewish self-criticism and does not address the question of the *converso*. See Hermes ("Author" 90–99).

political order, new institutions, and a new official language, Latin.[6] While historians of medieval Iberia, and in particular those of Aragon, have not hesitated to refer to the Christian conquests of al-Andalus as a colonial project (Linehan, *History* 95–127; Maravall, *Concepto* 269–87; O'Callaghan, *Reconquest* 4–7),[7] and scholars of medieval European literature have not hesitated to publish postcolonial readings of the medieval European perceptions of and experience in the East,[8] Hispanists have almost completely avoided postcolonial readings of the Christian conquest of al-Andalus.[9] Despite the substantial differences between medieval and modern colonialisms as regards political reality, public discourse, and the construction of subjectivity, one may safely argue that the Christian conquests of al-Andalus were a colonial endeavor, one of several studied by historians of medieval Europe.[10]

Petrus Alfonsi writes his rational yet highly personal response to his experience as a convert to Christianity in colonial Aragon into the *Dialogus* and the *DC*. The *Dialogus* is a literary dramatization of the internal debate between his Jewish and Christian selves, while the *DC* is a collection of material drawn from Arab and Jewish tradition placed in the service of medieval Latin (and therefore Christian) literature. In so producing a Latin, Christian work of didactic literature, he legitimizes himself as a Christian author while simultaneously maintaining and capitalizing upon his relationship with his Jewish Andalusī background. If the *Dialogus* is a literary record of the internal crisis accompanying Petrus Alfonsi's religious and cultural crossing, the *DC* is the literary fruit of this process. Both works result from the author's ongoing attempt to reconcile his Andalusī Jewish past with his Christian present and future. They are a literary reflection of life on the cultural frontier.

---

[6] Arabic was used only occasionally in official contexts in Christian Iberia, such as in the Mozarabic community of Toledo or in the bilingual surrender treaties administered by Alfonso I and Jaume I of Aragón. See González Palencia (*Mozárabes*), Burns et al., and Stalls. However, Latin was overwhelmingly the language of the dominant Christian religion and government. See López-Morillas ("Language" 51).

[7] Historians have been studying medieval Spain as a colonial problem for decades. See, for example, Burns (*Islam*) and Lourie. Angus MacKay describes *repobladores* ('re-settlers') quite plainly as "colonists" (36).

[8] See, for example, Dagenais and Greer ("Decolonizing"), as well as the other essays published in *Journal of Medieval and Early Modern Studies* 30.3 (2000). Contributions by Hispano-Medievalists are conspicuously absent from the collections of essays edited by Jeffrey Cohen and Kabir and Williams. For an excellent overview of medieval postcolonial criticism, see Holsinger.

[9] For one exception, see Hanlon ("Islam").

[10] Historians of medieval Europe have likewise begun to view aspects of European trade and crusade in the East as colonial activities. See, for example, Balard and Ducellier, and Bartlett.

Biography

Born Moshé in the last quarter of the eleventh century, Petrus Alfonsi lived in the majority Muslim, arabophone city of Wāškā (Huesca) in Aragon.[11] He received a secular education in Arabic and a religious one in Hebrew.[12] In his lifetime he was to live through Aragon's political and cultural transition from Islam to Christianity, and his life experience is emblematic of the cultural change and synthesis that characterized Christian Iberia during its conquests of al-Andalus. He received a double education in classical Arabic literature, philosophy, and the sciences, as well as in Hebrew and the Jewish rabbinic and literary tradition.[13] In all respects he was typical of the Jewish intellectuals of his time, even down to his occupation—that of physician. He grew up in a society where the dominant religion was Islam, the official language of government and education was Classical Arabic, and the colloquial tongue either Andalusī Arabic or Romance. He is the product of the twelfth-century sunset of the great flowering of Andalusī Jewish intellectual culture, one of the last of what Ross Brann has described as the "courtier-rabbis":

> The courtier-rabbis of the Hebrew "Golden Age" in Muslim Spain (c. 950–1150) were a most improbable breed of literati and an even more unlikely brand of clerics. On the one hand, they were deeply attached to Jewish tradition and meticulous in their observance of Jewish law; on the other, they were aficionados of Arabic *paideia* (cultural education) in Hebrew dress. (*Compunctious* 9)

In this description, Brann captures the essence of the Andalusī Jewish intellect, that ability to move between faith and science, Hebrew and Arabic, divine and temporal. María Rosa Menocal has written that what best characterizes Andalusī culture through the thirteenth century is this very ability to thrive on contradictory values and that the tenth-thirteenth centuries in al-Andalus constituted a

---

[11] Tolan has shown that many of the assumptions made by scholars regarding the details of Petrus Alfonsi's life are not supported by archival evidence (*Petrus* 213 n. 13–17). For example, references in much of the secondary literature to Moshé "Sefardí" are unfounded; Petrus Alfonsi refers to his past self only as "Moyses" in the *Dialogus*. Also spurious are Ashtor's claim that Moshé was a leader of the Jewish community of Huesca (2: 273), or Baer's assertion that he was converted by French Benedictine monks (1: 159).

[12] For an excellent overview of Jewish intellectual life in al-Andalus, see Brann ("Arabized"). On the cultural scene of medieval Aragon in particular, see Lomba Fuentes. Another, more renowned Jewish polymath of the time was Abraham ibn Ezra (1089–1164). While Petrus Alfonsi disseminated Andalusī learning to Latin Western Europe, Ibn Ezra did the same (in Hebrew) for the Jewish communities of Italy and France (*EJ*, "ibn Ezra, Abraham"; Sela).

[13] On the life of Petrus Alfonsi, see Alvárez ("Petrus Alfonsi" 282–84).

> genuine, foundational European cultural moment that qualifies as "first-rate," in the sense of F. Scott Fitzgerald's wonderful formula...that "the test of a first-rate intelligence is the ability to hold two opposed ideas in the mind at the same time." In its moments of great achievement, medieval culture positively thrived on holding at least two, and often many more, contrary ideas at the same time. (*Ornament* 11)

These courtier-rabbis lived biculturally, moving back and forth between two cultures. Gustavo Pérez Firmat writes of a similar type of biculturality, that experienced by Cuban-Americans, who are divided between the country they consider their legitimate ancestral home and the one in which they make their homes and futures. For him,

> biculturation designates not only contact of cultures; in addition, it describes a situation where the two cultures achieve a balance that makes it difficult to determine which is the dominant and which is the subordinate culture. [It] implies an equilibrium, however tense or precarious, between the two contributing cultures. [Cuban-Americans'] hyphen is a seesaw: it tilts first one way, then the other. (6)

What most distinguishes Petrus Alfonsi from the courtier-rabbis is his conversion to Christianity, which gained him entry into the highest levels of Christian society and enabled him to refashion himself into an intellectual who participated fully in the culture of the Christian majority. This change came at a cost: while the bicultural courtier-rabbis were able to move back and forth between Muslim and Jewish cultures while still maintaining their distinct religious identity, the *conversos* inhabit a space between identities: they are stuck on the up-side of Pérez Firmat's seesaw, with no way to come down.

Medieval Christianity's relationship with Judaism was dynamic and emergent, but nearly always conflictive (Dahan 14–17). Medieval Christian doctrine is inconsistent regarding the position of Jews within Christian society. While theologians were in agreement that Judaism was a false religion, some of them held that the Jews nonetheless served an important function within the Christian world, serving as a living example of those who would reject and betray Christ.[14] Canon Law stipulated unequivocal protections for Jews regarding their property and well-being, but made it clear that they were legally and socially subordinate to Christians. Not surprisingly, treatment of Jews by both Church and secular authorities was not always in

---

[14] For an exhaustive study of the legal status of Jews in medieval Christianity, see Pakter.

accordance with doctrine and in any event varied significantly depending on time and place.[15] In the same year that Sancho Ramírez conquered Huesca (1096), the launch of the First Crusade and the anti-Semitic massacres that accompanied it signalled a downward trend in Christian-Jewish relations and the beginning of a period of unprecedented violence against Jews in Christian Europe, especially in France.[16]

It is in this climate that Petrus Alfonsi makes the decision to convert. In the *Dialogus*, he is faced with the problem of how to characterize in writing the conflictive relationship between the religions of his former and present selves. He internalizes and records this conflict in the *Dialogus*, struggling with the memory of his Andalusī Jewish self. Despite significant historical and circumstantial differences, his situation prefigures that of the thousands of Castilian and Aragonese *conversos* of the late fourteenth- and fifteenth-centuries. Even when accepted as Christians, *conversos* were marked by difference.[17] In the case of Petrus Alfonsi, this difference propelled him to great success as a courtier and an intellectual, but the identity crisis he suffered as a *converso* left its mark on his writings.[18] This crisis begins with his conversion, and no personal crisis takes place in a social vacuum. Although the available information concerning his personal circumstances is scarce, we do know a good deal about the times in which Petrus Alfonsi lived. Aragon in the twelfth century was a frontier society in the throes of dramatic social and political transition. Even in such a setting, it is no small matter for a man to change his religion, his identity, and his language of written expression in adulthood. While these changes enabled Petrus Alfonsi to have a career as a member of the dominant culture of his times, they must also have brought about some measure of personal crisis. In order to better understand the *Dialogus* and the *DC* as records of Petrus Alfonsi's conflicted identity, we must situate the man in his times.

---

[15] On this disjuncture, see Jeremy Cohen ("Christian"). This extended equivocation gave rise to a tradition of disputation between Christianity and Judaism to which the *Dialogus* belongs. For a brief history of this tradition, see Sapir Abulafia.

[16] See Chazan ("Anti-Jewish"). For a study of the martyrological poetry resulting from the violence, see Einbinder.

[17] In the introduction to their English translation of the *DC*, Joseph Jones and John Keller comment that "Pedro Alfonso, once a Sefardic Jew, was always, even though a convert to western Christianity, a quasi-Sefardic personality" (19).

[18] The modern Tunisian Jewish writer Albert Memmi has commented that "the Jew who becomes a Christian does not completely break with the world of his past. He finds a new perspective, one which is cursed and abhorred by his people, but which unquestionably derives from his past" (*Jew* 74).

In the battle of Alcoraz (1096), the armies of Sancho Ramírez of Aragon (r. 1094–1101) overcame the forces of al-Mustaʿīn just outside of Huesca.[19] At this time, Moshé was already an adult. He fared quite well in the transition to Christian sovereignty under Pedro I (1101–1104). His medical expertise and prestigious Andalusī education afforded him access to the highest levels of society. Despite his position at court, Moshé was still a member of a religious minority in a society where this posed an insurmountable obstacle to full participation in Latin intellectual life. Jews under Christian rule did not enjoy the rights guaranteed by *ḏimmī* status under Islam. Catholic doctrine had long held Judaism in open contempt, and any privileges conceded to the Jewish subjects of a Christian monarch were by nature transitory.[20] Moshé belonged to a class of Andalusī Jews accustomed to full participation in the intellectual life of the dominant Arabic culture. He must have anticipated that he would not be able to continue this participation as a Jew in a Latin environment, and that the intellectual biculturality enjoyed by the courtier-rabbis would not survive the transition to Christian government. Andalusī Jews were educated in Arabic, but the Jews of Christian Spain—with very few exceptions—did not learn Latin,[21] and in their secular literary practice they gradually abandoned Arabic in favor of Hebrew.[22] These circumstances suggest that Petrus Alfonsi converted in order to enjoy full participation in the intellectual life of Christian Europe, but we can never know for a certainty. In 1106 he converted to Christianity, taking the names of Saint

---

[19] A certain Castilian hidalgo mercenary by the name of Rodrigo Díaz de Vivar ('el Cid') had fought in the service of both al-Mustaʿīn as well as his father, al-Muʿtamin (*EI*, "Hudids"). On the Battle of Alcoraz, see R. Menéndez Pidal (*España* 2: 562–64).

[20] "Life under Christian rule could not duplicate or genuinely imitate that of the Islamic period, essentially because of the very nature of Catholicism with its built-in deprecation of Judaism" (Levine Melammed, *Question* 4).

[21] Even by the late thirteenth century, "knowledge of Latin amongst Spanish Jews was a rare accomplishment, in effect limited to professional translators and their circles" (Loewe, "Introduction" lxix). Still, by the fourteenth and fifteenth centuries, only a few Jewish scholars were known to have translated from and into Latin. Significantly, these included rabbis who translated into Hebrew the Latin texts of Christian theologians such as Thomas Aquinas (Gutwirth, "Actitudes"; Miller 76–80).

[22] On the Jewish communities of Northern Spain in transition to Christian rule, see Ashtor (3: 167–240) and Baer (1: 39–77). Never having been a natural, colloquial language among the Jews of al-Andalus, Hebrew was confined to the synagogue and the literary academy, while Arabic was the primary language of secular learning. Beginning in the late twelfth century, Jews (mostly immigrants from al-Andalus) living in Christian kingdoms began to translate Arabic-language learning into Hebrew. The same translators involved in this effort, among them Judah al-Ḥarīzī, then began to compose original works of secular literature in Hebrew. For a general overview of Jewish language use in medieval Iberia, see López-Morillas ("Language" 41–46), Miller, and Morag. On al-Ḥarīzī, see Schirmann (*Hebrew Poetry* 2: 97–103), Schirmann and Fleischer (145–221), Sadan, and Blau and Yahalom.

Peter and of his godfather, none other than King Alfonso I of Aragon. He recounts the event in his prologue to the *Dialogus*:

> Cum itaque divine miserationis instinctu ad tam excelsum huius fidei gradum pervenissem, exui pallium falsitatis et nudatus sum tunica iniquitatis et baptizatus sum in sede Oscensis civitatis in nomine Patris et Filii et Spiritus Sanctui, purificatus manibus Stephani, gloriosi et legitimi eiusdem civitatis episcopi.
>
> Hora etiam baptismatis preter ea, quae premissa sunt, credidi beatos apostolos et sanctam ecclesiam catholicam.
>
> Hoc autem factum est a nativitate comini anno millesimo centesimo sexto era millesima centesima quadragesima quarta, mense iunio, die natalis apostolorum Petri et Pauli.
>
> Unde michi ob venerationem et memoriam eiusdem diei et apostoli nomen, quod est Petrus, michi imposui. Fuit autem pater meus spiritualis Alfunsus gloriosus Hyspaniae imperator, qui de me sacro fonte suscepit, qua re nomen eius prefato nomini meo apponens, Petrus Alfunsi michi nomen imposui. (6)
>
> (Seeing that I had arrived, by divine compassion, to such a high degree in this faith, I cast off the veil of falsehood and took off the tunic of iniquity and was baptized in the cathedral of the city of Huesca in the name of the Father and the Son and the Holy Spirit, purified by the hands of Stephen, glorious and legitimate Bishop of that city.
>
> In the very moment of baptism, aside from all that I had already promised, I pledged my faith in the holy Apostles and the Holy Catholic Church.
>
> This happened in the year 1106 of our Lord, 1144 of the [Spanish] era, in the month of June, on the day of the birth of the Apostles Peter and Paul.
>
> Whereas, out of veneration and in memory of that day and that apostle, the name, which is Peter, was placed upon me. It was my spiritual father, Alfonso, glorious Emperor of Spain, who took me from the sacred font, for which, adding his name to my previously mentioned one, I took the name Petrus Alfonsi.)

The Christian Petrus Alfonsi wasted no time in capitalizing on his new social status. He obtained a respectable command of Latin[23] and wrote treatises on various topics in the sciences, most of which have been regarded as mediocre by Andalusī standards, but were nonetheless groundbreaking in Western European Christendom.[24] Petrus Alfonsi made available for the first time a wide variety of writings in mathematics, astronomy, and most importantly for us, the short narrative tradition of the East. The *DC* in particular was

[23] Marcelino Menéndez y Pelayo alone dissents, claiming that Petrus Alfonsi's Latin was quite deficient and that "la rara sintaxis que el autor usa tiene más de semítica que de latina" ('the strange syntax that the author uses is more Semitic than Latin.') (*Orígenes* 1: 62).

[24] His scientific work is now regarded as having been mediocre, and his chief accomplishment seems to have been the inspiration of his students, who quickly surpassed him (Alvárez, "Petrus Alfonsi" 286–87).

very successful and was influential in the development of European narrative through its influence on authors such as Don Juan Manuel, Boccaccio, and Chaucer.

The role of Jews and *conversos* as intermediaries in medieval Iberian frontier culture is familiar to students of medieval and early modern Spanish literature. Petrus Alfonsi is a unique case in the panorama of Spanish Jews and *conversos* whose literary output bridged Arabic, Hebrew, and Latin literary culture. He precedes but shares the historical stage with two groups: the Jewish translators of the twelfth and thirteenth centuries and the *conversos* of the fifteenth and sixteenth. The translators worked alongside their Christian colleagues under the direction of Archbishop Raymond of Toledo (late twelfth century), who sponsored the translation of texts from Arabic into Latin, and under that of Alfonso X the Learned (late thirteenth century), who commissioned texts in Castilian.[25] These men were learned in Hebrew and Arabic scientific and literary tradition and would have been fluent speakers of Iberian Romance languages. As translators, they helped connect Latin readers with Arabic and Hebrew texts, but did not author original works in Latin. Therefore, their individual voices would not reach Christian audiences, and consequently little is known about their lives and characters; they remain shadowy figures, relegated to footnotes.[26] Their work, if not their personal fame, crossed cultural and linguistic boundaries. To wit, while the Castilian translation of the Arabic *Kalīla wa-Dimna* was widely read and eventually appeared in print in Latin and Castilian,[27] its anonymous translator did not accompany his work into the literary limelight. Moshé/Petrus Alfonsi, however, did cross these boundaries, albeit at the price of a fragmented identity. This crossing enabled him to make his voice heard in the Christian society that had suddenly become his home. If

[25] On the translation activity sponsored by Archbishop Raimundo of Toledo, see González Palencia (*Arzobispo*), Burnett ("Arabic"; "Institutional"; "Translating"), and Jacquart. On the activity of Jewish Alfonsine translators, see G. Menéndez Pidal, Gil, Romano Ventura ("Papel"; *Ciencia*), Sáenz-Badillos ("Participación"), Foz, and Barroso. For an overview of extant manuscripts of translations from Arabic and Hebrew into Iberian Romance languages, see Faulhaber ("Semitica Iberica").

[26] We know, for example, that Juan de Sevilla, known before his conversion to Christianity as Salomón ibn Daud (fl. 1135–1153), was responsible for the first translations of Avicenna (980–1037) into Latin (González Palencia, *Arzobispo* 121–22). In Barcelona, Abraham bar Ḥiyya (Savasorda in Catalan) collaborated with Plato of Tivoli (fl. 1134–1145) in his translations of several Arabic texts, such as the *Quadripartitum* of Ptolemy, the *De electionibus* of al-Imrānī (d. 955–956) and the *Liber Abulcasim de operibus astrolabiae* of the Cordovan Ibn al-Saffar (d. 1035) (González Palencia, *Arzobispo* 165–66).

[27] For a full discussion of *Kalīla wa-Dimna* and its translations, see chapter 3.

Moshé found himself thrust into this new Christian world, Petrus Alfonsi made a conscious decision to enter it. Therefore, while by upbringing and education Petrus Alfonsi had a great deal in common with the translators who would later work for Archbishop Raymond and Alfonso X, the fact of his conversion to Christianity adds a psycho-social problematic to his work that is absent in that of his former fellow Jews who did not convert. That is, the religious and political frontiers that he personally crossed are very much present in his text.

The Dialogus contra judaeos

The *Dialogus* offers the reader a great deal of insight into the mindset of the man who wrote the *Disciplina clericalis*, a man whose literary career was made by crossing borders. It is an anti-Judaic polemic in which Petrus Alfonsi attempts to prove the truth of Christianity and the errors of Judaism through rational argumentation. It is part of a well-represented tradition of polemical texts in Latin which dates to early medieval Christianity.[28] As we read Petrus Alfonsi employ rationalist philosophical discourse in a strictly religious debate, it becomes clear that the *Dialogus* is written across frontiers both intellectual and personal. On the one hand, he is using the intellectual tradition of the conquered Jewish and Muslim Andalusīs against them in an effort to discredit their religions. But when one stops to consider that Petrus Alfonsi was one of these very Andalusīs (at least until his conversion to Christianity), one realizes that he is arguing not only across an intellectual frontier, but across the frontier of his own divided self; indeed, in the debate, Petrus Alfonsi's adversary is none other than Moshé (Lat. *Moyses*), the name with which he was born.

The *Dialogus* stands apart from later anti-Jewish polemic texts such as Ramon Martí's *Pugio fidei* ('Dagger of Faith') and Peter the Venerable's *Adversus judaeos* in that Petrus confines himself to a strictly rational argument against the tenets of the Jewish religion, avoiding *ad hominem* attacks against the personal characteristics or behaviors of the Jews themselves. Barbara Hurwitz ascribes this even-handedness to Petrus Alfonsi's origins in the Jewish community (169), but the matter deserves a bit more nuancing. In the *Dialogus*, Petrus Alfonsi demonstrates a persistent attachment to

[28] See A. Williams, Dahan, Schreckenberg (*Christlichen; Christliche*), Limor and Stroumsa, and Sapir Abulafia (*Christians*).

his former Jewish self by casting Moshé—himself—as his interlocutor. His interior struggle, inaugurated by his conversion to Christianity, motivates a compelling literary display of conflicted identity in the *Dialogus*, played out by his two selves in dialogue. In the introduction, Petrus Alfonsi explains how Moshé sought him out upon receiving word of the apostasy/conversion of his alter ego:

> A ternera igitur pueritiae aetate quidam michi perfectissimus adheresat amicus nomine Moyses, qui a primaeva aetate meus consocius fuerat et condiscipulus. Ad hunc cum pervenisset sermo, quod ego paterna lege relicta, Christianam delegissem fidem, relicto suae stationis loco, ad me festinus pervenit, in ipso adventu quendam vultum ferens hominis indignantis et increpans salutavit me more non amici, sed quasi alieni... (8)

> (Thus, since a tender age, a fast friend by the name of Moses was by my side; since my earliest years, he had been my companion and classmate. When word had reached him that I had abandoned our paternal law and chosen the Christian faith, he left his usual place, quickly came to me, his face that of an indignant man, and began by greeting me not in the manner of a friend, but as if I were a stranger...)

Christian doctrine regarding conversion to Christ frames the experience as the resolution of a conflict, a rebirth, a cleansing of sin, or as a completion or a union of a "divided self." In the Catechism it came to be described metaphorically in terms of the return of the Prodigal Son.[29] Medieval Christian writers describe conversion as a personal union with God or a turning of the heart to God. Petrus Alfonsi clearly states that he writes the *Dialogus* in order to justify his conversion. He argues that he was motivated not by material or political gain (as one might well suspect of a man whose prospects were ultimately limited by virtue of his being a Jew), but by the undeniable truth of Christian revelation and inconsistency and falsity of Jewish law:

> Cumque notum esset Iudeis, qui me antea noverant, et probaverant peritum in libris prophetarum et dictis doctarum, partem etiam, licet non magnam, habere omnium liberalium artium, quod legem et fidem accepissem Christianorum et unus essem eorum, quidam eorum arbitrati sunt me hoc non fecisse, nisi quia

[29] Luke 15: 11–24. On Catholic doctrine concerning conversion, see *Catechism* (§ 1493) and Hudson. It should be noted that the medieval Christian understanding of conversion was quite different from that of other religions. For example, despite the fact that the expansion of Islam depended heavily upon conversion, it was not institutionalized in Islam as it was in Christianity (Morrison, *Understanding* xiv and 5–6). For a more complete personal account of the Jewish-Christian conversion experience in the twelfth century, see the case of Herman-Judah (Morrison, *Conversion* 39–113).

adeo amnem abieceram verecundiam, quod et deum et legem contempscram. Alii vero proterea me fecisse dicebant, quod non, ut decuerat, prophetarum et legis verba intellexissem. Alii autem vanae gloriae imputabant et me hoc fecisse calumpniabantur ob honorem seculi, eo quod Christianorum gentem ceteris omnibus superesse conspicerem.

Hunc igitur libellum composui, ut omnes et meam cognoscant intentionem et audiant rationem, in quo omnium aliarum gentium credulitatis destructionem proposui, post hec Christianum legem omnibus prestantiorem esse conclusi. Ad ultimum etiam omnes cuiuslibet Christiane legis adversarii obiectiones posui positasque pro meo sapere cum ratione et auctoritate destruxi.

(And, as it was known by the Jews who knew me previously and who regarded me as an expert in the books of the Prophets and sayings of the doctors, and in part, albeit not large, of the liberal arts, that I had accepted the law and faith of the Christians and that I had become one of them, some of them thought that I had only done so because at that point I had shed all modesty, for I hated God and his law. Others said that no, I had done it because I had not understood well the words of the Prophets and the law. Still others attributed it to vainglory, and insulting me by [implying my] worldliness, said that I had seen that the Christian people were surpassing all the others.

Therefore, I composed this book, so that all might know my intentions and hear my reasoning, in which all I proposed the destruction of the belief of all other peoples, that they might quickly conclude that the Christian law is superior to all others. Finally, I also expound all of the objections of any adversary of Christian law, and once expounded, I refuted them according to my knowledge, with reasoning and authorities.)

Critics are in disagreement as to the specific motives of Petrus Alfonsi's conversion, and although we may speculate as to its sincerity, his thorough rationalist consideration of both faiths confirms that it was a deliberate act and that he had meditated upon the personal and spiritual ramifications that it would have in his life.[30] Despite his protestations, and particularly in light of the fact that the King himself was his godfather, one cannot help thinking that contemporary politics played an important part in bringing Moshé to the baptismal font.

The dialogue genre is hardly an innovation on the part of Petrus Alfonsi. It was widely cultivated in Arabic poetry and especially in Arabic philosophical texts by both Jews and Muslims.[31] It would also become increasingly popu-

[30] On the question of Petrus Alfonsi's motives for converting, see Jeremy Cohen ("Mentality" 27–28) and Tolan ("Pedro Alfonso" xv).

[31] On the dialogue in Arabic poetry, see Scott Meisami and Starkey (191) and Scott Meisami (*Structure* 139 and 211–13). For an example of its cultivation in eleventh-century

lar in both Latin and the Romance vernaculars during the fourteenth and fifteenth centuries. By the time Petrus Alfonsi writes his *Dialogus*, there is already a well-represented tradition of such anti-Jewish polemics in dialogue. But the dialogue between self and self is unique to Petrus Alfonsi's *Dialogus*. That his major innovation in the dialogue genre was the introduction of the auto-dialogue between his Jewish and Christian selves is telling. One must, therefore, ask the question: why did Petrus Alfonsi cast himself as his own interlocutor, and what does this move mean in the context of his conflicted identity as a *converso*? Why put his identity crisis on display? One possible answer is that in making a public display of his inner dialogue he sought to satisfy those skeptics (whom he mentions in the prologue) of the sincerity of his conversion. Perhaps he felt that his Jewish self would gracefully retire into obscurity after being defeated publicly in a fair fight, just as an imaginary friend might disappear after being convinced he was not real.

We have a clue to this mystery in the decidedly anti-climactic conclusion of the *Dialogus*. Where one might logically expect Petrus Alfonsi's superior logic to result in Moshé's conversion, instead Moshé merely concedes, in typically rationalist fashion, that although Petrus' reasoning is superior, it does not necessarily reflect divine will:

> M.—Multum certe suae tibi deus dedit sapientiae et te magna ilustravit ratione, quem vincere nequeo, immo tu obiectiones meas confutasti ratione.
>
> P.—Hoc procul dubio donum est Spiritus Sancti, quem in baptismo recipimus, qui et corda nostra illuminat, ne falsum quid credere presumamus. Quod si tu, quod credimus, ipse etiam crederes et baptizari te feceres, eandem Spiritus Sancti illustrationem haberes, ut, quae vera sunt, cognosceres et, quae falsa, respueres. Nunc autem quoniam super te pietatem habeo, dei misericordiam imploro, ut Spiritus sui plenitudine te illustret et finem meliorem quam principium tibi prestet. Amen. (193)
>
> (M.—It is certain that God gave you much wisdom and granted you great reasoning, things which I cannot defeat; yet on the contrary, it is you who refuted my objections with your arguments.

al-Andalus, see *EI* ("Ibn Burd"). On its use in works of *kalām* (rationalist philosophy), especially in the eleventh and twelfth century, see Ben-Shammai (122). Its best-known examples in Hebrew (both Spanish) are the *Meqor Ḥayyīm* of Shlomo ibn Gabirol (c. 1020–c. 1057) and the *Kuzarī* of Yehudah Halevi (d. 1141). On the florescence of the dialogue genre in Hebrew after the *Kuzarī*, see Chazan (*Fashioning* 331–32).

P.—Without doubt this is a gift from the Holy Spirit, that we receive in baptism and that illuminates our hearts so that we believe nothing false. And if you also believed that which we believe and were baptized, you too would have that same illumination from the Holy Spirit, that you might know truth and reject falsehood. And now, given that I feel pity for you, I implore God's mercy that he illuminate you with the fullness of his Spirit and that he grant you a better end than a beginning. Amen.)

In essence, Moshé concludes that Petrus is the better philosopher, but that human reason does not equal divine revelation. That is, Petrus may be able to argue adeptly for the superiority of Christianity, but the fact of his powers of reasoning being God-given does not make his arguments true. This argument is typical of the doctrine of free will (*ikhtiyār*) espoused by such rationalist Andalusī philosophers as Maimonides and Ibn Rushd (Averroes).[32] They believed that reason is God's gift to humanity, but humans are ultimately responsible for practicing it responsibly. Here, the author's ambivalence comes to the fore: Petrus claims a logical victory, and though Moshé admits he is bested in the debate, he does not appear to embrace Christ as a result. Here Moshé and Petrus split into two distinct personalities: Petrus the Christian and Moshé the Jew. Thus the discussion ends, leaving Petrus at the top of Pérez-Firmat's see-saw, with no way to come down.

The Disciplina Clericalis

In *Dialogus*, we learn that Petrus Alfonsi's Andalusī education served him well in Christendom. His training in rational philosophy and both Jewish and Christian religious tradition enabled him to write one of the most adept religious polemics of his time, bringing the work of Jewish and Muslim Andalusī philosophers to bear against their own religions. The result is a curious blend of religious intolerance and intellectual cosmopolitanism characteristic of Christian Iberia in the late Middle Ages. His religious border crossing is a conflictive experience in which he is bound to denigrate his former religion in order to be accepted in his new one.

However, his fate as a frontier storyteller is different. While life on the frontier is conflictive when viewed in terms of religion, it is in storytelling that coexistence is more easily mediated, and with rich results. If the *Dialogus* is the story of an identity crisis, the *DC* is its more felicitous, less

[32] On the doctrine of *ikhtiyār*, or free will (a better translation is, perhaps, 'freedom of decision') see Watt, *EJ* ("Free Will"), and *EI* ("Ikhtiyār").

problematic literary outcome. This collection of tales and gnomic lore, with its combination of elements from Christian and Andalusī tradition, is Petrus Alfonsi's productive response to the challenge of being a *converso* intellectual in a colonial environment. The portrait of Petrus Alfonsi in the *Dialogus* is that of a man unable to reconcile his past and present selves. However, this same author who seems incapable of integrating his divided self proves much more so in reconciling the storytelling cultures of his past and his present. In the *DC* we see a Petrus Alfonsi who harkens back to the courtier-rabbis of al-Andalus, who moves between secular and religious, Arabic and Latin, Andalusī and Aragonese. Storytelling, including its literary forms, is rooted in popular oral culture, and the tales and fables that make up collections such as the *DC* owe less to the values of Church, Synagogue, or Mosque than those of home, hearth, and table. Popular narrative crosses linguistic and cultural border more readily than other genres—such as the type of debate found in the *Dialogus*—that directly reflect institutional religious values.

The content of the *DC*, like that of *Kalīla wa-Dimna*,[33] centers on object lessons of practical wisdom. A number of its *exempla* are related by the teacher as he answers the student's questions on topics such as the acquisition of wisdom, self-preservation, ethical treatment of others, and how to evade the wiles of women. As in the case of Boccaccio (1313–1375), who wrote numerous religious and scholarly treatises in Latin but is overwhelmingly remembered as the author of the *Decameron*, Petrus Alfonsi's other writings are largely overshadowed by the modern reception of the *Disciplina clericalis*, which survives in over 70 Latin manuscripts and was translated into several European languages and now attracts more scholarly attention than his other works, including the *Dialogus*.

Although the *Disciplina clericalis* may have been completely novel to Latin audiences in terms of its narrative structure and its use of sources drawn entirely from the Arabic and Hebrew tradition, it was not at all innovative in the context of Arabic and Hebrew literature. His most significant achievement with the *DC* was to introduce Latin readers to a well-established genre of courtly literature from Arabic tradition: *adab*.[34] The Arabic word *adab* is associated with a broad range of meanings that include "proper conduct" or "manners" as well as "education" or "literature" (Bonebakker 25). In the early period of Islam, through roughly the eighth century, an *adīb*, or cultured man, was one who had mastered the poetic and anecdotal traditions of the

[33] See chapter 3.
[34] On *adab* literature, see Bonebakker.

pre-Islamic *jāhilīyya* age (*EI*, "Djāhiliyya"). During the cultural flowering of the ʿAbbāsid period (8th–9th c.) it came to mean one who was versed not only in Arabic poetics but also in the gnomic and narrative literature absorbed from Indian and Persian traditions and the practical philosophy of the Greeks (*EI*, "Adab"). In short, *adab* is the forerunner of the secular liberal arts education. By the beginning of the ninth century, *adab* also came to signify such social graces as the ability to entertain others with verse, amusing anecdotes, and of course, stories (Bonebakker 23). At times, what made these anecdotes and tales amusing was their claim to didactic authority. That is, many of the stories that were counted as *adab* literature were not intended as serious moral lessons, but as ironically didactic bits of entertaining narrative (Jones and Keller 20). It is also important to remember that the narrative genres that eventually came to be recognized as *adab* were introduced as part of the adaptation of Persian material into Arabic literature that characterized the ʿAbbāsid period.[35]

Eventually, there appeared compilations of *adab* literature, miscellanies and anthologies that served as handbooks for courtiers aspiring to eloquence and witty discourse of the type that facilitate one's career. It was the tenth-century Andalusī author Ibn ʿAbd al-Rabbih who first consciously referred to his own writing as *adab* (Bonebakker 28). In the introduction to his *ʿIqd al-farīd*, or 'Unique necklace' he writes the following:

> I have composed this book and selected its gems from the best gems of *adāb*; it is the result of the compilers of clarity and was the gem of gems and the pith of piths; surely within it is compiled the choicest of selections, the best of anthologies, a mantle upon the breast of every book; it has no equal among the captured aromas of the sayings of the learned, and the achievements of the sages and the literati (*ʾudabāʾ*). And the selection of wise sayings is more difficult than their composition, for they have said: "man's freedom of decision is the ambassador of his intelligence." (1: 2)

In his introduction to the *DC*, Petrus Alfonsi echoes Ibn ʿAbd al-Rabbihi's description of the author of *adab* as a compiler and anthologizer, listing the various sources upon which he draws:

---

[35] This transculturation of narrative is a gradual process. When *Kalīla wa-Dimna* first appeared in the eighth century, Arabic prose fiction was a marginalized genre, and considered morally suspect. On the legitimation of fiction in Classical Arabic literature, see Drory (*Models* 37–47). Over time, the quality of Ibn al-Muqaffaʿ's Arabic prose and the work's sheer entertainment value prevailed; *Kalīla wa-Dimna* entered the canon of *adab* literature and is to this day considered one of the best-loved classics of Arabic literature. In fact, it was so important in Andalusī literary culture that it was the first translation from Arabic to Castilian commissioned by Alfonso el Sabio, who was still the *Infante* Alfonso when he ordered its translation in 1251.

> libellum compegi partim ex proverbiis philosophorum et suis castigationibus, partim ex proverbiis et castigationibus Arabicis et fabulis et versibus, partim ex animalium et volucrum similitudinibus. (2)
>
> (I have put together this book, partly from the sayings of wise men and their advice, partly from Arab proverbs, counsels, fables, and poems, and partly from bird and animal similes.) (104)

As an Andalusī intellectual, Petrus Alfonsi would have been well-versed in *adab* and in all likelihood would have known Ibn ʿAbd al-Rabbih's work, as well as other works of *adab* literature such as the Arabic *Kalīla wa-Dimna*.

Petrus Alfonsi's appropriation of *adab* for Christian Europe must be understood in terms of the colonial reality in which he lived. Compiling a work of *adab* in al-Andalus, where it was part of an established tradition, is one thing; introducing such a book in Latin literary culture is another. His conversion and entry into the newly dominant culture of his time put him in a position not unlike that of the Europeanized native elites of French North Africa or British South Asia. Part of Petrus Alfonsi's genius was his ability to thrive during a time of political and social transition, and this quality is borne out in the pages of the *DC*. The Christian conquest of al-Andalus was a colonial project, motivated primarily by material concerns and justified by the idea that the Christians of Castile and Aragon had a historic right to the whole of the Iberian Peninsula by virtue of their "Visigothic" lineage.[36] In this spirit, the *DC* is a transculturation of the purely secular *adab* literature of the colonized Andalusīs in a lightly Christianized, Latin format.

Transculturation is a term coined by the Cuban anthropologist Fernando Ortiz in 1947 in his landmark study, *Contrapunteo cubano del tabaco y el azúcar*. His thesis is that the culture of a colonized people does not disappear upon their adoption of a colonial culture, but rather engages the colonial culture in a process of transculturation that results in a unique new culture that bears elements of both but that is entirely its own (260). In the 1970s and 80s, the Latin American literary critic Angel Rama used the term to demonstrate how South American authors consciously introduced elements of indigenous culture into their work in order to resist urban and Europeanizing literary values. He described the colonial author as a "genial tejedor" ('good-natured weaver') (19) who picks and chooses from among the repertoire of conquered and conqueror, selects and adapts, and so produces a new, unique literature neither indigenous nor colonial. More recently,

[36] See n. 7, above.

Mary Louise Pratt has written of transculturation in the context of colonial and postcolonial travel narrative in her book, *Imperial Eyes*. For Pratt, the term transculturation describes "how subordinated or marginal groups select and invent from materials transmitted to them by a dominant or metropolitan culture" (6).

There are, granted, some crucial differences between twentieth-century Latin America and twelfth-century Aragon, hinging on questions of political power and cultural prestige. First, the Andalusī culture that Petrus Alfonsi represented to the dominant colonial power of Christian Aragon was prestigious by Western European standards. Though Islam and Judaism were abhorred by Spanish Christians, the science, philosophy, and art of Andalusī Muslims and Jews were highly prized. By contrast, Spanish *conquistadores* considered the indigenous Americans to be subhuman and barely capable of reason.[37] This inversion notwithstanding, the power dynamic between conquered Andalusī and conquering Spanish Christian is colonial, and Petrus Alfonsi works both the prestige of Andalusī learning and the power of Christian rule to his advantage. Therefore, while the mechanism of transculturation as described by Ortiz and Rama is similar in the *DC*, the terms of engagement are somewhat different.

Confident that his store of Andalusī knowledge is in high demand, and writing in Latin as a Christian of very high standing, the "genial tejedor" Petrus Alfonsi is at liberty to pick and choose his materials. His effort to frame his work in terms of Christian morality is decidedly *pro forma* and is largely passive. His work contains no material of specifically Christian provenance and does not illustrate Christian doctrine nor recount miracles of Saints. The only specific references to Christianity are found in the prologue:

> Vitandum tamen decrevi pro possibilitate sensus mei, ne quid in nostro tractatu inveniatur quod nostrae credulitati sit contrarium vel a nostra fide diversum. Ad quod adiuvet me omnipotens Deus cui supernitor. Amen. (2)
>
> (On the other hand, I decided that, within the capabilities of my senses, everything must be avoided in this book that might be found contrary to our beliefs or different from our faith. To do which may Almighty God to whom I dedicate myself, help me. Amen.) (104)

[37] The sixteenth-century polemics of Juan Ginés de Sepúlveda and Gonzalo Fernández de Oviedo y Valdés famously described indigenous Americans as bestial and subhuman (Keen 78–82; Arrom 69–79).

Thus, by his own admission, Petrus Alfonsi did not set out to write a book of teachings based on Christian doctrine, but rather one of secular Andalusī teachings that would not offend Christian sensibilities. Of the thirty-odd stories in the collection, there are only three that deal with moral issues, and even these fit equally well within the framework of Islam, Judaism, or Hinduism.[38]

In the first of these, "The Half Friend," a father teaches his son that only a truly selfless person can be a friend and that one should consider one's self lucky to have made half such a friend in an entire lifetime. The value of self-sacrifice for others is also the focus of the follow-up to "The Half Friend," the tale of "The Perfect Friend" (perhaps the best-known tale of the collection). In it, two merchant friends, one from Baghdad and the other from Egypt, demonstrate their loyalty to each other. First, the merchant from Baghdad falls in love with the intended bride of the Egyptian, who surrenders her to his friend in order to save him from a fatal case of lovesickness. Years later, the Baghdādī repays the Egyptian the favor by confessing to a murder for which the latter had been accused. Both tales illustrate the virtue of charity, a value taught by nearly every religious tradition and prominently so in Judaism, Christianity, and Islam. Perhaps the only tale in the collection with a patently religious didactic message is "The Prudent Son of the Royal Wazir," in which the son of a king's favorite counselor is criticized for spending his entire fortune on sustaining his king's subjects during a severe famine and drought. When questioned as to his motives, he replies that he had not squandered his fortune, but merely invested it in the world to come. In this way, writes Petrus Alfonsi, he acted just like the advice given by a philosopher to his son: "Fecit sicut philosophus filio suo praecepit dicens: 'Fili, vende hoc saeculum pro futuro et utrumque lucraberis'" (29). ('My son, sell this world for the next, and you will be rich in both') (158).

Given the complete absence of specifically Christian values in the tales and proverbs he brings together in the *DC* and his skillful blending of Eastern material and Latin rhetorical sensibility, we see that Petrus Alfonsi was a medieval version of Rama's "genial tejedor." True to Ibn ʿAbd al-Rabbih's ideal author of *adab*, he sets forth his *ikhtiyār*, or freedom of decision, as the ambassador of his intelligence. He picks and chooses from his warehouse of Andalusī learning, fitting it into his understanding of a Christian literary framework, yet emphasizing that man, as God's creation, is a rational being

[38] See Hermes ("Author" 18). For the *exempla* in question (nos. 1, 2, and 29), see *DC* (3–6 and 42–43; trans. 106–09 and 56–58).

whose purpose on earth is to use his intellect to better comprehend the world and its creator:

> Cum enim apud me saepius retractando humanae causas creationis omnimodo scire laborarem, humanum quidem ingenium inveni ex praecepto conditoris ad hoc esse deputatum, ut quamdiu est in saeculo in sanctae studeat exercitatione philsophiae, qua de creatore suo meliorem et maiorem habeat notitiam, et moderata vivere studeat continentia et ab imminentibus sciat sibi praecavere adversitatibus eoque tramite gradiatur in saeculo, qui eum dicat ad regna caelorum. (1)
>
> (For while I toiled to learn the causes of man's creation by every means and by frequent ponderings, I have found that the human spirit has been set down for this very purpose by the precept of the creator, that so long as it is in the world it may study and busy itself with holy philosophy, to have thereby a better and greater knowledge of its creator, to live in moderation and continency and to learn to protect itself in the midst of the supporters of ungodliness, and to follow that path in the world which will lead it to the kingdom of heaven.) (103)

His claim is that this book will help the reader in studying "holy philosophy," the better to understand the Creator. Yet there is very little mention of God or religion in the *DC*, and in order to better understand God, one would be better served by reading works of *kalām* by authors such as Ibn Rushd or Maimonides, or perhaps the theosophy of the Kabbalists. Petrus Alfonsi here is engaging in a bit of "bait and switch" rhetoric: he promises holy philosophy and delivers mostly practical wisdom. In doing so, he exercises the rational selectivity that for Ibn ʿAbd al-Rabbihi is the essence of *adab* and for Rama is characteristic of the transculturation of prose narrative.

Petrus Alfonsi is clearly conscious of his role as cultural intermediary and takes steps to emphasize this role in his writing. Well aware of the prestige accorded to Arabic learning in twelfth-century Christian Europe and eager to borrow some of its authority for his own work, he deliberately calls attention to the fact that he compiled the *DC* from Arabic sources (2; trans. 104). In fact, he tells the reader, not only does he compile his text from authentically non-Latin sources, he even composed it in another language (which we may assume to be Arabic) before translating it into Latin.[39]

[39] "Deus igitur in hoc opusculo mihi sit in auxilium, qui me librum hunc componere et in latinum transferre compulit" (1). ('Therefore may God be my help in this undertaking. He, who has compelled me to write this book and translate it into Latin') (103). Tolan surmises that he "composed and translated at the same time" (*Petrus* 76).

He wants his audience to know that his work is not merely a Latin composition of remembrances from an Andalusī education, but an original anthology of "authentic" Arabic lore. To this end, he puts many of the wise sayings and *exempla* in the mouths of known figures from Arabic tradition such as Idrīs and Luqmān, authorities familiar to Arabic audiences from Quranic, legendary, and gnomic sources, but quite novel and perhaps exotic to his readers in Western Christendom.[40]

For example, in the prologue, he attributes proverbs on the fear of God to a certain "Enoch philosophus, qui lingua arabica cognominatur Edric" (2) ('The philosopher Enoch, called Edris in Arabic') (104).[41] In the same section, he places a series of exemplary proverbs on the ant, the rooster, and the dog in the mouth of "Balaam, qui lingua arabica vocatur Lucaman" (3) ('Balaam, who in Arabic is called Lukaman') (105).[42]

Other times he attributes material to anonymous Arabs, either poets or fathers instructing their sons. The narrative convention of placing wisdom in the mouth of a father or teacher instructing a son or pupil was common to many forms of wisdom literature, some of which were already known in the West by the appearance of the *Disciplina*. Yet the fact that Petrus Alfonsi designates these fathers and teachers as Arabs (2, 3, 7, 9, 26, 31, 33, and 39; trans. 104, 06, 12, 13, 16, 35, 42–43, and 44), but not as specific historical or mythical individuals, suggests that he does so in order to infuse his work with a bit of the authority of the exotic, alien yet scientifically superior culture that the Arab world represented to Christian Europe at the turn of the twelfth century, only a few years after the First Crusade was launched in 1096, the same year in which Huesca fell to the Christians.[43]

---

[40] "In Arab Adab literature many wise sayings are ascribed to the sage Idrīs as well as to Lukman" (Schwarzbaum, "International" 1961: 287). This article is the first in a three-part series by the same title, all published in consecutive numbers of *Sefarad*. On the Arabic proverbial tradition attributed to Luqmān, see *EI* ("Luḳmān"), Halawah, Kafumah, Marzūq, and Yūsuf.

[41] It is worth noting that the Hebrew *Sefer Ḥenokh* ('The Book of Enoch') (Constantinople 1516 and Venice 1544) is a Sephardic Hebrew translation of the first two *exempla* of the *DC* (Schwartzbaum, "International" 1961: 286).

[42] Balaam would become known to readers of medieval Castilian through *Barlaam e Josafat* (ed. Keller and Linker). On *Barlaam*, see De Haan. The same work became the basis for Don Juan Manuel's *Libro de los estados* (Funes, "Leyenda").

[43] "[Readers of the *DC*] have noticed that the author of the *DC* belongs to a foreign world. The comparison of the work with Alexander's letter on the marvels of India, or with the *Historia Alexandri Magni*, which describes the amazing lands and peoples of the East, or with a section from another work by Petrus Alfonsi, the so-called *De Machometo*, bears testimony to the active desire of Western man to learn and know something about that

A number of Petrus Alfonsi's *exempla*[44] are set in the Arab world. The best known tale in the collection, that of the "Perfect Friend" (no. 2),[45] begins "Relatum est mihi de duobus negotiatoribus, quorum unus erat in Aegypto, alter in Baldach" (4) ('I have been told of two merchants of whom one lived in Egypt, and the other in Baghdad') (107). The settings are in no way essential to the development of the tale, but rather are conserved in order to appeal to the Latin reader's association of such cities with material sophistication and cultural authority. The tale of "The Two Townsfolk and the Countryman" (no. 19) is even set on the pilgrimage to Mecca, which anticipates (or perhaps inspires) the setting of Chaucer's *Canterbury Tales*: ("Dictum fuit de duobus burgensibus et rustico causa orationis Mech aduentibus quod essent socii victus" (27) ('The story is told of two men and a countryman who were making the pilgrimage to Mecca') (136). Again, while the tale warns that betraying the trust of a traveling companion may backfire and that it is imprudent to judge a person by their appearance, the specific setting is incidental window dressing. Another example (no. 15, "The Ten Chests") relates the experiences of an Andalusī on *hājj* to Mecca: "Dictum fuit mihi quod quidam Hyspanus perrexit Mech, et dum ibat pervenit in Aegyptum." (20) ('I was once told of how a Spaniard journeyed to Mecca, and while on his journey went through Egypt.') (128).[46] The pilgrim seeks to deposit his money in a safe place in Egypt before continuing across the desert to Mecca. Curiously, the Andalusī protagonist is referred to simply as "Hispanus" and not as "Maurus" ('Moor') or "Saracenus" ('Saracen').[47] With this, Petrus Alfonsi includes Spain—or at least the Spain of his youth—within the Arab world, as a source of exotic wisdom and lore.

distant foreign world that had suddenly attained such importance in the age of the crusades" (Hermes, "Author" 33).

[44] Tolan prefers 'fables' to '*exempla*' because the latter is commonly associated with twelfth- and thirteenth-century collections of Latin tales by Franciscan and Dominican preachers intended for inclusion in sermons (*Petrus* 82).

[45] The tale is well-attested in collections of *adab* literature (Schwarzbaum, "International" 1961: 289).

[46] There are a number of versions of this tale in the Talmud and in other Rabbinic sources (Schwarzbaum, "International" 1962: 32). Among these is an eleventh-century Judeo-Arabic version by Nissim ben Yaʿqob ibn Shāhīn (104–10; trans. Brinner 26–27).

[47] According to Fletcher, "early Medieval writers commonly employed the term *Hispania* to indicate what Arabic speakers called al-Andalus, that part of the Iberian peninsula under Muslim rule" (87).

By contrast, the only place in the Latin world he mentions by name is Rome, in "The Weeping Puppy Dog" (no. 13).[48] In it, a young nobleman leaves his chaste wife at home while he travels to Rome to study rhetoric.[49] In his absence, an old woman tricks her into taking a lover. Here again, the choice of setting is incidental and noteworthy only in that it is the sole mention of any specific location in the Latin world, among many such mentions of Eastern locales such as Egypt, Baghdad, and Mecca.

The life and work of Petrus Alfonsi remind us that the cultural achievements of *convivencia*—and by extension of all frontier culture—exact a human price. Petrus Alfonsi was indeed a remarkable man, if not a unique one in a time and place that was home to so many frontier crossers. In a time of political and cultural upheaval, he was able to preserve his status as an important courtier. Even more, he was able to trade on his conversion to Christianity in order to achieve intellectual celebrity in Latin Europe. He single-handedly introduced Europe to the courtly genre of *adab* literature, one of the essential hallmarks of an educated man in the Arab world. Underlying all these successes is a hint of personal pain. The *Dialogus* is testimony to a personal conflict, an internal struggle between Jew and Christian, Andalusī and Aragonese, that fueled Petrus Alfonsi's considerable creativity and personal accomplishment. In this way, he embodies the conflicts inherent in colonial society and the transculturation characteristic of it.

The *DC* demonstrates how tales, fables, and anecdotes common to folk narrative, easily travel across linguistic and cultural boundaries. The transculturation and recombination of narrative traditions within its pages are the blueprint for the type of synthesis and fusion that make medieval Iberian narrative unique in Christian Europe during the Middle Ages. In its pages, one sees narrative materials, techniques, references to familiar places and authorities that were the stock-in-trade of a twelfth-century Andalusī *adīb*. Petrus Alfonsi recontextualizes all of these within a Latin text that is foundational to the Romance-language narrative practice of late medieval Iberia. His personal experience (as a bicultural, polyglot convert) made possible important innovations in Latin and Romance narrative that would forever change the way Christian Europeans would tell stories in literature.

---

[48] This tale appears in the Castilian *Sendebar*, and Petrus Alfonsi's most likely source would be the Arabic original. See *Sendebar* (ed. Lacarra 108–11) and Schwarzbaum ("International" 1962: 24–28).

[49] "Contigit forte quod orationis studio Romam vellet adire" (17). ('It happened by chance that he desired to go to Rome to study oratory.') (124).

In sum, Petrus Alfonsi is a crucial link between the literary practices of al-Andalus and those of Christian Iberia. He is very much the literary grandfather of thirteenth- and fourteenth-century figures such as Alfonso X, Don Juan Manuel, and Juan Ruiz (whose work we will discuss in subsequent chapters), a man whose written work tells the story of a life lived across boundaries—religious, political, and cultural.

CHAPTER TWO

STORYTELLING AND PERFORMANCE IN MEDIEVAL IBERIAN FRAMETALE AND *MAQĀMA*[1]

The Andalusī literary culture from which Petrus Alfonsi emerged into Latin Christendom was home to a sophisticated tradition of literary prose narrative. Andalusī authors and audiences were heirs to two genres of narrative collections cultivated in ʿAbbāsid-era Arabic literature, the frametale and *maqāma*. In the years following the appearance of the *Disciplina clericalis*, Andalusī authors (and later Jewish authors living in Christian Iberia) cultivated both of these genres, and by the fourteenth century the distinctions between frametale and *maqāma* became increasingly blurred.

Both frametale and *maqāma* are collections of stories told—performed—within a story. It is a genre that portrays storytelling within a literary text. The way in which people tell stories, whether in social settings or in literary texts, differs according to the cultures in which storytellers and authors participate. The storytelling traditions that converged in al-Andalus (and later in Christian Iberia) had distinct practices of storytelling and popular narrative, and authors of frametales and *maqāmāt* drew on these practices in the ways in which they encoded storytelling events in their texts.

In al-Andalus, the story of the frametale and *maqāma* can thus begin to be told in terms of how these works render storytelling and performance in a textual setting. If the frametale is a story about storytelling, its critical study demands attention to how storytelling and performative practices are encoded and decoded by authors and audiences of frametales. In this way, we can begin to tell the story of performance in Andalusī literary culture and of how Andalusī authors of frametales and *maqāmāt* drew on Muslim and Jewish traditions of live and textually encoded performance in the literature they read and in the world they inhabited.

In this chapter, I will first discuss the encoding of storytelling performances in *Kalīla wa-Dimna*, a framed collection of fables that by the twelfth century

[1] A previous version of this chapter, titled "The Performativity of Ibn al-Muqaffaʿ's *Kalīla wa-Dimna* and *al-Maqāmāt al-Luzūmīyya* of al-Saraqusṭī" appeared in the *Journal of Arabic Literature* 34 (2003): 178–89.

had become a widely read classic of Arabic literature.[2] The popularity of *Kalīla* and its influence on later Arabic, Latin, and Castilian literature makes it quite likely that it would have served as a model for the textual encoding of performance for later works of fiction in Arabic. Two centuries after the appearance of *Kalīla*, and perhaps in reaction to the tradition of fictional storytelling encoded within it, the Arabic *maqāma* genre of prose fiction introduces a different model of performance in literary narrative, one based on the oral transmission of *ḥadīṯ*, the sayings of Muhammad.

The *maqāma* was first introduced to Arabic literature by Badiʿ al-Zamān al-Hamaḏānī in the late tenth century, in Baghdad. Al-Hamaḏānī strove to reproduce in literature the antics of the highly eloquent street preachers, performers, and hustlers known collectively as the Banū Sasān (Bosworth 1: 20). Various urchins, conmen, and ascetics of questionable intent are combined in the rogue character, an itinerant opportunist who dazzles his audiences with his rhetorical acrobatics and invariably leaves them penniless, bidding them farewell with a poem that lays bare the deception into which they have just fallen. In al-Hamaḏānī's *maqāmāt*, the narrator ʿIsā ibn Hishām recounts fifty such deceptions suffered at the hands of the rogue Abū-l Fatḥ al-Iskandarī, who appears each time in a different guise, as old man, youth, Bedouin, wanderer, and preacher. Only after ʿIsā bin Hishām is fleeced does he recognize the rogue and marvels at his excellent rhetoric as al-Iskandarī makes off with the narrator's cash. The *maqāmāt* of al-Hamaḏānī were imitated and greatly popularized by al-Ḥarīrī[3] in the Muslim East and in al-

[2] *Kalīla wa-Dimna* (= *Kalīla*) was first composed in Sanskrit by a Vishnuite Brahmin in the beginning of the fourth century. It was then translated into Pahlavi (Old Persian) by the order of the Sassānian King Khusraw Anushirwān in the second half of the sixth century by his physician Burzoē. About two centuries later it was translated into Arabic by ʿAbdallāh ibn al-Muqaffaʿ. For a complete discussion of the textual tradition and its transmission, see *EI* ("*Kalīla wa-Dimna*"), Penzol, and Montiel. A more detailed discussion of the work is found in chapter 3. Because this study is concerned with the reception of *Kalīla* in Castilian, I cite Cacho Blecua and Lacarra's edition of the thirteenth century Castilian translation, *Calila e Dimna* (= *Calila*), and reference the Arabic edition of Cheikho. His is accepted as the most authoritative, though it should be noted that it differs considerably from the Castilian translation in some places. The problem of the Arabic mansucript tradition is discussed in chapter 3. Another Arabic frametale, *Sindibād*, which we can assume to have circulated in al-Andalus owing to its translation into Castilian in 1253 (*Sendebar*) by Don Fadrique (brother of Alfonso X), would also have contributed to Andalusīs' understanding of textually encoded storytelling performance. Though it might serve as an equally productive example of the Arabic frametale in al-Andalus, we do not believe that the performances encoded within it differ significantly from those found in *Kalīla* for purposes of the present study. In any event, the Arabic original is lost, although several of its stories are included in the *Alf layla wa-layla* ('Thousand and One Nights').

[3] He is Abū Muḥammad al-Qāsim ibn ʿAlī al-Ḥarīrī al-Baṣrī (1054–1122), a high-level government official, poet, and philologist resident of Baghdād (*EI*, "al-Ḥarīrī").

Andalus as well, where they inspired al-Saraqusṭī to write his own *maqāmāt* sometime during the first half of the twelfth century, in Cordova.[4]

Andalusīs read *Kalīla* and Andalusī authors (most notably al-Saraqusṭī) cultivated the *maqāma* genre (Arie). Some years after the appearance of al-Saraqusṭī's Arabic *Luzūmīyya*, Jewish authors in Christian Spain began to cultivate the *maqāma* genre in Hebrew. Judah al-Ḥarīzī[5] writes his *Taḥkemonī* in imitation of the Arabic *maqāmāt*, bringing to his work notions of performance and transmission of narrative material reflective of Jewish law and tradition. At approximately the same time, Ibn Zabāra[6] writes the *Sefer Šaʿašūʿīm* ('Book of Delights', = *Šaʿašūʿīm*), interpreting the generic conventions of the Arabic *maqāmāt* more liberally and also drawing on the inspiration of frametales such as *Kalīla* in his textual encoding of narrative performance. From *Kalīla* to Arabic and then Hebrew *maqāmāt*, a picture of a specifically Andalusī tradition of textually encoded performance begins to emerge, one that inherits aspects of performative practice and transmission from the Sanskrit origins of *Kalīla*, the practice of popular preaching and storytelling in medieval Islam, and Jewish traditions of rabbinic and folk narrative. As I will argue in later chapters, the techniques and practices developed by these Andalusī authors in Arabic and Hebrew later enter Castilian and Catalan literary culture, both through the translation of texts and

---

[4] Abū-l Ṭāhir Muḥammad ibn Yūsuf al-Tamīmī al-Saraqusṭī ibn al-Aštarkūnī (d. 1143), an Andalusī scholar and writer whose literary legacy includes, apart from his *al-Maqāmāt al-Luzūmīyya* (= *Luzūmīyya*), a philological work on rare words in the Arabic language, and fragments of poetry. In addition, various references by contemporary writers to al-Saraqusṭī indicate that he was an active writer during much of his life, although the biographical information about him is scarce (Monroe, "Preliminary" 18–40). See the modern Arabic editions of Ḍayf and al-Warāglī, the English translation of Monroe, and the Spanish translation of Ferrando Frutos. I cite the English translation of Monroe and reference the edition of al-Warāglī.

[5] Judah al-Ḥarīzī (1165–1225) was born in Spain and traveled widely throughout Provence and the Islamic Mediterranean. He was a prolific translator of Arabic literature into Hebrew as well as a poet and author in his own right (*EJ*, "al-Harizi, Judah ben Solomon"). For his work *Taḥkemonī*, see the edition of Toporovsky and Zamora, the literal prose English translation of Reichert, the rhyming prose English translation of Segal, the Spanish translation of Del Valle Rodríguez, and the partial Spanish translation of Navarro Peiro (*Narrativa* 100–22). On al-Ḥarīzī's adaptation of Arabic poetics, see Drory (*Models* 215–32). All citations to *Taḥkemnonī* are from the Hebrew edition of Toporovsky and Zamora, and the English translation of Reichert.

[6] Joseph ben Meir Ibn Zabāra was a physician resident of Barcelona, born ca. 1140. See the edition of Davidson, the Catalan translation (with an excellent introduction and notes) of González-Llubera, the English translation of Hadas, the Spanish translation of Forteza-Rey, (including a general introduction giving an excellent overview of Hebrew literary production in medieval Iberia), the partial Spanish translation of Navarro Peiro (*Narrativa* 123–46) and the Dutch translation of Fontaine et al. I cite the English translation of Hadas and reference the Hebrew edition of Davidson (Berlin, 1925).

through indirect oral transmission occasioned by social contact and conversion. Thus, the development of textually encoded performance in Arabic and Hebrew frametales and *maqāmāt* sets the stage for canonical works of Castilian literature such as the *Libro de buen amor* of Juan Ruiz and the *Conde Lucanor* of Juan Manuel, in which storytelling and the dynamics of performance figure prominently.

The frametale and *maqāma* genres contain frequent representations of performances, such as storytelling events, and encode in writing discursive features common to verbal performance genres. An important intermediary between a live storytelling act and modern prose fiction, the frametale calls attention to the relationship between storytelling and story writing. Performance is present in the frametale and *maqāma* in two ways. First, because medieval audiences experienced reading primarily as a performance, the *maqāmāt* are a part of a literary culture that favors the utterance over the written word as text.[7] Within the text itself, a frametale is a series of textually encoded performances that portray characters in the act of storytelling. In frametale and *maqāma*, this orality or aurality is expressed primarily in the contextualization of tales, in the representation of their delivery to the audience. It is a question of performance.

Performance and Performativity

Performance is a highly reflexive genre of discourse that—as opposed to non-performative conversation and interaction—calls attention to its existence and purpose as a genre. According to Richard Bauman, it is unique among modes of human discourse in that its very existence "highlights the social, cultural, and aesthetic dimensions of the communicative process" ("Performance" 41). The performer and audience are both made aware of the roles they play within the context of performance, and the performance event draws attention to the social value of these roles within the context of the performance.

[7] Reading in the European Middle Ages was largely public, a heavily aural experience (Coleman 28). Clanchy maintains that the medieval "recipient [reader or audience] prepared himself to listen to an utterance rather than to scrutinize a document visually" (214). Hamesse similarly argues that in the medieval world "orality predominated over writing" (104). Sells explains that the "sound vision"—the "relation of sound to meaning" (12) in the audience experience of the Qur'ānic recitation—permeates the aesthetic values and experiences of many other verbal performance genres in the Islamic world (20).

A performance, therefore, creates a frame that alerts the audience to choose the appropriate interpretative filter. This filter will vary according to the genre of the performance: an audience has different conventional expectations of a wedding song than of a ghost story or dirty joke. The frame emphasizes the social and aesthetic aspects of the performance and "assigns to an audience the responsibility of evaluating the relative skill and effectiveness of the performer's accomplishment" (Bauman, "Performance" 44). Performance presupposes the audience's ability to decode culturally specific norms of performance (attitudes, codes, behaviors, expectations, participation and analysis) on the part of the participants, all of whom are active in the creation of the meaning of a performance.

A storytelling performance is a speech act[8] that delivers a message in a way distinct from casual conversational speech. It activates socially constructed norms and categories of participation (performer, audience) specific to a performance that are essential to the production of meaning.[9] The reflexive nature of a performance such as a storytelling event calls attention not only to the formal aspects of a given performance (language use, extra-linguistic information such as tone, gesture, etc.), but also to the function of narrative in performance. Richard Bauman has written that

> performance is formally reflexive—signification about signification—insofar as it calls attention to and involves self-conscious manipulation of the formal features of the communicative system... making one at least conscious of its devices. At its most encompassing, performance may be seen as broadly metacultural, a cultural means of objectifying and laying open to scrutiny culture itself, for culture is a system of systems of signification. ("Performance" 47)

A storytelling performance, then, in addition to being an occasion for narrative, is itself an opportunity for reflection on the social function of narrative. This is aptly illustrated in *Kalīla*, in which characters frequently conclude their performances of tales with a brief explanation of its purpose. For example, Dimna concludes his tale of the louse and the flea: "et yo non te di este enxenplo sinon por que sepas et entiendas que el mal omne sienpre está aparejado para fazer mal..." (ed. Cacho Blecua 153; cf. ed. Cheikho 93)

---

[8] According to Kent Bach, "speech acts are acts of communication. To communicate is to express a certain attitude, and the type of speech act being performed corresponds to the type of attitude being expressed. For example, a statement expresses a belief, a request expresses a desire, and an apology expresses a regret. As an act of communication, a speech act succeeds if the audience identifies, in accordance with the speaker's intention, the attitude being expressed" (81). The classic study on speech acts is that of Searle. On the role of speech acts in power and influence, see M. Williams.

[9] For a discussion of the formal aspects of storytelling events see Georges.

('and I have only given you this *exemplum* so that you might understand that the bad man is always disposed to do wrong...').

The context of a storytelling event, far from being a mere physical and temporal setting for such a performance, is also a group of processes by which the speech community (the performer, audience, and community) creates and extracts meaning from the performance. That is, a storytelling event is best understood as an emergent, dynamic process or set of social practices by which meaning is constituted, as opposed to a static text that is delivered in a static social setting.[10]

What, then, is the role of performance in the frametale and *maqāma*? I will limit my discussion of performativity in these works to the way in which aspects of storytelling and popular preaching are encoded or entextualized in the literary text. I will not consider how works such as *Kalīla* and *Luzūmīyya* were themselves performed or read publicly, though such a study is certainly possible. Neither do I intend to prove that the storytelling practices encoded in these works were accurate representations of storytelling practices that obtained in the social environments of the authors under consideration here. Rather, I believe that a careful analysis of the way in which performance is encoded in these texts can enhance our understanding of the development of the frametale as a genre of medieval Iberian literature that is characteristic of a literary culture in which authors and audiences of varying religious and linguistic backgrounds participated. I use performance as a lens through which to study medieval Iberian culture as it is reflected in literature. Because performance is socially and culturally specific, one can trace the development of prose narrative in al-Andalus by studying the way in which performance is encoded in literary texts. Andalusī authors collaborate across several centuries in creating a style of textually encoded performance that is unique to the medieval Iberian frametale, a genre that displays several different currents of literary narrative practice that converge in a common—yet complexly diverse—geographic and cultural experience—one not uniquely Christian, Muslim, or Jewish, nor expressed in any single literary language.

First, the reception of the Arabic *Kalīla* in al-Andalus introduces the concept of fictionality to Arabic prose narrative, with its encoded performances of fables from Eastern tradition. Next, the *maqāma* brings to Andalusī literary culture its parody of traditional Muslim genres of religious

[10] For a thorough review of the literature on the poetics of performance as a social phenomenon, see the study of Bauman and Briggs. On the emergent nature of performance, see Bauman ("Verbal" 179–83).

oral narrative such as the *ḥadīṯ*. Al-Saraqusṭī nuances the performativity of the *maqāma* by introducing the unreliable narrator, whose misleading performances undermine the integrity of the *ḥadīṯ* model of narrative and call into question the value of the storytelling event and its transmission. In adapting the Arabic *maqāma*, al-Ḥarīzī infuses his Hebrew *maqāmāt* with specifically Jewish notions of storytelling and fictionality. Blurring the distinction between author and fictional narrator, he complicates the notion of the encoded performance without straying far from the formal models of narrative performance in the Arabic *maqāma*. Finally, Ibn Zabāra's work re-incorporates elements of encoded performance from classical frametales such as *Kalīla* while further nuancing the figure of the unreliable narrator. These models of performance and narrativity are further developed in later medieval Iberian frametales such as Juan Ruiz's *Libro de buen amor* and Jaume Roig's *Spill*, which I discuss at length in chapters 5 and 6 respectively.

In discussing performance in frametale and *maqāma*, I stress two aspects of performative discourse in the texts: the way in which authors make use of elements of performative discourse in their framing and retelling of narrative, and the direct portrayal of storytelling performances by literary characters created by the authors. In discussing individual tales, I distinguish between the mode of performance (explicit or implicit) and the mode of tale (anecdote or fable). The former refers to the way in which the storytelling event is encoded in the text, the latter to the type of tale being told. With some exceptions, *Kalīla* is a series of explicitly encoded fables, the *maqāmāt* implicitly encoded anecdotes. In the *explicit* mode of performance, the performer is directly constituted in the text in the act of performance. The author describes the storyteller and audience before, during, and after the performance. By way of example, let us refer to the Castilian *Calila e Digna*, in which Calila narrates to Dimna the story of the Monkey and the Wedge:

> Dixo Calila:—E tu, hermano, ¿que as que preguntas lo que non as menester, nin te tiene pro en lo preguntar?.... E dexate desto, e sabe que el que se entremete de dezir e de fazer lo que non es para el, que le acaesçe lo que acaesçio a un ximio artero, que se entremetio de lo que non era suyo nin le pertenesçia. Dixo Dina:—¿Commo fue esto?
>
> Dixo Calila:—Dizen que un ximio vido unos carpinteros aserrar una viga, e estava el uno ençima. E commo yvan aserrando metian una cuña e sacavan otra por aserrar mejor. E el ximio vidolos, e en tanto que ellos fueron a comer, subio el ximio ençima del viga e asentose ençima e saco la cuña. E commo le colgavan los compañones en la serradura de la viga, al sacar de la cuña apreto la viga, e tomole dentro los conpañones, e machucogelos, e cayo amortesçido. Desy vino el carpintero a el, e lo que le fizo fue peor que lo que le acaesçio.

> E dixo Dina:—Entendido he lo que me dexiste, e oy el enxenplo que me dexiste.... (125–6; ed. Cheikho 65)

> (And you, brother, what motivates you to ask what you should not, that would not even profit you to ask? Leave this, and know that to whoever makes it his business to do or say what is not his, will happen to him what happened to the monkey, who got involved in that which was not his [affair] and did not belong to him.
>
> Said Dimna:—How did it this happen?
>
> Said Calila:—They say that a monkey saw some carpenters hewing a beam, while he was up above them. And as they were hewing, they placed a wedge and took another out the better to hew. And the monkey saw them, and as soon as they went to eat, the monkey came down on top of the beam and sat down and took out the wedge. And as his testicles were hanging in the area where the beam was being cut, when he took out the wedge they became caught in it and were crushed, and the monkey fell senseless. Just then the carpenter came to him, and what he did to him was worse than what had just happened.
>
> And Dimna said:—I have understood what you have told me, and heard the *exemplum* you have told me...)

The effect for the audience of the text is something like that of watching a puppet show in which one puppet narrates a tale to another. The discussion between Calila and Dimna leading up to the performance is described, Calila's tale is reported as direct discourse, and the literary audience of *Kalīla* experiences the performance alongside Dimna, whose reaction to the tale is also portrayed.

In a performance that is encoded *implicitly*, the narrator is mentioned as having performed, ("x narrated to y") but is not directly represented in the act of narration. Neither are the setting and circumstances of the performance described in the narrative. While performer and audience are referenced, their appearance and their behavior as participants during the storytelling event are not described in detail. As I will discuss below, the implicit mode of encoded performance depends on the audience's familiarity with the narrative features of *ḥadīṯ* (traditional sayings of the Prophet Muhammad). In its reception of the *maqāma*, the audience decodes the performance in accordance with its understanding of *ḥadīṯ* narrative.

For purposes of the present discussion, a tale (or the text of any encoded storytelling event within a frame tale) can be classified as either anecdote or fable. According to the *Bedford Glossary of Critical and Literary Terms*, an anecdote is

> a brief account of some interesting or entertaining and often humorous incident. Lacking the complexity of the short story, an anecdote simply relates a particular episode or event that makes a single point. Since an anecdote is supposed to be

> true, the incident described and the point made by the anecdote are typically more important than *how* the anecdote is told—that is, the artistry or style involved in the telling. Anecdotes frequently relate an incident in a particular person's life that reveals a character trait. (Murfin and Ray 19)

The tales related by narrators of *maqāmāt* (but not classical frametales such as *Kalīla*) push the envelope of this anecdotal genre. First, they typically involve both a protagonist and an antagonist (the narrator and the rogue). Second, while they are intended to demonstrate the character of the protagonist, they are also a showcase for the rhetorical virtuosity of the narrator. Nevertheless, the pretense of nonfictionality, supported by formal conventions intended to establish the integrity of the narration such as the *isnād* (chain of transmission), brings the tales narrated in *maqāmāt* down on the side of the anecdote, as opposed to the fable.

The fable, by contrast, is a

> short, fictional (nonhistorical) prose or verse tale with a specific moral. As allegorical works, fables are told to illustrate a particular point or lesson, which is often explicitly expressed at the end of the tale via an epigram. Fables often feature animals (personified) as their principal characters. (Murfin and Ray 150)

Unlike the anecdote, the narrator of the fable makes no claim to the historicity of the tale; consequently no suspension of disbelief is required on the part of the audience. That is, if a character in *Kalīla* tells a tale about a talking bird, it is not expected that the audience understand the tale as a reflection of a possible reality.[11] In the *maqāmāt* of the Andalusī author al-Saraquṣṭī, the anecdotal frame of performance suggests a continuity between the world of the tale and that of the audience, with the narrator linking the two through first person perspective (i.e., "I saw x happen and now I relate it to you"). It heralds the introduction of plausible fictionality to medieval narrative. The anecdotal mode of tale-telling underpins the development of the fictional *maqāma* genre that, it is tempting to suggest, culminates in the European picaresque novel.[12] However, while the narrative resources

[11] Rina Drory has dealt admirably with the question of fictionality in light of an ongoing debate between Arabic critics at the time the *maqāma* was moving from novelty to established literary genre (ca. 1140–1200) (*Models* 22–27).

[12] James Monroe has written that "the extreme enthusiast of genetic theories could posit a series of influences that would embrace [the *maqāma*] ... and the subsequent development of the European picaresque novel down to our times" (*Art* 15–16). However, such an argument is limited by a lack of textual evidence for the means of transmission between authors of *maqāmāt* and of the modern novel (Hämeen-Anttila, *Maqama* 298–99).

of the *maqāma* seem logically to prefigure those of the modern novel, it is impossible to prove the transmission of these resources from author to author down to modernity.

Performance—storytelling in particular—is a social phenomenon. No storyteller, story text, or performance thereof exists outside of the context of a speech community.[13] Accordingly, some of the social practices that constitute the storytelling event are encoded in the frametale text: the relationship between performer and audience, the performer's introduction of his material, the audience's reactions, and other features of a storytelling event. As in real life, storytellers in literary settings are "communicatively accountable" (Bauman, "Performance" 44); they have a responsibility to communicate effectively their message to an audience. This was also realized by medieval authors: without someone to tell it and someone else to listen to it, there is no story. Performer and audience are active participants in a social process. This process—or aspects of it—is encoded, if not accurately and realistically reproduced, in the frametale and *maqāma*.

Each of the four texts I will examine demonstrates a unique innovation in the narrative resources used to represent performance. In a cumulative and diachronic collaboration, authors of *maqāmāt* and frametales make incremental innovations in the textual encoding of performance. They are products of very different cultural moments within the medieval Iberian cultural panorama, but are brought together in their reception by successive generations of medieval Iberian audiences. In this way, the authors of these texts are participants in the development of a genre that transcends several languages, religions, and historical moments, but that is representative of all of them. *Kalīla* is the product of the encounter between Arab and Persian culture in the ʿAbbāsid Empire of the eighth century (*EI*, "Adab"). The *maqāmāt* of al-Saraquṣṭī were written in the intellectual hotbed of the Taifas (minor kingdoms) of al-Andalus in which he lived as a scholar on the move.[14] Finally, the Hebrew *maqāmāt* by al-Ḥarīzī and Ibn Zabāra are products of the Iberian diaspora of the Andalusī Jewish elite, who wrote

[13] For an example on the social contexts of tribal poetic production in Yemen, see Caton (65–76). On narrative in the Western Apache community, see Basso (99–137). On the social uses of performance in oral tradition, see Vansina (95–114). On the Palestinian folktale tradition, see Muhawi and Kanaana. In his study of the same tradition, Patai stresses the participation of the audience, which he describes "so intense that the *qaṣṣāṣ* [storyteller] seemed to be leading the audience as if it were a large orchestra" (1–2).

[14] On poetic and intellectual activity in the Taifas (Ar. *ṭawāʾif*), see Jayyusi, Dodds ("Arts" 606–11), and Garulo.

Hebrew literature informed by Arabic models in Christian Iberia (Drory, "Models" 216; Sherwood, "Introduction" 5–8).

Kalīla and the *Luzūmīyya* of al-Saraqusṭī are representative of the prose narrative tradition of Arabic literature that had taken root in al-Andalus; a tradition without which the innovation of such works as *Sefer Šaʿašūʿīm* ('Book of Delights') of Joseph ibn Zabāra and the subsequent *Libro de buen amor* of Juan Ruiz would have been impossible. The textual encoding of performance in *Kalīla* and the *Luzūmīyya* are the models available to later medieval Iberian authors of frametales such as the *Conde Lucanor* and the *Libro de buen amor*. *Kalīla* and the *Luzūmīyya* therefore provide the building blocks of the Andalusī and Castilian frametale.[15] I shall examine examples of the textual encoding of performance in these texts in terms of the performative mode of the storytelling events represented in the works, the narrative mode (anecdote or fable) of the tales themselves, and the textual encoding of the social practices associated with the storytelling event.

Kalīla wa-Dimna and al-Saraqusṭī's *al-Maqāmāt al-Luzūmīyya* encode performance textually as a way of providing a context for the anecdotes and fables narrated by the characters in each text. Textually encoded performance reflects the cultural and literary heritage of the author, as well as the performative nature of medieval Arabic literature in general. The two texts represent a convergence of oral narrative traditions: in *Kalīla* the Eastern animal fable tradition; in the *maqāma*, the Arabic tradition of popular preaching and storytelling framed by *ḥadīṯ*-style markers of performative transmission.

Each of these authors, writing in a different moment in medieval Iberia, responds differently to the challenge of reconciling their literary and religious values with the demands of encoding performance in the literary text. The way in which any given author will encode performance will depend both on available literary models of performance, prevailing narrative practice, acceptable attitudes toward such practice, and of course, individual preference and innovation.

[15] Our observations on the *maqāma* genre are centered on the work of al-Saraqusṭī and not al-Ḥarīrī because the former was active in al-Andalus, as were the rest of the authors (or translators, in the case of *Kalīla*) dealt with in this study. It is fair to assume that the *maqāmāt* of al-Ḥarīrī influenced medieval Iberian writers. In fact, al-Saraqusṭī is quite clear that he wrote his *maqāmāt* in imitation of those of al-Ḥarīrī (ed. al-Warāglī 17; trans. Monroe 113). The models of performativity in al-Ḥarīrī's *maqāmāt* do not differ significantly from those adopted by his imitator al-Saraqusṭī and therefore a separate study of al-Ḥarīrī's text is not warranted here.

Kalīla wa-Dimna

Translated into Arabic from Pahlavi in 748 by ʿAbdallāh ibn al-Muqaffaʿ, *Kalīla wa-Dimna* is the first work of literary prose narrative in Arabic. It was originally composed in Sanskrit as the *Panchatantra* in India around the year 300. There are subsequent translations into Pahlavi by Burzoē, physician to the Sasānian king Khūsraw Anuširwān (531–579), and then into Arabic (*EI*, "*Kalīla wa-Dimna*"). As a work it has two significant performative features. First, the text presents a series of storytelling events: characters narrate animal fables to one another. These scenes portray at least some aspects of live storytelling or performance event as defined by anthropologists such as Alan Dundes, Robert Georges, and Richard Bauman.[16] There is a storyteller, an audience, and a social context. The tales told by the characters are of a genre recognizable to their immediate audience (the other characters within the text who are experiencing the tale as performed by a fellow character) as well as to the fictive audience (the reader or audience of the text).

In framing the performance of these tales socially, authors of frametales and *maqāmāt* are continuing a long tradition of cross-pollination between oral and written storytelling genres. The tales narrated by characters in *Kalīla* have a history of real-life performance. Drawn from popular tradition, they were originally collected by Hindu preachers who used the fables as exemplary tales in their sermons, much like the Dominican and Franciscan friars of Western Europe in the thirteenth and fourteenth centuries.[17] The compiler of the tales included in the original *Panchatantra* was a Brahmin, a clergyman from the upper ranks of organized religion, who was assembling material drawn from performances of tales current in Indian oral tradition.[18] In contrast, orthodox Islam did not approve of the religious use of narratives apart from those found in the Qurʾān or the traditions of the Prophet Muḥammad; such tales were the currency of the *qaṣṣ* (popular preacher and storyteller) and did not bear the stamp of approval of organized religion (*EI*, "Ḳaṣṣ"). Therefore, *Kalīla* can be seen as a literary performance setting for tales that were historically performed (and transmitted) orally.

[16] In addition to the works by these authors cited above, see Dundes, the volume by Bauman and Babcock, and the essay by Bauman and Braid.

[17] For the *exemplum* in medieval Christian literature, see Welter (*L'exemplum*).

[18] On the origin and structure of the *Panchatantra*, see Keith (242–63) and Olivelle (ix–xlv).

Like *Kalīla*, the *maqāma* genre also provides a literary setting for storytelling events, but with some crucial differences. The narrator is performing (implicitly) tales in the anecdotal mode, and so the distance between audience and tale is reduced. That is, the narrator is recounting events that he claims to have experienced himself, whereas a narrator of fables (as in *Kalīla*) cannot possibly claim to have witnessed a discussion between two talking animals. Furthermore, the narrator of *Kalīla* is fictional, by the admission of al-Saraqusṭī himself.[19] Both the setting and the tales are pure fiction, yet the first person stance of the narrator invites the reader to identify with the narrator-as-character within the tales, while the chain of transmission (*isnād*) recalls the narrative authority of *ḥadīṯ*. The *maqāma* combines the implicit performance of the *ḥadīṯ* with the episodic fictionality of *Kalīla*. By building on the model of literary prose narrative introduced by *Kalīla*, the *maqāma* introduces suspension of disbelief into medieval literary prose narrative.[20]

Performance in Kalīla wa-Dimna

Performance creates a unique frame for the delivery of a message, a frame that alerts the audience to choose the appropriate interpretative filter. This filter will vary according to the genre of the performance: an audience has different conventional expectations of a wedding song than of a ghost story or dirty joke. The frame emphasizes the social and aesthetic aspects of the performance and, writes Richard Bauman, "assigns to an audience the responsibility of evaluating the relative skill and effectiveness of the performer's accomplishment" ("Performance" 44). It is fitting, then, that the frametale—a literary prose genre so inherently focused on verbal performance—be the vehicle for the debut of literary prose narrative in a literary culture dominated by performative, lyric genres.[21] The precise constellation of performer, message, audience, and context that obtains for a given performance can never be

---

[19] Despite the fact that al-Saraqusṭī provides an *isnād* that indicates Ibn Tammām as narrator, he takes credit for the work as his own literary creation in the colophon (ed. al-Warāglī 3; trans. Monroe 113).

[20] Rina Drory writes that "in Arabic the major difficulty in accepting the *maqāmāt* consisted in the novelty of overt fiction, which violated the norm of faithfully reporting on reality" ("Maqama" 200).

[21] The question of whether or not frametales and *maqāmāt* were written in order to be performed falls outside the scope of the present study. Much of the experience of a live storytelling event cannot be encoded in a literary text. Subsequently, modern ethnographers have developed notational systems for recording such events (Fine).

reproduced. Performances in *maqāmāt* and frametales are entextualized or encoded, not reproduced; much of the experience of a live storytelling event cannot be encoded in a literary text.[22]

While many aspects of a real-life storytelling event are not typically accounted for in a literary setting, some aspects, such as the relationship between storyteller and audience, are portrayed textually. In *Kalīla* the performative frame and context of the storytelling event are constructed in a fictional environment. The author creates an opportunity for a character to tell a tale by having another character request advice of the first. The request can be direct ("tell me the fable about...") or indirect ("I have such and such a problem, please advise me..."). Even this rudimentary performative frame reproduces some of the interaction between storyteller and audience characteristic of a storytelling event. Consider, for example, the interaction between Dimna and the lion before and after Dimna's performance of the tale of the Fox and the Drum:

> —Veo, señor, que ha tienpo que estás en un lugar, que te non mudas. ¿Esto por qué es?
>
> Et el león non quería que sopiese Dina lo que lo fazía con cobardez, et dixo:—Non es por miedo.
>
> Et estando amos así bramó Çençeba muy fuerte, et tamaño fue el miedo que ovo, que le fizo [dezir]:—Esta voz me tovo aquí en este lugar et non sé qué es. Enpero, veo que la persona que la faze deve ser tan grande commo la boz, et su fuerça tan grande commo la persona. Et si esto así es, non moremos en este lugar.
>
> Dixo Digna al león:—Escandalizástete de otra cosa fuera desta. Ca si non te fizo ál pavor sinon esto, non deves dexar tu posada, ca la flaqueza es ocasión de la pelea, et la mezcla es ocación del amor, et la grant boz es ocación del flaco coraçón. Et esto se departe en un proverbio que dize:—Non se deve omne temer de todas bozes.
>
> Dixo el león:—¿Cómmo fue eso?
>
> Dixo Digna:—Dizen que una gulpeja fanbrienta pasó por un árbol, et estava un atanbor colgado del árbol; et moviόse el viento et firiénronlo los ramos, et sonava muy fuerte; et la gulpeja oyó aquella boz et fuese contra ella fasta que llegó allá. Et en que vio que era finchado, cuidóse que era de mucha carne, que avía de mucha gordez, et fendiólo et vio que era hueco, et dixo:—Non sé; por ventura las más flacas cosas han mayores personas et más altas bozes.
>
> Et fuese dende.

[22] Physical environment, gesture, and tone of voice are among some of the aspects of storytelling events not commonly recorded by ethnographers (Dundes). Georges and Jones refer to the "paralinguistic" and "kinesic" (317) modes of coding a message that are often lost in transcription.

Et yo, señor, non te di este enxenplo sinon porque he esperança que sea esta cosa, cuya boz te espantó, atal commo el atanbor; et si a ella te llegases, más lijera te semejaría que tú non cuidas. Et señor, si fuere la tu merçed, enbíame a ella et está tú en tu lugar fasta que yo torne a ti con lo que sopiere de tu fazienda.

Et desto que dixo Dina plugo al león, et díxole:—Pues vete. (134–35; ed. Cheikho 73–74)

(—I see, Sire, that for some time you have stayed in the same place and not moved. Why is this?

The lion did not want Dimna to know that it was from cowardice, and said:—It is not from fear.

At that moment, Sençeba bellowed very loudly, and such was the fear of the lion that he said:—This voice is what keeps me in this place, and I don't know what it is. However, I think that the person behind it must be as large as the voice, and his power equally great. If it is thus, we cannot stay here.

Digna said:—They say that a hungry fox passed by a tree, and there was a drum hanging from the tree; and the wind moved it and the branches hit it, and the drum sounded loudly; and the fox heard the noise and went toward it. When she saw that the drum was inflated, she thought that it was meaty and fat, and in striking it and seeing it was only empty, said:—I don't know; it seems that the flimsiest things have bigger bodies and even bigger voices.

And she went on her way.

I, Sire, have only told you this fable because I have hope that this thing, whose voice frightened you, is like the drum, and if you go to it, it will be much less significant than you think. And Sire, if it please you, send me to it and you stay in your place until I return to you with whatever I find out about the situation.

The lion was pleased by these words of Digna [Dimna] and said to him:—Go, then.)[23]

Dimna tells the tale in order to ingratiate himself with the lion by explaining away the latter's preoccupation with the unidentified loud noise. The circumstances of the telling are part and parcel of the audience's experience of the tale. Therefore, viewing Dimna's tale as a performance leads us to consider carefully the relationships involved in the storytelling event. In *Kalīla*, the relationship is between a fearful ruler (the lion) looking to his advisor for guidance and a wily advisor (Dimna) seeking to capitalize on his master's fear. After gaining an audience with the lion, Dimna notes his recent changes in behavior: "—Veo, señor, que ha tienpo que estás en un lugar, que te non mudas. ¿Esto por qué es?—(134; ed. Cheikho 73) ('I see, Sire, that for some time you have stayed in the same place, and do not move. Why is this?').

[23] The tale is Aarne-Thompson type J 262.1, *noisy things often empty* (Thompson 33).

Well knowing it is because the lion fears the loud braying of the bull Sençeba, Dimna suggests that the lion find out more before fearing the unknown. He tells the lion a proverb: "It is not necessary to fear all voices."[24] The lion then asks Dimna to tell the tale illustrating the proverb. Dimna has a motivation for telling the story: he is attempting to quell the lion's unreasonable fear. He is also acting on the knowledge that in his role as storyteller he has the duty to "formulate, encode, and transmit" the tale according to the rules of a storytelling event. The lion has a motivation for listening to and reacting to the story: he wants to believe that the unknown voice poses no real threat. As audience, he has the right and responsibility to "receive, decode, and respond" to the story (Georges 318). These motivations cue the characters to provide markers for the performative frame. The lion requests an elucidation of a proverb by a performance of the related tale: "What tale is that?" Dimna then provides a marker for the beginning of his performance: "They say that..." and tells the tale.

Dimna's words alert the audience that what follows is lore; this information brings the audience (the lion) into the storytelling event. Once the narrative marker focuses the attention of the audience and prepares it to hear a *story* (as opposed to any other type of verbal utterance), the performance can proceed. Such formulas are common to all popular narrative traditions. In English, one might mark the beginning of a tale with "once upon a time" and conclude with "and they lived happily ever after."[25] Dimna marks the end of his performance with an explanation of why he told the particular tale: "Verily I have coined this tale in order to that you might learn that...." (135; ed. Cheikho 74) and so closes the performative frame.

Kalīla's mode of performance is explicit, meaning that the author describes the performer and audience, and explains the context, setting, and/or act of performance. The fictive audience "watches" the character (Kalīla) preparing to tell and listen to tales, and is witness to the reactions of the fictional audience (the lion). With the exception of the tales interpolated in Ibn al-Muqaffaʿ's introduction (89–98; ed. Cheikho 51–61), the performance of every tale that appears in the work is described by the author. More often than not, the tales are told as part of a piece of advice that is sought by one

[24] The Arabic text reads "*laysà kulu-l-aṣwātin tuhābu*" (ed. Cheikho 73).

[25] Compare, for example, with traditional rhyming concluding formulas in Spanish ("colorín, colorado, este cuento se ha acabado" ['colorful, red, this story is finished']) and Catalan ("i aquí hi ha un gos, i aquí hi ha un gat, i aquest conte s'ha acabat" ['and here there is a dog, and here there is a cat, and this story is finished']).

of the characters. Dimna, in seeking to ingratiate himself with the lion king, introduces him to the ox Sençeba. The lion takes an instant liking to the ox, who replaces Dimna as the king's favorite. When Dimna realizes that he has undercut himself, he goes and complains to Kalīla:

> Et quando vio Dina que el león se apartava con Sençeba sin él et sin la otra conpaña, pesóle, et ovo ende grande enbidia, et querellóse a su hermano Calila, et díxole:—Hermano, non te maravilles de mi mal seso et de mi locura, et de cómmo pensé en pro del león, et trabajé en le traer el buey que me ha echado de mi dinidat.
>
> Dixo Calilla:—Pues acaesció a ti lo que acaesçió al religioso.
>
> Dixo Dina:—¿Et cómmo fue eso? (137; ed. Cheikho 77)
>
> (And when Dimna saw that the lion was alone with Sençeba without him and the other courtiers, he was distressed, and was very envious, and complained to his brother Kalīla, and said to him:—Brother, do not be surprised at my stupidity and my madness, and at how I only thought of the lion's benefit, and worked to bring him the ox who has removed me from privilege.
>
> Kalīla said:—Well, then, what happened to the ascetic has happened to you.
>
> Dimna said:—And how was that?)

By way of illustration, Kalīla then goes on to narrate the tale of the hermit who invites a thief into his home and is dumbfounded when the thief robs him of some expensive textiles.[26] Nearly all the tales performed in *Kalīla* are fables; that is, they portray a reality not intended to resemble, nor to be directly contiguous with, that of the audience. They are generally stories of anonymous animals and humans who live in a nameless, timeless place. The storyteller does not often claim to have any personal experience of what he narrates, and the first person perspective is never used. The narrative markers, brief formulas used to frame a tale's performance, overwhelmingly refer to anonymous traditional authority. The most common narrative marker in *Kalīla* is "Dizen que…" ('they say…,' Ar. '*zaʿamū ʾanna…*').[27] This references a speech act, a type of performance in itself. It describes the transmission of a tale in purely anonymous terms, told in the fabulistic mode:

[26] This tale includes Aarne-Thomspon motif K346: *Thief trusted by cleric to guard goods steals them and runs off.* It is also attested in *Exemplario contra los engaños y peligros del mundo* (Goldberg, *Motif-index* 95).

[27] In *ḥadīt*, the formula is *ḥadatanā*, rendered in Aljamiado texts as "fue recontado." For examples, see López-Morillas (*Textos* 96 and 118).

> Dizen que un cuervo avía su nido en un árbol en el monte; (143; ed. Cheikho 83)
> Dizen que un león estava en un valle çerca del camino; (158; ed. Cheikho 101)
> Dizen que en una tierra avía un mercador pobre. (175; ed. Cheikho 118–19)
>
> (They say that a crow had his nest in a tree in the thicket;
> They say that a lion was in a valley near the road;
> They say that in a certain land there was a poor merchant.)

Less frequently, tales are introduced as anecdotes, with proper nouns designating either the protagonist, the city in which the tale takes place, or both:

> Dizen que avía en una villa un rico omne que 'l dezían Morzubem....[28] (198; ed. Cheikho 149)
> Dizen que en tierra de Duzat, çerca de una çibdat que dezían Muzue, avía un lugar de caça do caçavan los paxareros...et avía ý un nido de un cuervo que dezían Geba. (202–03; ed. Cheikho 153)[29]
> Dixo el filósofo:—Señor, dizen que en tierra de Gurguen avía un rico mercador, et avía tres fijos. (122; ed. Cheikho 61)
> Dizen que en una çibdat que dizían Quertir, que es en tierra de Yabrit, avía un rico mercador. (184; ed. Cheikho 131)[30]
>
> (They say that there was in a town a rich man named Morzubem...
> They say that in the land of Duzat, near a city called Muzue, there was a hunting ground where the fowl hunters went...and there was the nest of a crow named Geba.
> The philosopher said: Sir, they say that in the land of Gurguen there was a rich merchant, and he had three sons.
> They say that in the town of Quertir, that is in the land of Yabrit, there was a rich merchant.)

While these examples do not go as far as the first-person perspective in linking the reality of the tale with that of the audience, they do attempt to locate the tale in a specific geographic location, albeit one unrecognizable to the audience. It is tempting to assume that the Castilian translator

[28] The Arabic text is "*fī baʿdi-l-mudūn, rajul min al-marāzibatin*" ('in a certain city, one of the provincial governors') (Ar. *marāziba*, sing. *marzubān*). The Castilian translator seems to have mistaken the man's office for his name. The effect is that of "there once was a man named King...".

[29] The Arabic does not name a specific city, but uses the formula "*fī baʿdi l-mudūn*", meaning "in a certain city." Also, the crow is only described with the Arabic word for crow, *ġurāb*, which may have yielded the proper noun "Geba" in the Castilian.

[30] The Arabic version is set in Kashmir.

programmatically introduced the use of proper nouns in narrative markers in order to give the tale an anecdotal feel, following what may have been a contemporary trend in the novelization of traditional tales. However, since we do not have the manuscript from which he worked, it is impossible to determine if the increased use of proper nouns is attributable to our translator or to the editor of one of the Arabic manuscripts of *Kalīla* produced in the roughly four hundred years between Ibn al-Muqaffaʿ's translation and the 1251 Castilian version.

The few examples given above are the only ones in *Kalīla* of tales in the anecdotal mode,[31] perhaps because this is a mode that is only later introduced in Arabic genres such as the *maqāma*. There is, however, the very occasional anecdotal marker that places the tale within the personal realm of experience of the narrator. For example, the rat in "El ratón cuenta su historia" ('The Rat Tells His Story') introduces his tale as taking place in the house where he was born: "do yo nasçí fue en casa de un religioso que non avía muger nin fijos" (210; ed. Cheikho 161) ('I was born in the house of a monk/sūfī who had neither wife nor children.') However, he does not attempt to link the characters in the tale to his own experience, nor does he cast himself as a character or active observer of the actions he narrates. This glimmer of anecdotal storytelling is developed more fully in the *maqāma* and later in such Castilian texts as the *Libro de buen amor* and the *Conde Lucanor*.

The Social Dimension of Performance

Because a performance is a social phenomenon and cannot exist without the active participation of both performer and audience, a significant aspect of the frametale is the construction of the relationship enjoyed between performer and audience. Characters who perform and who listen to tales are defined in large part by their actions as performers and as audiences. The nature of this relationship can affect greatly the way in which a tale is delivered and received. For the literary critic, an understanding of the relationships portrayed between the characters of the frame is indispensable in the study of the frametale and *maqāma*. In *Kalīla*, because the mode of performance is explicit, these relationships are portrayed openly, especially in comparison to the *maqāmāt* of al-Saraquṣṭī, in which the implied performance of the

[31] That is, tales that reference a specific place, person, or event as opposed to tales in the fabulistic mode, which are not bound in space and time.

narrator is indicated only telegraphically in the chain of transmission. The author deliberately characterizes the personalities of the two jackals, Kalīla and Dimna, advisors apparent to the Lion:

> Et entre los otros vasallos qu'él allí tenía avía dos lobos çervales. Et al uno dizían Dina et al otro Calila, et eran muy ardides et agudos. Et era Dina de más noble coraçón, et de mayor fazienda, et el que menos se tenía pagado por el estado en que era; et el león non los avía conosçido, nin era(n) de la privança fasta allí. (125; ed. Cheikho 65)

> (Among the other vassals that he had, there were two jackals. The one they called Dimna and the other Kalīla, and they were very astute and very intelligent. Dimna was of nobler heart, and of greater station, and least satisfied with his condition; and the lion did not know them, nor were they in his confidence.)

In the course of the work, this characterization of the two jackals is supported by the tales they tell: Calila's tales promote caution and good conduct, Dimna's opportunism and Machiavellian politics. At the beginning of Book 3, when the lion is afraid of the loud braying of the bull Sençeba, Dimna observes the lion's fear: 'está el león en su lugar recachado, que non se mueve nin se solaza commo solía fazer' (125; ed. Cheikho 64) ('the lion is withdrawn in his place, he does not move about nor enjoy himself as he used to'). When he suggests to Calila that they take advantage of the lion's weakened position, the latter responds with the cautionary tale of the monkey and the carpenter (reproduced in full above). To this Dimna responds: '¿cómmo fue esto?,' ('how was that?') indicating an active participation in the event and prompting Calila's response, which will in turn further define the "good cop-bad cop" relationship between the two jackals for the audience. This is the most frequent type of exchange between storyteller and audience that elicits a storytelling event, a formula along the lines of "et el enxemplo desto es tal commo de las tres truchas" (149; ed. Cheikho 90) ('and this fable is like that of the three trout'), or ¿non te dixeron de cómmo mató un cuervo a una culebra? (143; ed. Cheikho 82) ('Didn't they tell you about how a crow killed a serpent?'). These are simple formulas of exemplarity designed to elicit a request for a performance of the tale alluded to.

There are also examples of audience members' more active involvement in the selection of the specific tale performed. In the example that follows, the audience (King Dabšalīm) actively participates in the selection of the topic, perhaps attempting to elicit a specific tale. This is behavior characteristic of an oral audience, one in direct social contact with the performer. It is similar to that of the members of a musical audience who request a tune whose title they cannot remember, and so instead they hum a bar or two of the melody (i.e., "sing us the one that goes *dum de dum dum dum de dum de dum*"). In this case, the storyteller (the philosopher Baydabā) is a repository of common lore who is able to call up and perform tales that are already familiar to the audience:

> Dixo el rey a su filósofo:—Esto oído lo he. Dame agora enxemplo de los dos que se aman et los departe el mesturero, falso mentiroso, que deve ser aborresçido como la viganbre, et los faze querer mal...
>
> Dixo el filósofo:...Esto semeja lo que acaesçió al león et al buy [sic].
>
> Dixo el rey: ¿Cómmo fue eso?
>
> Dixo el filósofo:—Señor, dizen que en tierra de Gurguen avía un rico mercador, et avía tres fijos. (122–23; ed. Cheikho 61)[32]

> (The king said to his philosopher:—This much I have heard. Now give me an example of the two who love each other and how the meddling, false liar, who deserves to be abhorred like vinegar, tears them apart and wishes to do them ill...
>
> Said the philosopher:...This is like what happened to the lion and the ox.
>
> Said the King: How was that?
>
> Said the philosopher: Sire, they say that in the land of Gurguen there was a rich merchant who had three sons...)

In this type of storytelling event, the audience takes on a much more active role than if the story had simply been framed by an independent statement made by the storyteller (i.e., "this is a story about..."). Here, the audience introduces the story and becomes an indispensable part of the storytelling process. The King summarizes the previous story told by Baydabā and then takes the reins, adding commentary and prompting the philosopher to conclude the story:

> Dixo el rey al filósofo:—Ya oí lo que fizo Digna por ser tan pequeña et el más vil de todas las bestias selvajes al león et al buy [sic]....
>
> Et los omnes entendidos deven perseguir las mentiras et falsedades; et perseguir los mezcladores et escodrinar tales cosas....
>
> Pues dime agora quál fue su escusación de Digna et qué çima ovo por este fecho. (178; ed. Cheikho 121)

> (Said the king to the philosopher:—I have heard what Digna, being the lowest and basest of all the wild animals, did to the lion and the ox....

[32] In Cheikho's edition, the tale is set in Dastabā, which he explains is 'a large town in Persia between Rayy and Hamadān' (61 n. 1).

> And men of understanding should persecute lies and falsities; and persecute the meddlers and scrutinize such cases....
> Then tell me now what was Digna's alibi, and how did it all end?)

The King provides a brief synopsis of the previous tale and its moral application and indicates his desire to hear how the story ends. In a sense, he is directing the performance of the Philosopher. This type of involvement in the selection of narrative material has its analogues in the performance of folktales. Ethnographic observers of folktale performances have noted how the audience will request elaboration in certain areas of a tale and will in fact interrupt the storyteller in order to make a "request" or a correction in the narrative.[33]

Storytelling and Literature

Readers of modern prose fiction in the West do not generally experience reading as a performance or as a social activity, and so would not tend to draw on such experience in the act of reading. It is far more likely for a reader in current-day Los Angeles, Athens, or Seoul to read a novel alone and in silence than aloud to an audience.[34] The contrast between medieval and modern modes of reading literary prose thus puts a great deal of distance between the modern critic and the medieval reality of reading (Saenger; Coleman 23).

When today's reading public thinks of performance, its thoughts turn to drama, music, perhaps to poetry. However, readers of medieval Arabic literary prose would have brought to their readings very strong associations with orality and performance. When the formative works of Arabic literary narrative were being composed, reading was most often a performance. Because of this, written literature enjoyed a fairly immediate sense of aurality, and a performative context. The earliest audiences of Ibn al-Muqaffaʿ's *Kalīla* and al-Saraqusṭī's *al-Maqāmāt al-Luzūmiyya* would have heard them read aloud (Monroe, "Preliminary" 2). These works were composed during

[33] This is especially true of oral traditions that are well known by the audience, such as epic song and myth. See, for example, the transcripts of performances of Egyptian oral epic poet ʿAwadallah ʿAbd al-Jalīl ʿAlī (Slyomovics) or those from North American Apache tradition (M. Jacobs). It also obtains for stories narrated to an audience as yet unfamiliar with the story (Bauman, *Story* 101–06). See also above, n. 13.

[34] Only recently have linguistic anthropologists turned a critical eye to studying reading habits in developed societies (J. Boyarin, *Ethnography*).

a time when lyric was the prestige literary genre and narrative was held in lower regard, for it was largely the province of popular *quṣṣās*, storytellers, and preachers (*EI*, "Ḳaṣṣ."). The exemplary tale told by a popular preacher or storyteller would have been familiar to Ibn al-Muqaffaʿ's courtly audience as well, but would have been accorded a lower level of prestige, since performers making use of such tales would not have been associated with organized religion.[35] Literary connoisseurs of the day showed a distinct preference for lyric and generally held poetry in higher regard than prose narrative.[36] The Andalusī thinker Ibn Rushd[37] explains this distinction in his commentary on Aristotle's *Poetics*:

> He said: from what has been said about the intention of poetical statements, it is clear that representation that comes about by means of false inventions—namely the things called parables and stories like what is in *Kalīlah wa-Dimnah*—is not part of the poet's activity. Indeed, the poet speaks only about existing or possible matters.... Those who do make parables and stories are making something other than what poets make, even if they have made those invented parables and tales in metered speech. (trans. Butterworth 76–77; ed. Butterworth and Harīdī 83–84)

In fact, Ibn al-Muqaffaʿ's aim in translating *Kalīla* was not so much to promote prose narrative as a literary genre as it was to use it as a vehicle to display a highly polished rhetorical style (*EI*, "Maḳama").

Translated works such as *Kalīla* play an important (but often minimized) role in the development of a literary tradition—because they often fill gaps in the literary system of the target culture. At times such gaps are due to a change in the demand for literary texts.[38] In the case of the introduction

[35] While such popular preachers were originally admitted to mosques, particularly in Iraq, they eventually began to take liberties by mixing non-Islamic material into their performances and thus earned the scorn of orthodox Islam. This disdain on the part of Islamic scholars was probably affected by the fact that the *quṣṣās* attracted larger crowds than the former (*EI*, "Ḳaṣṣ"). In general, a "certain mistrust of narrative literature" that could not be readily Islamicized obtained in medieval Islam (*EI*, "Ḥikāya").

[36] Stefan Leder (35 and 43) maintains that fictionality was difficult to accept for medieval Islam in general and was made obvious only in the *maqāma* genre.

[37] Abū l-Walīd Muḥammad Ibn Rušd (1126–1198), known in the West as Averroes (*EI*, "Ibn Rušd").

[38] Even-Zohar writes of "historical moments where established models are no longer tenable for a younger generation" ("Position" 48). In the case of *Kalīla*, the historical moment is when Arabic literary culture encompasses non-Arab groups, such as Persians, who cultivated genres without analogues in Arabic literature. Ibn al-Muqaffaʿ was himself a Persian of noble origin who converted to Islam only in adulthood (*EI*, "Ibn al-Muḳaffaʿ). Therefore it is safe to assume that he had had a literary education in Pahlavi and was well acquainted with genres from that tradition, such as the frametale.

of a genre previously unknown in the target culture, translated works stand as a challenge to authors working in the target language to assimilate the new genre by creating original works in their own language. This process of appropriation leads to innovation and the development of new, hybrid genres that combine aspects of the original and target cultures.[39] Ibn al-Muqaffaʿ's translation clothed the tales of the Pahlavi *Kalīla* in the Arabic rhetorical style so redolent of performance and was instrumental in opening avenues of innovation in Arabic prose narrative.[40] His introduction of episodic prose narrative paved the way for later authors of *maqāmāt* such as the innovator Badīʿ al-Zamān al-Hamadānī, al-Ḥarīrī, and the Andalusī al-Saraqusṭī.

Kalīla has been historically classified as a work of gnomic literature. As such it is believed to have been written for the education of royalty, though the lessons contained within it obviously have application for anyone concerned with pragmatic philosophy and political strategy.[41] The model of the overall frame is that of a conversation between student and teacher. In *Kalīla*, the philosopher Baydabā relates to King Dabšalīm the tale of the Lion, the bull Šanzaba, and the two jackals, Kalīla and Dimna (122–23; ed. Cheikho 61). The frame of the work is recursive, meaning that further tales are narrated by the animal characters themselves. Also, the relationships between characters in the frame are reproduced in the interpolated tales themselves. For example, just as Baydabā acts as counselor to his king, Dimna (unknown at court at the tale's beginning) aims to position himself as counselor to his king, the lion. He explains his ambition to his brother Calila, who is wary of Dimna's ambition:

> Dixo Calila:—¿Qué te semeja si el león non te llegare a sí, nin pudieres fablar quando quisieres con él? ¿Qué será de ti?
> Dixo Digna:—Así es commo tú dizes. Mas sepas que los que son con el rey non fueron con él sienpre, mas con su femençia alcançaron las dignidades del rey, et son con él et lléganse a él después que son lluene dél. Et yo trabajarme he de fazer otro tal…(129; ed. Cheikho 68)

[39] The concept of transculturation is useful in considering the adaptation of technologies and cultural practices (including literary genres) across social and cultural boundaries. Just as Petrus Alfonsi was instrumental in the transculturation of the frametale from the Arab to the Latin world, Ibn al-Muqaffāʿ effected its transculturation from Persian to Arabic literary culture. On transculturation, see Ortiz (260), Rama (19), and Pratt (6).

[40] Ibn al-Muqaffaʿs translation of *Kalīla* introduced prose fiction as courtly genre of Arabic literature (Latham 53). On the legitimation of fiction in Classical Arabic literature, see Drory (*Models* 37–47). It is also noteworthy that *Kalīla* was thrice rendered into Arabic verse (perhaps in an attempt to increase its prestige) in the eighth, twelfth, and thirteenth centuries (*EI*, "Kalīla").

[41] For a complete discussion of the didactic orientation of *Calila*, see Parker (*Didactic*).

(What if the lion does not draw you to him, and you are not able to speak with him when you wish? What will be of you?

Said Dimna: Then it will be as you say. But know that those who are with the king were not with him always, but attained the attentions of the king by means of their effort, and are with him and draw near to him after they are far from him. And so I will work on doing likewise...)

In this way, Dimna earns the attention of the lion and serves as his counselor, along with Kalīla. While Kalīla is upright and gives his advice only to forward the lion's best interests, Dimna is more ambitious and far less scrupulous, plotting the ox's death in order to improve his own standing at court. This setting provides the context for the majority of tales whose performance is encoded in the text. They are exemplary tales told by royal advisors in order to illustrate points of political advice and practical strategies for success in worldly matters. Most of the interpolated tales warn against misleading appearances and deceptive behavior.[42]

The Maqāmāt al-Luzūmīyya *of al-Saraquṣṭī*

The *maqāma* is the product of a different cultural moment, and as such is very different from *Kalīla* in terms of structure, discourse, and in the ways performance is manifest in the text. It consists of a series of some 50 independent episodes narrated by an unreliable and sometimes inconsistent narrator, who is also the protagonist of each episode. The hapless narrator al-Sā'ib ibn Tammām relates the repeated misfortunes he suffers at the hands of the wily orator al-Sadūsī.[43] In each episode, ibn Tammām encounters an eloquent rogue, always played by al-Sadūsī, usually shabby in appearance. The rogue may appear as a young boy, an old man, a drifter, or a *šaykh* (religious scholar). In the course of each narrative, the rogue, dazzling the narrator with his eloquence, relieves him of his money and/or property. The relationship between narrator and character is an inversion of the student/teacher roles played by the lion and the jackals in *Kalīla*.[44] In *Kalīla*, the characters narrate

[42] For example, "la zorra y el tambor" ('The Fox and the Drum'), "la rata transformada en niña" ('The Rat Transformed into a Girl'), and "el palomo y su hembra" ('The Dove and His Wife') (135, 244, and 291; ed. Cheikho 74, 195–97, and 230–31).

[43] For example, at the end of *maqāma* 8, the narrator relates, "When dawn came, I found myself bound with some ropes, and wrapped in a threadbare mantle" (trans. Monroe, 166; ed. al-Warāglī, 81).

[44] Drory notes that the originator of the *maqāma* genre, al-Hamaḏānī, developed his *maqāmāt* as "parodic variations on familiar, much-studied pieces of *adab* knowledge" ("Maqama" 191), among which one may count *Kalīla*.

tales of the shortsightedness and gullibility of others. In the *maqāma*, the teacher/rogue consistently deceives the student/narrator, who in turn narrates the tales of his own gullibility.

Similarly, the *maqāma* was not originally valued for the quality of the narrative it presented, but rather as a showcase to parody existing genres of Classical Arabic literature.[45] These works began as literary experiments; *Kalīla* applied a literary Arabic register to translations of foreign prose, while the *maqāma* parodied (in Arabic) established Arabic literary genres. Over time, both *Kalīla* and the *maqāmāt* of such authors as al-Hamaḏānī, al-Ḥarīrī, and al-Saraqusṭī ended up as classics in their own right.

Ḥadīṯ *and Early Prose Fiction in Arabic*

By the time of al-Saraqusṭī, the popularity of *Kalīla* in the Arab world had already established a model of the frametale with an explicit mode of performance, in which the storytelling event is portrayed within the text, as in the discussions between Kalīla and Dimna. The relationship between performer and audience is described, not simply referenced. In the *maqāma* model, the storytelling event is implied by the reproduction of the *maqāma*'s chain of narrative transmission, or *isnād*. In the Arabic *maqāma*, the narrator's reliability is established by a chain of transmission leading from the fictive narrator/character to the author through two or three intermediaries.[46] In the *maqāmāt* of al-Saraqusṭī, the chain is represented as follows:

> The author said:
> Al-Munḏir ibn Humām narrated and said:
> Al-Sā'ib ibn Tammām narrated to us and said:
> I was in a certain country... (trans. Monroe 114; ed. al-Warāglī 14)

This means that before the narration reaches the reader, it has to pass from al-Sā'ib ibn Tammām, to al-Munḏir ibn Humām, to al-Saraqusṭī, to whomever is transcribing al-Saraqusṭī's words.[47]

---

[45] Monroe has commented that "the work of Hamaḏānī was conceived, at one level at least, as a parody of certain noble genres that already existed in Arabic literature, among them, *ḥadīṯ*, *sīra*, and the lyric" (*Art* 38). The *maqāmāt* were heavily laced with allusions and quotations from *ḥadīṯ* literature (Zubaidi 343).

[46] The *fictional audience* is the characters portrayed as the direct audience in the physical presence of the performer described in the work; the *fictive audience* refers to the "reader" or "auditor" of the text.

[47] However, we are later assured that it is al-Saraqusṭī who "composed" these *maqāmāt*, because in the colophon he assures us as much: "Let it be known that the following are fifty

In Islamic tradition, the record of the chain of transmitters of a narrative text recalls the *isnād* cited at the beginning of a *ḥadīṯ*, or sayings of Muhammad.[48] These texts are central to orthodox Sunnī Islamic law, and educated Muslims are intimately familiar with them and the means of their transmission. Each *ḥadīṯ* is passed along orally through a chain of transmitters until it arrives to the compiler, who preserves this chain in writing. During the life of Muhammad, the *isnād* introducing a *ḥadīṯ* consisted of but a few transmitters at most and was easily verified.

Over the years, as *ḥadīṯ* literature proliferated, and false versions of the Prophet's sayings were transmitted alongside those believed to be genuine, there was a need to determine both the authenticity of the *ḥadīṯ* and the soundness of the *isnād* recounting the chain of transmission. This was achieved by verifying the moral integrity of the transmitters. The jurist Al-Imām Abū ʿAbdāllah Muḥammad ibn Idrīs al-Shafiʿī (b. 767) set the standard for the acceptable narrator of *ḥadīṯ*:

> Each reporter should be trustworthy in his religion; he should be known to be truthful in his narrating, to understand what he narrates, to know how a different expression can alter the meaning, and report the wording of the hadith verbatim, not only its meaning. (trans. Khadduri 239–40; ed. Shākir 369–70)

By the ninth century a new genre dedicated to reporting on the behavior of the transmitters of *ḥadīṯ* was born (*EI*, "ḥadīṯ"). Thereafter, the reliability of the *ḥadīṯ* is determined by the morality and judgment of the transmitter.

Traditional Anecdote and the Maqāma

This discussion addresses two ways in which performance is encoded in the *maqāma*. The first is in the narrative frame established by the *isnād*. As opposed to the explicit framing in *Kalīla* in which characters are described in the act of storytelling, the narrative frame of the *maqāma* is implicit, and the act of narration is simply referenced in the *isnād* that begins each individual *maqāma*. Performance is also explicitly encoded in the *maqāmāt* in the actions of the rogue character (Abū Ḥabīb al-Sadūsī in the *Luzūmīyya*

maqamat composed by Abū-l Ṭāhir Muḥammad ibn Yūsuf al-Tamīmī al-Saraquṣṭī in Córdoba, one of the cities of al-Andalus [Spain]" (trans. Monroe 113; ed. al-Warāglī 17).

[48] On *ḥadīṯ* literature, see ʿAlī and al-Bukhārī, J. Burton, Guillaume, Hasan, and Siddiqi and Murad.

of al-Saraquṣṭī), who often appears as a popular preacher or *qaṣṣ*, exhorting and entertaining a crowd in hopes of monetary gain. Thus we see in the *maqāmāt* two types of performance: the authoritative performance of the transmission of textual tradition (in imitation of the *ḥadīṯ*), and the subversive performance of the popular preacher or storyteller, the *qaṣṣ*.

In both cases, the *maqāmāt* establish the performative frame using markers that are specific to traditional genres of Arabic literature and public oratory. Because the *maqāmāt* are believed to be parodies of a variety of classical genres including *ḥadīṯ*, their performative pretext lies in their transmission, after the manner of *ḥadīṯ* literature. Like *ḥadīṯ*, each *maqāma* begins with an *isnād* which traces the chain of transmission from the eyewitness to the author. Each link in the chain constitutes a performance of its own and suggests, as in *ḥadīṯ* literature, that the integrity of the message relies upon the narrative accuracy (and moral integrity) of each transmitter, or performer.[49]

While the narrative description of the performance event in this case is minimal, it does posit a performance and means of transmission of a type with which the audience would be quite familiar. Monroe maintains that the *isnād* of the *maqāma* (referring to those of al-Hamaḏānī) was intended as a parody of established genres of Arabic literature (Monroe, *Art* 99). Therefore, one can conclude that in the *maqāma*, the need to construct directly the storytelling event that obtains in *Kalīla* is obviated, because the *maqāma* draws on the audience's familiarity with the oral settings of the *ḥadīṯ* genre that it parodies. The audience of the *maqāma*, hearing the *isnād*, recalls the sound vision of the transmission of a *ḥadīṯ*. There is no need for the author to paint the storytelling event in detail within the *maqāma* itself. For example, the carefully placed narrative markers characteristic of *Kalīla* are absent in the *maqāma*; their function is fulfilled by the reproduction of the *isnād* at the beginning of each episode.

Storytelling and Popular Preaching in Medieval Islam

This *isnād*-like frame of narrative transmission sets a familiar stage for the audience of the *maqāma*. Within this frame that recalls the learned narrative

[49] There was a practice among popular storytellers (*quṣṣās*) of inventing *ḥadīṯ* "to which they attached seemingly impeccable *isnād*s, their purpose being to astonish the common people and receive payment for their stories" (*EI*, "Ḥadīth"). This closely resembles the activity of the rogue character (as well as the narrator) of the *maqāmāt*, who dazzles townsfolk with his oratory in hopes of being paid for it.

of *ḥadīṯ*, a second, more popular form of performance is portrayed: that of the popular preacher/storyteller, the *qāṣṣ*. The figure of the *qāṣṣ* as depicted in medieval Arabic literature is a dubious one at best; he tends to operate on the margins of society, exploiting the ignorance and/or goodwill of his audiences, and by charming and dazzling them with his rhetorical skills, lines his pockets. He is the medieval Islamic cousin of the snake-oil vendors of the nineteenth-century American West. Though shunned by established religion, he is embraced by the man on the street, a living example of the powerful social value of rhetoric in medieval Islam.

The importance placed on *balāġa* (eloquence) and *khaṭṭāba* (rhetoric) in Arabic culture lends its literature a performative aspect. The Arabic tradition of *balāġa* is highly performative, in that its aim is to draw attention to the artifice of the speaker's words in order to invest them with authority. Systematic analyses of *balāġa* by medieval authors[50] made frequent reference to the figure of the *khaṭīb* or orator, thus reinforcing the performative and oral nature of *balāġa*.[51]

The *maqāma* incorporates traits of such rhetorical performance. The name itself suggests a public act of oratory. Since one of the definitions of *maqāma*, like *majlis*, is an assembly of important people,[52] and since such a meeting is a common forum for eloquent oratory, it is a natural metonymy for the word *maqāma* to denote the act of oratory itself (*EI*, "Maḳama"). Even the *sajʿ* (rhymed prose), in which much of the *maqāmāt* are composed, has its roots in oral composition and performance.[53] While by the time of al-Saraqusṭī, *sajʿ* had evolved into the standard genre for all official correspondence and had very solid footing as a genre composed in writing (but read aloud), its history is rooted in orality and performance as a genre utilized by oracles and popular orators. Originally the pre-Islamic oracles (*kuhān*) used *sajʿ* to announce an "oracular utterance" (*EI*, "Sadjʿ"). The Qurʾān later drew on the spiritual authority of *sajʿ* by using it in several *sūras*, for example *Sūrat*

[50] Among these are the *Kitāb al-badīʿ* (887–888 CE) of Abū ʿAbbās ʿAbd Allāh ibn al-Muʿtazz, the *ʾAsrār al-balāġa* of ʿAbd al-Qāhir al-Jurjānī (d. 1078 CE), and the third chapter of the *Miftaḥ al-ʿulūm* of Abū Yaʿqūb Yūsuf al-Sakkakī (d. 1226 CE).

[51] "The demand for skill in improvisation and the recurring references to the *khaṭīb* (or orator) in connexion with the discussion of the concept" was central to literary treatments of *balāġa* (*EI*, "Balāgha").

[52] The lexicographer Ibn Manẓūr defines *maqāma* as *al-majlis* (11: 362). Ibn Qutayba (d. 278 AH/889 CE) uses the term *maqām* in his *ʿUyūn al-akhbār* with the sense of "pious harangue" (Blachère 646–52). This recalls the oratory of the popular preachers described in the two poems titled "Qaṣīda sasāniyya" of Abū Dulaf and Ṣafī al-Dīn (trans. Bosworth 2: 197, v. 56 and 296, v. 14; ed. Bosworth 2: 13 and 45) and depicted in the *maqāmāt* of al-Saraqustī (ed. al-Warāglī 41; trans. Monroe 130).

[53] On *sajʿ* and its use in the *maqāma*, see D. Young (*Rogues* 21–43).

al-nās (114).[54] In every instance, *sajʿ* is associated with performance genres, more often than not popular genres which orthodox Islam came to regard with suspicion.

During the ʿAbbāsid period, storytelling and storytellers continued to be an object of scorn for religious officials and thinkers, who sought to restrict the activity of popular preachers whose public performances in the mosques captivated the attention of the common folk and were therefore a potential threat to the social order. ʿAbd al-Raḥmān ibn ʿAlī al-Jawzī,[55] in his treatise on popular preachers and storytellers (*Kitāb al-quṣṣāṣ*), argues for the legitimacy of storytelling in Islamic tradition and establishes a taxonomy of proper and improper uses of storytelling in popular sermons. He warns against the abuse of storytelling and oratory in popular preaching for purposes of stirring the lust of the audience or for falsifying *ḥadīṯ* and other religious materials. Similarly, Ibn al-Ḥājj, in his *Madkhal al-šarʿ al-šarīf* ('The Way of the Noble Law'), differentiates between meetings dedicated to religious instruction (*majlis al-ʿilm*) and those dedicated to storytelling devoid of moral or religious value (*majlis al-qaṣaṣ*) (Berkey 71).[56] In his own condemnation of such false *quṣṣāṣ*, al-Ghazālī[57] condemns those who tell stories in *sajʿ*:

> It is not permitted to gather a crowd around oneself and narrate stories in mosques... as for those who adorn themselves and whose master is lust, and tell [their stories] in rhymed prose and sing them... such a deed is considered an unforgivable sin and should not be permitted even outside the mosques.[58]

Apparently such *quṣṣāṣ* were a widely known social phenomenon in medieval Islam, for there are vivid accounts of them in literature meant to amuse and edify, not censure. The "Qaṣīda sasāniyya" of Abū Dulaf (fl. tenth century) contains a verse inventory of beggars, petty con artists, and street performers, among them "the one who tells stories about the history and legends

---

[54] For this and subsequent references to the Qurʾān, see *Holy Qurʾān*.

[55] Ibn al-Jawzī (1126–1200) was born to a well-to-do family in Baghdad. For biographical information, see Ibn al-Jawzī (15–38) and *EI* ("Ibn al-Jawzī").

[56] Ibn al-Ḥājj was a Mālikī jurist born in Cairo in 1336 (*EI*, "Ibn al-Ḥājj"). While Ibn al-Ḥājj lived somewhat after the period of literary production in question, he draws on materials dating from early Islam forward.

[57] Islamic jurist and theologian Abū Ḥāmid Muḥammad ibn Muḥammad al-Ghazālī (1058–1111) (*EI*, al-Ġazālī, Abū Ḥāmid Muḥammad b. Muḥammad al-Ṭūsī).

[58] From al-Ghazālī's *Kīmīyā-yi Saʿādat*, his own translation into Persian of his Arabic *Iḥyā ʿulūm al-dīn* (ed. Amram 404–06; trans. Omidsalar 206). For an English translation of the entire work, see al-Ghazālī (*Alchemy*, trans. Claud Field).

of the Jews, or who relates a series of brief anecdotes one after another" (trans. Bosworth 2: 195, v.41; ed. Bosworth 2: 9). Somewhat later, Safid-Dīn (1278–1349) in his own "Qaṣīda sasāniyya" describes a similar type of character: "and how often have I acted as a popular preacher and storyteller (i.e. as a *qāṣṣ*), making people absorbed and enraptured by my stories and verses, and how often have I addressed them in a mad, deranged fashion, swinging my head from side to side whilst declaiming" (trans. Bosworth 2: 297, v. 25; ed. Bosworth 2: 47). Al-Saraqusṭī describes just such a character in his fourth *maqāma*:

> When I was in the district of Oman, by turns experiencing poverty and prosperity, I encountered group after group of people going down, singly and in pairs, to where a man was standing telling stories and tales, and enduring weariness and fatigue in the course of his preaching. At times, he spoke in verse, and at times in prose, moving fluently, without stumbling in his discourse. (trans. Monroe 130; ed. al-Warāglī 41)

The activities of such *quṣṣāṣ* were especially curtailed in al-Andalus, where the prevalent Māliki school of Islamic law "would scarcely tolerate them" (*EI*, "Ḳaṣṣ"). The performances of these *quṣṣāṣ* in mosques or other public places constituted a live storytelling event. In a literary setting such as the frametale or *maqāma*, the author's aim in encoding the storytelling event is not to record the performance as would an ethnographer, but rather to set up a meaningful didactic relationship between the tale and the situations faced by the characters. In other words, the tale must be told for a reason, and it must serve a function within the narrative frame.

Performance in al-Saraqusṭī's Luzūmīyya

We have noted that the characters in *Kalīla* tell mostly fabulistic tales in the explicit mode: they are described in the act of storytelling. In contrast, the characters in the frame story of the *maqāmāt* of al-Saraqusṭī are portrayed as telling anecdotal stories in the implicit mode. Instead of showing us and describing the storytelling act, the author simply mentions that it occurred, relying on the familiar structure of the *ḥadīṯ* in which the narrator only states the chain of transmission by which the anecdote has reached him:

> The author said:
> Al-Munḏir ibn Humām narrated and said:
> Al-Sā'ib ibn Tammām narrated to us and said: (trans. Monroe 114; ed. al-Warāglī 14)

The *isnād* of each *maqāma* recalls two successive performances of an anecdote: al-Sā'ib ibn Tammām narrates an anecdote to al-Mundir ibn Humām, who in turn narrates it to the author, who writes it down. As we have discussed, this frame itself indexes these two performances, but does not describe them explicitly. Rather than describe a storytelling event, the author encodes the performance with the *isnād* formula, familiar to the reader from *ḥadīṯ*. This is one of the most salient imprints of Islamic literary culture on the representation of storytelling in the *maqāmāt*.

Like the characters in the frame story of *Kalīla*, however, the characters portrayed *within* the anecdotes recounted by the narrator in al-Saraqusṭī's *maqāmāt* (almost always the ubiquitous rogue al-Sadūsī) also give explicit performances, not of tales, but of oratory—they are literary versions of the very real *quṣṣās*, those street preachers and confidence men condemned by religious authorities such as Ibn al-Ḥājj and al-Ġazālī.

There is an important connection in the *maqāmāt* of al-Saraqusṭī between the implicit performances of the transmitters and the explicit performances of the rogue al-Sadūsī. In each *maqāma*, the rogue uses his superior rhetorical skills to deceive the narrator al-Sā'ib ibn Tammām. This trickery, the only constant uniting the fifty episodes of the *maqāmāt*, is a literary representation of the *Banū Sasān* portrayed by Abū Dulaf and Ṣafī al-Dīn. For example, al-Saraqusṭī's *maqāmāt* 35 and 38 portray trainers of a bear and an ape, and Abū Dulaf describes the "cunning youth who goes round with performing monkeys or bears, begging by means of them" (trans. Bosworth 2: 205, v. 104; ed. Bosworth 2: 25). Similarly, Ṣafī al-Dīn's poetic voice boasts of having "done tricks with performing monkeys, and hav[ing]...put on a show with dancing bears" (trans. Bosworth 2: 299, v. 51; ed. Bosworth 2: 51). Al-Saraqusṭī's *maqāma* 46 portrays al-Sadūsī and an accomplice as a faker of seizures and a quack doctor who pretends to heal him, and Abū Dulaf mentions "the feigned madman and madwoman" (trans. Bosworth 2: 192, v. 30; ed. Bosworth 2: 6). Finally, al-Saraqusṭī's *maqāma* 50 features a con man posing as a *ṣūfī* ascetic. The narrator al-Sā'ib ibn Tammām relates:

> a man descended upon us, who had set out from Kufa and who belonged to the *sufi* order, the hair of whose temples had turned white, and whose cheeks pensiveness had furrowed, whom worship and asceticism had inflamed, and whom work and exertion had emaciated, for he did not cease exhorting people to practice piety and virtue, and to adopt no more than what was absolutely necessary and moderately sufficient to sustain life...(trans. Monroe 490; ed. al-Warāglī 461)

The false ascetic is revealed as the trickster Abū Ḥabīb al-Sadūsī, who uses the disguise as a ruse to win Ibn Tammām's money. This is precisely the same type of street preacher derided by Ibn al-Ḥājj and al-Ghazālī, and described by Abū Dulaf (trans. Bosworth 2: 195, v. 42; ed. Bosworth 2: 9). All these performances are carried out by the rogue al-Sadūsī in his perennial mission to dupe the narrator, Ibn Tammām. From a narratological standpoint, the most interesting of these performance ruses is the 'sob story' in which the performer relates his misfortunes in hopes of a handout. In his "Qaṣīda Sasāniyya," Abū Dulaf describes

> the one who slashes himself, alleging that he has been mutilated by assailants, or the one who darkens his skin artificially, pretending that he has been beaten up and wounded.
>
> *Shattaba* is when he slashes himself with a razor and then starts to give out mendacious accounts about the Bedouins and Kurds and robbers [and how they did this to him]. *Rakkaba* is when he smears his body with sesame oil so that his skin becomes black; he then makes people believe that he has been flogged or that the Jinn have beaten him up during the night....
>
> And the one who parades in the garb of an ascetic, or who begs on the context that he is a pilgrim. (trans. Bosworth 2: 195 v. 42; ed. Bosworth 2: 9)

Many of the confidence strategies described by Abū Dulaf have counterparts in the anecdotes related by al-Saraqusṭī's narrator Ibn Tammām.[59] However, in each *maqāma*, he is left penniless, cheated by al-Sadūsī. The fictional rogue's sob stories, told in hopes of winning the sympathy (and money) of his fictional audience Ibn Tammām, are identical to those of the Baghdādī street cons described in Abū Dulaf's poem. In short, the explicit performances described in the *maqāmāt* are a reminder that the implicit performance (that of al-Sā'ib Ibn Tammām to al-Mundir bin Humām, the transmitter) is a fiction and that the reader should take nothing at face value. While the *isnād* style of chain of transmission used parodically by the authors of the *maqāmāt* suggests a solemn recitation of reported speech (as in *ḥadīt*) in a study session, the content of Ibn Tammām's narrations suggests the carnivalesque milieu described by Abū Dulaf. In the end, it is entirely possible that the narrator Ibn Tammām is not just a repeat victim of al-Sadūsī's trickery, but is himself another silver-tongued performer, telling his own sob story, looking to pass on his misfortune to a dupe of his own. His is a performance, if you like, of desperation.

The models of performance and its encoding first introduced to Arabic literature in *Kalīla* are diversified and nuanced in the Arabic *maqāma* by

[59] For example, in *maqāma* 41, Ibn Tammām is left fleeing a band of Berbers eager to kill him for stealing their money (having been framed, of course, by al-Sadūsī) (trans. Monroe 418–24; ed. al-Waräglī 385–92).

drawing on the narrative resources of the *ḥadīṯ*, as well as actual performance practices of street preachers and storytellers in the medieval Islamic world. In his *maqāmāt*, al-Saraqusṭī ironically frames his accounts of the subversive, popular performances of street preachers and storytellers (*quṣṣāṣ*) with the authoritative performance of traditional narrative (in his parody of the transmission of *ḥadīṯ*). In doing so, he questions the integrity of both types of performance, underscoring the need for audiences to read and listen critically, lest they themselves be duped like the hapless Ibn Tammām.

Performance in Hebrew Maqāmāt

By the end of the twelfth century, the *maqāma* began to be cultivated by Hebrew writers living in al-Andalus and Christian Iberia. In their adaptation of the genre, the representation of performance undergoes a number of changes. While the essential features remain consistent in the Hebrew *maqāmāt*, a number of specifically Jewish cultural and literary features are present in the work of writers such as al-Ḥarīzī and Ibn Zabāra, contributing to the uniqueness of the Hebrew Iberian *maqāmāt*. They provide a different solution to the problem of narrativity and fictionality inherited from their Arabic predecessors, and this difference affects the way performance is represented in the texts.

Al-Ḥarīzī and Ibn Zabāra wrote during a period when the tradition of secular literature in Hebrew was relatively new. Hebrew poets did not begin to produce profane compositions regularly until the end of the tenth century. At this time, a group of poets in al-Andalus began to write secular poetry in Hebrew, adapting Arabic poetic metrics, themes, imagery, and metaphors.[60] These highly Arabized Jewish intellectuals moved freely in Andalusī intellectual and political circles. Their adaptation of Arabic poetics was second nature. In both cultures, writers of secular poetry and prose

[60] The most prominent of these poets were Shmuel (Samuel) Hanagid ibn Nagrela (993–1055 or 1056), Shelomo (Solomon) ibn Gabirol (c. 1020–c. 1057), Moshe (Moses) ibn Ezra (c. 1055– after 1138), and Yehudah (Judah) Halevi (before 1075–1141). For English works on Spanish Hebrew poetry in general, see Scheindlin (*Gazelle*), Brann (*Compunctious*), and Pagis. The definitive work on Hebrew poetry in Spain is Schirmann (*Hebrew Poetry*). On Arabic themes in Hebrew poetry, see Schippers (*Spanish*). For a selective Spanish edition and translation see Pérez Castro. See also the Spanish translations by Sáenz-Badillos and Targarona of the poetry of Shmuel Hanagid (*Poemas* and *Poemas II*) and Yehudah Halevi (*Poemas*), Sáenz-Badillos' translation of the poetry of Shelomo ibn Gabirol (*Alma*), and Sáenz-Badillos and Targarona's dictionary of Sephardic authors (*Diccionario*).

were constantly challenged by what might be called the anxiety of scriptural authority. Early Islamic writers (and poets in particular) had constantly to reconcile their work, clothed as it was in the language of the Qurʾān, with the tenets and cultural norms of Islam.[61] While the Qurʾān was viewed as the paragon of literary style, one had to take pains to avoid dishonoring it by abusing its language. This model of scriptural literary authority was adapted by Hebrew writers in order to justify using the language of the Torah for secular ends.[62] Two factors distinguish the timing of the introduction of secular literature in the Muslim and Jewish traditions. First, the Arabic language already possessed a considerable corpus of pre-Islamic poetry, a poetics, and a culture of secular literature among the nomadic tribes of the Arabian Peninsula.[63] Second, since the destruction of the first Temple by the Babylonians (586 BCE), Hebrew had not been used as a vernacular by Jews, who typically adopted the vernacular of the people amongst whom they lived. Hebrew was restricted to liturgical and legal usage. While this liturgical usage included devotional poems (Heb. *piyyūtīm*, sing. *piyyūt*), the Hebrew used in composing such religious poetry was post-biblical, in an often obscure idiom (Pagis 6). There was no tradition of secular Hebrew literature before the Andalusī Hebrew poets of the tenth century. What this means is that when the authors of the Hebrew *maqāmāt* were writing, the performative context of the biblical Hebrew from which they wrought their verse was strictly liturgical, and every word of their poetry resonated with the public recitations of the Hebrew Bible performed on market days, the Sabbath, and holidays.[64]

However, the language used by authors of Arabic *maqāmāt* was associated with a great variety of performative contexts, both religious and secular: Qurʾānic recitation, sermons, legal proceedings, political addresses,

---

[61] In Islam, there is a problematic division between orthodox religious writing and poetry. This division has its origins in the Qurʾān, which inveighs vehemently against poets and their perceived moral failings: "And the poets—the perverse follow them; hast thou not seen how they wander in every valley and how they say that which they do not?" (26: 224). Therefore, the Qurʾān, despite being written partly in rhymed prose (the *sajʿ* used by authors of Arabic *maqāmāt*), "is the speech of a noble messenger. It is not the speech of the poet…" (69: 41).

[62] "The formal mechanism by which this cultural transfer was put into practice was to regard the Hebrew Bible as a 'Jewish Qurʾān', that is, to consider biblical form aesthetically and stylistically perfect just as its content was considered authoritative" (Brann, *Compunctious* 23).

[63] The classic collection of such pre-Islamic poetry is the *Muʿallaqāt*, (the Suspended). See the edition of al-Zawzānī, the English translations of both O'Grady and Sells, and the Spanish translation of Corriente.

[64] On reading as speech act in antique and medieval Jewish culture, see D. Boyarin.

and the type of popular oratory described in the *maqāmāt* themselves and contemporary texts such as the "Qasīda Sasāniyya" of Abū Dulaf.[65] Authors of Hebrew *maqāmāt* were opening new territory in the performativity of the Hebrew language.

Aspects of performativity in the Arabic *maqāmāt* unique to Islam were received differently by Hebrew authors and audiences. For example, the parodic use of the *isnād* or chain of transmission of the *ḥadīṯ* tradition did not have the same significance in Jewish culture, which favored other models of narrativity and peformance. The structure of the *isnād* reflects an insistence on fidelity to an original and absolutely authoritative source: there is but one way to relate a tradition and one admissible chain of transmission. Because this model of transmission of the *ḥadīṯ* is absent from Jewish religious culture, its use in Hebrew *maqāmāt* would not have the same resonance as in Arabic texts. By contrast, Talmudic discourse is not so concerned with transmission-based authority (providing the definitive answer) as it is with dialectic and polyglossia (debating the question). A *ḥadīṯ* is a statement made by one person to another. A page of Talmud, however, is an asynchronous discussion between several rabbis across centuries (J. Rosen 9–10). The Talmud contains a great deal of narrative content, mostly exemplary in nature, which means that a Jewish Andalusī sense of didactic narrative would be indebted to Talmudic and midrashic *aggadah*, narrative material used by the rabbis in teaching "conduct and ethics" (Steinsaltz 251).[66]

The problem of fictionality first broached by the Arabic *maqāmāt* is reiterated, with variations, in the Hebrew *maqāma*. While the directive in Arabic literature, exemplified by the use of the *isnād*, was to ensure a work's concrete historicity,[67] Jewish religious literature sought a more abstract reality.[68] The concept of faithful representation of reality central to Islamic literature did

[65] See the medieval Islamic authorities on the subject of preaching and storytelling brought together by Berkey (22–35).

[66] On the folktale in Jewish literature, see Yassif. For an exhaustive collection of *aggadah* from various rabbinical sources, see Bin Gorion. On medieval collections of *aggadah*, see Gaster.

[67] "Classical Arabic literature claims to make absolute, definitive statements about the course of history.... The major poetic claim of classical Arabic literature is its historicity; the claim is so authoritative that it is made in all prose genres, even in those that have no direct association with religion" (Drory, *Models* 12).

[68] "Traditionally, Jewish literature...was not so much interested in portraying reality as in representing the correct order of things. Its main concern lay in theological and moral paradigms rather than in their particular, transient, historical manifestations...." (Drory, "Maqama" 200).

not obtain in Talmudic literature. Instead, a different model of orality and transmission prevailed: one of a cacophonous, Bakhtinian heteroglossia, where rabbis held disorganized discussions juxtaposed across the centuries in a kind of proto-hypertext originally transmitted orally but finally set down in writing by the sixth century.[69]

Storytelling and Performance in the Jewish Context

Just as the culture of popular and religious narrative in Islam is brought to bear on the encoding and decoding of performance in *Kalīla* and the Arabic *maqāmāt*, Jewish traditions of narrative, particularly Talmudic and Midrashic *aggadah*, inform readers and audiences of Hebrew *maqāmāt* such as al-Ḥarīzī's *Taḥkemonī* and Ibn Zabāra's *Sefer Šaʿašūʿīm* ('Book of Delights').

Aggadah, literally 'telling', is a form of exegetic literature that seeks to explain obscure biblical passages with bits of short narrative. It is a narrative genre, one that is conversational in nature, as befits its origin in transcriptions of rabbinic discourses and study groups. There are abundant examples of *aggadah* in the Talmud, the Midrash, and other works of Jewish exegesis. *Aggadah*, while useful in explaining and expanding on biblical narrative, is not considered sound basis for religious law, and so its validity in legal argumentation has been criticized by the rabbis, and even more so by Muslim and Christian polemicists seeking to discredit the textual foundations of Jewish law. Although *aggadah* is found in written sources, its tone is conversational and recalls the performative context of a religious study group or perhaps a sermon.[70]

The idea that *aggadah* was a distinct subgenre within exegetic literature, one primarily speculative and narrative as opposed to authoritative, is reflected in sources from medieval Iberia. When the prominent Catalan rabbi Nahmanides was called upon to defend the integrity of the Talmud in the Disputation of Barcelona (1263), he explained to his adversary, Pablus Christiani, that the *aggadah* was more homiletic than doctrinal:

---

[69] On heteroglossia, see Bakhtin (67–68). On the dialogic nature of rabbinic exegetical narrative, see Levinson. For a discussion of Talmudic and digital discourse, including hypertext, see J. Rosen. On *aggadah* in rabbinic tradition of thirteenth-century Provence, see Saperstein. On the oral-textual nexus in the transmission of Jewish tradition, see Elman and Gershoni.

[70] For an ethnographic account of a contemporary Talmudic study group, see J. Boyarin ("Voices").

> We have another, third type of book called *midrash*, which means *sermones*,[71] as when the hegemon [bishop] stands and gives a *sermón*, and someone from the audience likes it and writes it down. As regards this type of book, if one should believe in it, good, and if not, there is no harm in it... and we also call it *aggadah* literature, which means *razonamiento*, which means it contains only things that a man might tell to his friend. (trans. Saperstein 11; ed. Chavel 1: 308)[72]

Aggadah is a narrative genre, part of exegetic discussions and sermons that would later be committed to writing. Therefore, the distinction between authoritative exegesis and fanciful narrative—even within the same document—was drawn at an early stage in the development of Hebrew literature. By the Middle Ages, it was clearly delineated, as the comments of Nahmanides demonstrate. As such, *aggadah* literature was a profound influence on the literary imagination of medieval Jewish writers, whose sense of narrative, especially literary narrative, would have been nurtured by extensive exposure to *aggadah* during religious study. A survey of modern histories of Hebrew literature reveals that medieval Hebrew narrative is often considered as an extension of rabbinic *aggadah* (Yassif 246–48). The major literary innovation of writers like al-Ḥarīzī and Ibn Zabāra was the introduction of narrative modes and materials from *aggadah* and folktale into a secular literary context. These influences, along with the authors' reworking of the performative model of Islamic *ḥadīṯ* adapted from the Arabic *maqāma*, contribute to the textual encoding of performance in the Hebrew *maqāma*.

While the *ḥadīṯ* model of performance and narrative transmission was developed out of a concern for accuracy and secure transmission of religious material that was the basis for Islamic law, *aggadic* material in the Talmud was not considered valid basis for legal argumentation. Rather, it was considered useful for illustrating concepts and principles involved in legal discussion. Given these differing—yet convergent—narrative legacies, Hebrew *maqāmāt* are more concerned with non-realistic fiction than with verisimilitude and historical accuracy (Drory, "Maqama" 205). This sense of non-realism comes across in the *maqāmāt* of al-Ḥarīzī and—decidedly more so—in those of

---

[71] One wonders why the Catalan speaker Nahmanides would have used the decidedly Castilian forms "sermones" (in place of the Catalan *sermons*) and "razonamiento" (Cat. *raonament*). It is possible that the original text contained the Catalan, but that a later Castilian- or Judeo-Spanish-speaking scribe—or perhaps Chavel, the editor of the printed edition cited here—emended the forms to reflect Castilian usage.

[72] On the Disputation of Barcelona, see Chazan (*Barcelona*), Maccoby, and Riera i Sans and Feliu.

Ibn Zabāra. In the case of al-Ḥarīzī, the break from reality is established by means of a disclaimer given by the author in his introductory *maqāma*:

> And all the words of this book I have put upon the tongue of *Heman, the Ezrahite*, and in the name of *Heber, the Kenite*, I have founded and built them, although neither of them live in our generation, and all that I have mentioned in their name never was and never happened, but is only fiction.[73] (trans. Reichert 1:40; ed. Toporovsky and Zamora 15)

Thus it is made clear to the reader—in keeping with the nature of traditional Jewish literature—that what follows is not intended to be a faithful representation of reality. However, because al-Ḥarīzī is—by his own admission—closely following the model of the Arabic authors of *maqāmāt* such as al-Ḥarīrī and al-Saraqusṭī, his fiction is still largely plausible.[74] That is, there is little of the fantastic, magical, or marvelous in the world he constructs. His characters are similar to those in the Arabic *maqāmāt*, and like al-Saraqusṭī's rogue al-Sadūsī, Heber the Kenite is a gifted orator in search of recognition and cash. By contrast, the *Sefer Šaʿašūʿīm* of Ibn Zabāra, less closely patterned after al-Ḥarīrī's *maqāmāt*, strays from the conventions of the genre, including that of realism. The reality of Ibn Zabāra's *maqāmāt* is somewhat more fantastic than that of his predecessors.

While al-Ḥarīzī makes a formal disclaimer to free himself from the responsibility of reporting faithfully on reality, Ibn Zabāra does no such thing. He takes one step away from the performance model of *ḥadīṯ* as an occasion for the transmission of authoritative narrative tradition and toward the modern conceit of fiction. Far from distancing himself from the narrator by declaring him fictional, he goes the other way and closes the narrative gap between author and narrator by making himself the narrator. The work begins:

> There lived a man in the city of Barcelona whose name was Joseph ben Zabara. From his youth up had he dwelt at ease, in amity with his friends and comrades. All that knew him became his friends, and they that were his friends loved him;

[73] Allusion to the Talmudic saying "*Lo hayah ve-lo nivrah, ʾela mašal hayah*," in reference to story of Job (*Talmud Bavlī*, Bava Batra 15a, cited in Drory, *Models* 200–01).

[74] Although his work assumes the formal characteristics of the Arabic *maqāmāt* such as those of al-Ḥarīrī, al-Ḥarīzī openly frames the *Taḥkemonī* as a Hebrew response to the challenge posed by the virtuosity of al-Ḥarīrī's Arabic text: "Now the thing that stirred up my spirit to compose this book was that a wise man among the sages of the Arabs and one of the choicest of the enlightened whose tongue is powerful in Arabic poetry and through whose mouth the vision of song is spread abroad—he is the famous al-Ḥarīrī, all the authors of poetry except him are barren—he composed a book in the Arabic tongue that offers goodly words" (trans. Reichert 1: 35; ed. Toporovsky and Zamora 11).

> among them he was respected and esteemed, bound to all by ties of affection. He for his part honored and exalted them, served them and healed them. For those of them that were sick he compounded suitable remedies, in accordance with his knowledge and his skill. In his love and charity he busied himself with his patients whether old or young, and served them, and ministered to them. Everyone, then, loved Joseph and sought his company eagerly, but as Scripture hath it [Psalms 117:5], Joseph was sold for a servant.
>
> Came then a night when I, Joseph, was sleeping upon my bed. My sleep was sweet upon me, for that alone was my portion for all my labor.... (trans. Hadas 47; ed. Davidson 7)

His way of indicating the work's fictionality is more subtle: he sets his narrative in a dream dreamt by the narrator. Joseph relates: "and it came to pass as I slumbered that I saw an appearance before me[75] in my dream, in the likeness of a man exceeding tall, who did then rouse me as is the wont of a man who arouseth another from his sleep" (trans. Hadas 48; ed. Davidson 8). The "appearance" he sees is his companion Enan Hanatas, Ibn Zabāra's equivalent of al-Ḥarīzī's rogue, Heber the Kenite. Since dream reality is not bound by the same rules as waking reality, Ibn Zabāra signals his work's fictionality by the dream state of his narrator. The dream state justifies the instances of the supernatural that pepper Ibn Zabāra's narrative: his riding ass speaks (trans. Hadas 146; ed. Davidson 127); his traveling companion Enan is eventually revealed to be not a man, but a demon, "Enan the Satan, son of Ornan the demon" (trans. Hadas 147; ed. Davidson 128); and certain of the residents of Enan's hometown are described as "great and tall, yea mountainous, as unicorns" (trans. Hadas 149; ed. Davidson 132).

Because the narrator and the author are the same, there is no need (or place) for the *isnād*-style chain of transmission that signals the implicit mode of performance in the Arabic *maqāmāt* and in the Hebrew *maqāmāt* of al-Ḥarīzī. Therefore, the tales told in the *Sefer Šaʿašūʿīm* must be delivered explicitly, before the "eyes" of the fictive audience, as in *Kalīla*. Ibn Zabāra, working outside the performative conventions of the "classical" *maqāma* to which al-Saraqusṭī and al-Ḥarīzī so faithfully adhered, is free to experiment with other narrative devices. What he comes up with is a frame story that is narrated explicitly yet is still narrated as if it were anecdote (and not fable), as author and narrator are one and the same person.

---

[75] Note the language: Ibn Zabāra writes "an appearance... in the likeness of a man" (Heb. '*kemar'eh adam temūnato*') he does not simply state "I saw a man." This phrasing suggests that Enan Hanatas is perhaps something other than human. Additionally, his name (minus the Hebrew definite article *ha*), spelled in reverse, is 'Satan'.

With regard to the contextualization of performances, Ibn Zabāra's work falls somewhere between frametale and *maqāma*. The interpolation of performances, particularly of tales, in *Sefer Šaʿašūʿīm* at times resembles the request-for-advice pretense used in *Kalīla* and at times the various performative contexts of the *maqāmāt*. The innovation of Ibn Zabāra is in the combination of the explicit mode of performance typical of *Kalīla* with the fictionality of the *maqāma*. From the point of view of a reader of modern fiction, this explicit mode of performance is richer and affords more opportunities for characterization and novelistic detail than the implicit. Tales performed in the explicit mode lead the fictive audience to a more nuanced understanding of the function of tales within the frame story. The result is a more sophisticated system of framed storytelling, one that allows for a closer identification of the audience with the narrative material than *Kalīla*, while making available to the author narrative resources more varied than those of the "classical" *maqāma*. In *Šaʿašūʿīm*, as in the *maqāma*, Ibn Zabāra tells tales in the first person; as in *Kalīla*, he frames them explicitly, describing the storytelling act as it happens. This style of narration presages the direction later taken by such European works as Boccaccio's *Decameron* and especially Chaucer's *Canterbury Tales*.

A review of the narrative strategies of tales interpolated in the frame story of the *Sefer Šaʿašūʿīm* reveals at least three distinct methods: fabulistic, nested exemplary tales (like those found in *Kalīla*), fabulistic tales introduced by a proverb summarizing the tale, and anecdotal tales introduced by their significance to the actual geographic location of storyteller and audience. In each case, the framing strategy offers another opportunity for the characterization of Joseph and Enan in their interaction and in the portrayal of the role of performance in their relationship.

In chapter 2, Joseph explains that he is hesitant to trust Enan and to follow him in his travels, for Joseph's physiognomic analysis of his companion indicates that the giant may have a less than trustworthy character: "every tall man is a fool, sinful in speech, blind and a follower of lust" (trans. Hadas 55; ed. Davidson 19). He gives voice to his fear of placing his safety in the hands of an untrustworthy character by telling the tale of the Leopard who followed (and was deceived by) the Fox:

> I replied: "A leopard once lived in content and plenty: ever he found easy sustenance for his wife and children. Hard by there dwelt his neighbor and friend, the fox. The fox felt in his heart that his life was safe only so long as the leopard could catch other prey. 'If other prey should be wanting for a single day he will seize me in his might and slay me in the strength of his wrath, for he is in truth but shameless and he will apportion me unto himself and his sons

> as viands. Surely I must bespeak him cunningly and beguile him with words of deceit; mayhap I shall prevail by wile and cast from my neck the yoke of his burden. "Before the evil cometh," the sage hath said, "counsel is good, but after trouble hath arrived it is but vain." Therefore will I remove him from my dwelling place and cause him to depart from my habitation. I will banish him from his place ere he swallow me, and cast him from his station ere he cast me down and devour me. Perhaps I can lead him in the path of death, for have not our sages of blessed memory declared, "If one come to slay thee, arise thou betimes and slay him?"' (trans. Hadas 55–56; ed. Davidson 20–21)

Joseph then goes on to tell the entire tale of how the Leopard is turned against the counsel of his own wife by the Fox. Eventually, the Leopard moves his family to a dry riverbed on the advice of the Fox, and his entire family is drowned at the first rainfall. It becomes apparent to Enan that Joseph identifies himself with the Leopard, and Enan with the Fox. Enan is outraged to think that Joseph should mistrust him so:

> Then Enan Hanatas turned toward me and gnashed his teeth and sharpened his eyes against me as a sword is ground against an enemy and said: "I marvel at thee. Against whom hast thou uttered this long speech, hast thou lifted thy proverbs, hast thou named me *fox* and thyself *leopard*? Thinkest thou that I am affrighted of thee as was the fox of the leopard? Thinkest thou that I blinded thine eyes when I spake unto thine ears? Truly the sage has said, 'In the multitude of words there wanteth not sin.' As my soul liveth, because of thee almost would I despise all my comrades and reject all my friends. Cease then from words of jest and mockery, for they are vanity, deeds of folly." (trans. Hadas 69–70; ed. Davidson 34–35)

While in *Kalīla* the discussions of political problems between the characters (and the tales used to illustrate such problems and possible solutions) refer to relationships outside that of advisor-advisee, here there is a conflation of roles; the tale narrated by Joseph to Enan refers reflexively to the relationship between the two. In *Kalīla*, a character such as Dimna will narrate a story to illustrate a problematic relationship between the Lion and a third party. Here the anecdotal mode of narration of the *maqāma* is combined with that of the fable: the analogy is drawn between the narrator's own behavior and that of the characters within the fable he himself narrates. It is a self-contained social universe wherein the performer, the audience, and players in the social milieu whose actions are being analyzed and explained are all found in the frame characters, Joseph and Enan. The very referent of performance is the relationship between performer and audience, not that between the audience and the outside world, as in *Kalīla*.

We have another example of such socially reflexive performance in chapter 3, where with a seemingly enigmatic proverb Enan invents a pretext for being invited to tell a tale to Joseph. Here Enan's tale is itself a story about storytelling and its social value (Bauman, "Performance" 47):

> And it came to pass after we had gone a furlong, each riding upon his ass, that Enan said to me: "Do thou carry me or I will carry thee; do thou lead me or I will lead thee." I said to him, "But thou art riding upon thine ass and I upon mine: how then may I carry thee or thou me? How can I lead thee or thou me?" "That," he replied, "is the story of the countryman and the kings' eunuch." (trans. Hadas 71; ed. Davidson 36)

In this tale a King has a disturbing dream and dispatches his eunuch to the home of a "wise man" who lives in the countryside. Riding a donkey, the eunuch comes upon a peasant, likewise riding a donkey, who invites the eunuch to his home. On the way, the eunuch makes a number of enigmatic statements, the first of which echoes the exchange between Enan and Joseph:

> And it came to pass in the morning that he met a certain countryman who was riding upon an ass. The eunuch hailed him, "Peace to thee, thou worker of the earth, who art thyself earth and yet eat earth." The countryman laughed at his words. "Wither goest thou?" asked the eunuch. "To my house," the countryman replied. Then the old eunuch said, "Carry thou me or I will carry thee." The countryman replied, "But, my lord, how may I carry thee when thou ridest upon thy mule and I ride upon my beast?" (trans. Hadas 72; ed. Davidson 37)

In the tale, the eunuch poses a series of such statements to the countryman to test his intelligence in order to ascertain if he is indeed the "wise man" whom the King has dispatched the eunuch to find. The countryman, unable to grasp the meaning of any of them, considers the eunuch foolish. However, the countryman's daughter explains that the eunuch's "meaning was that everyone that goeth upon the way with his neighbor and relateth sayings and stories, and cites puzzles and proverbs, doth thereby carry his neighbor and lead him on, and relieve him of the weariness of the journey and remove him from troubling thoughts" (trans. Hadas 73; ed. Davidson 38). She then goes on to explain all of the eunuch's riddles, and so it is revealed that she is the wise "man" sought by the King. Brought to court to interpret the King's dream, she does so with such aplomb that the King marries her.

Within the tale, the phrase "carry thou me…"[76] serves to establish relative intelligence between eunuch and countryman. It serves as a sort of enigmatic proverb marking the beginning of a performance: a series of riddles by which

---

[76] The Hebrew text is "*saʾeni o ʾesaʾekha, ve-nahalenī o anahalekha*" (ed. Davidson 36).

travelers might dispel some of the boredom of the road. It is a performative marker, an invitation to a reciprocal performance of wisdom lore. The countryman is too ignorant to recognize both the marker and the meaning of the riddles subsequently posed by the eunuch. In a sense, the ability to recognize the code as a performative marker serves as a kind of intelligence test for the countryman. Similarly, Joseph reveals his own ignorance by failing to understand Enan's use of the proverb, as befits his role of narrator/dupe in the traditional scheme of the *maqāma* genre.

Taken out of the context of Enan's telling, the moral of the tale is that the judicious application of wisdom is rewarded with an upgrade in social status. However, in the context of the exchange between Enan and Joseph, the former uses it as a way to test the latter's ability to interpret enigmatic statements, i.e. Joseph's intelligence. But since he is both author and narrator, he is testing his *own* intelligence. Why, then, is this particular phrase "carry thou me..." used to tie this particular narrative into Ibn Zabāra's work? It does not necessarily speak to the moral of the inserted tale (i.e., the judicious application of wisdom can further one's social position). Its significance within that tale is negligible at best, yet it is the guide for Ibn Zabāra's inclusion of the tale in his work. Enan uses the phrase to demonstrate Joseph's proverbial ignorance and thereby to define the performative relationship between the two men: Enan as the skilled performer and Ibn Zabāra as the less-than-savvy audience. As in al-Saraqusṭī's case, where he invites the reader to apply metaphorical interpretation (*taʾwīl*) to his text,[77] the perceptive reader of Ibn Zabāra's work will draw the same conclusion: that one must apply such interpretation to the words of others.

Ibn Zabāra's contextualization of the tales interpolated within his frame story not only provides such opportunities for characterization, it also aids in encouraging the fictive audience to sympathize with the characters portrayed in the tales. To this end, Ibn Zabāra builds on the practice (found only occasionally in *Kalīla*) of framing tales anecdotally by assigning proper nouns to places and characters and thereby according the tales' personal relevance to those characters who tell them.[78] In chapter 5, Enan frames the tale of the "Clever Judge" anecdotally. As he and Joseph arrive in a "certain city" (Ibn Zabāra does not name it), Enan begins to cry. When Joseph asks him why, Enan replies: "in this city did my beloved friend and comrade perish; 'tis

[77] This is found in one of the colophons of the manuscripts examined by al-Warāglī (ed. al-Warāglī 467; trans. Monroe 202).

[78] This practice is adopted more regularly by Don Juan Manuel in his *Conde Lucanor*, and even more so by later authors of European frametales such as Chaucer and Boccaccio.

for him that my tears flow" (trans. Hadas 80; ed. Davidson 43).[79] Here he claims personal acquaintance with the setting and the characters of the tale. It is no longer "a tale about a judge," but the story of a dear, departed friend. The audience now has more reason to sympathize with Enan and access to more details that contextualize the tale within the frame story.

Ibn Zabāra is the last in a succession of medieval Iberian authors of frametales and *maqāmāt* in which performance plays an important role in the development of fictionality and literary narrative technique. Between *Kalīla* and *Šaʿašūʿīm* our authors have incorporated and synthesized a great deal of influences ranging from Arabic rhetoric, Muslim *ḥadīṯ* and popular preaching to Talmudic *aggadah* and both Muslim and Jewish notions of literary fictionality. In addition, each author, as an artist in his own right, has left his signature on the literary articulation of performance in the texts.

A clearer understanding of how performance is encoded in frametale and *maqāma* affords us a broader preparation in reading Castilian and Catalan contributions to the genre. Only by studying the various varieties of the frametale and *maqāma* being cultivated in medieval Iberia can we begin to develop a picture of how performance emerges as one of the most important prose narrative strategies of the Middle Ages. As we shall discuss in chapters 5 and 6, the narrative strategies of Hebrew *maqāmāt* were most likely transmitted indirectly to authors working in Castilian and Catalan; however, the translation of *Kalīla* commissioned by the Infante Alfonso (soon to be Alfonso X of Castile and León) would make those of the frametale directly accessible to readers of Castilian.

79 Ibn Zabāra here is referencing the *topos* of the *nasīb*, or lament over the abandoned campsite of the beloved, from classical Arabic poetry. On the *nasīb* in the Arabic *qaṣīda* (ode) see Allen (102–03) and *EI* ("Nasīb").

CHAPTER THREE

THE CULTURAL CONTEXT OF THE TRANSLATION OF *CALILA E DIMNA*

In 1251, in Toledo, an anonymous scholar translated the popular collection of tales known as *Calila e Dimna* from Arabic into Castilian. He first produced a rough, direct translation from the Arabic, then a second version which was more polished and Castilian-sounding. The man who commissioned the translation was Alfonso X the Learned, who was about to become the King of Castile and León (1252–1284). He was a great patron of science and literature, in particular of the translation of scientific treatises from Arabic into Castilian. He could not have predicted the influence his translation of *Calila e Dimna* would have on the development of Western literature, no way to know that it would inspire such canonical works as Don Juan Manuel's *Conde Lucanor,* Chaucer's *Canterbury Tales*, and Boccaccio's *Decameron*. At the time he was merely doing his part to bestow upon Castile a unique cultural patrimony drawn from the centuries-old tradition of Arabic scholarship in Iberia and for the first time, rendered into the official language of his kingdom, Castilian.

Because my argument is that the frametale was a medieval Iberian genre that engendered a common literary experience across religious, linguistic, and political groups, I am most concerned with how this text was *experienced* by Arabic and Castilian audiences. Accordingly, the present study centers more on the cultural significance of certain symbolic values of characters and situations within the narrative of the Arabic and Castilian translations of *Kalīa*, rather than on analysis of individual tales or of the textual history of the work.[1] The translation of a work as popular as *Kalīla* brings about a commonality between audiences of the Arabic and Castilian versions—a secular commonality defined not by a common religion or language, but by a common literary experience. My aim is a reading of *Calila* as a window

[1] On these topics, see Montiel and Penzol for the textual history of *Calila e Dimna*, and Marsan on the individual tales in the context of medieval Iberian short narrative. Of particular interest is Girón Negrón's recent study of the artistic specificity of the Arabic, Hebrew, and Castilian translations of the tale of the barber, the shoemaker, and their wives ("Go-between").

into the medieval Castilian cultural personality and how it set the stage for the flourishing of the frametale genre in such works as Don Juan Manuel's *Conde Lucanor* and Juan Ruiz's *Libro de buen amor*.

In this chapter I will locate the translation of *Kalīla* into Castilian in its political and cultural context, focusing on the importance of translation in the development of the emergent Castilian literature and culture of the late Middle Ages. I will demonstrate that one of the chief reasons for the successful reception of *Calila* is that its moral didactic program was compatible with the experience of Christian Castilian audiences, despite the work's origin in a Muslim, Arabic milieu.

For this type of analysis, it is more productive to study *Calila* as an act of translation and reception within a literary system, rather than as a textual artifact, a translated text.[2] Here *Calila* as an object of analysis is not simply a physical text, but as a group of interlocking literary activities: the act of translation, the production and consumption of the translation, and the significance of these activities for the emergent Castilian literary system.

The concept of the literary polysystem was pioneered by Itamar Even-Zohar, whose work on the interrelated Russian, Yiddish, and Hebrew literatures of Europe and Israel signalled a need for a functionalist approach that could be applied to literary systems producing texts in more than one language. This concept has been cultivated as an analytical tool primarily by scholars examining European literary systems featuring two or more languages in close contact.[3] Building on Roman Jakobson's ideas on spoken communication, Even-Zohar conceived the literary system as a set of relationships and activities. This approach goes beyond the study of a canonical list of "masterpieces" to embrace all types of literary activities, and all types of texts, regardless of the literary value subsequently placed on those texts by critics and institutions. The polysystem approach represents itself as more empirical than traditional literary studies that are controlled by institutional factors, such as canonicity, and turns a critical eye on the institutions themselves that foment literary activities.

---

[2] Even-Zohar defines a literary system as "the network of relations that is hypothesized to obtain between a number of activities called 'literary,' and consequently these activities themselves observed via that network" ("Literary System" 28).

[3] Even-Zohar first introduced his theories in "Israeli." He then published his and others' work on the topic in the inaugural issue of *Poetics Today* (1979). On the theory's application to cultural studies see Cattrysse, Even-Zohar ("Factors" and "Making"), and the other essays included in the *Canadian Review of Comparative Literature* 24.1 (1997). See Iglesias Santos on its application to Latin American literary systems and Codde for a comprehensive overview of polysystems theory and its reception.

The study of medieval Iberian literature has traditionally been partitioned into Romance, Hebrew, and Arabic sectors. Hispanists study works of vernacular Castilian, Portuguese, or Catalan, Hebraists study works in Hebrew, and Arabists study works in Arabic. The political and cultural background of this state of affairs is complex, and while deserving of further investigation, cannot be addressed here.[4] This compartmentalized approach necessarily minimizes or ignores aspects of literary activity that cross linguistic and cultural boundaries and tends to yield limited results. Perhaps the most notable example of this problem is that of the study of the Romance *kharjāt* (Sp. *jarchas*), final couplets found in Hebrew and Arabic *muwaššaḥāt* (strophic poems) by eleventh- and twelfth-century authors.[5] These couplets, examined outside the context of the Hebrew and Arabic poems of which they form a part, are extremely enigmatic. However, taken in the context of the entire poem, they can be appreciated and understood more fully. Just as the *jarcha* is only a small segment of the *muwaššaḥ*, the Castilian literature of the thirteenth and fourteenth centuries represents only a small segment of the literary environment from which it springs.

While Alfonso's translation activities are proof of literary activity bringing Castilian into contact with Hebrew and Arabic, such activity also occurred in Latin as well as a number of other Romance dialects.[6] Producers and consumers of Castilian texts were also producers and consumers of Hebrew and Arabic texts. Much of what makes Castilian literary culture unique is owed to this fact. Alfonso's 1251 translation of the Arabic *Kalīla* into the Castilian *Calila* as an example of literary practice is emblematic of the cultural personality of early Castilian literature in that it represents literary activity in Castilian, Arabic, and possibly Hebrew.[7]

[4] On the question of the Balkanization of medieval Iberian studies, see Menocal ("Bottom").

[5] For an excellent overview of the debate surrounding the *kharjāt*, and particularly of the heated exchanges published throughout the 1980s in *La corónica*, see Armistead ("Brief History"). See also Jones, Hitchcock and Harvey, eds. and Corriente ("By No Means"). More recent studies include those of Armistead ("Kharjas"), Galmés de Fuentes (*Jarchas*), and Zwartjes.

[6] Poets were active at his court in a variety of Romance Languages as well: Guiraut Riquier (d. 1292) in Occitan, Gil Pérez Conde (fl. 1269–1286), Gonzalo Eanes do Vinhal (fl. c. 1280), Airas Nunes, and João Airas de Santiago (1230–1265) in Galician-Portuguese (O'Callaghan, *Learned* 144). It is also noteworthy that Todros Abulafia, a Hebrew poet, also enjoyed Alfonso's patronage (Doron, "Dios").

[7] That is, it is a Castilian translation of an Arabic text which was quite influential in al-Andalus. Its translation most likely involved the cooperation of Christian and Jewish scholars working together with Castilian as their common language. Although the resulting text is in Castilian, it represents a series of activities and readings in various languages.

Up until the time of the translation of *Calila*, the use of Castilian as a literary language was limited to the transcription of epic poetry such as *El Cantar de Mio Cid*, and works of *clerecía* such as the anonymous *Libro de Alixandre* and the poems of Gonzalo de Berceo.[8] Its use as a language of administration began during the reign of Fernando III.[9] In any event, the Castilian literary system was, at the time of *Calila*'s translation, in its infancy, its repertoire quite limited. *Calila* was the first work of Arabic to be translated into Castilian and perhaps the first work of literary prose narrative in Castilian.[10] It is curious that, while the Romance genre was well established north of the Pyrenees by the twelfth century, it does not appear in Castilian until the anonymous *Libro del cavallero Zifar* at the close of the thirteenth century or beginning of the fourteenth.[11] *Calila* is the first example of literary prose narrative in Castilian. It could just as well have happened that a Castilian author, with direct or indirect knowledge of the Arabic *Kalīla*, sat down and wrote a new frametale in Castilian. But this is not what happened—the translation of *Calila* was a conscious act of appropriation of a literary genre, not a casual imitation. Alfonso purposefully commissioned a translation of the Arabic *Kalīla* in order to make it available to Castilian readers. The frametale structure introduced by Alfonso's *Calila* significantly captured the imagination of Castilian audiences, for it not only precipitated the translation into Castilian of *Sendebar* (1253),[12] but inspired Juan Manuel to write his own original frametale, the *Conde Lucanor*, some eighty years later. In short, *Calila* introduced Castilian audiences to a new way of telling stories, just as the *Disciplina clericalis* had done for Latin audiences in the previous century.

The study of *Calila e Dimna* in the cultural and political context of its translation touches on some of the most fundamental problems of the study of medieval Iberia. In the second half of the thirteenth century, Christian Iberia found itself for the first time in a position of relative security. After the decisive battle of Navas de Tolosa (1212) and subsequent conquest of

---

[8] The poetic form *mester de clerecía*, or *cuaderna vía* is written in regular verses of 14 syllables. It is an adaptation of the Alexandrine verse form, which first appeared in Spain in the Latin epic poem *Alexandreis* (Walter of Châtillon).

[9] For a rigorous study of the emergence of Castilian prose literature, see Gómez Redondo (63–76 and 157–61).

[10] The one possible exception is that of the *Libro de los doze sabios*, which Walsh dates ca. 1237 (1).

[11] On the medieval French Romance, see D. Kelly.

[12] See Lacarra's introduction to her edition of *Sendebar* (19).

the greater part of the peninsula by the monarchs of Castile and Aragon,[13] Muslim polities no longer posed a significant military or political threat. At the same time, some of the lands newly opened to Christian rule were populated in considerable part by Muslims (and Jews), who continued to exert a strong cultural influence in the area.[14] Christian Iberia was now faced with the challenge of integrating the Arabic, Muslim past into the multicultural present and future of Spain. What remained to be seen was how Andalusī culture would be assimilated by a society dominated by Christians, whose literary language was primarily Latin and only provisionally Castilian.

Calila e Dimna is an ideal cornerstone for a study of Castilian-Andalusī acculturation, because it represents the first stage of a complex cultural process of integration and synthesis: contact and translation. This differs from the dynamics of transculturation as observed in Petrus Alfonsi's *Disciplina Clericalis* on two points. First, the translator of the Castilian text is not personally present in *Calila*, as is Petrus Alfonsi, and so his role in encoding meaning in the text is difficult to discern. This is particularly true when one takes into account the lack of evidence (apart from the very existence of the Castilian translation) of any reliable original Arabic manuscript. Second, while Petrus Alfonsi derives his cultural authority from institutions with which his audience most likely identified (Church, monarchy), *Calila* derives its authority from the intellectual legacy of Andalusī learning.

The fact that *Calila e Dimna* began life in Castilian as a translation, and not a newly composed text, is significant: an original text may be read with the assumption that the work represents the culture of the author. In the case of a translation, it is difficult to assess its significance to the target culture on the basis of the text alone—one must examine the reception and significance of the translation to its target audience. That is, in order to understand the translation and reception of *Calila e Dimna*, to understand how the Castilian reader of the thirteenth century would have *experienced* the text, and produced meaning from it, one cannot rely on the text alone, but must attempt to constitute the "horizon of expectations"[15] of the audience. Because this type of analysis of a work in translation is so heavily dependent on an examination of the target culture, it is necessarily less dependent on a

[13] Mallorca (1230), Ibiza (1235), Cordova (1236), Valencia (1238), and Seville (1248) (Lomax 141–56).

[14] Due to the "survival of a massive Muslim population" in Valencia, "the new [Christian] institutions were...designed to emphasize and strengthen the position of a ruling minority in a still alien society" (Lomax 148).

[15] The term is Jauss's, and refers to the aggregate of personal experience, education, and predispositions of the reader (or audience) before the text (*Toward* 23–24).

close reading of the text and more dependent on a close reading of the target culture itself. Here, the production of meaning in the Castilian reception of *Calila* resides primarily with the audience. Therefore, we must attempt (insofar as is possible) to get inside the mind of the thirteenth-century audience of the Castilian *Calila*.

Calila e Dimna: *Origins and History*

Calila boasts an impressively complex textual back story, and its translation from Arabic to Castilian comes relatively late in its trajectory. The collection began literary life as the Sanskrit *Panchatantra*, which was composed around the year 300 by a Vishnuite Brahmin. The tales contained within the *Panchatantra*, probably culled from popular sources, were thought to have been used in preaching to the public. The text then embarked on a long and complex journey. From Sanskrit it was translated into Pahlavi (Old Persian) and Syriac around 570 at the translator's school in Yundai Sapur, Persia. After the ʿAbbasids moved the Caliphate to Baghdad in 750, they set about translating works of Persian learning into Arabic. A Zoroastrian convert to Islam, ʿAbdallah Ibn al-Muqaffaʿ, undertook the translation of the Pahlavi translation of the *Panchatantra* made by the Persian physician Burzoē for King Khūsraw Anuširwān in the sixth century. The result was Ibn al-Muqaffaʿ's *Kalīla wa-Dimna*, which circulated widely in the Arab world and became known (and still is known) as a classic. Five hundred years later, Alfonso decided to add it to his own library and ordered its translation. This is an abbreviated version of a long and extremely tangled web of transmission and translation.[16] While the Castilian translation is most important for the study at hand, the text most influential to European literature in general is a thirteenth-century translation of the Arabic text into Hebrew, by an author known only as Joel. His translation served as the base text for the Latin translation of Johannes de Capua, an Italian Jew who had converted to Christianity. De Capua's text, translated sometime between 1263 and 1278, entitled *Directorium humanae vitae*, was translated into Spanish three centuries later and widely distributed in a printed edition entitled *Exemplario contra los engaños y peligros del mundo* (*EI*, "Ibn al-Muḳaffaʿ").[17] It was the

[16] For a full accounting of the textual tradition, see Alemany Bolufer, Montiel, and Lacarra's introduction to Ibn al-Muqaffaʿ (ed. Cacho Blecua and Lacarra 15–22).

[17] See Derenbourg's edition of De Capua's Latin text, the fifteenth-century Castilian translation (*Texto*), and Sánchez Salor's modern Spanish translation of the Latin. There is

Directorium that achieved wide distribution throughout Europe and, along with the *Disciplina clericalis*, likely influenced such authors as Chaucer and Boccaccio to try their hand at the genre in their respective vernaculars.[18]

However, the Castilian *Calila* was influential in its own right. Its translation into Castilian inspired the translation from the Arabic of *Sendebar* (1253) only two years later by Alfonso's brother Don Fadrique.[19] Together, the two works provided a structural model for Don Juan Manuel's *Conde Lucanor* (1340).[20] Several other frametales and similar types of didactic narrative appeared throughout Europe in the following century, including the *Novellino* and *Decameron* in Italy, the *Roman de Renart* in France, *Barlaam e Josafat* in Spain, and the *Canterbury Tales* in England.

Why is *Calila* significant to the study of medieval narrative? To begin with, it was the first example of literary prose narrative in Castilian (as Ibn al-Muqaffaʿ's translation was in Arabic). Also, it was the first Castilian effort to recontextualize the popular didactic tale in a work of written prose.[21] The Castilian *Calila*, written as it was in the vernacular, would more closely approximate the language of popular storytelling than texts in learned languages. Since literary Arabic and Latin were not natural languages of everyday conversational discourse, they are ill-equipped to represent the speech of a popular storyteller.[22]

---

also a second, incomplete Hebrew translation (ostensibly from the Arabic) by Yaʿqob ben Elʿazar (late twelfth-thirteenth c.) of Toledo, also edited by Derenbourg (*Deux*). See Navarro Peiro's study of the Hebrew translations ("Versión"), as well as her partial translation of ben Elʿazar's text (*Narrativa* 228–32).

[18] See Lacarra's introduction to Ibn al-Muqaffaʿ (ed. Cacho Blecua and Lacarra 42). There is also a secondary Latin version of the *Directorium* prepared in France in 1303, Raimundus de Biterris' *Liber Kalile et Dimne* (B. Taylor).

[19] See Lacarra's introduction to her edition of *Sendebar* (18–21).

[20] *Calila e Dimna* is "el más antiguo libro de (cuentos) en nuestra lengua, y... precedente forzoso de las obras originales del incomparable don Juan Manuel" ('the oldest book of stories in our language, and... clear precedent of the original works of the incomparable Don Juan Manuel') (Menéndez y Pelayo 1:45).

[21] An oral work is not necessarily popular. Therefore, the dichotomy is not oral/literary, but oral/written (Stock 31–33).

[22] While developing textual culture (i.e., works in Classical Arabic such as *Kalīla*, or in Latin such as *DC*) often imitated the structures of orality, it did not faithfully reproduce the reality of an oral culture (Stock 36). In Europe, Latin-based literacy ensured a distance from the structures of oral discourse based on colloquial, natural language. However, with the advent of vernacular literature and in particular the frametale genre, a new current of orality appeared in written literature: the language used in texts was the same (or virtually the same) as the language used in day-to-day speech. Therefore, a vernacular text representing a story-teller would have a better chance of "ringing true" than would a Latin text. On the expanded mimetic potential of the vernacular *novella*, see Jauss (*Toward* 82–87).

As we have seen in the preceding chapter, the textual encoding of storytelling in literature is subject to religious and cultural norms of "live" storytelling. In a storytelling culture, the frame is the physical performance of the folk tale, the physical setting and social context of the performance, and the participation of the audience. In the case of a literary work in which storytelling is textually encoded, if the author and audience share a common language and culture—as in the case of the *Conde Lucanor*—the task of approximating the audience's reception of the work is simplified: we can assume that the audience will respect (at least some of) the institutions and conventions from which the author derives his authority, that they will be familiar with the cultural world he portrays. In the case of Don Juan Manuel, a high ranking nobleman, the audience would in all likelihood be familiar with the author himself. In the case of *Calila*, however, we are not afforded this luxury. The original author of the Sanskrit version remains quite distant both temporally and culturally. Even Ibn al-Muqaffaʿ, the known translator most proximate to the Castilian version, lived half a millennium before the Castilian translation and did not share a common language, religion, ethnicity, or culture with the Castilian audience. Given this distance between author and audience, how is it possible to determine how *Calila* was experienced by an audience in (for example) early fourteenth-century Seville?

In such a case, we must focus on the way in which the audience produces meaning from Ibn al-Muqaffaʿ's text. How to begin articulating the experience of the audience? According to Jauss, we can begin by assessing the audience's "horizon of expectations":

> A literary work, even when it appears to be new, does not present itself as something absolutely new in an informational vacuum, but predisposes its audience to a very specific kind of reception by announcements, overt and covert signals, familiar characteristics, or implicit allusions. It awakens memories of that which was already read, brings the reader to a specific emotional attitude, and with its beginning arouses expectations for the "middle and end," which can then be maintained intact or altered, reoriented, or even fulfilled ironically in the course of reading according to the specific rules of the genre or type of text. (*Toward* 23)

As regards literary culture, we can consider their likely familiarity with storytelling, or with the frametale as a literary genre. On a textual level, is the world depicted by the author consonant with the reality of the audience? How does the social and political behavior of the characters reconcile with the prevailing ethical system of the audience? Such an analysis is clearly not an exact science and runs the risk of essentializing the audience: clearly no two medieval Castilians will experience a given text in identical fashion. They will not share the exact worldview or personal experience. However, a careful examination of an audience's culturally specific values and experiences can be productive in reckoning their reception of a text. To this end, we will be reading *Calila* with an eye not toward its structure or style, but toward the "horizons of expectations" of the Arabic and Castilian audiences.

The Alfonsine Culture of Translation

In order to come to an understanding of the cultural reality of the audience of the Castilian *Calila*, one needs to examine the intellectual, political and cultural context of its translation. Castile, and Toledo in particular, had long been a center of translation of Arabic learning. Toledo had been the capital of the kingdom of the Visigoths in Spain from 507 until the Muslim invasion of 711. Under Islamic control, Toledo's Christian community was culturally arabized and greatly reduced through conversion, but even so survived.[23] When Toledo was reconquered in 1085, it was restored to primacy as a religious and therefore an intellectual center. Throughout the twelfth and thirteenth centuries, Toledo was a relatively peaceful multicultural city, in which Christians, Muslims, and Jews lived and worked alongside one another. After the fundamentalist Islamic Berber Almohads overran al-Andalus (Islamic Spain) in 1147, a steady stream of intellectual Jewish families poured into the lands of the Christian North, enlarging the Jewish communities in Toledo, Aragón, Catalonia, and even in the south of France (Baer 1: 76–77). In Toledo, scholars from these communities, learned in both Hebrew and Arabic, found employment as translators under Archbishop Raymond in the first quarter of the twelfth century. Under his direction, scholars from Spain and elsewhere in Europe worked to translate Arabic works of philosophy and science, most notably the commentaries on works of Aristotle by al-Farabī (d. 950) and Ibn Sīnā (980–1037), known in the West as Avicenna.[24]

The teams involved in these translations were commonly comprised of a Jewish scholar who would render the Arabic text into the Romance vernacular and a Christian scholar who would render the Romance into polished Latin prose.[25] This phase is significant in two ways: first, it establishes a precedent of

---

[23] This period has been documented by González Palencia (*Mozárabes*).
[24] See González Palencia (*Arzobispo* 126–32).
[25] See chapter 1, n. 25.

institutional support for organized, systematic translation of Arabic learning on Spanish soil; second, it begins to elevate Hispano-Romance to the status of a literary language. While working on a text, the translators had to communicate with each other in their common Romance vernacular. In practice, these translations were from Arabic to Castilian, and then into Latin.

In this process, the vernacular Romance spoken by the translation teams working under Archbishop Raymond had to evolve in order to express and support scientific and philosophical ideas and discourses that had been developed over hundreds of years by scholars working in Arabic. Therefore, a century before Alfonso X launched his ambitious project to put Castilian on the map as a language of science and literature, a small group of Hispano-Romance speakers had already begun to do this, although there is no explicit documentation of their work procedures. That is, they had been using Castilian (or perhaps Andalusī Romance) as a language of literary activity, but not as a language of literary texts.[26]

In the following century, at the time of the translation of *Calila*, Castilian literature was undergoing a period of self-definition in which it strove to distinguish itself from the Latin, Hebrew, and Arabic cultures that surrounded it, while still maintaining a comfortable level of identification (whether positive or negative) with these cultures that so strongly contributed to the Castilian cultural personality (Márquez-Villanueva, *Concepto* 12). Contact with the literatures of other languages, whether in the original language or in translation, plays an especially important role in the development of a young national language. Itamar Even-Zohar explains that the innovation of new genres results almost exclusively from contact with foreign works:

> Through the foreign works, features (both principles and elements) are introduced into the home literature which did not exist there before. These include possibly not only new models of reality to replace the old and established ones that are no longer effective, but a whole range of other features as well, such as a new (poetic) language, or compositional patterns and techniques. (*Position* 47)

Translation and translated works play a crucial role in enriching a national literature's literary repertoire. Before *Calila e Dimna*, readers of Castilian unfamiliar with Arabic did not know the work; after its translation, this genre

[26] This is an excellent example of how polysystem theory can provide a framework for the study of medieval Iberia and how it can be productive to study linguistic phenomena that left no materials fit for traditional philological analysis.

went on to become enormously influential, not only in Castilian literature but in Latin and the major literatures of Western Europe.

The Castilian translations sponsored by Alfonso X were completed in a Castile quite different from that where, in the previous century, Archbishop Raymond commissioned translations into Latin. With the taking of Seville in 1248 by Fernando III, the overwhelming majority of the Iberian Peninsula now lay in Christian hands. By the time Alfonso X ascended to the throne in 1252, Castile's energies, once singularly devoted to fighting the Muslims, could be directed inward, toward the definition of a Castilian culture. This also meant that Castilian intellectuals could now afford to *choose* to resist foreign (especially French) influences and *choose* to be open to no-longer-foreign Semitic influences (Galmés de Fuentes, *Influencias* 230–32). Alfonso even went so far as to establish a school of Arabic and Latin studies at Seville in 1254, a decision that demonstrates the institutionalized assimilation of Andalusī culture as a defining characteristic of the emergent Castilian culture (Márquez-Villanueva, *Concepto* 158).

After ascending to the throne in 1252, the year after the translation of *Calila e Dimna*, Alfonso became the patron of a considerable body of translation work by a number of scholars who have come to be known collectively as the Alfonsine school of translators.[27] It was Alfonso's aim to provide his new and expanding kingdom with a cultural patrimony that would distinguish it from both its Muslim past and its Latin neighbors throughout Europe. The translation activity Alfonso sponsored was driven more by a need to define the identity of Castilian as the language of a specific political, scientific, and literary enterprise than to increase knowledge of specifically Arabic or Hebrew scholarship (Harvey, "Alfonsine" 111; Bossong 16).

The role of monarch as literary patron was not invented by Alfonso. His most immediate model (and also his cousin on his mother's side) was Holy Roman Emperor Frederick II of Hohenstaufen (r. 1211–1250). Frederick was a pioneer in the cultivation of court poets working in the vernacular (here Sicilian). Himself a composer of poetry in Sicilian, he employed a host of poets at court, including the brothers Reginald, Jacob, and Monaldo of Aquino, Jacopo Mostacci, Reginald of Palermo, and the foremost poets of the group, Piero della Vigna and Giacomo da Lentini. Frederick also sponsored a great deal of translation work, in particular that of Michael

[27] While some of this activity is known to have taken place in Toledo (by then a well-established center of learning and of translation), there is no evidence that the translators working in the service of Alfonso had any group consciousness, nor even that they were based in Toledo (Márquez Villanueva, *Concepto* 179; Roth "Collaborators" 58).

Scot, whose accomplishments include Latin translations of Arabic versions of Aristotle's *De caelo* and *De anima*, along with the commentaries of Ibn Rushd (Kantorowicz 331–42).[28] In France, Louis IX (r. 1226–1270) was also an active patron of letters and kept poets and encyclopedists at court (Le Goff 585–92). In these two Christian monarchs, Alfonso had models of imperial monarchs who regarded the cultivation of vernacular literature as an important part of their royal activities. Long before Louis, Holy Roman Emperors Charlemagne (r. 771–814) and Alfred the Great (r. 871–899) provided historical precedents as patrons of letters who supported foreign scholars at court and put into motion sweeping reforms in Latin education in order to consolidate their empires (Westra 61; Anderson 257–307).

Alfonso's unique contribution to imperial literary patronage was the use of the vernacular for legal and scientific texts. By delivering sources of Arabic learning directly to readers of Castilian, Alfonso made great strides in boosting the reputation of Castilian as a learned language throughout Europe, for Arabic learning was very much in demand in the thirteenth century.[29] The emergence of such vernacular literature heralded two important changes: it shifted the center of intellectual activity from the Church to the Court and widened the definition of literacy from Latin to Castilian. That is, whereas the ability to read Latin required the study of an entire language, under Alfonso X it became possible for a Castilian speaker to become literate simply by mastering the Roman alphabet. In the span of a few years, the potential audience for texts that were previously inaccessible (except to the clergy) expanded exponentially. Any one wealthy enough to have access to a library and who could invest the time necessary to learn the alphabet could now consult arcane works of law, astronomy, philosophy, and governance. Latin now had to share the stage of intellectual life in Castile with its vernacular offspring.

The translation activity supported by Alfonso X was significantly different from that of his Toledan predecessor Archbishop Raymond in that its patron was a secular figure as opposed to an ecclesiastical one, and the language of translation was Castilian, not Latin. This shift in patronage from ecclesiastical

---

[28] For general histories of Frederick II, see D. Abulafia and De Stefano. For studies of poetic activity in his court, see Gensini, Magaletta, and Panvini. On Frederick II and the sciences, see Toubert and Paravicini Bagliani. Of particular interest is Mallette's chapter on Frederick's relationship with Arabic letters (47–64).

[29] While there was a trend in Western Europe in the thirteenth century toward the use of the vernacular in royal documents, Alfonso X led the way, with France and England following suit only toward the close of the century (Márquez-Villanueva, *Concepto* 35–38).

to royal precipitated a parallel shift in the dynamic between the Jewish and Christian translators. The teams working on translations under Alfonso differed from those of Archbishop Raymond in that the importance of the Latin scholar (a Christian cleric) was minimized. Under Archbishop Raymond, Jewish translators relied on their Christian counterparts to produce a sound Latin translation; those working under Alfonso were there to put an official stamp on the endeavor. Unlike the Christian clerics working under Raymond, those in Alfonso's employ did not have the opportunity to leave a significant literary mark on the texts (Procter 8). The Jewish translators working under Alfonso had a deep knowledge of the Arabic and Hebrew texts with which the teams worked, and they translated the texts from Arabic or Hebrew directly into Castilian. This marginalization of Latin in the translation process inevitably shaped the nature of the Castilian translations. Because they were written in Castilian (and not Latin) by Jews educated in Hebrew and Arabic, the language of the texts would have been influenced far more by Arabic, Hebrew, and Castilian than by Latin.[30] Therefore, the Semitic acculturation, in semantic and syntactic terms, of spoken literary Castilian that had begun with the translators of Archbishop Raymond was now being committed to writing and would become an important stratum in the early development of literary Castilian.[31]

Alfonso's project of developing Castilian as a literary language was not an isolated phenomenon in Western Europe. By the thirteenth century, French, Italian, Provençal, and Catalan were well under way in their development as literary languages. In Italy, Dante would soon write his groundbreaking *De vulgari eloquentia* (c. 1304), in which he sought to define a literary Italian vernacular worthy of an imperial court.[32] As in Castile, the refinement and canonization of the vernacular is carried out with political goals in mind—specifically, Dante and Alfonso both make an effort to unify politically and linguistically diverse areas by constructing a vernacular that draws upon the most desirable components of each regional dialect. Both Dante and Alfonso sought to create a language in which natives of each region of

---

[30] Judah ibn ʿAbbās, writing in thirteenth- c. Castile-León or Aragon, reports that the secular curriculum for Jewish students over the age of 18 included medicine, mathematics, astronomy, logic, and the natural sciences, all of which would have been studied in Hebrew and Arabic texts (*EJ*, "Education, Jewish"; Guedemann 58–62).

[31] For the linguistic influence of Arabic on early literary Castilian, see Galmés de Fuentes (*Influencias*).

[32] *De vulgari eloquentia* was groundbreaking because it was the first effort to bring Scholastic analysis to bear on a vernacular language and the first systematic effort (in the West) to fashion a literary register from a vernacular language (Botterill xiii).

the empire could see their own linguistic contribution reflected (Niederehe 429). In this way, the development of a vernacular that represents all areas of the empire and not just the capital has been seen as essential in the nation-building process.

However, the composition of vernacular poetry alone (such as Alfonso's *Cantigas de Santa Maria*, composed in Galician-Portuguese) is not sufficient to raise the prestige of a given court (Bossong 13–14).[33] It was the translation of Arabic science, unavailable elsewhere in the Latin world, into Castilian that would best promote the reputation of Alfonso's kingdom as a prestigious center of learning. While there *is* poetry in Alfonso's output, he inaugurates his translation project with a work of didactic prose, *Calila*, and not one of poetry.[34] Because by Alfonso's time there was already an established tradition of courtly poetry in Romance, there was no need to translate such texts from the Arabic or from non-Hispanic Romance (French, Italian, etc.). Nevertheless, *Calila* cannot be read simply as a scientific or philosophical text; it is in fact a wolf in sheep's clothing, a complex, innovative literary genre qualifying as a work of political philosophy or wisdom literature.

What precipitated this sudden interest in vernacular didactic prose, when the translations sponsored by Archbishop Raymond in his previous translation effort had been limited to scientific and philosophical texts? The Christian conquests of al-Andalus had generated a great deal of wealth—tremendous amounts of land and property changed hands from Muslim to Christian rulers. In periods of relative peace and affluence, resources that would be directed in times of war to military concerns can be dedicated to other, more humanistic projects. This economic opportunity characterized Castilian literature from its origins and is evident not only in the circumstances of literary production in Castile but also in the way literary content was shaped (J. Duggan 20).

If the boom in Castilian literary production was facilitated by the material reality of the Christian conquest of al-Andalus, it was given shape and direction by the distinct personality of Alfonso's imperial ambition and tempered

[33] In any event, Castilian did not become an acceptable vehicle for courtly lyric poetry until the final years of the fourteenth century, when it finally edged out Galician-Portuguese and Occitan (Deyermond, *Historia* 234–37).

[34] "The emergence of prose, especially of narrative fiction, is a more important step towards status improvement than the emergence of lyrical or epical [sic] poetry" (Bossong 13). Therefore, Alfonso's translation of *Calila* (and not of French Romance, for example) can be understood as a deliberate effort to raise the status of Castilian (and therefore of his court).

by a calculated humanism that strove to perfect human knowledge.[35] Alfonso's aims transcended those of a national king; as claimant to the Holy Roman Empire, he regarded his court as the seat of that empire. That such a temporal power be so concerned with worldly learning is not uncharacteristic of the times. In the twelfth and thirteenth centuries, the transfer of learning from Church to Crown was in progress all over Europe, and the crown as well as the nobility strove to support the sciences and letters. They put into practice the vision of humanity as an active custodian of God's creation, bearing a responsibility to understand, master, and perfect the Deity's work (Duby 248–62). In this new environment, the king had a responsibility not only to rule justly, but to fund letters and arts. Within the distinctively Hispanic context of Alfonso X's scientific and literary patronage, it is also quite possible that the Wise King may have looked upon the cultural activities of Hispano-Arabic *ṭaifa* monarchs as precedents for his own initiatives.[36]

The monarchs of the time did not, however, promote art strictly for art's sake; rather, they enlisted their poets and sages to further their political interests. As was the case with Frederick II in Sicily (d. 1250) during the first half of the thirteenth century, part of the imperial enterprise was to promote the use of a language of empire. In Sicily, Frederick employed at court poets who wrote in the Italian vernacular.[37] Alfonso X likewise envisioned literary Castilian as a means of uniting scholars from the Latin, Arabic, and Hebrew traditions of his kingdom. This environment should not, however, be understood in terms of a modern, secular, pluralistic democracy. As with Frederick II, it was an attempt at intellectual, not political, pluralism. While Muslims and Jews were hardly considered the equals of their Christian neighbors, the cultural output of their respective traditions was still regarded as valid and useful. Despite his clearly parochial social policies,[38] Alfonso sought to maximize the potential and prestige of his intellectual projects by drawing on the resources of scholars from both Christian and non-Christian traditions (González-Casanovas 436).

That Arabic scholarship played a central role in the definition of Alfonso's Christian kingdom is the hallmark of a secular consciousness that recognized the value of the cultural production of all the groups resident in what had

---

[35] On Alfonso's imperial ambitions, see Ballesteros Beretta and Rodríguez Llopis (175–212).

[36] On poetic activity sponsored by the *mulūk al-ṭawā'if*, see chapter 2, n. 14.

[37] See D. Abulafia, Tronzo, and Panvini.

[38] For example, there are several strictures on social contact between Jews and Christians in Alfonso's *Siete Partidas* (Carpenter, *Alfonso X* 85).

recently become Christian territory. This trend of cultural appropriation and translation was not invented by Alfonso; he simply lent institutional authority to an aspect of the local culture that had long been a reality. Alfonso's endeavor is distinct in that it was a purposeful initiative by a Christian monarch, not a spontaneous cultural synthesis occurring in a popular context.

While traditional twentieth-century Spanish historiography tended to describe the Muslim period of Spain (711–1492) as an unfortunate and incredibly long "occupation,"[39] recent scholarship has tried to achieve a more integrated vision of the Christian, Islamic, and Judaic cultural elements of what was to become Spain.[40] Looking backward, one can see that even in the earliest literature of the Reconquest, there was a tendency on the part of the Christian conquerors, whether Castilian, Aragonese, or Catalan, to incorporate the culture of the conquered rather than simply to obliterate and replace it. Take for example the epic poem *Cantar de Mio Cid*, most likely recorded in the early thirteenth century, which details the exploits of Rodrigo Díaz de Vivar, a powerful late-eleventh-century Castilian warlord. The poem, incidentally, is the cornerstone of the traditional canon of medieval Spanish Literature, much like the *Chanson de Roland* for French. El Cid, as his name suggests (Ar. *sīdī*, 'my Lord') (Corriente, *Dictionary* 266b), is a bicultural and very successful mercenary whose respect for Islam and Andalusī culture is exceeded only by his material ambition. However, while his French counterpart Roland is quite clearly characterized as a Christian hero, it is el Cid's material and political ambition, and not his religious ideology, that determine his treatment of the Muslim occupants of the towns he conquers. After taking the Moorish-held town of Alcocer, Rodrigo speaks to his men:

---

[39] See the introduction to the present volume, n. 12. The best known detractor of Castro is Sánchez Albornoz. The thrust of his argument is that Castro overvalues the contribution of Jews and Muslims to what will later become Spanish culture. In fact, he dedicates an entire chapter to refuting the influence of Andalusī culture on modern Spanish culture, aptly titled "No se arabiza la contextura vital hispana" (*España* 189–240).

[40] See the collection of historical essays edited by Subirats. On literature, see Márquez-Villanueva ("Hispano-Jewish"); Menocal (*Arabic*); Menocal, Scheindlin and Sells; Gutwirth ("Hispanicity"); and Hamilton, Portnoy and Wacks. As early as 1976, Hillgarth maintains that "the Christians of the peninsula were linked to Western Europe by their religion, and, increasingly, by their laws and political concepts. They were bound to Islam by the weight of the past, the Islamic culture which had dominated the Iberian world for four hundred years; by the daily presence among them of Muslims and of Jews trained in Arabic culture; by the physical setting in which they lived, the Islamic cities which covered the peninsula from Toledo and Saragossa southwards, which, for centuries, the conquerors hardly attempted to change" (*Kingdoms* 161).

Los moros e las moras vender non los podremos,
Que los descabeçemos nada non ganaremos;
Cojámoslos de dentro, ca el señorío tenemos;
Posaremos en sus casas e dellos nos serviremos
(*Poema de Mio Cid* 139–40, vv. 618–22)

(We cannot sell the Muslim men and women,
in beheading them we gain nothing;
Let us take them inside the city, over which we now rule;
We will stay in their houses and make use of them.)

These verses are emblematic of the *zeitgeist* of the Christian conquest of al-Andalus. Because the conquered pose no threat, there is no harm in making use of their property, their artistry, their science, even their literature. There was nothing distasteful about secular Arabic culture to the Christians of medieval Iberia, provided that Christians were not subject to Islamic rule. While it is true that emphasis was placed on rallying behind Santiago Matamoros (St. James the Moor Slayer)[41] in conquering the lands of the south from the Muslims, the most likely motivation for taking land held by Muslims was material: there were large amounts of land and property at stake,[42] and once the Muslim nobility had been beaten and sent packing to Granada or North Africa, their entire holdings and households were transferred to the conquering Christians.[43]

If the Cid advocated appropriation of the material culture of the conquered Muslims, the Castilian translators of the twelfth and thirteenth centuries advocated, and brought into practice, the appropriation of the Muslims' intellectual assets. The translation efforts supported by Archbishop Raymond (carried out during the time that the *Cantar de Mio Cid* was most likely being composed) and Alfonso X brought dozens of Arabic scientific and medical texts into Latin and Castilian, echoing the Cid's suggestion, "de ellos nos serviremos" ('let us make use of them'). In the absence of an Islamic polity to lend institutional and military force to Islam, the translation and

[41] See, for example, Castro (*Santiago*), Cabrillana Ciézar, and Márquez-Villanueva (*Santiago*).

[42] Lomax plainly states that "booty was an important motive for fighting, and as well as slaves, gold, silver, precious stones and cloths it normally included sheep and cattle." In fact, livestock became so recognized as booty that the word used to refer to it was "ganado" ('winnings,' lit. 'won') (101).

[43] For example, after the conquest of Seville, all of its lands passed to the Christian conquerors (Lomax 154–55). For a study of the *Libros de repartimiento* that documented the material transition from Muslim to Christian rule, see Glick (*Fortress* 127–66).

appropriation of scientific, philosophic, or literary texts in Arabic was wholly unproblematic; indeed it was much desired by Christian Iberians.[44]

The Purpose of Translating

One of the most enduring aspects of the Christian Iberian culture of conquest is the recontextualization of Islamic monuments and institutions within a Christian society: mosques are converted into churches, banners are lowered and new ones raised over fortresses, monuments are changed to reflect the culture of the conquerors.[45]

Unlike the Muslim religious activity housed by a mosque, the content of *Kalīla* posed no significant theological threat to Christianity and was quite consonant with the values of Christian Castilian audiences. Just as the *Disciplina clericalis* contained no specifically Christian teachings in the *exempla* Petrus Alfonsi culled from Semitic tradition, the lessons offered to the audiences of *Calila* are chiefly pragmatic. Part of what made *Calila* such a great success over the centuries, and what enabled its parent texts, the Sanskrit *Panchatantra* and the Arabic *Kalīla wa-Dimna*, to cross cultural lines and be translated into several different languages, was its universality. It deals with practical political and strategic matters that are common to all cultures, and so it is understood in much the same way from one audience to another.[46]

In particular, the audiences with which we are concerned, thirteenth-century Iberian readers of Arabic and Castilian, lived realities that had a great deal in common, and therefore would be similarly predisposed toward many aspects of the text. Thirteenth-century Castilians were surrounded by

---

[44] Márquez-Villanueva notes that Alfonso "reconocía, por fin, el hecho palmario de que en los últimos cuatro siglos la lengua del progreso había sido el árabe y no el latín. Rompía con esto la actitud cristiano-medieval de la admiración vergonzante y de préstamos silenciados de la cultura musulmana" ('recognized, at last, the obvious fact that in the previous four centuries the language of progress had been Arabic and not Latin. This broke with the medieval Christian attitude of guilty admiration of and not-talked-about borrowings from Muslim culture') (*Concepto* 134).

[45] Glick notes that the function and social context Muslim *ḥuṣūn* (castles) were recast when they became Christian *castillos* (*Fortress* 150–51). At the same time, in some cases the appropriation of the built environment of al-Andalus impacted administrative and cultural practices of Christian society, as Ribera y Tarragó has argued (*Orígenes*). Ecker has demonstrated how the conversion of neighborhood mosques into parish churches in Seville influenced ecclesiastical and tax administration ("Masjid" and "Administer").

[46] For a complete study of the didactic orientation of *Kalīla*, see Parker.

and borrowed freely from secular aspects of Andalusī culture.[47] As an eminently secular text, *Calila* fell into that category. The experiences it describes would be equally familiar to its Arabic and Castilian readers, regardless of their religion.

For example, consider the social mores demonstrated by the tale of "El carpintero, el barbero, y sus mujeres" ('The Carpenter, the Barber, and Their Wives'), in which the carpenter asks his wife to take care of a visiting ascetic while he goes out drinking:

> Desí amanesçió et fuese el religioso a buscar el ladrón a otro lugar, et ospedóle un ome bueno carpentero. Et dixo a su muger:—Onra a este ome bueno, et piensa bien dél, ca me llamaron unos amigos a bever et non me tornaré sinon bien tarde (139; ed. Cheikho 78)
>
> (Then day broke, and the ascetic went to look for the thief in another place, and a carpenter, a good man, took him in for the night. The carpenter said to his wife:—Honor this man, and look after his needs, for some friends have invited me to go out drinking, and I will be coming home late tonight.)

With this he leaves the house and sets the tale in motion. The Arabic version is essentially the same, except that the carpenter's friends do not invite him out explicitly in order to drink. His words are "*daʿānī baʿadu al-aṣḥābī illà daʿwatin.*" In Classical Arabic, *daʿwa* (in this context, 'invitation,' 'gathering,' or perhaps 'banquet') does not imply the consumption of alcohol; still, it hardly needs arguing that Muslim al-Andalus was home to many an accomplished winebibber.[48] More telling than his drinking is the fact that the carpenter is leaving his wife alone with a strange man (even a wandering ascetic), a serious error for a medieval Mediterranean of any religion or language group. Coming home stone drunk and passing out cold is not considered exemplary behavior in any culture, medieval or otherwise, of which I am aware. These are situations, characters, and values that easily transcend religious and linguistic boundaries.

---

[47] For example, Feliciano notes that "Andalusi textiles were central to the formative process of the medieval Iberian aesthetic vocabulary. . . ." (103).

[48] See, for example, the bacchic poetry of Ibn Quzmān (ed. Corriente and Makkī; trans. García-Gómez). On the tradition of Arab bacchic poetry in the Andalusī *maqāma*, see D. Young ("Wine").

Adaptation of the Frame

The frametale, as introduced to Europe through Petrus Alfonsi's *Disciplina Clericalis* and then by the Castilian *Calila*, served as a catalyst for the development of the short narrative in Europe.[49] The nested tale technique (or *mise en abîme* structure) used in *Calila* is not native to Latin tradition, and although there are hints of it in some Classical works such as the *Metamorphoses* of Ovid and the *Asinus aureus* ('Golden Ass'), it is unknown in Europe before the translation of *Calila*.[50] The frametale is the product of a world view considerably different from that of Christian Europe, one shaped by the Hindu, Persian, and Arabic cultures that nurtured the genre. Once the translation of *Calila* made the genre available, European authors adapted it to their own worldviews and cultural reference points, thereby making it a European genre.[51] The frametale is a literary palimpsest upon which each generation of authors writes its cultural signature. The manner in which each author does so can reveal much about the culture from which he writes. Authors such as Don Juan Manuel, Chaucer, and Boccaccio infused the frametale with their own outlook and under the influence of Scholasticism stressed structural integrity, order, and symmetry.[52]

Because *Calila* is concerned primarily with the problem of human behavior, the most salient issues are of a political, ethical, or religious nature. There are questions of loyalty, deception, and hospitality. We see portrayals of moderation, leadership, and other specific political characteristics of leaders; theological issues, such as miracles, the afterlife, free will, and divine justice are also addressed. Although they do not represent any particular religion or philosophy, ascetic religious characters (Sp. *religioso*, Ar. *nāsik*) appear. Finally, the text depicts aspects of daily life, such as animals, drinking, and language. The animals are particularly important in anticipating how the audience will decode the text for their double significance; their workaday reality (if the animal is found in the environment of the culture in question) and their symbolic value. Educated medieval Iberian Christian and Muslim

---

[49] While the *DC* can be considered a frametale by the strictest definition, *Calila* exhibits a much more developed frame and a more sophisticated and self-conscious *mise en abîme* narrative structure, in which the tales are nested one within the other (i.e., a character in one tale will narrate a tale of his own that is pertinent to the theme at hand).

[50] On the frametale in the Classical tradition, see Cooper (6), Gittes (18–19), Lacarra's introduction to her edition of *Sendebar* (50), Clements and Gibaldi (36–37).

[51] See my discussion of Petrus Alfonsi's transculturation of *adab* literature in chapter 1.

[52] See my discussion of the structure of Juan Manuel's *El Conde Lucanor* in chapter 4.

readers would not have had significantly different understandings of either the daily reality or symbolic values of the animals portrayed in Calila.

Ethics and Reception

One of the reasons that *Calila* has been so portable across cultures is that it does not promote an ethical or moral system specific to any one religion or culture. While Keller ("Literature") has argued that the function of such didactic frametales as *Calila* and *Sendebar* is to entertain rather than to instruct, Parker (14) has argued the opposite, that it is the universally applicable, practical political wisdom taught by the book (and not its entertainment value) that is responsible for its proliferation across so many languages, so large a geographic area, and so many centuries. What had proven useful for the Indian Buddhist of the third century proved equally so for the sixth-century Zoroastrian, the eighth-century Arab, and the thirteenth-century Castilian. While each translator will inevitably leave his mark on the text, the core values expressed in the tales are universal—the work's adaptability is the key to its longevity.

The Arabic translator, ʿAbdallah ibn al-Muqaffaʿ, is a curious link in the transmission of the ethical content of the text. Ibn al-Muqaffaʿ's literary works dealing with morality, of which *Kalīla* is the most popular, represent an early effort to reconcile the Islamic ethical standards promulgated by the *ḥadīṯ* (traditions of the Prophet Muhammad) with wisdom literature received from pre-Islamic sources, among them works of Indian, Greek, and Persian provenance.[53] This synthesis was brought to its apogee in the *ʿUyūn al-akhbār* of Ibn Qutayba (d. 889–90), who, by suppressing the most offensive elements of the pre-Islamic ethical traditions, ensured that his work would become the standard manual of Islamic ethics (*EI*, "Akhlāḳ"). It is noteworthy that *Kalīla*'s ethical stance predates this reconciliation and that, as I shall discuss in my treatment of religious issues found in *Kalīla*, our translator Ibn al-Muqaffāʿ was by no means an orthodox Islamic fundamentalist. Like Petrus Alfonsi, he was a convert who came to a new religion and literary language in midlife. His other works, most notably his *Adāb kabīr* ('A Mirror of Princes'), espouse practical morality which favors the clever manipulation of human passions over religious and ethical practices. In this, his outlook

[53] On problems related to the transmission of *Kalīla*, see López-Morillas ("Broad").

more resembles that of his cosmopolitan Andalusī rationalist readers than that of orthodox Muslims from the East (*EI*, "Ibn al-Muḳaffaʿ").

Therefore, while Qurʾānic and traditional Muslim understandings of the world should be taken into account when attempting to understand the mindset of the Andalusī audience of *Kalīla*, one must realize that many of Ibn al-Muqaffaʿ's readers would have been rationalist free-thinkers and intellectuals who did not comply with orthodox Islamic doctrine on issues of theology, morality and religious practice. Accordingly, the moral universe of *Kalīla* (or that of its Andalusī readers) cannot be taken simply to represent orthodox Islamic ethical teachings. To complicate matters further, we must also keep in mind that we have not even a scrap of the original version of Ibn al-Muqaffāʿ's Arabic text. The two extant textual traditions of the Arabic *Kalīla* are so different, and date so much later than the Castilian translation, that we cannot with certainty maintain that any given passage of the text originated from the pen of Ibn al-Muqaffāʿ himself (*EI*, "Ibn al-Muḳaffaʿ"). For example, we can reasonably state that the changes in the introductory material that are reflected in the Castilian translation are the work either of an Andalusī copyist or of the translator of the Castilian version. At the very least, we know that the work was popular in al-Andalus and therefore stimulated significant literary activity in the Andalusī polysystem in the form of reading, listening, referencing, copying, and so forth.

If the information we have concerning the life and deeds of Ibn al-Muqaffaʿ is relatively scant, the information regarding the Castilian translator is even more so. We have a date (1251) and a sponsor (Alfonso X), but no further information concerning the man or men who introduced the Western world to the genre which would inspire some of the most popular—and to this day the most widely taught—works of medieval European literature. In sum, it is extremely difficult to assess the individual contribution(s) of the translator of the Castilian version due to the following: the absence of the Arabic manuscript from which he worked, the highly irregular manuscript tradition of the Arabic *Kalīla*, and the lack of biographic information regarding the translator himself. As in the case of Ibn al-Muqaffaʿ, we can only make educated guesses as to the translator's worldview, based on what we do know about Alfonso's translators and daily and intellectual life in thirteenth-century Castile.

The Meaning of Animals

Reception Theory teaches us that each reader or auditor experiences a text differently; the text itself is only one component of the "work" considered as a cultural phenomenon. The total work is the combination of the author's text and the reader's interaction with it. A living author affords a good deal of information about his or her life, education, experiences, everything that comprises one's "horizon of expectations." Similarly, we know a great deal about living readers and their particular horizons of expectation because we share those horizons, if only in part. In this way, once the author puts down his or her pen, the recently encoded text becomes a static object, which demands the active participation of the reader in order to decode it. Just as the script of a play is interpreted and produced by a cast and crew, the text is not itself the product, but only one component of what Wolfgang Iser has called a "structured act of comprehension" (8) that also includes the active participation of the audience in processing and experiencing the text. Therefore, understanding a work of literature entails study of the text, the reader, and an attempt to reconstruct the reader's experience of the text.

For medieval works, the question of constituting the reader is made difficult by the paucity of information available regarding the work's audience. The trick, then, lies in constituting the Arabic and Castilian readers of *Calila e Dimna* in order to approximate the meaning of the text for its Castilian audience. Particularly because they are focused through the lens of *Calila*'s decidedly secular moral orientation, the "horizons of expectation" of the work's thirteenth-century Christian and Muslim readers will be remarkably similar, and so will the audience's "performance of meaning." That is, the way in which they make sense of the text in a given reading will have far more to do with individual ethical disposition than with religious or linguistic difference.

Ibn al-Muqaffaʿ himself seems to anticipate modern Reception Theory in his introduction, in which he guides the audience's understanding of the moral value of the tales he translates. He addresses the need for the reader to be properly informed in order to receive the maximum benefit from the work:

> Pues el que este libro leyere sepa la manera en que fue conpuesto, et quál fue la entençión de los filósofos et de los entendidos en sus enxemplos de las cosas que son aí dichas; ca aquel que esto non sopiere non sabrá qué será su fin en este libro. (91; ed. Cheikho 51–52)

(Who reads this book should know the way in which it was composed, and what was the intention of the philosophers and the sages in its examples of the things that are said in it; for he who does not know this will not know its purpose in this book.)

While Ibn al-Muqaffaʿ does not go so far as to assert that the reader is essential to the work's existence as such, he does imply that the work will not be able fully to serve its function without the involvement of an educated audience who is able to decode the work competently. Assuming that such audiences existed, how do we attempt to determine the meaning of the text to them? Even more importantly, how do we constitute the differences between these audiences? How to construct the actual and symbolic value of such animals as the lion, ox, and jackal for Arabic and Castilian (and not by any means mutually exclusive) audiences?

Since animals play an important role in *Calila e Dimna* and their significance is magnified by the fact that they have both concrete and symbolic value in the original and target cultures, any attempt to envision the reception of the Castilian translation must examine the historical and symbolic realities of the animals portrayed: the two jackals, Calila and Digna, the ox Sençeba, and the Lion are particularly important because of the centrality of their characters, and therefore are likely objects of analysis here.

What, then, might these animals *mean* to the thirteenth-century Arabic or Castilian audience? There are two often conflicting realities that contribute to the reader's experience of a given animal: actual and symbolic. The actual experience would be the reader's day-to-day contact with the animal. This familiarity could be with a domestic farm animal or pet, with an animal the reader has hunted or fished or seen on a trip abroad. It could have been (in the case of the monkey) an animal brought to town by a traveling band of entertainers. In some cases, more than one context might apply: one could have experience of a bear both in the wild and as a tamed beast.

In medieval sources, animals' symbolic value is more clearly articulated than their physical natures. The medieval mind valued the symbolic and allegorical over the realistic in art (Eco 52–64), and so we have far more medieval allegorical bestiaries than manuals of zoology. In the thirteenth century, the scientific study of animals was as yet unknown. However, systematic allegorical studies of animals—bestiaries—were quite widespread. Because animals have been the protagonists of short didactic tales since ancient Egypt and India, Greco-Roman writers like Pliny used such tales in sections of scientific compendia cataloging the characteristics of animals. Early Christian texts adopted this tradition, giving the tales a Christian moral value and relating the characteristics of these animals to biblical references, both direct and allegorical.[54] The most important of these early Christian bestiaries is the *Physiologus*, written in Greek by an anonymous author in Alexandria, probably in the second half of the second century. Highly influential throughout the Middle Ages, this work was widely paraphrased and referenced. Latin bestiaries of the high and late Middle Ages show a strong influence from the *Physiologus*, and the text enjoyed wide circulation in Western Europe (Baxter).

The bestiary and Hellenistic fable traditions developed in parallel, and both contributed to the Castilian reader's horizon of expectations regarding animals. Hellenistic fable material reached Castilian readers through both Latin collections in the Hellenistic tradition (Babrius, Avianus, Romulus, etc.) and through Petrus Alphonsi's *Disciplina clericalis*, in which appear several stories of Aesopic origin. This fable tradition also gave rise to a tradition of illustration that was influential in the formation of Medieval European images of specific animals (Salisbury 109).

Since *Calila* can be seen as a collection of *exempla* (indeed, the title of its Latin translation, *Directorium humanae vitae*, is translated into Spanish as "*Exemplario*"), the behavior of its animal characters is intended to be exemplary of human behavior. This is at odds with the Christian bestiary tradition, which portrays animal behavior as allegorical and prophetic. With the advent of the *Physiologus*, the Christian allegorical meanings it attributed to animals outweighed the social exemplarity of the Aesopic fables. It was not until the High Middle Ages that authors began to break from the bestiary tradition and explore non-allegorical representations of animal behavior more typical of the Classical Aesopic tradition. This was begun by Odo of Cheriton in the twelfth century, was continued in the *Lais* of Marie de France, in the *Roman de Renart*, and by the translator of *Calila* in the thirteenth.[55]

In constituting the horizon of expectations of Castilian readers of *Calila*, one should also consider the influence of encyclopedic texts, many of which contained a chapter on animals in the tradition of the Latin bestiary. The Florentine author Brunetto Latini (c. 1220–1294) penned the ambitious *Livres dou tresor* in Old French. This text is particularly useful in assessing the medieval Castilian literary conception of animals, because Latini was Florence's ambassador to the court of Alfonso X in 1260 and had considerable

---

[54] That is, they commented on direct references to the animal in biblical texts as well as the Christ-like or other allegorical value of the animal.

[55] However, in Byzantium the Hellenistic collections of fables were preserved in a form much freer from Christian allegorical readings (Rodríguez Adrados and van Dijk 2: 559–628, especially 620–21).

contact with intellectuals of Alfonso's court during this time (Holloway 109–13). In addition, his *Livres dou tresor* was translated into Castilian in the late thirteenth century and Aragonese in the fourteenth and has been regarded as a highly influential text in Castilian literature. The Castilian version, which survives in 27 manuscripts, was quite popular (Baldwin viii).

In sources from Arabic, Muslim tradition, the symbolic values suggested by texts portraying animals are, by and large, analogous to those in the Christian tradition. This suggests compatible readings of *Calila* by readers of the Arabic and Castilian versions. While references to animals abound in Arabic poetry and in the Qur'ān, there is no Arabic equivalent to the Medieval Latin and Romance bestiary. The only work devoted specifically to classifying animals (as opposed to, for example, works on hunting, falconry, or veterinary science) is the *Kitāb al-ḥayawān* ('The Book of Animals') by al-Jāḥiẓ (776–868). His work is primarily one of *adab* literature, courtly belles-lettres considered required reading for aspiring courtiers and intellectuals. Basing his entries primarily on Aristotle's treatises on animals, al-Jāḥiẓ also draws on Arabic literary tradition. Like the *Physiologus*, the *Kitāb al-ḥayawān* is more homiletic than scientific.[56] Animals received extensive treatment by Arab poets, and it is quite common in both pre-Islamic and Islamic poetry to describe animals literally or allegorically whether in panegyric or invective simile.[57] In one very well-known example, the pre-Islamic poet Ṭarafa ibn al-ʿAbd (fl. ca. 500) dedicated a lengthy section of his *muʿallaqa* (ode) to his riding camel (Jumʿah 74–75).

The Meaning of Animal Behavior in Calila e Dimna

In *Calila*, animals are represented with varying degrees of anthropomorphization. Some act as humans (i.e., carry on conversations in human language), some simply as animals. This suggests an accumulation of narrative material from traditions that differ in their epistemological treatment of animals. At the beginning of chapter one, the reader is informed that the book "departe por enxemplos de omnes et aves et animalias" (69) ('is divided into exemplary

[56] Its function is to explain the relationship between God and Man by celebrating God's creation; it does not (like the *Physiologus*) assign an allegorical value to each animal. Rather, the work aims to glorify God's wisdom in creating only useful animals. Even malicious or dangerous ones have been created as a "test" for humans (*EI*, "Animals"). On animal books in Arabic literature, see McDonald.

[57] For animals in Arabic poetry, see Ḥaṣan, Jumʿah, and Šukr. For animals in Hispano-Arabic poetry, see Pérès and Khidr.

tales of men and birds and animals.')[58] The characters in the primary frame of the story, the Lion, the Ox, and the two jackals Calila and Digna, are anthropomorphized, in the sense that they speak, think abstractly, and themselves tell tales. Many of the animals featured in the tales throughout the work are also anthropomorphized to various degrees. More often than not, animals that share the stage with humans in a tale are not anthropomorphized and do not speak either to humans or to animals. However, animal protagonists of tales involving only animals almost always speak.[59]

When the animal talks and behaves as a person (but yet acts according to the perceived nature of that animal), its behavior serves to illustrate a human attribute. In the case of "El piojo y la pulga" ('The Louse and the Flea'), the two insects converse as humans do, but still act as parasites, feasting on the flesh of their host human:

> Dixo Digna:—Dizen que un piojo estava muy viçioso en un lecho de un rico omne, et avía de su sangre cada día quanta quería, et andava sobre él muy suavemente que lo non sentía él. Desí fue así que le demandó una pulga una noche ospedadgo, et él ospedóla, et díxole:—Albergad comigo esta noche en sabrosa sangre et mollido lecho.
>
> Et la pulga fízolo así, et alvergóse con él; et en echándose el omne en su lecho, et mandó sacodir su sávana et catar si avía alguna cosa; et saltó la pulga et estorçió a una parte; et fallaron al piojo mal andante, et tomáronlo et matáronlo. (152–53; ed. Cheikho 93)

> (Digna said:—They say that a louse lived viciously in the bed of a rich man, and every day drank as much of his blood as he wanted, and walked over him so lightly that he could not feel him. And so it was that a flea asked to stay with him one night, and he accommodated her, and said to her:—Stay with me tonight; enjoy tasty blood and a soft bed!
>
> And the flea did so, and stayed with him; and before getting into bed, the rich man had his bedclothes shaken out to see if there was anything inside; and the flea jumped out and got away to one side, but they found the poor louse, and took him, and killed him.)

Here the literary animals act in accordance with the behaviors of their flesh-and-blood counterparts: lice do indeed live in human hair and fleas inflict painful bites. At other times, however, certain animal characters display

---

[58] The passage is absent in Cheikho's edition.

[59] See the tales "El piojo y la pulga" ('The Louse and the Flea'), "El camello que se ofreció al león" ('The Camel Who Offered Himself to the Lion'), and "Los monos, la luciérnaga, y el ave" ('The Monkeys, the Firefly, and the Bird') (152–53, 158–62, and 170–71; ed. Cheikho 93, 101–05, and 113–14).

behaviors that are not known to be characteristic, whether in real life or in literary and/or artistic sources. Take for example the tale of "La garza, las truchas y el cangrejo" ('The Heron, the Trout, and the Crab'), in which the perceptive crab outwits the heron:

> Dixo el lobo çerval:—Dizen que era una garça, et avía fecho su nido en una ribera muy viçiosa, do avía muchas truchas. Et envegeçió et non podía pescar, et ovo fanbre, et trabajóse de engañar a aquellas truchas et aquel pescado, et demostró muy grant tristeza et cuidado. Et viola un cangrejo de alueñe, vínose para ella, et díxole:—¿Qué as, que estás triste et cuidosa?
>
> Dixo ella:—Más mal que bien. Yo solía bevir de las truchas, et acaesçió oy que vi dos pescadores venir a este nuestro lugar, et dixo el uno al otro:—¿Por qué non echamos alguna vez la red aquestas truchas que son en aqueste lugar?
>
> Dixo el otro:—Mas vayamos a un lugar que yo sé do ay muchas truchas et comencemos ý, et desí vengamos acá et abarrerlas emos.
>
> Et yo sé que, si ellos oviesen ya acabado de pescar aquellas a que fueron, que ya tornados serían, et non fincaría aquí ninguna que las non pesquen; et en esto es mi muerte et mi desfalleçimiento.
>
> Et fuese el cangrejo a todas las truchas et pescados, et fízogelo saber; et viniéronse todas para ella, et dixiéronle:
>
> —Venimos nós para ti que nos consejes, ca el omne entendido non dexa de consejar con su enemigo, seyendo de buen consejo, en las cosas que se puede dél ayudar. Et en bevir nós as tú pro, et bien puedes conseja[r]nos.
>
> Díxoles:—Nós non lo podemos contrastar, mas yo sé un lugar de un piélago muy grande do ha mucha agua et mucho bien; et si vós quisierdes, vayámosnos allá, ca en esto vos yaze pro et salud.
>
> Dixieron ellas:—¿Et quién nos fará este bien sinon tú?
>
> Dixo ella:—Fazerlo he a honra de vos.
>
> Començó a levar dellas dos a dos cada día, et levávalas a una ribera, et comíalas. Et vínose a ella el cangrejo, et díxole:—Yo miedo he en este lugar, et si tú me levares, farías bien.
>
> Llevólo fasta que llegó al lugar do las comía, et vido el cangrejo las espinas de las truchas ayuntadas. Entendió que ellas las comía et que otro tal quería fazer a él, et dixo en su coraçón:—Quando el omne se fallas con su enemigo en los lugares do sabe que lo matará, deve lidiar con él por honra o por guarda de sí, querer vençer o non, et non se le omille ni se le meta en poder.
>
> Et travó con sus tenazas al cuello de la garça, et apretóla tanto que la mató. Desí tornóse el cangrejo a las truchas, et díxoles las nuevas de la garça et de las truchas que levava cada día et las comía, et que la avía muerta, et moráronse en su lugar. (143–45; ed. Cheikho 83–85)
>
> (Said the jackal:—They say that there was a heron, and she had made her nest on the bank of a rapid river, where there were a lot of trout. The heron grew old and could no longer fish, and was hungry, and then tried to trick the trout. A crab saw her from afar, came toward her, and said to her:—What's wrong? Why are you so sad and worried?

> She said:—I've been better! I used to live on these trout, and today I saw two fishermen come here to our place, and one said to the other:—Why don't we cast our nets to catch these trout here?
>
> Said the other:—First let's go to another place that I know has a lot of trout; we'll start there and then we'll come back here and get them, too.
>
> And I know that once they finish fishing the other trout, they will come back here, and soon there will not be any more trout for me to fish, and in that is my death and demise.
>
> The crab went straight away to the trout and other fish, and let them know; they all went to the heron and said:
>
> —We have come for advice, for the wise man does not hesitate to seek counsel even from his enemy, if he is a wise enemy, and may be of help. Our survival benefits you, so you are fit to advise us.
>
> She said to them:—There's no doubt about that! I know a place far out at sea where there is lots of water and good things; and if you want, we can go there, for in this is your health and your benefit.
>
> They said:—Who else would treat us so well?
>
> She said:—I do it to honor you!
>
> So she began to take them there two by two, each day, and carried them to a riverbank, and ate them. And the crab came to her and said:—I'm scared here, and if you can take me out of here, I'll make it worth your while.
>
> So she carried him to the place where she had been eating the trout, and the crab saw the pile of trout bones. He realized that the crane had been eating them, and would do the same to him, and said to himself:—When a man finds himself with his enemy in a place where he knows he will be killed, he must fight in his honor or his defense, whether he win or not, and not let himself be humiliated or overtaken.
>
> So he took the neck of the heron between his claws, and squeezed it so hard that she died. Then he went back to the trout, and told them the news about the heron, how she had been taking them and eating them up, and how she had died, and they all lived together in their place.)

Here the crab is rather randomly characterized as perceptive and fearless, qualities that are not attested elsewhere (nor, do I believe, are commonly held to be true). In terms of the narrative, what is more significant are the physical capabilities of the fish, the heron and the crab, and not any behaviors that might correspond to human traits.

However, when animals are portrayed in tales alongside human protagonists, they simply act as animals, and the human weakness illustrated by the tale is expressed not through the actions of the animals but through those of the humans. In the tale of "Los papagayos acusadores" ('The Accusing Parrots'), the bird protagonists do not have conversations or display any kind of human intelligence or linguistic capacity—they are simply parrots:

Dixo Digna:—Dizen que avía en [una] villa un rico omne que l'dezían Morzubem, et era noble et de grand fecho, et avía una muger muy fermosa et buena et leal. Este rico omne avía un sirviente açorero, et amava a su señora, et avíale demandado su amor muchas vezes; et ella non tornava cabeça por él et amenazólo muy mal. Et quando fue desfuziado ella, pensó de buscarle mal con el marido. Et salió un día a caçar, et priso dos pollos de papagayos; et apartólos el uno del otro, et enseñó al uno dezir: "Yo vi al potrero yazer con mi señora en el lecho"; et enseñó al otro dezir: "Pues yo non quiero dezir nada." Et aprendieron esto los pollos en lenguaje de Balaf, que non sabían los de aquella tierra, et tomólos et diolos a su señor. Et cantavan ant' él et plazíale con ellos, et non sabían qué dezían.

Et un día viniéronle huéspedes de tierra de Balaf. Et después que ovieron comido, mandó traer las aves ant' ellos por les fazer plazer, et cantaron. Quando ellos oyeron lo que los pollos cantavan, catáronse unos a otros et abaxaron las cabeças de vergüenza que ovieron. Díxol' el uno dellos:—¿Sabés que dize el uno destos papagayos? Non te ensañes contra nos si te lo dixiéremos, ca fablan en lenguaje de Balaf.

Dixo él:—Non me ensañaré, ca ante me plazerá.

—Sabed que dize:—El potrero yaze con mi señora en el lecho de mi señor; et el otro dize:—Pues yo non quiero dezir nada. Et nós avemos por ley de non comer en casa de omne que su muger sea mala.

Quando esto ovieron dicho, dixo el siervo que estava ý çerca:—Verdad es, et yo só ende testigo que lo vi muchas vezes y non lo osé dezir.

Et el señor de casa, quando esto vido, mandó matar a su muger. Et ella enbiól' rogar que pesquisase bien lo que le dixeran, et dixo:—Demanden et pregunten a los papagayos si saben más deste lenguaje de Balaf, et fallarán que esto ha fecho tu açorero; ca él me pidió mio amor et yo non quise.

Et ellos fiziéronlo así, et vieron que non sabían más fablar, et entendieron qu'el açorero los enseñara. Et quando esto vieron que la muger era sin culpa et al açorero era mintroso, et mandáronlo llamar. Et él entró muy atrevido, et traía en la mano un açor. Et díxole la muger:—Di tú, ¿me viste fazer esto que dizes?

Dixo él:—Sí.

Quando esto ovo dicho, saltóle el açor al rostro, et sacóle los ojos con las uñas. Dixo la mujer:—Vees, traidor, la justiçia de Dios qué aína te avino et te conpreendió porque testimoniaste falso contra mí de lo que non sabías nin acaesçió. (198–200; ed. Cheikho 149–151)

(Said Digna:—They say that in a town a rich man by the name of Morzubem, noble and accomplished, had a very beautiful, good, and loyal wife. This rich man had a servant, a falconer, who loved his lady, and had begged for her love many times. She never once looked at him, and threatened him badly. And when he felt he had been rejected, the falconer thought to turn her husband against her. He went out one day to hunt, and caught two parrots. He separated them, and taught the first one to say: "I saw the colt herder sleep with my lady in her bed"; and taught the other to say: "I don't want to say anything." And the two parrots learned this in the language of Balaf, that the locals did not

> know, and the falconer took the two parrots to his lord. And they sang for him, and he enjoyed them, and did not know what they were saying.
>
> One day came some guests from the land of Balaf. After they had eaten, the man had the parrots brought out to entertain them, and they sang. When the guests heard what the parrots were singing, they looked at one another and hung their heads in shame. One of them said to him:—Do you know what these parrots are singing? Don't get mad at us, they are speaking in the language of Balaf!
>
> He said:—I won't get mad, I promise.
>
> —He's saying:—The colt herder sleeps with my lady in my lord's bed, and the other says:—I don't want to say anything! And our law says that we cannot eat in the house of a man whose wife is wicked.
>
> When they had said this, the servant who was close by said:—It's true! I witness that I have seen it many times but didn't dare say anything.
>
> And the lord of the house, when he heard this, ordered that his wife be killed. And she begged him to investigate what they said, and said:—Go ask and interrogate those parrots to see if they know any more of the language of Balaf, and you will find that this is the work of the falconer, for he asked for my love and I refused him.
>
> And they did just that, and they saw that the parrots didn't know any more speech, and understood that the falconer had taught it to them. And when they saw that the wife was innocent and the falconer was a liar, they called him in. He came in nervously, carrying a falcon. The wife said to him:—Tell me, you, have you seen me do this thing that you claim?
>
> He said:—Yes!
>
> When he said this, the falcon jumped to his face, and scratched out his eyes with its talons. The woman said:—You see, traitor, that God's justice is brought upon you, because you bore false witness against me for something you didn't know of and that never even happened!)

Far from being actors in the narrative, the parrots are only the unwitting tools of the scheming falconer who is eventually exposed and punished. They are the least anthropomorphic of animals, but they share the stage with other animals who talk, think independently, and act much as humans do.

None of the five tales that Ibn al-Muqaffāʿ relates in his introduction features animal characters.[60] The first animal protagonist encountered by the reader is Sençeba, the Ox, who is serving as beast of burden to a traveling merchant when he falls into a disused grain silo and is gravely injured. The

[60] The tales are: "El hombre engañado por los cargadores" ('The Man Deceived by the Porters'), "El ignorante que quería pasar por sabio" ('The Ignorant Man Who Wanted to Pass for a Learned Man'), "El hombre que dormía mientras le robaban" ("The Man Who Slept While They Robbed Him'), "El hombre que quería robar a su compañero" ('The Man Who Wanted to Rob His Companion'), and "El pobre que se aprovechó del ladrón" ('The Poor Man Who Took Advantage of the Thief') (89–98; ed. Cheikho 51–60).

merchant assigns a servant to stay with the ox until he is healed and then bring him along with the rest of the caravan. The servant, resentful of being left behind, leaves Sençeba and tells the merchant that his ox has died. However, Sençeba eventually recovers and wanders off, until he ends up within earshot of the court of the Lion. Once freed from his role as beast of burden and accessory to a human, he gains the power of speech and enters into the world of anthropomorphic animals who become animated only in the absence of humans, like the toys in the movie *Toy Story* who spring to life only when their owner is out of the room. This episode is a unique bridge in the work between the world of humans and the world of anthropomorphic animals. It marks an important shift in the characterization of Sençeba. In the human world, he is a mute and expendable beast of burden. In the animal world, he is a potential rival to the highly placed advisors of the Lion, the jackals Calila and Digna.[61]

The Animal Imaginary of Andalusī and Castilian Audiences of Kalīla/Calila

In determining the historic and symbolic values of an animal for Andalusī and Castilian audiences of *Calila*, one can have recourse to several resources: textual clues as to the animal's meaning to a reader and non-textual sources that contribute to a sense of each animal in the *gestalt* of the audience. The latter consist of various types of cultural production of the time (plastic arts, literary, religious, and scientific texts) and whatever historical or archeological evidence may be available regarding the actual existence of the animal in the region where the audience lived. For Islamic sources, one may consider the Qur'ān, the *sunna* or practices of the Prophet Muhammad, the *ḥadīṯ* or traditions of the Prophet, and the various commentaries thereupon. These texts will consider the animal primarily as food (whether permitted

[61] It is possible that this shift is a literary manifestation of the doctrine of metempsychosis (Ar. *tanāsukh*), the belief in several Eastern religions that the human soul can migrate, in reincarnation, to animal, vegetable, or mineral hosts according to the quality of the soul's conduct in the previous life. In so doing, every man reaps the fruit of his actions in previous lives. In Hinduism, the wicked are reborn as dogs, pigs, or insects. Augustine condemned the doctrine in his anti-Manichean writings because it flew in the face of the Christian belief that one's actions in this world are addressed only by divine judgment (Eliade). The tale of a jackal who had been a sinful king in his previous life is omitted from the Arabic *Kalīla*, perhaps in an effort to suppress features of the work that were potentially offensive to Islam (Lacarra, Introduction to Ibn al-Muqaffaʿ 14).

or forbidden), as raw materials for industrial use (hides, various body parts for medicinal purposes), or perhaps as regards their relationship to the life of the Prophet.[62]

Familiarity with a given animal as food would certainly affect one's perception of that animal in literature. Consider, for example, the impression a meat-eater will have of a chicken or a cow, as distinguished from a lion or bear. These religious texts differ in their treatment of animals from, for example, poetry (which tends toward the symbolic) or fables (which tend toward the didactic). As concerns the representation of animals in the plastic arts, the Islamic evidence is more limited than the Christian, for the representation of animals and people was regarded as sacrilegious by the greater part of the Muslim world (*EI*, "Animals in art" and "Sūra"). Therefore, Muslim audiences may not have had reliable access to a visual image of an animal not native to or otherwise present in their home environment and would therefore rely more on other sources of information. For Christian audiences, one must consider the appearance of animals in the New and Old Testaments, but dietary laws, for example, do not figure as strongly as they would in determining a (devout) Muslim's experience of an animal.

This pulse-taking of the audience's *gestalt* is not an exact science. Henderson warns against pigeonholing medieval authors and reminds us that "we can catalog options known to be open to our authors, but we cannot predict their choices among options" (46). He also maintains that authors of medieval fables insert or overlay their own perceptions (of animals) and agendas when recasting beast fables. Christian authors, particularly in the High Middle Ages, employ an exegetical style that goes beyond simple moralizing. They apply the allegorical approach to existing material. In this way, the same beast, or even the same specific behavior of a beast, could be used to illustrate different points according to the author in question.

Because our focus is on the values of the reader, not the author, we can approximate this set of associations by examining images of these animals in materials to which the medieval reader may reasonably have had some form of access, direct (reading, listening) or indirect (illumination, oral paraphrase). Here we will include materials both contemporary with the translation of *Calila* as well as some slightly later texts that can be held to represent the

[62] For example, while *ḥadīṯ* permits the killing of roosters and fleas, it forbids "reviling" these animals because they were said to have been helpful in waking the Prophet in time for prayer. Different schools of Islamic Law (there are four recognized by orthodoxy) sometimes take different positions on a given animal. For example, the monkey is considered forbidden (as food) by all major schools except the Mālikī, the most prevalent in al-Andalus (*EI*, "Animals").

symbolic value of the animal in question for the audience of the Castilian *Calila*.

How, then, would the medieval readers of *Calila* have approached the images of animals encountered in the text? I shall limit my investigation of this question to the three primary characters in the frametale, the Lion, the ox Sençeba, and the eponymous jackal characters, Calila and Digna. The way the reader will bring previous experiences and images to interact with those in the present text will depend on how the animals are characterized in *Calila*. Because the book is not a work of natural history, a bestiary, or a work of strictly recreational fiction such as a romance, it serves a didactic purpose; the way the animals are characterized is informed by the work's function as a text that purports to train humans in political matters. The introduction to *Calila* identifies the work as one dealing with animals as exemplars for human behavior. Ibn al-Muqaffāʿ states this quite clearly in his introduction (99).[63] Once beyond the introduction, the frame story is presented as the story of the "león et...buy [sic]" (122; ed. Cheikho 61). This is the philosopher Berzebuey's response to his King's request for a story that exemplifies "dos que se aman et los departe el mesturero, falso, mentiroso..." ('two that love each other and who are driven apart by the meddling, false, lying man...') (122; ed. Cheikho 61).[64] He wants to hear a story of intrigue, and Berzebuey tells him of the Lion, the Ox, and the Jackals. The lion is so universally charged with symbolic value that it would be impossible to track all of its manifestations in art and literature. However, we can cite a great many texts to which a thirteenth-century Castilian audience might have had access.

The Old and New Testaments offer a wealth of references to the lion in several capacities. In the Old Testament, the lion is most frequently cited for its ferocity, most usually in metaphoric application either to God (when angered)[65] or to an individual or army when described as a military foe.[66] Occasionally it is used descriptively to demonstrate how God's power can overcome even the strongest or most powerful forces.[67] In the OT the lion

---

[63] There is no corresponding text in Cheikho's edition.

[64] This motif is Aarne-Thompson K 2131.2, Envious jackal makes lion suspicious of his friend, the bull (Goldberg, *Motif-index* 110).

[65] "Ne quando rapiat ut leo animam meam" (Psalms 7:3). For all citations of the Vulgate see *Biblia Sacra Iuxta Vulgatam Clementinam*.

[66] "Dan catulus leonis, fluet largiter de Basan" (Deuteronomy 33:22), "Susceperunt me sicut leo paratus ad praedam: et sicut catulus leonis habitans in abditis" (Psalms 16:12).

[67] "Rugitus leonis, et vox leaenae, et dentes catulorum leonum contritii sunt" (Job 4:10); "Et fortissimus quisque, cujus cor est quasi leonis, pavore solvetur" (2 Kings 17:10).

is also symbolic of the tribe of Judah, for their bravery in battle.[68] In later Jewish tradition, the lion comes to represent any valiant or brave person, and even an accomplished scholar. There are multiple references to the lion, especially as symbolic of Judah, in the Talmud and Midrashic texts. Later commentators widened the semantic field associated with the lion so that by the mid-fourteenth century, Jacob ben Asher (1270?–1340) of Toledo uses the lion to signify an outstanding scholar (*EJ*, "Lion" and "Jacob ben Asher").

In the New Testament, the lion receives scant treatment in the Gospels and is used only in Timothy to describe an escape from danger[69] and in Peter to describe the ferocity of the Devil.[70] In Revelation the lion is featured several times in descriptions of visions and fantastic creatures whose various body parts recall those of lions.[71] It is also worth noting that the lion has been traditionally associated with the evangelist St. Mark in early Christian writings (i.e., St. Augustine and St. Jerome) and in medieval Christian art. According to Augustine,[72] Mark is metonymically associated with the lion because he was responsible for calling attention to the kingly nature of Christ, and the lion has always symbolized royalty. In addition, there are many representations of Mark as a lion in illuminated manuscripts, mosaics, and stained glass windows throughout Europe.[73]

The *Physiologus* introduces the allegorical value of the lion in its tripartite presentation of the animal. It explains that the lion covers his tracks with his tail when he senses a hunter, just as Christ hid his divine nature from the "unbelieving Jews" who sought to foil his ministry. The lion's vigilance, demonstrated by sleeping with its eyes open, recalls the flesh of Christ sleeping on the cross while his divine nature remains vigilant, protecting humanity.[74] Finally, the lioness is known to guard her stillborn cub for three days, until the lion can arrive to see the body. This vigil is likened to the three days Christ lay dead after his crucifixion and before his resurrection. Such allegorical readings, because of their incongruence with the vast majority of available

[68] "Catulus leonis Iuda a praeda fili mi ascendisti requiescens accubuisti ut leo et quasi leaena quis suscitabit eum" (Genesis 49:9).

[69] The Apostle Paul describes how he was strengthened by God at a particularly difficult point in his ministry: "et liberatus sum de ore leonis" (2 Timothy 4:17).

[70] "Quia adversarius vester diabolus tanquam leo rugiens circuit" (1 Peter 5:8).

[71] "Et animal primum simile leoni" (Revelation 4:7); "Et habebant capillos sicut capillos mulierum; et dentes earum sicut dentes leonum erant" (Revelation 9:8); "et os ejus sicut os leonis" (Revelation 13:2).

[72] *De consensu evangelistarum* 1.6.9, cited in Just.

[73] For the symbols of the Evangelists, see Just.

[74] This is a reference to Matthew 26:64, which in turn is interpreted as a gloss on Psalms 121:4: "Ecce non dormitabit neque dormiet, qui custodit Israël."

images of lions, would probably not leap to the fore in a reading of *Calila*, particularly as they are not in keeping with the exemplary function of the stories in the text. Readers of *Calila* would more likely draw on images of the lion as a ferocious foe and fearless monarch of the animal world. Such images are supported by bestiaries based on the *Physiologus*, by early Castilian literature, and by what little we know of the lion's physical presence in Europe during the Middle Ages.

Owing to its association with power and military might, the lion had been a popular animal with royalty since antiquity. Medieval monarchs were known to present one another with lions, and Henry I of England kept lions in his menagerie. Lions at this time were still wild in North Africa and were commonly found as caged animals in Iberian courts as well (George and Yapp 48). This courtly context of the lion in medieval Iberia is portrayed in the *Cantar de Mio Cid*. At the beginning of the third *cantar*, while the Cid is napping, his captive lion escapes from its cage. The Cid's men surround their leader to protect him while they deal with the lion. Finally the Cid wakes up and heads for the lion, who recognizes the warlord's valor and hangs his head low as the Cid takes him by the neck and leads him back to his cage (ed. R. Menéndez Pidal 227–28).

The lion also appears in several works of literature contemporary with *Calila*. In the *Libro de Alexandre* several similes compare men in battle to the lion. Menelaeus is referred to as "tan rauioso; cuomo un leon yrado" (f. 30v). Similar references to the lion in the coetaneous *Poema de Fernán González* (circa 1250) refer to men's ferocity in battle: "commo leon brrauo ansy dio vn gemjdo" (transcr. Geary f. 24r). The lion appears in a discussion of the movements and significance of the constellation Leo in *Judizios de las estrellas* (1254). These references are even more abstract than those in the *Physiologus* and probably cannot be held to contribute greatly to a reader's interaction with the lion of the *Calila*.[75] Finally, there is a single image of a lion in the *Milagros de Nuestra Señora*, where the Virgin intercedes to save one of her faithful from a lion:

[75] See also the discussion of stones corresponding to astrological properties of the lion sign in Alfonso X's *Lapidario* (1250) (89), and the explanation of the lion piece in chess in his *Libro de ajedrez, dados y tablas* (1283). In the latter, the physical properties of the lion correspond with the game play of the namesake chess piece: "E el Leon es bestia otrossi muy fuerte & salta mucho en trauiesso o en derecho; mas que otra bestia quando quiere tojmar alguna cosa. E a essa semeiança lo pusieron aqui & salta a quarta casa la una en derecho & las dos en trauiesso" (fol. 81v) ('the Lion is also a very strong animal and jumps far either backward or forward; more than any other animal when he wants to take something. And in this image they put him here, and he jumps to the fourth square, one forward and two sideways').

veno sancta María: como solié uenir
con un palo en mano pora'*l* león ferir
(Berceo, *Obras* 2:153, st. 476b–d)

(Holy Mary came, as she was wont
with a staff in hand to wound the lion)

Andalusī Muslim audiences of *Calila* would have brought similar imagery to bear in their understanding of the lion. As in Christian Europe, the lion (Ar. *qaṣwara, ʾassad, layṯ, abū ḥāriṯ*) in Islam is commonly associated with royalty. Caliphs traditionally went lion-hunting, kept lions in zoological gardens, and used them as trained beasts. The animal was often used as personal name or family name, such as Assadī and Laythī (*EI*, "al-Asad"). Pre-Islamic poets would often use the image of the lion as a steadfast warrior and fierce defender in elegiac or panegyric descriptions of Bedouin leaders (Jumʿah 33–35). Consider Zuhayr ibn Abī Sulmā's[76] description of his patron:

Is he not a valiant warrior in striking with his sword,
and in freeing the bound prisoner from his shackles?
Like a lion, Abū Šiblayn defends his lair
When he meets with adversity he does not flee![77]

The lion was also identified in poetry as ruler of the animals of the wilderness (Ar. *ġāba*,) who watched over them as a human ruler would his subjects, as in these lines by Layla al-Akhyālīyah (sixth century):

He appeared as a lion of the thicket defending his lair,
whose cubs and wives were pleased with him;
Loving and mild when asked for clemency,
a merciless killer when striking his prey at its most vulnerable spot.[78]

In the Arabic tradition, the lion is described in al-Jāḥiẓ's *Kitāb al-ḥayawān* as fleet of foot, having very sharp claws for tearing apart his prey, the mightiest of all animals, a voracious hunter, and as a frequent subject of poets (1: 228, 6:11, 8:132, 1:229, 2:13, 3:306, 2:213, 4:104, 4:223, and 5:488).

Some of the behaviors of the lion enumerated in the *Physiologus* are also found in the *Kitāb al-manāfiʿ aʿdaʾ al-ḥayāwān* by the Syrian Ibn Bakhtīšūʿ

---

[76] One of the authors of the pre-Islamic *muʿallaqāt*, or desert odes. See also the Spanish translation by Corriente (*Muʿallaqat* 91–98), and the English translation by O'Grady (32–36).

[77] Traditional text of Zuhayr cited in Jumʿah (34).

[78] The Arabic text of Layla is cited in Ḥaṣan (212). For further treatment of the lion in Classical Arabic literature, see Ḥaṣan (212–19).

(d. 1058) (38).[79] This work enjoyed diffusion across the Arab world, and may well have been read in al-Andalus. Ibn Bakhtišūʿ reports the following:

> The authors of books of animals mention three properties of the lion: the first, that when it smells the scent of the hunters, it wipes out its footprints. The second is that the lioness gives birth to her cubs without moving, watching them attentively for three days.... The third, that it sleeps with its eyes open and eats no meat that it has not hunted itself. (38)

It is not surprising that some of the Arabic sources, particularly the scientific texts that draw on classical authors (such as *Kitāb al-ḥayawān* and *Kitāb al-manāfiʿ*), should resemble Latin and Romance texts. Much of the lore regarding animals in circulation around the Mediterranean during the Middle Ages is common to Arabic and Latin tradition. Also, the Arabic poetic tradition and the Biblical Hebrew poetic tradition (reflected in the Vulgate and influential in subsequent Christian literature) draw on the same imagery concerning the lion that was common to the societies of the fertile crescent in antiquity.

Sources prior to and contemporary with *Calila* associate the lion with royalty and in particular with military prowess, ferocity, and raw strength. While there are scattered references to the lion as a monarch, as an allegorical Christ, and as an actual lion in the wild, the overwhelming majority portray the lion's strength and physical supremacy. This is the backdrop which the medieval Castilian reader brings to the lion in the *Calila*. Images of lions in Arabic sources are practically identical, tending to focus on the lion's valor, bravery, and ferocity.

The second animal of significance in *Calila* is the ox Sençeba, who vies with the jackals Kalīla and Dimna for the favors of the lion. Omnipresent in the agricultural life of medieval Europe, the ox would have had immediate and familiar associations for the Castilian readership of the *Calila*. In addition, it is featured in many bestiaries and other popular texts. In the medieval plastic arts, the ox is generally depicted as a friendly domesticated animal, together with its companion under the yoke. The ox is social—when its companion is absent the ox lows in distress. Normally it is portrayed standing. In the illuminations it is very similar to the typical Spanish bull, which was thought to have been among the first kinds domesticated (George and Yapp 104). It is not, however, mentioned in the *Physiologus*, although it is featured in several of the bestiaries. Old Testament sources refer to the

---

[79] I translate from the Spanish translation of Ruiz Bravo-Villasante. No edition of the Arabic text (found in Escorial ms. 893) is available.

ox's intelligence,[80] compliance,[81] and value as an animal fit for important sacrifices in the Hebrews' biblical religious observance.[82] New Testament references generally concern the ox in relation to commerce, as property, or as part of the marketplace environment.[83]

As with the lion, the imagery used to describe the bull (but not the ox specifically) in Arabic sources is analogous to that in the Christian sources. The pre-Islamic poets often make reference to the bull in recalling an anecdote in which a bull is beaten for roiling the drinking water of a well, when it was the cows who were drinking from it. The anecdote reproaches those who would unfairly punish one member of a group for a crime committed by another member. Ultimately, however, this anecdote stresses the leadership of the bull over the rest of the cattle, and therefore the responsibility of leaders for the actions of their subjects (as in *Kitāb al-ḥayawān*) (Jumʿah 138). Although it has a sizeable sura titled "The Cow" (6, *al-Baqara*), the Qurʾan is fairly silent on the neutered male of the species (Ar. *ṯawr*), but makes several general references to bovines in reference to ritual sacrifice,[84] Jewish dietary law,[85] and in the retelling of the biblical story of Joseph.[86] The bull is mentioned several times in the *Kitāb al-ḥayawān*, for his leadership of all cattle (1:19), his horns (2:234; 8:192), his snub nose (3:309), and his natural enmity with the wolf (2:10). The *Kitāb al-manāfiʿ* mentions simply that the bull has a great appetite for mating and that his ability to work is compromised if he does not have sufficient opportunity to indulge this appetite, especially when young (Ibn Bakhtīšūʿ 9).

The eponymous characters *Calila* and *Dimna* are jackals (Ar. *ibn ʾawā*, Sp. *lobo çerval*). These animals, while known to medieval Europeans, do not enjoy the widespread familiarity or symbolic value of the lion and the ox. There is also confusion as to exactly what they are. They seem to be interchangeable to a certain extent with the wolf and the hyena. In the Castilian text, the two characters are referred to as "lobos çervales" which,

---

[80] "Cognovit bos possessorem suum" (Isaiah 1:3).

[81] "Numquam rugiet onager cum habuerit herbam? Aut mugiet bos cum ante praesepe plenum steterit?" (Job 6:5).

[82] "Et placebit Deo super vitulum novellum" (Psalms 68:32); "immolabat bovem et arietem" (2 Samuel 6:13).

[83] "Et alter dixit: Juga boum emi quinque, et eo probare illa: rogo te, habe me excusatum" (Luke 14:19); "et invenit in templo vendentes boves..." (John 2:14).

[84] "Of camels a pair, and of oxen a pair" (6:144).

[85] "For those who followed the Jewish Law, we forbade every (animal) with undivided hoof" (6:146).

[86] "And the king said, 'I saw in a dream seven fat kine, and seven lean ones devouring them" (12:43).

as defined in the *Diccionario de la lengua española*, is equated with "lince" or lynx—which would make it a feline. The jackal in the Old Testament is a symbol of desolation; in the Prophets it is used to predict the fate of civilizations that resist the law of God—i.e., they will be turned into a "acervos arenae, et cubilia draconum") ('a heap of ruins, and a haunt of jackals') (Jeremiah 9:11).[87] The New Testament ignores the jackal completely, but the *Physiologus* briefly mentions the "brute" or hyena, citing it from Leviticus 11:27 and Jeremiah 12:9.

In Arab tradition, the jackal is known for cowardice (it only leaves its lair at night), and because of its impurity before Qurʾānic law, it is generally regarded as a pariah in Islamic countries. Interestingly, it was known as a source of hides that were traded in Muslim Spain and North Africa, and so Andalusī readers of *Kalīla* may have worn the animal's hide as clothing or used it as a bag (*EI*, "Ibn Awā"). Al-Jāḥiẓ follows the biblical descriptions of the jackal as being a resident of the wilderness and not coming near human settlements (6: 209). The jackal is also mentioned in the *Risālat ḥayāwān wa-l insān*, an extract from the *Risālat ikhwān al-ṣafāʾ* ('Treatise of the Brothers of Purity'), a text portraying a court case between the humans and the animals presided over by the king of the Jinn. When the jackal is called to bear witness, he is called by the name "Kalīla," in reference to Ibn al-Muqaffāʿ's work (Ikhwān al-Ṣafāʾ, ed. Asín Palacios 51; trans. Goodman 86–87).[88]

Lion, Ox, and Jackal in Calila

In *Calila*, the jackals Calila and Digna, characterized as "muy ardides et agudos"[89] ('very wise and astute') (125; ed. Cheikho 64), are portrayed as advisors to the Lion. Readers familiar with the characterization of the jackal in prior sources would add to this: "advisors not to be entirely trusted," as the jackal in Biblical and Arabic sources is anti-social, cowardly, and untrustworthy

[87] Also: "faciam planctum velut draconum" (Micah 1:8); describing utter dejection: "frater fui draconum, et socius struthionum" (Job 30:29); a symbol of desolation: "et replebuntur domus eorum draconibus" (Isaiah 13:22); as the wildest elements of nature: "Glorificabit me bestia agri, dracones et struthiones" (Isaiah 43:20).

[88] This text is also of importance to the literary culture of medieval Iberia because it was adapted by the Catalan Franciscan friar, Arabist, and convert to Islam, Anselm Turmeda. See Llinarès' modern edition of the surviving 1554 French text *Dispute de l'ane* and the modern Catalan translation thereof by Olivar, *Disputa de l'ase*. On Turmeda's use of the Arabic original, see Alvárez ("Beastly").

[89] The Arabic reads "*wa-kulāhumā ḏū ʾadabin wa-dahāʾin*" ('Both of them were subtle and clever').

(*EI*, "Ibn Awā"). Already the reader is predisposed to characterize the jackals before they act. The lion is then brought into the picture, when he becomes aware of Sençeba's off-stage lowing, which terrifies him:

> Et çerca de aquel plado avía un león que era rey de todas las alimanias, et en aquel tienpo estavan con el león muchas dellas. Et este león era muy loçano, et quando oía la boz de cómmo el buey bramava, en que non tal cosas avía oído, espantávase mucho, mas non quería que gelo sopiesen sus vasallos. (125; ed. Cheikho 64)
>
> (And nearby that meadow there was a lion who was king of all the animals, and at that time many of them were with him. This lion was very strong, but when he heard the voice of the ox bellowing, the likes of which he had never heard before, he was very frightened, but did not want his vassals to know.)

This is not insignificant, as the lion is described as "muy loçano"[90] ('vigorous' or perhaps 'proud') (124; ed. Cheikho 64) before we discover his fear of Sençeba's voice. Digna, who seeks to capitalize on the lion's fear of the unknown, characterizes the lion as "de flaco consejo e de flaco coraçón, et es escandalizado en su fazienda con sus vasallos" ('of weak counsel and weak heart, and is scandalized in his dealings with his vassals') (128; ed. Cheikho 67). Thus the jackals of *Calila* are shown to be consistent in their behavior with portrayals of jackals in sources available to medieval readers of the Arabic *Kalila* and the Castilian *Calila*.

Traditional characteristics of the lion and the jackal as discussed above are born out in *Calila*, even nuanced to some degree. The lion is generally powerful and brave, the jackal wily and antisocial. The lion of the frame story, with Sençeba, Calila and Digna, is not the only lion in the text. In general, the lion is portrayed as a strong ruler who is in need of guidance—his intelligence does not match his might. This leaves him susceptible to deception and makes him a potential deadly weapon in the hands of the untrustworthy. Other animals often intrigue against the lion (precisely because he is king), as in "Las liebres y el león" ('The Hares and the Lion') (146–49; ed. Cheikho 86–88), where the rabbit tricks the lion into seeing another enemy (the lion's own reflection in the pond) and through misdirection fools him into drowning. In the tale "El camello que se ofreció al león" ('The Camel Who Offered Himself to the Lion') (158–62; ed. Cheikho 101–05), the lion is again represented as being a leader in need of counsel and not always aware of what is going on below him. Although the lion has brought the herbivore Camel into his closest confidence (as with fellow herbivore Sençeba in the

[90] The Arabic text is "*mazhūwwān munfaridān*" ('haughty and solitary').

frame story), when resources are scarce, the other meat-eaters conspire to convince the camel to offer himself up as food for the community. The lesson: while herbivores may be good-natured and gentle advisors, they lack the killer instinct to make it in politics. Conversely, while the carnivorous lion may be a strong ruler, he depends on good counsel to maintain his power. Therefore, let the advisors advise and the rulers rule.

In the tale "Del arquero et de la leona et del axara," ('The Archer and the Lioness and the Jackal') (300–02; ed. Cheikho 284–87) the lioness, powerful but not judicious, is convinced by the jackal (Ar. *al-šaʿhar* > O. Sp. *axara* or *anxara*) to give up meat in favor of fruit once her two cubs are skinned by a hunter. Then, when the jackal complains that she is endangering the fruit supply, she "metióse a comer yervas, et a fazer vida de religioso" ('took to eating herbs, and to lead the life of an ascetic') (302; ed. Cheikho 407). Here the jackal is again portrayed as advising the lioness (or lion) against its nature and possibly to its detriment. The jackal is a counselor from the school of self-preservation, when what is needed is one with a more altruistic approach, who will help the lion toward decisions that will benefit the entire community and secure the lion's position.

This lesson of adhering to one's nature is also the subject of the tale "Del león et del anxahar religioso"[91] ('Of the Lion and the Ascetic Jackal') (305–15; ed. Cheikho 259–81). A jackal goes against jackal culture and leads an ascetic life, abstaining from killing and meat-eating. The lion king hears of this jackal and invites him to court to serve as an advisor. The jackal protests that politics is no place for an honest ascetic and that other, more rapacious members of the court will devour him. He finally accepts the king's invitation on the condition that his safety be guaranteed irrespective of the claims of his competitors. The king agrees, and the jackal comes to serve at court only to be schemed against as predicted. He then asks the lion to return him to his previous state.

All of these portrayals in *Calila* are based on the general characteristic of the lion being the most powerful, but not the smartest of animals. None is based on actual observations of specific behaviors, and so are understood to be symbolic of behaviors of lion-like (powerful yet not particularly insightful) humans. The tale structure involving the lion king and the jackal advisor is reproduced several times in *Calila e Dimna*. However, the tales featuring lions and jackals that do not refer to the eponymous characters are only told by Berzebuey once the Calila and Dimna tale is closed, (i.e., once

[91] According to Cacho Blecua and Lacarra's glossary to their edition of *Calila, anxahar* ('jackal') is interchangeable with *lobo çerval* (362).

Calila and Dimna are no longer telling tales to the lion king). This seems to indicate that the structure of the lion being advised by the jackal was a known trope before the invention of the *Calila* frame, and that the *Calila* frame is a literary innovation based on the Lion and Jackal characters in these independent tales.[92] That is, the *Calila e Dimna* frame story represents a novelistic innovation and elaboration of a motif identifiable in independent tales apart from the context of a narrative frame. The early development of a frame from two characters of an independent tale signals the further narrative evolution that occurs when the genre is taken up by European authors in the fourteenth century.

Such portrayals of animals in *Calila* will compete (or at least interact) with other representations that will combine to form an organic whole of what a lion, or an ox, or a jackal *means* to a reader or audience. Based on my analysis of ethical behavior and the animal imaginary, this meaning generated by the interaction of Castilian and Arabic readers with Ibn al-Muqaffaʿ's text would not differ significantly. That is, both audiences would have had much in common in the way they understood the work, despite their linguistic and (perhaps) religious differences. This common performance of meaning in reception serves to define these two audiences as a single community of reception, much as a common language defines a group as a speech community.

The absence of significant cultural or ideological obstacles in the Castilian reception of *Calila* may help to explain the work's success in Castilian and why Alfonso might have chosen it to be his first commissioned translation of a work of Arabic literature. Because *Calila* is devoid of specific references to Islam, or to values that would be offensive to Christians, and because its treatment of animals and other material is consonant with the horizon of expectations of a Castilian reader, the matter of adapting and incorporating the Arabic *Kalīla* into the nascent Castilian literature was unproblematic. The translation and reception of the Castilian *Calila* is characteristic of the assimilation and incorporation of aspects of Andalusī culture into that of expansionist thirteenth-century Christian Iberia. The increasing cultural supremacy of the courts of Catholic monarchs such as Alfonso X and James I of Aragon and the further development of secular literature in the vernacular both set the stage for the appearance, in the next century, of the first frametale in a European vernacular, Don Juan Manuel's *El Conde Lucanor*.

[92] The tale is Aarne-Thompson type K2141 (Goldberg, *Medieval* 110).

CHAPTER FOUR

RECONQUEST IDEOLOGY AND ANDALUSĪ NARRATIVE PRACTICE IN THE *CONDE LUCANOR*

In the tenth century, when Cordova was the richest and most populous city in Europe, and the ʿUmayyad Caliphate was setting the standard for cultural florescence in the Islamic world, a group of Christian nobles in the rocky precincts of northernmost Spain sought to expand their territorial holdings southward, into al-Andalus. Their aim was to unseat Islamic political power on the Iberian Peninsula, and they sought to authorize this project by discrediting Muslim leaders as the usurpers of a Christian political dynasty to which the Christians were rightful heirs. In their view, Christian conquests of al-Andalus were not truly conquests; they were the recuperation of lands that, in the eyes of God himself, belonged to them. Thus, the Christian conquests of al-Andalus came to be known as the Reconquest.

Spanish culture as we know it today is the product of this medieval frontier society, in which Christians and Muslims—during a span of some 700 years—continuously negotiated a political border that was culturally quite porous. By the middle of the thirteenth century, Christian rulers had gained control of the large majority of the Iberian Peninsula, including the populous and important cities of Cordova and Seville in the south. The Christians who populated these newly conquered lands found themselves in close contact with a sizeable population of Andalusī Muslims (and Jews and Christians) who had remained. The conquering Christians were great consumers of Andalusī culture in general, especially arts and sciences, and even literature. At the same time, they viewed Islam, the dominant religion of al-Andalus, as a purely illegitimate basis for political power and social organization.

If the official narrative of Reconquest argues for tidy cultural purity and conformity, the reality on the ground is, in contrast, a messy and emergent pluralism.[1] This is the contradiction faced by Don Juan Manuel, author of

[1] Modern scholars of the Reconquest and of *convivencia* have commented extensively on this disparity. For a deconstruction of the Reconquest as a purely religious enterprise, see Maravall ("Idea" 1–37 and *Concepto* 263–312). His argument has been reevaluated more recently by Hillgarth ("Historiography"). Castro likewise has noted that military orders in

the *Conde Lucanor* (1340) (= *CL*).[2] Juan Manuel was the most powerful nobleman of his time and held extensive lands in Murcia, which retained a far higher proportion of its pre-Reconquest Muslim population than did neighboring Castile and Leon (O'Callaghan, *History* 459). While his military and political career depended on eradicating Islam from the Iberian Peninsula, he earned his literary renown—in part—by imitating and incorporating Andalusī narrative tradition and history into his own writings. In Juan Manuel's adaptation of the frametale genre, the *CL*, this dissonance between the religious and political agendas of the Reconquest manifests in narrative. If the *CL* shows us the ideology of the Reconquest, it also offers the reader a reflection of the more complicated and nuanced reality of daily life and human behavior characteristic of Reconquest-era Castile-Leon (Linehan, "Frontier" 53).[3] In it, Juan Manuel distills the political realities, religious discourse, and cultural interaction of the time into the first original frametale in any European vernacular.[4]

Juan Manuel's religious agenda and frontier political philosophy come across quite clearly in the 50 *exemplos* of the *CL*. The idea of the Christian nobleman's duty to wage war against Islam permeates the work, most starkly in these words of the Count's advisor Patronio: "...Dios vos poblo en tierra quel podades seruir contra los moros" ('...God has given you towns in the land so that you might serve him against the Moors') (2: 58). At the same time, Juan Manuel's willingness to embrace Andalusī narrative genres and materials, including a number of proverbs which he quotes in the original Arabic, seems on the surface to run counter to his official narrative of Reconquest. This type of apparent contradiction is typical both of the frontier society in which Don Juan Manuel came of age and of his genre of choice in writing the *CL*. The frametale genre itself is didactically ambiguous, depending as it does on exemplary tales (and not direct discourse alone) to illustrate

---

Reconquest-era Spain (those of Calatrava, Santiago, and Alcántara) were "más política[s] que religiosa[s]" ('more political than religious') (*España* 181). For a re-evaluation of the medieval Iberian frontier as a culturally porous space, see Linehan ("Frontier").

[2] The *Conde Lucanor*, or *Libro de Patronio* of Don Juan Manuel is extant in seven manuscripts (Madrid: Nacional, 19163; Madrid: Nacional, 19426; Madrid: Nacional, 4236; Madrid: Nacional, 6376; Madrid: Academia Española, 15; Madrid: Academia de la Historia, 9–29–4/5893; and Santander: Menéndez y Pelayo, M-92) (*PhiloBiblon*). All quotations of original texts by Juan Manuel are from the edition of Blecua (*Obras* 2: 9–503). For a complete study of the manuscript tradition of the *Conde Lucanor*, see Hammer.

[3] That is, in any historical moment there are marked inconsistencies between belief, ideology, and practice (Housley 104–19, especially 115).

[4] The *Conde Lucanor* predates the better known medieval European frametales, Boccaccio's *Decameron* (ca. 1350) and Chaucer's *Canterbury Tales* (ca. 1400).

the didactic arguments of the main characters. Often there is a discrepancy between what the author purports to be teaching and the lessons the reader perceives. Therefore, in the way he tells stories and in the very stories he tells, Juan Manuel as author gives the reader a quintessentially Castilian text, the complex and compelling literary product of life in a frontier society. His is but one example of the impact of a centuries-long *convivencia* on the Castilian literary imaginary.

Reading the *CL* is not simply a question of identifying cultural elements originating in the culture of the Other, whether Muslim, Arab, or Andalusī; it is seeing how conflictive and colonial engagement between Christian polity and Muslim subject gives rise to new ways of telling stories and giving voice to one's experience. In the *CL*, Castilian readers experience a new way of telling stories that can accommodate the contradictions that characterize a frontier culture such as that of fourteenth-century Castile-Leon.

In this chapter, I will background the *CL* with a discussion of the political and religious discourses of the Reconquest, including other texts by Juan Manuel. I will then demonstrate how the *CL* reflects these discourses and how Juan Manuel's use of Andalusī narrative practices subverts his discourse of Christian Reconquest.

Colonizing the Frametale

Juan Manuel, in addition to being an actor in the political and military aspects of the culture of Reconquest, was also active in its literary manifestation. Just as the Christian *repobladores* ('settlers') took possession of Andalusī homes and fields, Juan Manuel appropriated the frametale genre from Andalusī literary practice. The frametale is a collection of stories framed by an overarching literary setting in which characters narrate stories to one another. The best known examples of the genre are the *Thousand and One Nights*, Chaucer's *Canterbury Tales*, and Boccaccio's *Decameron*. The genre was introduced to Castilian readers with the translation of *Kalīla wa-Dimna* into Castilian commissioned by Alfonso X (who was still crown prince at the time) in 1251. Alfonso's brother, Don Fadrique, not to be outdone by his higher-ranking brother, similarly commissioned a translation of *Sendebar* in 1253.[5] Having inherited the genre from his uncles' translations of *Calila*

---

[5] For an overview of the frametale literature of thirteenth- and fourteenth-century Castile, see Lacarra (*Cuentística* 11–31).

e Dimna and *Sendebar*, Juan Manuel writes the first frametale in a European vernacular language, inhabiting the genre as one inhabits a structure. In adopting the Andalusī practice of the frametale genre, he renders his rigid ideological program vulnerable to the more porous "border thinking" engendered by the frametale genre.

Walter Mignolo describes border thinking as a way of decentering the epistemological and hermeneutic habits of a post-colonial culture, by challenging the way we produce and disseminate knowledge. He advocates questioning the institutionalized linguistic hegemony of colonial languages such as Spanish and English in the study of post-colonial cultures that have become "transnational" and "transimperial" (250–66). Juan Manuel is a product of colonial Christian Iberia, and his work reflects the interplay between the culture of the conqueror and that of the conquered. The frametale, borrowed from Andalusī literary practice and inherently resistant to didactically fixed readings, destabilizes Juan Manuel's political and religious discourse of Reconquest. The frametale's portrayal of narrative as storytelling practice, as opposed to canonical authority, anticipates and encourages future retellings and recastings.[6] To live in an environment whose design is shaped by aesthetic values and cultural practices that are different from one's own is not a simple matter of a change of home décor. Living in the house of the Other can change one, or at least change the way one interacts with the built environment. According to Pierre Bourdieu's concept of the *habitus*, the built environment results from and perpetuates specific patterns of social practice ("Maison" and "Berber"). In the case of the Christian conquest of al-Andalus, Heather Ecker has demonstrated that the administration of neighborhood mosques in Seville very directly determined the administration of local parishes after the city changed hands in 1248 (Ecker, "Administer").

A similar dynamic obtains in the case of the *CL*. For Juan Manuel, this means that the frametale structure he adapts from Arabic works such as *Sendebar* and *Calila* affects not only the way in which he delivers his message, but also the message itself. While Juan Manuel's didactic intent is quite clear in his explicit verse summations of each *exemplum*,[7] the genre he chooses is inclined toward didactic ambiguity. This tension between the author's didactic rigidity and the inherent didactic ambiguity of his chosen

[6] Menocal ("Life" 487) notes that there is a discrepancy between the stated didactic purpose of each tale (as contextualized by the characters who tell them) and the implicit lessons understood by the reader. On the question of authority in the *Conde Lucanor*, see Gerli.

[7] At the end of each *exemplo*, Juan Manuel sums up the lesson learned in an original couplet.

genre exemplifies the complexity of life on the frontier, playing out on the pages of the *CL* the blurring of boundaries between the cultural legacies of conqueror and conquered.[8]

This contradiction is reflected in the very nature of the frametale genre itself, a genre that juxtaposes the explicit didactic program of the author with the more ambiguous lessons expressed by the tales themselves and decoded by the reader. This juxtaposition opens a space between our author and his narrative. It is a space where the storytelling process brings the contradictions of the colonial culture of Reconquest into relief: the conqueror occupies the physical and cultural spaces of the conquered and in doing so is conditioned by the *habitus* of the colonial environment.

The Christian Conquest of al-Andalus as a Colonial Enterprise

In modern scholarship, the idea of the Reconquest as a domestic crusade or as an expansionist land-grab has well overshadowed that of the Reconquest as a colonial endeavor.[9] However, the two approaches are in no way mutually exclusive. In fact, the shortest of backward steps takes us from the world of the *conquistadores* to that seal of the Reconquest, the 1492 capitulation of Granada to the Catholic monarchs. Where, if not in the centuries of Reconquest, did the *conquistadores* learn to conquer and colonize? Claudio Sánchez-Albornoz states this position quite clearly:

> Descubrimos, conquistamos y colonizamos América siguiendo la trayectoria multisecular de nuestro medioevo. No tuvimos que improvisar una política de expansión y de colonización más allá de las fronteras nacionales al comenzar la Edad Moderna. (*España* 2: 508)
>
> (We discovered, conquered, and colonized America following the multi-century trajectory of our Middle Ages. We did not need to improvise a policy of expansion and colonization beyond our national borders when the Modern Age began.)[10]

---

[8] This is but one example of how Spanish identity has been formed in terms of its relationship with al-Andalus and its Jewish and Islamic past. See, for example, Castro (*Realidad* 28), Goytisolo, and Barkai.

[9] For a brief overview of the crusade vs. materialist theses, see Linehan (*History* 205–08).

[10] On the Reconquest as the background for the conquest of the Americas, see Manrique and Taboada. On this trajectory in the writings of Columbus, see Bartosik-Vélez (35–37) and Taboada. On the use of the image of Santiago (patron saint of the Reconquest) in the conquest of the New World, see Cabrillana Ciézar; Díaz-Férnandez and Heliodoro Valle.

As we have mentioned, the political directive of the Reconquest is best summed up by the Cid's instructions to his men after they take the Muslim-held town of Alcocer: "posaremos en sus casas y dellos nos serviremos" ('we will stay in their houses and make use of them') (140, v. 22). This is colonialism in a nutshell; Christians are not to deport or kill Muslims, but to subjugate them politically and exploit them by occupying their space and appropriating their resources. It has been well established that the *Cantar de Mio Cid* is far more concerned with politics and economics than with religion (J. Duggan; Harney). Given this, I believe the Cid would agree with Albert Memmi's definition of the colonizer:

> Étranger, venu dans un pays par les hasards de l'histoire, il a réussi non seulement à se faire une place, mais à prendre celle de l'habitant, à s'octroyer des privilèges étonnants au détriment des ayants droit. Et cela, non en vertu de lois locales, qui légitiment d'une certaine manière l'inégalité par la tradition, mais en bouleversant les règles admises, en y substituant les siennes. (*Colonisé* 38)
>
> (A foreigner, having come to a land by the accidents of history, he has succeeded not merely in creating a place for himself but also in taking away that of the inhabitant, granting himself astounding privileges to the detriment of those rightfully entitled to them. And this not by virtue of local laws, which in a certain way legitimize this inequality by tradition, but by upsetting the established rules and substituting his own.) (trans. Greenfeld 9)

This is precisely the type of regime change implied in Reconquest: the supplanting of one political and social order for another, for the sake of material opportunity. The Christian conquest of al-Andalus facilitated an unprecedented measure of social mobility in a society where, historically, one's social standing was determined by that of one's father.[11]

For medievals, the most natural justification for such a colonial project (indeed for any war) would be religion; but this does not mean that a desire to convert Andalusī Muslims and Jews was the primary motivation of the Reconquest. Studies of the monastic and royal chronicles of the eighth to thirteenth centuries make it eminently clear that the ideological basis of Reconquest colonialism was to "recuperate" land to which Iberian Christians had a historical right.[12]

---

[11] "During the Central Middle Ages in Iberia social fluidity appears constant. Thus, the *peón* who desired to raise his legal position to that of a *caballero* usually had the capability to do so." (Powers 101). See also Glick (*Islamic* 162).

[12] See Maravall (*Concepto* 269–87), Linehan (*History* 95–127), and O'Callaghan (*Reconquest* 4–7). Historians have been studying Medieval Spain as a colonial problem for decades. See, for example, Burns (*Islam, Medieval*) and Lourie. MacKay describes *repobladores* quite

Unlike literary and cultural scholars, historians have not hesitated to describe the Reconquest as a colonial enterprise. In his study of the partition of Mallorca, Ricard Soto i Company follows Memmi quite closely in describing the Christian *repobladores* of Mallorca as opportunistic colonials whose low social standing or outright mediocrity would impede their progress in the home country:[13]

> A Mallorca s'hi instal·laren, més aviat, una sèrie d'administracions, tant reial com senyorials, que organitzaven la colonització per delegació. Els individus lligats a aquestes administracions, que hom no resisteix la temptació de qualificar de 'colonials,' trauran, a la llarga, el màxim profit de la colonització, i constituiran una classse privilegiada de la qual no formaven part possiblement al país d'origen. (Soto i Company 20)
>
> (Soon in Mallorca, a series of administrations were established, both royal and seigneurial, that organized the colony by delegation. The individuals associated with these administrations, that one cannot resist categorizing as "colonials," received, by and large, the maximum profit of the colonization, and constituted a privileged class of which they would not possibly have formed part in the country of origin.)

The members of this privileged class, Christian Castilians and Aragonese, were avid consumers of Andalusī clothes, textiles, weaponry, farming technology, architecture, and of course, literature.[14] Many of Spain's greatest architectural monuments were Andalusī-built: the Alhambra in Granada, the Giralda and Torre de Oro in Seville, the Cathedral of Cordova, and scores

plainly as "colonists" (36). However, most historians and literary scholars of medieval Iberia have yet to examine the cultural problematics of Reconquest in light of colonial and postcolonial critical theory. For a notable exception, see David Hanlon's insightful study on the representation of Muslims in medieval Castilian literature ("Islam"). More recently, Heather Ecker, a historian of architecture, plainly refers to the "Castilian conquests and colonizations" ("Administer" 45).

[13] Compare with the language of Memmi: "C'est le médiocre, enfin, qui impose le ton géneral de la colonie. C'est lui qui est le véritable partenaire du colonisé, car c'est lui qui a le plus besoin de compensation et de la vie coloniale.... Si tout colonialiste n'est pas un médiocre, tout colonisateur doit accepter en quelque mesure la médiocrité de la majorité des hommes de la colonisation." (*Colonisé* 75) ('It is the mediocre citizens who set the general tone of the colony. They are the true partners of the colonized, for it is the mediocre who are most in need of compensation and of colonial life.... Even if every colonist is not mediocre, every colonizer must, in a certain measure, accept the mediocrity of colonial life and the men who thrive on it.') (trans. Greenfeld 51)

[14] For an overview of the Spanish love affair with Andalusī and "mudéjar" material culture, see Dodds ("Arts" and *Al-Andalus*) and Feliciano. For photographs representative of Andalusī plastic arts, and a study of Mudéjar artistic production for Christian clients, see Ecker (*Caliphs* 78–108).

of provincial fortresses and churches predate the conquest of al-Andalus.[15] The *repobladores* (settlers) of the newly-conquered cities and towns of the south took possession of and adapted existing houses built to reflect Andalusī lifestyles and habits, and their descendents live there to this day. In fact, Castilians first experienced city life and urbanism itself owing to their conquest of cities such as Toledo, Cordova, Seville, and Murcia (Valdeón Baruque, Salrach i Marés and Zabalo Zabalegui 39). The *Libros de repartimiento* that document the material transition from Muslim to Christian rule detail the ways in which Christian colonizers (*repobladores*) adapted the houses built by Muslim former residents.

The Discourse of Reconquest

The Reconquest was an impulse both military and ideological. The term does not represent a discrete, fixed event or period, but a complex, multi-layered reality revealed in sources that vary in language, political orientation, discourse, and ideological program. The canonical narrative of the Reconquest, as first propagated in the Latin monastic and later Catalan and Castilian royal chronicles (Maravall, *Concepto* 261–312), is that the Muslim invasion of 711 and subsequent conquests left the Iberian Peninsula almost entirely under the control of the ʿUmayyads, with the exception of a small enclave in Asturias, to where the most loyal and valiant Christian Visigoths fled, rather than endure the bitter life of a protected minority (*ḍimmī*) under Islam. This is the narrative that took root in the official and popular imagination, persisted, and flourished through the fall of Granada in 1492.[16] This idea is

[15] For a visual introduction to Andalusī architecture, see Barrucand and Bednorz. For an exhaustive bibliography on the topic, see Montêquin. It is worth noting here that the very term "mudéjar" to describe a Muslim-"influenced" aesthetic has recently come under fire. On the tendency of art historians to essentialize the mudéjar style as a simple incorporation of Islamic decorative elements into an otherwise Christian aesthetic, see Robinson, and Robinson and Rouhi ("Editors'" 5). Putting aside for the moment the question of nomenclature, the Christian affinity for Muslim-designed built environments did not end with the Reconquest; in fact, the *mudéjar* styles of architecture flourished for centuries after 1492. On the *mudéjar* stylistic legacy in the Americas, see Toussaint, Aguilar et al., López Guzmán, and Moffitt.

[16] According to Maravall, the idea of the Reconquest was "[una] saeta que con incomparable fuerza recorre la trayectoria de nuestros siglos medievales, y que, conservándose la misma, llega hasta los Reyes Católicos" ('an arrow that ran with incomparable force the trajectory of our medieval centuries, and which, retaining the same force, arrives even to the Catholic Monarchs [Isabella and Ferdinand]') (*Concepto* 267 and "Idea" 4). This narrative persists in contemporary public discourse, for example in the 2004 inaugural address of Spanish President José María Aznar as Distinguished Scholar in the Practice of Global Leadership

expressed by Juan Manuel himself in the *Libro de los estados*, where he plainly states that war against Iberian Muslims is justified, because they

> se apoderaron de muchas tierras et avn tomaron muchas et tienen las hoy en dia, de·las que eran de los christianos que fueron conuertidos por los apostoles a·la fe de Ihesu Christo. Et por esto, a guerra entre los christianos et los moros, et abra fasta que ayan cobrado los christianos las tierras que·los moros les tienen forçadas. (1: 248)

> (assumed control, and even conquered many lands and hold them to this day, lands that used to belong to the Christians who were converted by the Apostles to the faith of Jesus Christ. And for this reason, there is war between Christians and Muslims, and will be until the Christians have recuperated the lands that the Muslims took from them by force.)

While these words of Juan Manuel are typical of the ideology of Reconquest, the reality of fourteenth-century frontier Castile in which he lived is far more complex and has more to do with politics than with religion.

In broad strokes, the political gamesmanship of frontier Castile during the fourteenth century was not much different from contemporary territorial struggles elsewhere in Western Europe.[17] The relative internal political stability afforded by the emergence of the nation state was still centuries in the future, and the prevalent political model was that of a balancing act between a monarch whose power fluctuated according to his or her fortunes, pitted not only against neighboring kingdoms but also against the domestic nobility. In Spain, Christian and Muslim monarchs were engaged in a continuous process of negotiating their territorial borders and political allegiances (Linehan, *History* 506–59). This held equally true for relations between Castile-Leon and Aragon as it did for those between Castile-Leon

at Georgetown University: "The problem Spain has with Al Qaeda and Islamic terrorism did not begin with the Iraq Crisis. In fact, it has nothing to do with government decisions. You must go back no less than 1,300 years, to the early eighth century, when a Spain recently invaded by the Moors refused to become just another piece in the Islamic world and began a long battle to recover its identity. This *Reconquista* process was very long, lasting some 800 years. However, it ended successfully."

[17] For example, during this time France had their own Granada in England, with whom they were engaged in the 100 years' war. French internal politics was characterized by the same struggle between nobility and crown that obtained in Spain (M. Jones). In Italy, the disunity and discord following the death of Frederick II of Hohenstaufen gave way to a scene of competing city states ruled by tyrannical dictators, papal states cutting a swath across the center of the peninsula, and a 90 years' war with the southern Kingdom of Sicily that was as devastating as France's with England (C. Duggan 46; Hearder and Morris 72–88; Larner 38–46).

and Granada.[18] Within Castile itself, the fourteenth century was particularly conflictive for the crown and nobility, a time of political strife, social upheaval, and economic depression (Valdeón Baruque, Salrach i Marés and Zabalo Zabalegui 54–81; Macpherson and Tate 30). Juan Manuel himself describes this period as a "doloroso et triste tienpo" ('doleful and sad time') (1: 208).

This is the political reality against which one must read the ideological discourse of the Reconquest. In twelfth- and thirteenth-century Castile-Leon, war against Islam provided a convenient pretense and rhetorical repertory for southward territorial expansion into al-Andalus.[19] When Christian fought Christian, wartime rhetoric hinged on honor, lineage, and historical right. When Christian fought Muslim, such nuances were conveniently replaced by the rubric of religious crusade. Christian-Muslim political antagonism in the Iberian Peninsula also resonated with the European crusades in the Middle East, whether Iberian monarchs sought to enlist the support of fellow Christians for campaigns against Muslim leaders or to excuse themselves from participating in foreign crusades, claiming the need to devote those resources to the "crusades at home." In fact, Spanish monarchs received many papal bulls institutionalizing the Reconquest as a crusade in the doctrinal sense (García-Serrano 14–16; Goñí Gaztambide; O'Callaghan, *Reconquest* 22). The religious rhetoric of the Reconquest addressed two perceived wrongs: the continued presence of Islam as a political power in the Iberian Peninsula and the persistence of Judaism and Islam as personal religions among subjects of Christian monarchs. While Catholic clerics, most frequently members of the Dominican order, were quite active in operationalizing the spiritual agenda of the Reconquest (Lawrence 15), men like Juan Manuel were active in its military and political aspects.

Juan Manuel's views of Islam as a religion are predictably in line with the prevailing religious polemical discourse of his day: it is a Christian duty to struggle against Islam on the Iberian Peninsula. In the prologue to *CL*,

---

[18] For example, in a letter dated January 1314, Nāṣir I of Granada describes the "amor bueno e leal e uerdadero" ('good and loyal and true love') that he has for Jaume II of Aragon. Only four months later, Jaume complains that Granadan troops are en route to attack him (thanks to none other than Juan Manuel) (Giménez Soler, *Juan Manuel* 445, no. 295 and 463–64, no. 320). There are many such examples in Juan Manuel's correspondence that portray a Castile defined by unstable borders and continuously shifting alliances between Castile, Aragon, and Granada. See also Maravall (*Concepto* 285).

[19] The occasional and transitory political and military alliances that were the basic building blocks of feudal politics were distinguished in Spain by being sporadically framed in terms of religious conflict when it was convenient to do so (O'Callaghan, *Reconquest* 20).

Patronio explains to the Count Lucanor his duty as a Christian nobleman to engage in armed struggle against the Muslim "occupiers" of the Iberian Peninsula. Upon this duty rest one's salvation and reputation:

> ...Dios vos poblo en tierra quel podades seruir contra los moros, tan bien por mar commo por tierra, fazet vuestro poder por que seades seguro de·lo que dexades en vuestra tierra.... Et faziendo esto, tengo que esta es la meior manera que vos podedes tomar para saluar el alma, guardando vuestro estado et vuestra onra. Et deuedes creer que por estar en seruicio de Dios non morredes ante, nin biuredes mas por estar en vuestra tierra. Et si murieredes en seruicio de Dios, biuiendo en la manera que vos yo he dicho, seredes martir et muy bien auenturado, et avn que non murades por armas, la buena voluntad et las buenas obras vos faran martir, et avn los que mal quisieren dezir, no podrian. (2: 58–59)
>
> (God has given you towns in the land so that you might serve him against the Moors, by land as well as by sea, exercise your power so that you may be sure of what legacy you leave in your land.... And in doing this, I hold that this is the best way to save your soul, defending your station and your honor. And you must believe that by being in the service of God you will not die any sooner; neither will you live longer by staying on your lands. And should you die in the service of God, living in the manner of which I have told you, you will be a martyr and very blessed, and even if you do not die in battle, your good intentions and good works will make you a martyr, and even those who might wish to speak ill of you, will not be able to.)

Patronio's words describe the Reconquest as a Christian Iberian struggle against Muslim Granada. The martyrdom he promises for those who engage in this struggle is not limited to those who die in battle but extends even to those whose "good intentions" support the cause. Patronio here describes the Reconquest mentality that underpins Juan Manuel's narrative: 'your purpose in life is to expel the Muslims from Iberian soil, and your salvation depends on the extent to which your thoughts and deeds are dedicated to this end.'[20] Patronio again reminds the *Conde* in *exemplo* 33 of his duty to wage war continuously against the Muslims:

> Segund el vuestro estado que vos tenedes, non le podedes tanto seruir commo en aver guerra con los moros por ençalçar la sancta e verdadera fe catolica, consejo vos yo que luego que podades seer seguro de·las otras partes, que ayades guerra con los moros. (2: 123–26)

---

[20] On the Reconquest as a "creencia de pura inspiración islámica" ('belief of pure Islamic inspiration') and a direct imitation of the Islamic concept of *jihād*, see Castro (*España* 198 and *Realidad* 419–29).

> (According to your station, there is no greater way for you to serve God than to wage war against the Moors to exalt the true holy Catholic faith, I advise you that once your other borders are secure, you should wage war against the Moors.)

This ideology of Reconquest is attested throughout the *CL*. *Exemplo* 15 describes the siege of Muslim Seville by Fernando III and the contest of bravery between three knights who taunt the besieged defenders by touching their lances to the city's gates. In *exemplo* 28, the protagonist Lorenzo Suarez Gallinato lives in Granada amongst the Muslims. In that city, a renegade priest who has converted to Islam stages a bogus mass in order to hand the consecrated host over to the Muslim crowd, who then abuse it. Don Lorenço intercedes, killing the transgressive priest and defending himself against the crowd of Muslims, now enraged for having been deprived of the host that they had been desecrating with gusto (2: 246–48). Finally, Fernán González, iconic figure of the Castilian Reconquest and protagonist of the thirteenth-century *Poema de Fernán González*, is depicted quite anachronistically as defeating Almanzor[21] in *exemplo* 37 (2: 305–06).

In addition to having his characters voice and enact Reconquest ideology, Juan Manuel describes Islam as a false religion through which one cannot achieve salvation: "En ninguna ley que sea dada nin sea natural non se pueden saluar las almas al tienpo de agora sinon en·la ley de·los christianos" (1: 241) ('under no law, given or natural, it is possible to save one's soul in this time except under the law of the Christians'). In his view Islam is incompatible with the spiritual goals of Christianity, and any Islamic government is illegitimate. It would then follow that Reconquest, the elimination of Islamic religion and political power, is the sacred duty of every Christian nobleman.

Dominicans and Reconquest

The Reconquest was conceived as a battle for both the bodies and souls of conquered Andalusī Muslims. Christian noblemen such as Don Juan Manuel occupied themselves with the worldly tasks of military conquest and colonial administration; the Order of Preaching Friars Dominican (Cast. *frailes*

[21] He is Abū ʿĀmīr ibn Muḥammad ibn ʿAbdallāh ibn Muḥammad ibn Abī ʿĀmīr al-Maʿarīfī (938–1002), known as al-Manṣūr bi'llāh ('he who is made victorous by God'). He ruled al-Andalus from 978 until his death in 1002 as *de facto* monarch, though acting officially in the office of *ḥājib* (i.e., chamberlain) during the minority of Hišām II. He was responsible for a series of devastating campaigns into Christian territory and is most notorious (in Spain) for having sacked the Cathedral at Santiago de Compostela in 997 (*EI*, "al-Manṣūr bi'llāh").

predicadores dominicanos) saw to the souls of the conquered *mudéjares* and Jews. The Dominicans' primary mission was to preach to the unconverted, be they Christian, Jew, or Muslim. Perhaps not coincidentally, the apogee of the Christian conquest of al-Andalus is coetaneous with the rise of the mendicant preaching orders, important actors in the cultural landscape of Reconquest Spain. The 1220s saw the establishment of Franciscan missions in Portugal and Spain, and the Dominicans raised a convent in Cordova in 1236, the same year it was won from the Muslims (Lawrence 15). According to tradition, Fernando III rode into newly conquered Seville (1248) in the company of two Dominican friars. In Aragon, a Dominican (and companion of St. Dominic), Miquel Fabra, aided King Jaume I in the conquest of Mallorca and was charged with preaching Christianity to its subject Muslim population (García-Serrano 13).

During the thirteenth and fourteenth centuries, the increasing importance of towns and the development of a merchant class fostered the rise of both the Franciscans and Dominicans. The mendicant orders thrived in cities, which offered twin attractions: a population of wealthy merchants and petty nobility (*caballeros villanos*) who could offer financial support to the orders, and significant populations of Jews, who might be converted by the friars. The Dominican order also provided opportunities for educated laypeople to participate more actively in religious life without isolating themselves as cloistered monks. They established schools to certify lay preachers, who would then have permission to preach in their district. The friars' original aim was to devote themselves to ministering to the poor denizens of an increasingly urban population. Eventually, the orders became powerful institutions that mediated between nobles like Juan Manuel, the Church, and the Crown (García-Serrano 15–25; Lawrence 120).

It should not be surprising, therefore, that a man such as Juan Manuel should have strong ties with the Dominican order. His title of *Adelantado de la frontera de Murcia* ('Governor of the Frontier of Murcia') made him one of the key political players of the fourteenth-century frontier with Granada, and his considerable political clout as the highest ranking Castilian nobleman of his time made him a natural ally of the preaching friars against the crown. His devotion to the order is most clearly evident in his construction of the Dominican monastery at Peñafiel, where he also deposited the autograph manuscript of his complete works.[22]

[22] In the prologue to the *Conde Lucanor*, Juan Manuel invites readers to check their copies against the autograph manuscript housed in the Dominican monastery at Peñafiel (2: 23).

Dominican Preaching and Castilian Literature

In order to reach the commoners, the Dominicans knew they would have to speak their "language," which meant preaching in the vernacular as well as adopting popular forms of narrative. The *exemplum*, or exemplary tale, was an important tool in their vernacular homiletic practice. Dominican friars made regular use of popular hagiographic and secular narrative to illustrate their sermons. To this end, they were the first Europeans to compile systematically organized collections of *exempla*, arranged according to the latest innovations in indexical technology.[23] In Spain, the Franciscan and Dominican orders placed a strong emphasis on preaching, which implied an increased use of the vernacular in sermons (especially those directed to lay people) (Zink 85–91; Martin 560–65; Bataillon 23). The vernacular sermon was pioneered by the Dominican friars as the surest way of delivering their message to the common folk, who were their target audience.[24] Despite their generally extemporaneous nature, such sermons were not totally improvised. Preachers made heavy use of exemplary tales—*exempla*—to structure the sermons, as well as to win the attention of their uneducated audiences. Dominican writers, with their emphasis on education and orderly classification, produced several collections of such *exempla*.[25]

Juan Manuel's association with the Dominicans left its mark on his work, in the dogmatic tenor of his prose, his selection of narrative material, and in the work's structure. Their influence is most evident in his popular, almost colloquial tone. Due to their commitment to vernacular preaching, to reaching the common people in their habitual environments, the Dominicans preached in the open air, in marketplaces and fields, placing their preachers and thinkers directly into the fabric of daily life, or, to use Juan Manuel's words, in the middle of "las cosas que acaesçieron" ('the things that happened,' i.e., daily life) (2:23). This focus on the mundane is evident in the

[23] During the thirteenth century, Cistercians, Dominicans, and Franciscans developed research tools such as the concordance, the alphabetical index, and tables of content, primarily for use in composing sermons. Already by 1230, the Dominicans had begun work on a verbal concordance of the Bible and were involved in the indexing of biblical texts (Rouse and Rouse 214–15, 239, and 248).

[24] "These [largely illiterate] audiences responded far better to local narratives and parables applicable to their own life situations than they would to official Latin mandates from the official clergy" (Lawless 54).

[25] See, for example the *Speculum laicorum, Tabula exemplorum*, Vincent of Beauvais, and Jacob of Voragine. In Catalan, see the *Recull de eximplis e miracles, gestes e faules e altres ligendes ordenades per A-B-C*. On the use of *exempla* in preaching, see Berlioz, and Berlioz and Polo.

prologue to the *CL*, where the author delineates his approach to realistic detail. In his *ejemplos*, he maintains, he offers a mirror of daily life, of the diversity of human experience. Everyone will be able to relate to what is narrated within, "e seria marauilla si de qual quier cosa que acaezca a·qual quier omne, non fallare en este libro su semejança que acaesçio a otro" ('and it would be a marvel that of all the things that might happen to any given man, that one might not find in this book a similar instance of it happening to another') (2: 23). Juan Manuel purports to offer his readers real-life experiences for the edification of Castilian audiences. This is not to say that *exempla* accurately illustrate daily life as experienced by the audience; rather, they are calculated to appeal to that audience and engage with it on its own terms, using types, events, and symbols with which it will be familiar and which will have meaning for it. Mark Johnston has challenged traditional scholarship's understanding of *exempla* as "illustrative of everyday life":

> Perhaps the charm of quotidian detail included in certain *exempla* will always discourage us from recognizing that those details are not necessarily meaningful in themselves, but "make sense" thanks to many other factors, such as the principle of decorum that urges the match of material to audience, and all the social, esthetic, or cultural distinctions that this principle assumes. Perhaps we value such *exempla* because they allow us to mediate the seemingly unreconcilable functions of "telling stories" and "presenting facts" that we demand of historical scholarship.

Therefore, the "realistic detail" so much lauded in the *ejemplos* of Juan Manuel may be constructed from bits of reality recognizable to the audience; but the mosaic they form does not necessarily resemble that of their own lives.[26] This method of appealing to the audience is drawn from the training received by Dominican preachers. Handbooks of preaching emphasize the importance of *decorum*, of tailoring the mode of discourse to fit the intended audience.[27]

Through their preaching, the mendicant orders contributed to the development of the literary vernacular, and more specifically to the development of the frametale in medieval Iberia. Juan Manuel demonstrated a moral and intellectual affiliation with Dominican thought—the order was the wellspring

---

[26] Several critics count Juan Manuel's ability to faithfully recreate reality as one of his best qualities as a writer. See, for example, Steiger (7–8), Ayerbe-Chaux (xvi–vii) and Menéndez y Pelayo (156).

[27] "The preacher should, moreover, exercise prudence, varying his sermons according to the type of his hearer" (Humbert of Romans 44). They should also tailor their content to fit the intended audience, with specific modifications for preaching to the youth, the poor, the rich, soldiers, the learned, clergy, nobles and royalty, married people, or virgins (Alain of Lille 146–49).

of his intellectual personality. Indeed, Peñafiel is his intellectual center both metaphorically and concretely: it is there where he deposited the autograph manuscript of his works. In the prologue to the *CL*, Juan Manuel explains that those readers who question the readings in their copies of his writings may refer to the originals kept there:

> A los que leyeren qualquier libro que fuere trasladado del que él compuso, o de los libros que él fizo, que si fallaren alguna palabra mal puesta, que non pongan la culpa a él, fasta que bean el libro mismo que don Johan fizo, que es emendado, en muchos logares, de su letra... E estos libros están en 'l monasterio de los fraires predicadores que él fizo en Peñafiel. (2: 23)
>
> (To those of you who read copies of any of the books that he wrote, if you should find a poorly copied word, do not blame him until you see the very same book that Don Juan wrote, which is emended, in many places, in his hand... And these books are in the monastery of the Preaching Friars that he built in Peñafiel.)

Given Juan Manuel's relationship with the Dominicans, it is logical that his work would bear their intellectual influence. Diego Marín suggests that Juan Manuel was personally familiar with the collections of *exempla* by members of the mendicant orders, particularly those of the Dominicans Jacob of Voragine (d. 1298; *Legenda aurea*) and Vincent of Beauvais (d. 1264; *Speculum maius*). Marín notes that Vincent himself sent a copy of his work to Alfonso X, who made use of it in *Las siete partidas* and the *General estoria*. At the same time, Marín admits that Don Juan Manuel might have become familiar with the *exempla* found in these collections not by reading them, but by having heard them in sermons given by Dominican friars (3–6). This supposition is borne out by Macpherson's comments on the colloquial nature of Juan Manuel's written discourse (2–6)—it is plausible that if his exposure to the narrative material of *exempla* was through oral diffusion, aspects of this mode of transmission would carry over into his adaptation of it.[28]

A good measure of content of the *CL* can be traced to Dominican sources. Overall, nine of the 51 *exempla* (nos. 3, 4, 14, 28, 31, 40, 42, 45, and 51) in the *CL* treat specifically religious themes. While that does not qualify the work as a collection of religious *exempla* such as the Catalan *Recull d'eximplis*, which is comprised of an overwhelming majority of religious *exempla*, it is a significant portion, especially when compared with the almost completely secular *Calila e Dimna*. According to the sources cited by Ayerbe-Chaux,

---

[28] On the question of orality in the *Conde Lucanor* and other works by Don Juan Manuel, see Biglieri, Seniff ("Así" and "Orality"), and Gerli.

thirteen of the fifty *exempla* of the *CL* are found in the collection of Jacques de Vitry and nine of these also appear in that of Etienne de Bourbon. A handful of others are found in the works of Vincent of Beauvais, Jacob of Voragine, the *Tabula exemplorum*, and the *Speculum laicorum*.[29]

Perhaps more importantly, the very structure of the *CL* is influenced by the Dominicans' methods and mentality. In Juan Manuel's adaptation of the frametale genre, the pragmatic (and essentially non-sectarian) moral orientation[30] and open structure of *Calila* comes into contact with the undeniably Christian moral universe and regular organization of the *CL*. Katharine Gittes has observed that the structure of a frametale is representative of the mindset of the culture that produces it. Therefore, the Sanskrit *Panchatantra* is characterized by the hypotactic (closed) thinking characteristic of Sanskrit culture, while its Arabic counterpart, *Kalīla wa-Dimna*, is characterized by a paratactic (open) structure identified with Islamic thought (Gittes 9 and 17). We would extend this idea to include the *CL*: its methodical organization and scholastic approach to framing the tales and to summarizing their didactic value owes much to the encyclopedic organization of collections of *exempla* authored by Dominicans.[31]

The key concepts in the difference of organization between *Calila* and the *CL* are clarity and regularity. The *mise-en-abîme* structure of *Calila*, with one tale nested within another, is replaced by the very clear-cut, repetitive, and closed structure of the *CL*, in which each *exemplo* stands alone and is not subordinated to the narrative of the frame story. Count Lucanor relates a situation in which he is involved (making no specific reference to previous situations), Patronio offers advice couched in an *exemplo*, and Juan Manuel garnishes the exchange with his *viesso* (summary couplet), distilling Patronio's advice in somewhat wooden verse. There is no confusion as to who is speaking and to what purpose.

---

[29] For a complete discussion of medieval collections of *exempla*, see Welter (*L'exemplum*).

[30] Within the ethical system of *Calila e Dimna*, "the tales urge application of knowledge to useful ends. The fables cited in support of theoretical arguments demonstrate the effectiveness or non-effectiveness of enunciated principles as tested by actual experience" (Parker 66).

[31] For example, the *Legenda aurea* of the Italian Dominican Jacob of Voragine (d. 1298) is ordered by the name of the saint protagonist of each *exemplum* (*Racconti* 2: 24–25). The anonymous *Tabula exemplorum secundum ordinem alphabeti*, compiled by a late thirteenth-century Dominican or Franciscan in Paris, is arranged alphabetically by the theme of each *exemplum* (Welter, "Introduction" xi–xii). Somewhat later than Don Juan Manuel, at the beginning of the fifteenth century, Filippo degli Agazzari compiles his *Assempri* numerically (*Racconti* 3: 280–81).

This clear-cut style of classification is characteristic of the Aristotelian idea that the world is ordered according to divine will (Soellner 53–55). There is a deliberate scheme to God's creation, and the scheme is meaningful. It is an expansion of the idea that each natural phenomenon is a rubric for some aspect of divinity. Juan Manuel's frame is informed by this very sensibility; MacPherson notes that "he considers clarity, concision, and completeness as the virtues for which he would like posterity to admire him" (9). This need for clarity, stressed by Dominican authors of manuals of rhetoric and preaching technique, is mirrored in Juan Manuel's carefully explicit titles for each of his *exemplos*. This attention to classification is brought into sharp relief when we compare the organization of the *CL* with that of *Calila*.

Calila is divided by Ibn al-Muqaffaʿ into eighteen chapters and an introduction, all of which are rubricated (according to the edition of the Castilian text by Cacho Blecua and Lacarra and that of the Arabic by Cheikho) far less regularly than those of the *CL*. Of these nineteen sections, twelve contain nested tales that are not indicated in the chapter title. For example, chapter three is titled, simply, "Del león et del buey," but contains nineteen nested tales that are told by characters within the tale indicated by the chapter title. Other chapters are similarly titled, such as chapter one, "Estoria de Berzebuey el menge," chapter six, "De los cuervos et de los búos," and chapter nine, "Del gato et del mur." The text does not display a need to identify the content of each tale to the reader before the tale is read. Rather, the nested structure is part of the play of reading, a way simultaneously to engage and reward the reader by keeping him slightly in the dark, alternating the techniques of *amplificatio* and *abbreviatio*.[32]

By contrast, Juan Manuel's numbering and identification of his *exemplos* is perfectly regular. Each *exemplo* is numbered and glossed by a subtitle identifying the main characters and often containing a subordinate clause describing a character or its actions, as in "Exemplo VI: De lo que contesçio a·la golondrina con las otras aves quando vio sembrar el lino" ('*Exemplo* VI: What happened to the sparrow with the other birds when it saw the linen being sowed.') (2: 77). The *CL* is also unique in that its characters are sometimes given personal names (often historical) that are reflected in the chapter headings, such as in "Exemplo XIV: Del miraglo que fizo sancto Domingo quando predicó sobre el logrero" ('*Exemplo* XIV: Of the miracle performed by Saint Dominic when he preached about the usurer'). The

[32] These techniques are well known to have been studied and taught by medieval rhetoricians. See, for example Geoffrey of Vinsauf (45–59).

frame characters, Patronio and Conde Lucanor, are not referred to in the table of contents, which amount to a simple inventory of the fifty *exemplos* identified by theme.

It is clear from the structure of the *CL* that Juan Manuel places a high priority on organization. Peter Dunn has commented that Juan Manuel's faith in organization imbued his arrangement of the *exemplos* and that the act of writing itself could provide a sense of order in a chaotic world, that narrative can "impose order upon the unruly world of human action" (Dunn, "Framing" 96). The scholastic sense of hierarchy and subordination inherited from the Dominicans comes through quite clearly in the organization of the *CL*. They also shaped the text of the *CL* in a way that distinguishes it from the frametales *Calila* and *Sendebar*, in which the *exempla* are subordinated thematically to the plot of the frame story. This structural synthesis of scholastic handbook and frametale, unique to the *CL*, is the framework upon which Juan Manuel assembles his frontier narrative. Within this same structure, the interpolated tales told by Patronio resist this narrative, reproducing in literary microcosm the intertwined legacies of conqueror and conquered that defined the cultural life of the frontier kingdoms of Castile-Leon and Aragon during the fourteenth century.

Juan Manuel and Andalusī Culture

Despite his clear condemnation of Islam, as a Christian of Reconquest-era Spain, Juan Manuel is at the same time quite approving, if not plainly covetous, of Andalusī technology, learning, and popular culture. In the *Libro de los estados* (ch. 76) his appreciation of Andalusī military prowess is unapologetic:

> Qvando an de conbatir algun lugar, comiençan lo fuerte et muy espantosa mente, et quando son conbatidos, comiençanse a·se defender muy bien a·grant marabilla; [et] quando vienen a·la lid, vienen tan reçios et tan espantosa mente, que son pocos los que non an ende muy grant reçelo. (1: 346–47)
>
> (When they attack, they do so fiercely and terrifyingly, and when they are attacked, they begin to defend themselves marvelously; when they join battle, they do so so ferociously and frighteningly, that there are few who are not very afraid.)

In fact, claims Juan Manuel, Muslim troops are so effective, that "mas tierra correran et mayor danno faran et mayor caualgada ayuntaran dozientos omnes de cauallo de moros que seyçientos omnes de cauallo de christianos" ('two hundred Moorish knights will cover more ground and do more damage and organize a more effective raid than will six hundred Christian knights') (1: 346).

Juan Manuel demonstrates a similar admiration for Andalusī narrative practice in his adoption of the frametale genre and in the inclusion of several Andalusī tales and proverbs in the *CL*. In this affinity, he follows the lead of his uncle Alfonso X, who commissioned the translation of numerous works of Arabic literature into Castilian, including the frametale *Kalīla wa-Dimna*, which along with *Sendebar* served as a model for Juan Manuel.

In his adaptation of tales of Andalusī origin, Juan Manuel is a pioneer in vernacular Romance literature. Other medieval authors made ample use of Eastern tales,[33] but Juan Manuel is unique in that he reproduces historical anecdotes from Andalusī tradition.

Part of colonizing a people is appropriating and cultivating their cultural forms.[34] In modernity, British and French colonial architects made a conscious effort to recast traditional indigenous architectural styles in the modern colonial cityscape as a way of appropriating the cultural authority of the traditional built environment (Chattopadhyay; Wright 9). Juan Manuel's appropriation and recasting of the frametale structure is a literary analogue of this process on both the structural and narratological levels. He appropriates the frametale genre from Andalusī literature and includes in his work three *exemplos* originating from Andalusī anecdotal proverbs (nos. 30, 41, and 47) which Juan Manuel quotes phonetically, then translates into Castilian (2: 257–59, 324–36, and 389–91). This suggests that his intended audience would include people who had at least some knowledge of Andalusī colloquial Arabic, even if they were not native speakers. In light of his liberal use of Arabic source material, there has been a good deal of scholarly speculation as to whether or not, or to what degree, Juan Manuel knew Arabic.

---

[33] While much Arabic narrative material had been made available to readers of Castilian by the translations of both *Calila e Dimna* (1251) and *Sendebar* (1253), these are not original in Castilian, do not refer to Castilian people or locations, and do not qualify in the same sense as original works of Castilian literature. Many other such tales had previously achieved wide diffusion by their inclusion in Petrus Alfonsi's *Disciplina clericalis* (Alvárez, "Petrus" 289; Tolan, *Petrus Alfonsi* 74). The anonymous *Libro del caballero Zifar* (late thirteenth century) contains a handful of tales from Eastern tradition (Hernández Valcárcel), as does the *Libro de buen amor* of Juan Ruiz (mid-fourteenth century) (Michael). Also, Ramón Llull included a paraphrased selection of tales from the Arabic *Kalīla wa-Dimna* in his *Llibre de les bèsties*, intercalated into his larger work *Llibre de meravelles*.

[34] On this problem in light of the contested meaning of the term "mudéjar," see Dodds ("Mudejar" 113–14).

Spanish scholars of the late nineteenth and early twentieth century such as Pascual de Gayangos, José Antonio Conde, Marcelino Menéndez Pelayo, and Angel González Palencia were in agreement that Juan Manuel could at least speak and understand some colloquial Andalusī Arabic, even if he were not literate in Classical Arabic. More recently, Juan Vernet (cited in Hitchcock 594–95) has asserted that Juan Manuel most probably spoke colloquial Andalusī Arabic. Richard Hitchcock maintains that Juan Manuel probably relied on written sources for the Andalusī anecdotes reproduced in the *CL*, but as a mere "occasional reader of Castilian" himself, it is highly unlikely that the author was able to read Arabic and probably had the anecdotes read and translated for him, as was his habit with Castilian texts (Macpherson 8–9; Hitchcock 597).

Regardless of his degree of proficiency in Arabic, he evidently believed that his audience would appreciate reading and hearing these anecdotal proverbs in the original. What most concerns us here is *why* he decided to include them. Juan Manuel's use of Andalusī narrative material (anecdotes and tales), and more specifically his use of the Arabic language itself, is meant to inject a bit of authority derived from the prestigious cultural legacy of al-Andalus. Structurally, Juan Manuel's use of Arabic is analogous to the homiletic function of a citation of Latin scripture (*thema*) in a sermon (Charland 136–49). A verse of Latin scripture authorizes, and serves as the thematic base of, a sermon. While it is not necessarily expected that the (probably illiterate) audience of the sermon understands the Latin, the sound vision of the language of scripture lends authority to the sermon which is based on it. In Don Juan Manuel's case, his use of Arabic language and Andalusī narrative material invokes the cultural authority of the Andalusī Caliphate (and later *Taifa* kingdoms) populated by the protagonists of his *exempla*. That is, he is borrowing from the nostalgic prestige of the al-Andalus of popular memory. In doing so, he is laying claim to the historical legacy of the al-Andalus colonized by his grandparents' generation.[35]

[35] Devoto argues that Juan Manuel is a proto-orientalist who prefigures the *maurofilia* of the sixteenth century and purposefully imbues his *exemplos* with "Arabic atmosphere" (433). Hanlon argues that stereotypes of Muslim figures in texts written by Castilian Christians reflected "anxiety on a cultural level about the ambiguous status of the Mudejar, of the Muslim as a subject to be governed within the frontiers of Castile and León" ("Islam" 479).

Don Juan Manuel's al-Andalus

As firm as he may be in his condemnation of Islam as a religion, Juan Manuel is quite ambivalent in the representation of Andalusīs and what he seems to perceive as Andalusī culture.[36] In broad terms, he portrays his Andalusī characters as decadent materialists, which points to a justification of the Reconquest as unseating a corrupt Islamic dynasty unfit to rule on grounds both theological and moral. David Hanlon has written that these stereotypes were "necessarily ambivalent forms of knowledge that justify a social hierarchy maintaining Mudejar subjects in positions of subordination" ("Islam" 480). I hold both to be true, and that stereotypes of Muslim characters in the *CL* served the double purpose of justifying the Castilian-Aragonese conquest of al-Andalus and the medieval colonialism that was its legacy.

As we have seen above, Juan Manuel held that Christianity is the sole path to salvation. It then follows that Islamic political rule is inherently morally corrupt. A survey of the behavior of Andalusī characters in the *CL* bears out this notion of Muslims as decadent materialists with skewed moral priorities. The two Andalusī monarchs, Alhaquem[37] and Abenabad,[38] are respectively portrayed as effete, frivolous, and inattentive to political matters (Alhaquem), or uxorious and indulgent (Abenabad). This decadence, coupled with the manifest religious error of Islam, justifies the Christian conquests of Seville (Abenabad) and Cordova (Alhaquem) in the previous century.[39] According to Juan Manuel, though the Andalusīs enjoyed a superior material culture, they were morally corrupt and politically inept, shortcomings that explain their defeat at the hands of Christian monarchs such as Fernando III and Jaime I of Aragon.

Non-historical and nameless Muslim characters are characterized as merely unscrupulous seekers of wealth. One is a young man who purposefully contracts a loveless but financially beneficial marriage and intimidates his new

---

[36] On the representation of Muslims in the writing of Juan Manuel, see Caldera.

[37] Alhaquem is al-Ḥakam II of Cordova, whose addition was indeed built during the years 962–966. He is protagonist of *Exemplo* no. 41 (2: 324–36).

[38] Abenabad is Muḥammad ibn ʿAbbād, known as al-Muʿtamid, who ruled Seville from 1069 to 1090. In 1071, he annexed Cordova into his kingdom, which explains the setting of this *exemplo*. He was ultimately deposed and sent into exile in Morocco by the Almoravid Yūsuf b. Tashūfīn (the "Rey Yúçef" of the *Cantar de Mio Cid*), who had originally come to al-Andalus to aid al-Muʿtamid against the Christians (*EI*, "Abbadids"). He is protagonist of *Exemplo* 30 (2: 257–59).

[39] Cordova (1236) and Seville (1248) were conquered by Fernando III ("el Santo") of Castile-Leon (Payne 1: 73).

bride with a display of brutal violence.[40] The other two are a brother-sister team of cowardly grave robbers who give no thought to mutilating the corpses of those whose tombs they raid.[41] In these *exemplos* featuring non-historical characters, Juan Manuel signals to his audience that the protagonists are indeed *moros* and that he has drawn the tale from Andalusī tradition with which he was so familiar. This is another way in which he demonstrates his knowledge of Andalusī culture and reinforces his authority as *Adelantado de la frontera* (Lida de Malkiel, "Tres notas" 155–94).

Juan Manuel's inconsistent relationship with Islam and Andalusī culture, demonstrated in his treatment of Andalusī Muslim characters, is amplified by his choice of literary genre. The structure of the frametale often highlights the discrepancy between the stated didactic intent of the author and the apparent message of the interpolated tale.[42] The two characters whose conversation provides the pretext for the work's 50 *exemplos* enjoy a relationship in which the power dynamic is clear: the *Conde* is the master, Patronio is his advisor and servant. One would suppose that Patronio's advice, illustrated by the 50 *exemplos* he relates, would serve his master's interests. Yet a closer examination of individual tales often reveals that Patronio's advice is not necessarily borne out by his *exemplos*. Quite often, the *exemplos* are only loosely illustrative of moral or object lessons explicitly stated by Juan Manuel in the *viessos* or couplets he furnishes at the end of each tale. Thus, the frametale genre is didactically unstable, which makes it better suited for conveying the experience of socio-political instability and cultural ambiguity than for communicating an ideologically consistent narrative. Juan Manuel's explicit didactic program, distilled in the *viessos* (couplets) in which Juan Manuel summarizes each *exemplo*, often seems to be at odds with the actions and words of the tales' protagonists. Part of this effect is the result of the opposite pulls of literary creativity and didactic intent: for every picture there

[40] The ever-popular *Exemplo* 35, "De·lo que contesçio a·vn mançebo que caso con vna muger muy fuerte et muy braua" ('Of what happened to a youth who married a very strong and fierce woman') (2: 285–89). On this tale in Arab tradition, see Wallhead Munuera (101–17) and El-Shamy (559–60).

[41] *Exemplo* 47, "De·lo que contesçio a·vn moro con vna su hermana que daua a entender que era muy medrosa" ('Of what happened to a Moor with his sister who made one think that she was fearful') (2: 389–91). On this tale and its relation to Andalusī oral tradition, see Monroe ("Salmà").

[42] In general terms, the open-ended and often ambiguous didacticism of the *Conde Lucanor* was owed in part to the vernacular, oral discourse of Dominican preaching (Lida de Malkiel, "Tres notas" 157). Menocal has noted that the *viessos* "are always grossly reductive and often have little to do with the story that has been told" ("Life" 487). On ambiguity in the *Conde Lucanor*, see de Looze ("Subversion") and England.

is a nearly infinite number of potentially suitable captions. Yet in another way, the dissonance between the aphorisms and *exemplos* of Juan Manuel is a literary reflection of the contradictions between the religious discourse of the Reconquest and its cultural reality.

Juan Manuel's "border thinking," evident in the tension between his explicit didactic message and the more ambiguous lesson that can be read in his narrative prose, comes through most clearly in two *exemplos* that deal with figures drawn from Andalusī history. The first of these is *exemplo* 30, "De lo que contesçió al rey Abenabet de Seuilla con Ramayquía, su muger" ('What happened to King Abenabet of Seville with his wife Ramayquía') (2: 257–59). In it, Abenabet is portrayed as an indulgent husband who eventually must chastise his wife for her ungrateful behavior. First, in Cordova she witnesses a freak snowstorm and is saddened at the thought of never being able to see snow on a regular basis. Abenabet then orders the planting of thousands of white-blossoming almond trees throughout the sierra of Cordova, so that every February Ramayquía might be reminded of snow by the sight of the almond trees in bloom. Her next request is met with an even greater display of indulgence. From her window, she sees women making adobe bricks by the river and wishes to do the same. Not about to let his queen muddy herself, but anxious to fulfill her whim,

> mando el rey fenchir de agua rosada aquella grand albuhera[43] de Cordoua en logar de agua, et en lugar de tierra, fizo la fenchir de açucar et de canela et de gengibre et espic et clavos et musgo et ambra et algalina, et de todas buenas espeçias et buenos olores que pudian seer; et en lugar de paia, fizo poner cannas de açucar. Et desque destas cosas fue llena el albuhera de tal lodo qual entendedes que podria seer, dixo el rey a·Ramayquia que se descalçase et que follase aquel lodo et que fiziesse adobes del quantos quisiesse.
>
> Otro dia, por otra cosas que se le antojo, començo a·llorar; et el rey preguntole por que lo fazia.
>
> Et ell dixol que commo non lloraria, que nunca fiziera el rey cosa por le fazer plazer. Et el rey veyendo que pues tanto avia fecho por le fazer plazer et conplir su talante, et que ya non sabia que pudiesse fazer mas, dixol vna palabra que se dize en·el algarauia desta guisa: "v. a. le mahar aten?", et quiere dezir: "¿Et non el dia del lodo?", commo diziendo que pues las otras cosas oluidada, que non deuia oluidar el lodo que fiziera por le fazer plazer. (2: 258)[44]

---

[43] Note that Juan Manuel here uses the Arabic word *buḥayra* (lake, pond, lagoon), the diminutive form of *baḥr* (sea), with the meaning of (an artificial) 'pool' or 'pond'. This usage persists in the Valencian and Mallorcan proper names for (natural) lagoons known respectively as *La albufera* and *S'albufera*.

[44] This anecdotal proverb appears in the late thirteenth-century collection of Andalusī proverbs by the Andalusī ethnographer Abū Yaḥyà 'Ubaid Allāh al-Zajjālī (Ould Mohamed

(the King ordered that great pond of Cordova be filled with rose water instead of water, and instead of dirt, he had it filled with sugar and cinnamon and ginger and spices and clove and musk and amber and algalina, and with all good spices and good aromas there were; and in place of straw, he had them put sugar cane. Once the pond was filled with a mud such that you could only imagine, the King told Ramayquía to take off her shoes and enjoy that mud and make as many adobe bricks as she wanted.

The next day she began to cry over something else she wanted, and the King asked her why she was doing it.

And she said that why shouldn't she be crying, that the King never did anything to please her. And the King, seeing as how he had already done so much to please her and satisfy her desires, and not knowing what else he could do for her, said to her in Arabic something like this: "wa lā nahār aṭ-ṭīn?", and it means: "And not the day of the mud?", meaning that since she had forgotten all the other things, she should not forget the mud that he made to please her.)

The *viesso* at the end of the *exemplo* distills the anecdote's object lesson as follows: "Qui te desconosçe tu bien fecho, non dexes por el tu grand prouecho" ('Whoever does not recognize your good deeds, do not grant him great advantage') (2: 259). Therefore, the stated didactic message is that you must be judicious in how you reward your subordinates, lest they begin to take your patronage lightly. Despite his extravagant indulgence of his wife's whims, Abenabet ultimately refuses Ramayquía, reminding her of her past ingratitude, and Juan Manuel seems to regard him as an example of a decadent, indulgent ruler who nevertheless is able to set limits when necessary.

The setting in Andalusī Cordova, together with Abenabet's exaggerated extravagance in fulfilling Ramayquía's wishes, communicates the implied message that even the most powerful Muslim kings are weak-willed when it comes to pleasing their wives and generally preoccupied with sensual matters. Underlying this criticism of Andalusī mores, however, is a begrudging and unvoiced admiration for, and perhaps jealousy of, the superior material culture of al-Andalus, which the "mud" made up of all manner of spices mixed with sugar cane represents. This material culture was an important part of the colonial legacy of the Reconquest, and the audience of the *CL* would have been very familiar with Andalusī (or *mudéjar*) textiles, architecture, agricultural science, and the like.

Baba 166, no. 1950; Al-Zajjālī 448). Its usage has continued into modern times and has been collected in Tetuan, Morocco (Dawūd 184). Therefore, it appears to have retained currency comparable to that of "let them eat cake" in English.

The other Andalusī ruler in the *CL*, al-Ḥakam II, is the protagonist of *exemplo* 41: "De·lo que contesçio a·vn rey de Cordoua quel dizian Alhaquem" ('What happened to a king of Cordova called Alhaquem'). In it, Alhaquem suffers the scorn of his subjects for failing to leave a legacy befitting of a Caliph:

> Et acaesçio que estando vn dia folgando, que tannian antel vn estrumento de que se pagauan mucho los moros, que a nonbre albogon. Et el rey paro mientes et entendio que non fazia tan buen son commo era menester, et tomo el albogon et annadio en·el vn forado en la parte de·yuso en derecho de·los otros forados, et dende adelante faze el albogon muy meior son que fasta entonçe fazia.
>
> Et commo quier que aquello era buen fecho para en aquella cosa, por que non era tan grand fecho commo conuinia de fazer a rey, las gentes, en manera de escarnio, començaron aquel fecho a·loar et dizian quando loauan a alguno: "V.a. he de ziat Alhaquim," que quiere dezir: "Este es el annadamiento del rey Alhaquem."
>
> Et esta palabra fue sonada tanto por la tierra fasta que·la ouo de oyr el rey, et pregunto por que dezian las gentes esta palabra. Et commo quier que gelo quisieran encobrir, tanto los afinco, que gelo ovieron a dezir.
>
> Et desque el esto oyo, tomo ende grand pesar, pero commo era muy buen rey, non quiso fazer mal en·los que dizian esta palabra, mas puso en su coraçon de fazer otro annadamiento de que por fuerça oviessen las gentes a·loar el su fecho.
>
> Entonçe, por que la mezquita de Cordoua non era acabada, annadio en·ella aquel rey toda la labor que y menguaua et acabola.
>
> Esta es la mayor et mas conplida et mas noble mezquita que·los moros avian en Espanna, et loado a Dios, es agora eglesia e llaman la Sancta Maria de Cordoua, et offreçiola el sancto rey don Fernando a·Sancta Maria quando gano a·Cordoua de·los moros. (2: 325)
>
> (It happened that while he was at leisure one day, that they were playing before him an instrument very popular among the Moors, called the albogón. And the king realized that it did not sound as good as it should, and took the albogón and added a hole in the lower part in line with the other holes, and since then the albogón makes a much nicer sound than it used to.
>
> And although that was a deed in its own right, because it was not a deed appropriate for a king, the people, by way of ridicule, began to praise it and said, in doing so: "*wa hāḏā zīyādat al-Ḥakam*", which means: "this is the addition of the King Al-Ḥakam".
>
> And this anecdote was repeated so often throughout the land that the King heard it, and asked why people were telling it. And although they wanted to keep it from him, he insisted so much that they had to tell him.
>
> As soon as he heard this he became very depressed, but as he was a good king, he did not seek to punish those who were telling this anecdote, but rather became determined to make another addition for which the people would have no choice but to praise his name.

> And so, because the Mosque of Cordova was not finished, that king invested in it all the necessary labor and completed it. This is the largest, grandest and noblest mosque that the Moors had in all of Spain, and, praise to God, is now the church called Santa María of Cordova, and the King San Fernando dedicated it to her when he won Cordova from the Moors.)

Juan Manuel's explicit message in the *viesso* that follows is that one should always try to accomplish the greatest deeds possible, for greatness is immortal: "Si algun bien fizieres/que muy grande non fuere,/faz grandes si pudieres,/que el bien nunca muere" ('If you achieve something/that is not very great,/[also] achieve greatness if you can,/for greatness does not die') (2: 326). In Patronio's version above, the public ridicule Alhaquem suffers opens his eyes to the necessity of establishing a legacy of great accomplishments. The message is clear: it is not enough to improve a musical instrument; the king must dedicate himself to statecraft and to kingly pursuits, lest his legacy suffer.

However, the implied message is somewhat more complex. Alhaquem's initial "accomplishment" of the addition of the extra hole in the *albogón* describes a young monarch who is frivolous by nature and who must be goaded into proper kinglike behavior by public ridicule. Eventually, he rises to the challenge and with the expansion of the Great Mosque, manages to change the meaning of "this is the addition of al-Ḥakam" from a backhanded compliment into a paragon of achievement.[45] While the *viesso* focuses on the need to strive for greatness, in the actual narration Alhaquem is characterized more by his error than by its correction. The same is true of the *exemplo* of Abenabad, in which the narrative is far more focused on his extravagant treatment of his wife than it is with his ability to admonish her for her lack of gratitude. In short, although Juan Manuel's *viessos* orient these anecdotes as positive examples by virtue of the kings' decisive actions, the narration orients them as negative ones by virtue of their material indulgence and moral decadence.

If we do give credence to the *viessos* that tell us that these are positive examples, we are faced with another contradiction: given that the Reconquest is justified by the illegitimacy of Muslim rule, why would a Castilian statesman such as Juan Manuel draw on the deeds of Muslim rulers for exemplary governance? These moments of ambiguity and indeterminacy are

[45] "Et el loamiento que fasta estonçe le fazian escarniçiendo lo, finco despues por loor; et oy en dia dizen los moros quando quieren loar algun buen fecho: 'Este es el annadamiento de Alhaquem'" ('And the praise that until then had been ridiculing him, was later turned into actual praise; and these days the Moors say, when they want to praise a good deed: "This is the addition of Al-Ḥakam"') (2: 326).

the result of Juan Manuel's attempt to press a genre that favors multivalence and critical reading into the service of a more rigid didactic position. The explicit message he delivers in the frame and the message implicit in the framed tale are different, and the tension between the two is part of what gives the genre its enduring appeal.

By way of conclusion, the tension between the sectarian rhetoric and colonial, frontier reality of the Reconquest is quite evident in the *CL*, particularly in Juan Manuel's ambiguous relationship to Andalusī history and culture. A Christian nobleman whose lands were won from al-Andalus, he enjoyed all the advantages of a colonizer, as well as the inherently problematic relationship with the colonized. His affinity for Andalusī culture reveals some of the contradictions of the frontier culture of Christian Iberia: Andalusī Muslims are unfit to rule, yet worthy of both high praise and imitation. Juan Manuel's enthusiasm for Andalusī literary technique and popular narrative tradition determined both the structure and (in part) the content of the *CL*. Like the Cathedral of Cordova, framed by the outer walls of the Great Mosque of Cordova, Juan Manuel's *CL* is framed by Andalusī narrative tradition and belongs to it as well as to Christian, Latin tradition. As one of the leading noblemen of Reconquest Spain, Juan Manuel is bound to undermine the political basis of the Andalusī culture he so admires. This contradiction is projected onto the pages of the *CL*. Don Juan Manuel's political and religious rhetoric is that of the Reconquest, but his narrative sensibilities are informed by Andalusī notions of what stories are and how they are told and written. The result is a narrative dissonance between the stories he tells and the stories he tells us he tells.

CHAPTER FIVE

THE *LIBRO DE BUEN AMOR* AND THE MEDIEVAL IBERIAN *MAQĀMA*[1]

Don Juan Manuel drew on many literary resources in composing the *Conde Lucanor*, including popular narratives from Andalusī oral tradition that had become part of Castilian lore. Generically, he adapted the *CL* from Castilian translations of frametales such as *Kalīla* and *Sendebar*. His contemporary, Juan Ruiz, does likewise, borrowing from the narrative strategies and content of the Arabic and Hebrew *maqāmāt* that were among the literary genres available to medieval Iberians.

In ultra-peninsular Europe, the thirteenth and fourteenth centuries saw the cultivation of two overlapping literary genres, the frametale (Chaucer's *Canterbury Tales*, Boccaccio's *Decameron*) and the pseudo-autobiography (Jean de Meun's *Roman de la rose*, Guillaume de Machaut's *Voir Dit*). Between the two sits the Castilian *Libro de buen amor* (= *LBA*) of Juan Ruiz.[2] This work has been canonized as a classic of Castilian literature and is commonly taught in university courses of medieval Spanish literature along with the anonymous *Cantar de Mio Cid* (1207), Juan Manuel's *El Conde Lucanor* (1340), and the *Celestina* of Fernando de Rojas (1499 and 1502). Yet it is a work with clearly evident roots in the Hebrew and Arabic literatures of medieval Iberia, roots that are indispensable in understanding Ruiz's work, particularly in dealing with the figure of the narrator, the Archpriest of Hita.

The Archpriest of Hita is author, narrator, and protagonist of his gleefully irreverent, highly innovative, and difficult-to-classify work. He wrote it in a troubadour-tinged *mester de clerecía*, or Alexandrine verse, a form cultivated in the first universities and the monasteries of Western, Romance-speaking Europe in the twelfth and thirteenth centuries (Deyermond, *Historia* 108–09). Juan Ruiz was active in a time and place whose residents read and wrote

[1] Portions of this and the following chapter have been published as part of an article entitled "Reading Jaume Roig's *Spill* and the *Libro de buen amor* in the Iberian *maqāma* tradition" that appeared in the *Bulletin of Spanish Studies* 83.5 (2006): 597–616.

[2] The *LBA* is extant in three manuscripts, G (1330), (Real Academia Española 19), S, (Biblioteca de la Universidad de Salamanca MS 2663) and T, (Biblioteca Nacional V^{a}–6–1). All citations are from the edition of Blecua. On the manuscript tradition of the *LBA*, see Ruiz (ed. Corominas 7–37; ed. Blecua xlix–xcvii) and Dagenais (*Ethics* 118–52).

in several languages. The city where Ruiz probably lived as a student and was later a canon of the Cathedral of Toledo as the Archpriest of Hita was a center of Jewish intellectual activity, a multilingual royal capital city whose residents were proficient and productive in Latin, Arabic, Hebrew, Castilian, and several other Romance dialects. They chatted, rhapsodized, argued, waxed lyrical, prayed, and cursed in all these languages. In this intensely multicultural environment, language use is difficult to stereotype according to religion: there are Jews who write Latin, Arabized Christians, and Hispanic Muslims.[3] To view Juan Ruiz's world through an exclusively Latin or Romance lens would be akin to approaching the cultural study of present-day New York or Los Angeles by engaging only Anglo-American art and literature.

While Ruiz's work is representative of a multilingual tradition of medieval Iberian collections of short narrative written in Arabic, Hebrew, and Castilian, the overwhelming majority of its content is drawn from Latin sources.[4] However, if the *LBA* is kin to the *Cantar de Mio Cid* and the *Celestina*, it also shares common literary ancestry and geography with such works as the Hebrew *Sefer Šaʿašūʿīm* (= *Šaʿašūʿīm*) of Joseph Ibn Zabāra (Barcelona, late twelfth or early thirteenth century) and the *Taḥkemonī* of al-Ḥarīzī, as well as the Arabic *Luzūmīyya* of al-Saraqusṭī.

Scholars have very clearly linked nearly every aspect of the *LBA*'s content to sources in the Latin tradition.[5] One consistent sticking point has been the question of genre. Critics have classified it variously as autobiography, love treatise, and satire, all well-known genres in the Latin tradition. Yet something about the *LBA* has prompted multiple generations of its critics to look beyond Latin to Hebrew and Arabic sources. As early as 1894, Francisco Fernández y González describes the *LBA* as having "la forma de *macama*" ('the form of a *maqāma*') (55), a comment he does not follow up

---

[3] To wit, there are legal documents from late thirteenth-century Toledo written in Castilian, yet signed in Arabic script by witnesses with names such as Pedro López, Fernán Pérez, and Felipe Fernández (León Tello 1: 392, no. 16, 94, no. 18, and 1: 401, no. 24).

[4] In any event, the game of Latin/Romance vs. "Semitic" influences in Castilian literature, and in particular the *LBA*, is too often framed as a zero-sum game (i.e., something is either "Western" or "Oriental") or a pseudo-science of ascribing discrete "elements" or aesthetic values to one or another tradition. As it is nearly impossible, in most cases, to do so, I propose a new question (which I cannot address here): what is the ideological underpinning of such an approach? What precisely is at stake in identifying an author, work, or literary element as either "ours" or "theirs"?

[5] See, for example, Lida de Malkiel ("Notas"; *Dos obras* 40–62), MacDonald, Vicente García, Jenaro MacLennan, Marmo, Burkard ("Pseudo"; *Archpriest*) and Deyermond and Walker.

with much in the way of exposition or evidence. More than half a century later, María Rosa Lida de Malkiel wrote an exhaustive study of the sources of the *LBA* in classical and Romance tradition ("Notas"), concluding that Latin and Romance sources alone would not bring scholars to a richer understanding of Ruiz's work (*Dos Obras* 22–26). The missing piece of the puzzle, she claimed, was to be found in the Hebrew *maqāmāt*, particularly Ibn Zabāra's *Šaʿašūʿīm*.[6]

Despite the many coincidences between the two texts, it is impossible to know how Juan Ruiz might have learned of Ibn Zabāra's work. To begin with, very little is known about Juan Ruiz himself. While earlier scholars were content to read autobiographical material internal to the poem as historical,[7] modern scholarship has not even been able to identify positively any historical Juan Ruiz as the author of the *LBA*.[8]

It would be foolhardy to argue that Juan Ruiz personally read *Šaʿašūʿīm*; it is highly unlikely that he knew any Hebrew at all.[9] How, then, might he have come in contact with Ibn Zabāra's work? Lida de Malkiel writes that Ruiz's demonstrated familiarity with Sephardic and Andalusī culture suggest that he was in a position to have been exposed to Ibn Zabāra's work indirectly:

> Sería insensato postular para Juan Ruiz lectura o imitación libresca de las *maqamat* hebreas, pero la preciosa confesión "después fiz muchas cánticas de dança e troteras/para judías e moras" y su familiaridad con la judería, prueban que bien pudo llegarle noticias de tales obras. (*Dos Obras* 33)

[6] While Moses Hadas had brought out his English translation in 1932, Ignasi González-Llubera had made Ibn Zabāra's work accessible to Romance language scholars with his 1931 Catalan translation, *Llibre d'ensenyaments delectables*, which includes an excellent introductory study and notes. Lida de Malkiel worked from the Catalan version.

[7] As late as 1930, Elisha Kane requests that he "be pardoned for raising certain doubts as to why the…lines [describing the Archpriest] should not be regarded as authentic self-portraiture" (103).

[8] We have only one piece of external evidence confirming the existence of an Archpriest of Hita named Juan Ruiz: a legal document dating from around 1330 detailing a lawsuit brought against the Chapter of Toledo by the clergy of Madrid. See Hernández. However, this evidence alone is insufficient when one considers the name "Juan Ruiz" is practically the Castilian equivalent of "John Smith" in English. More recent studies by Sáez and Trenchs and Márquez-Villanueva ("Nueva") identify Ruiz with Juan Ruiz de Cisneros, son of Arias de Cisneros, who fathered Ruiz while in captivity in Granada.

[9] The simplest solution to the problem of Ruiz's knowledge of Ibn Zabāra—and one for which no evidence whatsoever exists—was once suggested to me by Shamma Boyarin, after he was good enough to read a preliminary draft of this chapter. His idea was that Ruiz was himself a *converso*, which would also help to explain why so little is known about him (as Juan Ruiz). It was not at all unheard of for *conversos*—both before and after Juan Ruiz's time—to enter the clergy: Pablo Christiani (d. 1274), who debated against Nahmanides at the Disputation of Barcelona (1263), was a Dominican priest, and Pablo de Santa María (c. 1350–1435, formerly Solomon Halevi) became Bishop of Burgos.

> (It would be ill-advised to posit for Juan Ruiz the bookish imitation of the Hebrew *maqāmāt*, but the priceless confession: "Next after that I wrote the words to many a dancing song/ For Jewesses," and his familiarity with the Ghetto, prove that specific knowledge of such works may well have reached him.) (*Masterpieces* 23)

In this chapter, we will pick up the trail blazed by Lida de Malkiel (and her critics) in the consideration of Ruiz's familiarity with *Šaʿašūʿīm*. First, we will set the stage for Ruiz's putative exposure to Ibn Zabāra's work by discussing the presence of Jewish intellectuals in the courts of Castile and Aragon before and during the lifetime of Juan Ruiz. That is, we will look at the question of how and why Jews and Christians were in meaningful social contact. Next we will revisit and expand Lida de Malkiel's argument (as well as address some of the arguments of her critics) in order to trace Juan Ruiz's adaptation of the narrative resources of the Iberian *maqāma* in the *Libro de buen amor*.

Jewish and Christians at Court in Castile-Leon and Aragon

From long before the time of Juan Ruiz, during the period of Islamic rule in al-Andalus, it was not at all uncommon for Jewish physicians and secretaries to hold high-level administrative positions at court, both during the ʿUmayyad caliphate (711–1002) and later, during the period of the *mulūk al-ṭawāʾif*, or Taifa kingdoms (1002–86).[10] One early and notable example is Ḥasdai ibn Shaprūt (ca. 915–ca. 970), who served as physician, director of customs, and diplomat to the ʿUmayyad Caliph ʿAbd al-Raḥmān III (912–961) (Ashtor 1: 155–227). In the following century, Shmuel Hanagid Nagrela (993–1055) served Ḥabbūs, King of Granada, as vizier (Ashtor 2: 41–189). This state of affairs obtained until the Almohad invasions of the 1140s, when Jewish communities were ravaged and their members forced to convert to Islam or leave.[11] Many Jews left for the north, where they settled in

[10] After the disintegration of the Cordovan caliphate, al-Andalus devolved into a collection of independent city kingdoms whose monarchs were engaged in constant political struggle with and against the other Muslim and Christian monarchs of the Iberian Peninsula. For a thorough study of this period, see Wasserstein.

[11] The Almohad Berbers were fiercely fundamentalist Muslims who had little in common with the residents of al-Andalus, who were Romance and Arabic speakers and not particularly observant Muslims. Their arrival heralded a general quelling of intellectual activity, especially that of Islamic rationalists, who were considered heretics in the eyes of the Almohades. Among

Christian Provence, Catalonia, Aragon, Castile, Navarre, and Portugal. Like their Muslim counterparts, the Christian monarchs of Iberia soon realized the usefulness of their subject Jews. While Christian nobles often entered into political struggles against the crown, the Jews had no power base apart from the privileges granted to them by the king. Their utter dependence on the crown guaranteed their loyalty.[12] This fact combined with the Jews' range of administrative and artisanal skills to create opportunities for their advancement in the Christian North. Under Christian monarchs individual Jews enjoyed powerful positions as court physicians, secretaries, and tax farmers.

It was typical for such Jewish courtiers to be accomplished religious scholars and poets as well. Two of the foremost rabbis of Jewish tradition lived in medieval Iberia, somewhat before the period in question. Maimonides was the paragon of the medieval Iberian Jewish physician/rabbi. Born in Cordova, he practiced medicine in order to live, but his primary interest lay in rabbinical studies.[13] Another important figure of the medieval Iberian Jewish milieu, Nahmanides, (Moses ben Nahman) was born in Gerona (1194) and became a highly influential scholar and leader throughout the Jewish communities of the Crown of Aragon (*EJ*, "Naḥmanides").

For hundreds of years, men like these served the Christian monarchs and nobles of Aragon and Castile. As early as 1147, Alfonso VII of Castile (1126–1157) placed Judah ibn Ezra in charge of his fortress at Calatrava, and later at the head of his kingdom's central administration (Baer 1: 77). Alfonso II of Aragon (1162–1196) employed Don David ibn Aldaian as his personal *alfaquim* (Ar. *al-ḥakīm*, 'philosopher' or 'physician') (Baer 1: 82).

Jewish courtiers enjoyed particularly favorable circumstances under Alfonso X ("The Learned," r. 1252–1284), who surrounded himself with men of learning from all three of the region's major traditions. He employed several Jews as physicians, secretaries, and translators, among them Yehuda ben Salomon ibn Mosca, Abraham ibn Wakar, Samuel Halevi, and Isaac ha-Ḥazan ben Sid (Don Çag) (Hernández Morejón 83–85; Shatzmiller 41).

---

those forced to flee al-Andalus were the family of Maimonides (Moses ben Maimūn, b. 1131), who left Cordova for Fez when he was still a child (H. Davidson 9–18).

[12] This dependence was actually law: the *Fuero de Teruel*, an early Castilian law code, reminds us that "los jodíos siervos son del sennor Rey et sienpre a la real bolsa son contados" ('the Jews are servants of the Lord King and are counted among his assets.') (320).

[13] He lamented not being able to dedicate himself full-time to his scholarship on account of having to work as a physician (H. Davidson 35; complete biography on pages 3–74).

In particular, the renowned Hebrew poet Ṭodros ben Judah Halevi Abulafia (b. 1247) "enjoyed the confidence of Alfonso and his consort, Violante" (Baer 1: 119) and even accompanied them on Alfonso's unsuccessful trip to Beaucaisse in France in quest of the imperial crown in 1275. Abulafia's work is noteworthy in that he was a Hebrew poet writing in the court of a Christian monarch alongside other poets working in Galician-Portuguese and Provençal (Alvar 181–258; Millá y Fontanals, *Trovadores* 179–99; Doron, *Poet* 28–29; O'Callaghan, *Learned* 144). Aviva Doron has studied the results of his extended contact with his counterparts working in Romance languages and does not hesitate to describe him, without qualification, as a "Hebrew troubadour" (*Poet* 42). During this same period, the son of the renowned Catalonian Rabbi Naḥmanides[14] served at court in Castile (Baer 1: 120).

Most of the existing documentation regarding the involvement of Jewish intellectuals in Christian courts is legal in nature and details financial and other privileges conceded to the Jews by the king.[15] Sources on the daily life of Jewish intellectuals are limited, but the poetry of Abulafia provides ample (if anecdotal) evidence of the favorable conditions enjoyed by his peers at the Castilian court (Doron, *Poet* 41–48). The more ample documentation of the Crown of Aragon provides a great many references to Jewish translators, craftsmen, and physicians working in the service of the crown at the end of the thirteenth century and during the whole of the fourteenth. In these sources are several records of Jewish scholars contracted to translate Arabic books (primarily scientific works) for Christian patrons.[16]

---

[14] Nahmanides (known as Bonastruch Sa Porta in Catalan), aside from being a highly prominent scholar of Jewish law, also had the distinction of participating in the Disputation of Barcelona of 1263, in which he debated the legitimacy of the Jewish versus the Christian faiths with the *converso* Pablo Christiani. (Riera i Sans and Feliu; Chazan, *Barcelona* and *Daggers*).

[15] For example, several documents from the *Cartas Reales* (Escribà) in the Archives of the Crown of Aragon refer to a certain Alazar ("físico" or "físico real") during the period 1328–1333. One grants him the privilege of farming taxes from the *aljamas* of the Kingdom of Aragon (no. 603). Another assigns him to arbitrate a dispute between a prominent member of the Jewish community of Navarra and the royal treasurer (no. 738). A third orders Alazar to judge (according to Jewish law) a case of alleged excessive taxation brought by a resident of Murviedro (no. 880). For documents regarding the Jewish community of Toledo during this period, see León Tello.

[16] Among the Valencian documents edited by Rubió Vela (*Epistolari*) are work orders issued by Jaume II in 1294 to Jahuda Bonsenyor to translate a group of Arabic documents (no. 12) and in 1313 for the translation of an entire book (no. 29), a 1349 order from Pere III to Francesch Roys to hand over an Arabic book to be translated in Catalan by Mestre Salamó, payment orders and requests for delivery of astrolabes to be fashioned by Jewish craftsmen for the king (nos. 79 and 143), a request from Pere III in 1347 to ask his (Jewish) doctor, Mestre Cresques, to invite a Jewish silversmith (Mossé Jacob, "Argenter de

Alfonso's successor, Sancho IV of Castile (r. 1284–1295), likewise employed a number of influential Jews at court: Don Abraham El Barchilón served as paymaster and cloth purchaser and Abraham ibn Shoshan was a tax collector. Ṭodros ben Judah Halevi Abulafia, who had fallen out of favor at the close of Alfonso X's reign, was restored under Sancho and exulted in his renewed good fortunes:

> Now, with the help of God, the Rock eternal,
> My writs shall be signed and sealed...
> His kindness will fill my chambers with riches
> And fate will direct wealth into my home.
> (trans. Baer 1: 134; ed. Yellin 2: 99)

The fortunes of Jews at the court of Castile saw a short period of decline during the reign of Ferdinand IV (1295–1312). During the first segment of his reign, their position was weakened because of the increased power enjoyed by the nobility during Ferdinand's minority and the regency of his mother, María de Molina. After Ferdinand assumed the throne, it was further weakened by papal directives issued by Clement V (1305–1314) to abolish Jewish money lending (Baer 1: 309).

During the reign of Alfonso XI (1312–1350), contemporary with the life of Juan Ruiz and the appearance of the *LBA*, several Jews once again found high-level positions at court. Members of the Abenardut family were especially prominent; in 1330, Elazar ibn Ardut was named "physician to the most illustrious Lord King Alphonso" (Shatzmiller 61). Other physicians in service to Christian monarchs were named *alfaquim* or *familiaris* in official documentation, in order to denote their privileged relationship with the monarch (Shatzmiller 59). Don Samuel ibn Wakar (son of Abraham ibn Wakar) served as physician and astronomer and in 1331 was granted the concession of the royal mint (Baer 1: 326–27). Samuel's rival, Don Yuçaf de Écija (Joseph Halevi ben Ephraim ben Isaac aben Shabat), served as *almoxarife mayor* (i.e., chamberlain) to Alfonso. Pedro IV of Aragon (r. 1336–1387) had several Jewish physicians at court; and Enrique II of Castile (r. 1369–1379), despite having promised to rid his kingdom of the Jews, nevertheless kept several in his personal service (Assis 25).

To illustrate on a more personal level the types of relationships being forged between Christian nobles and Jews, we have the example of the Infante

Perpinyá") to come decorate the clocks of the Royal Palace in Barcelona (no. 85), and an order issued by Joan I in 1390 to protect the library of the Jewish community of Mallorca from confiscation (no. 330).

Don Juan Manuel. A contemporary of Juan Ruiz, Don Juan Manuel enjoyed a close friendship with his Jewish physician, Don Salamón, a relationship documented in Juan Manuel's *Libro enfenido*:

> Et como quier que don Salamón, mio físico, es judío et non puede nin deue seer cabeçalero, nin yo no lo fago mio cabeçalero. Pero por quello fallé siempre tan leal que abés se podría dezir nin creer, por ende rruego a mis fijos quel quieran para su serviçio et lo crean en sus faziendas et so çierto que se fallarán bien dello. Et si cristiano fuesse, yo sé lo que yo en él dexaría. Et eso mismo ruego a mis cabeçaleros, ca çierto so que commo me fue leal al cuerpo, que así lo farrá a la mi alma. (Giménez Soler, *Don Juan Manuel* 699)
>
> (Seeing as how Don Salamón, my physician, is a Jew and cannot be the executor of my estate, I do not make him my executor. Nonetheless, I have found him always so loyal that one would scarcely be able to say or believe, and therefore I beg my sons that they might want him in their service, and entrust their affairs to him, and I am certain that they will find themselves better off for doing so. And were he Christian, I am certain that I would leave my affairs in his hands. I likewise beg the same of my executors, for I am certain that as loyal as he was to my body, so shall he be to my soul.)

Here Juan Manuel leaves little doubt as to the extent of his trust: were the physician Christian, he would be executor of Juan Manuel's estate. Since Jewish physicians were generally highly educated in Hebrew literature, religious and secular,[17] it is not unlikely that the very literary Juan Manuel might have discussed Hebrew literature with Don Salamón.[18]

Authors of important works of medieval Hebrew Iberian literature had documented connections to courtly circles. Ibn Zabāra's sponsor, Sheshet ben Isaac Benveniste, to whom the author dedicates his book, served as *alfaquim* and *baile* (bailiff) to Alfonso II (r. 1162–1196) and Pedro II (r. 1196–1213) of Aragon. In 1208, Judah ibn Isaac ibn Shabbetay, author of the influential Hebrew *maqāma, Minḥat Yehudah, soneh hanašīm* ('The Offering of Yehu-

[17] As we have mentioned above, several of the most important Hebrew poets and religious scholars of medieval Iberia were also physicians, including Maimonides, Solomon ibn Gabirol, Naḥmanides, Joseph ibn Zabāra, and Ṭodros Halevi Abulafia. On the education and licensing of Jewish physicians in the Middle Ages, see Shatzmiller (14–35).

[18] This is the argument of Morón Arroyo, who claims that Juan Manuel learned of the frametale structure from Don Salamón, who may well have been familiar with such Hebrew frametales as the *Mišlei Sendebar* ('Parables of Sendebar,' the Hebrew translation of the Arabic *Sendebar*; see *Tales of Sendebar*, ed. and trans. Epstein), the Hebrew *Kalīlah et Dimnah* (late thirteenth century) (Ibn al-Muqaffaʿ, ed. Derenbourg), and Ibn Sahula's *Mešal haqadmonī* (ca. 1285). However, it is equally likely that Juan Manuel learned of the frametale through the Castilian *Calila*, to which he would have had access through his uncle Alfonso X, who commissioned the work in 1251 while still crown prince.

dah, Misogynist'), performed his work *Milḥemet ha-Ḥokhma ve-ha-ʿOšer* ('The War Between Wisdom and Wealth') at the court of Alfonso VIII (see ch. 6 n. 39). In short, there is a great deal of evidence placing Jewish intellectuals in close, prolonged, and meaningful contact with Christian rulers and courtiers.[19] It seems likely, therefore, that Ibn Zabāra had contact with Christians of high status, via his sponsor, Sheshet Benveniste.

Because so little is known about him, it is somewhat more difficult to place Juan Ruiz in documented contact with Jewish intellectuals. We do know, however, that his near contemporary Santob de Carrión (Shem Tov ben Isaac Ardutiel), author of the *Proverbios morales* (ca. 1360), had been at court. He dedicates his *Proverbios* to Pedro I of Castile (1350–1369);[20] in the same poem, he makes reference to other Jews who had also been recipients of royal patronage: "Que non so para menos/Que otros de mi ley,/ Que ovieron buenos/Doniados del Rey." ('Yet I am not worse than others of my religion who have received good gifts from the King') (ed. Perry 13, ll. 161–64; trans. Perry 19, § 161).

The work exists in manuscripts in both Latin and Hebrew script and was received by both Christian and Jewish audiences.[21] Given the activity of such men as Ṭodros Abulafia[22] at the court of Alfonso X and Santob de Carrión at that of Alfonso XI and Pedro I, it is more than reasonable to conclude that Hebrew and Christian men of letters were in contact and in all likelihood enjoyed mutual intellectual exchange.

---

[19] On Jewish intellectuals and doctors in the courts of Castilian monarchs in the thirteenth and fourteenth centuries, see also Castro (*Realidad* 443–92).

[20] "Señor Rey, noble, alto,/ Oý estes sermon/ que vyene desyr Santo,/ Judio de Carrion" ('Lord King, noble and high, hear this discourse, which Santob, the Jew from Carrión, comes forward to speak:') (ed. Perry 9, vv. 1–4; trans. Perry 17, vv. 1–4).

[21] On the extant manuscripts, see the introductions of Perry (10–19) and González Llubera (2–3) to their respective editions of Santob's text.

[22] The poet and financier Ṭodros ben Judah Halevi Abulafia is not to be confused with Ṭodros ben Joseph Abulafia (c. 1220–1298), the noted exegete and kabbalist. The former was a highly assimilated financier and libertine, who was known to consort with non-Jewish women at the court of Alfonso X, while the latter was a highly respected rabbi and kabbalist who inveighed against the moral decrepitude of such Jewish courtiers (*EJ*, "Abulafia, Todros ben Judah Ha-Levi" and "Abulafia, Todros ben Joseph Ha-Levi"; Sáenz-Badillos, "Ṭodros"). It happens that Alfonso promulgated a series of laws designed to prevent precisely the type of (social) intercourse with Christians in which Ṭodros ben Joseph indulged (Carpenter, *Alfonso X* 85).

Juan Ruiz and the Jews

The reality of the cosmopolitan, multicultural Toledo in which Juan Ruiz lived and wrote helped to shape his literary sensibilities. Through his Jewish and Muslim acquaintances, Ruiz would have had access to their religious, social, and literary traditions. Accordingly, much attention has been drawn to Juan Ruiz's familiarity with Jewish and Muslim culture.[23] Although scholars have identified references to Jewish religious practice and culture in the *LBA*, none has explained the significance of these references, nor how they differ from representations of Jews in authors contemporary with Ruiz.

Richard Burkard, in refuting Lida de Malkiel, argues that Ruiz's adoption of medieval anti-Judaic commonplaces typical of Christian literature are indicative of the author's own personal attitudes toward the Jewish community of Toledo.[24] However, Burkard fails to distinguish between party-line rhetoric and personal proclivity, a distinction that (as we have learned from our discussion of Don Juan Manuel) is key in understanding how a multicultural yet non-democratic society functions. As a Catholic priest, Ruiz would have been bound to uphold the position that the Jews were responsible for the death of Christ—in official, public discourse.[25] In practice, however, individuals are more complex than the institutional doctrines to which they nominally subscribe. Accordingly, Ruiz's references to Jews and Jewish culture in the *LBA* suggest that his formulaic anti-Judaism was but lip service paid to an official culture that held Judaism (if not individual Jews) in open contempt.[26]

---

[23] See, in addition to the work of Lida de Malkiel cited above, González Llubera ("Aspecte"), Lecoy (137–45), Aizenberg, Martínez Ruiz, and Rambaldo.

[24] "There is reason to believe he was personally supportive of the anti-Semitism of his day, a bias which would seemingly have caused him to keep his distance from Jewish religious practice and intellectual activity" (*Archpriest* 131).

[25] Burkard refers specifically to the stanzas describing the Passion of Christ (st. 1051–66, especially 1051 and 1063) and another reference blaming the Jews for Christ's death in st. 1657. Such anti-Semitism on the part of Ruiz, he claims, makes it "unlikely...that he should seek then in the very same work to imitate rabbinical literature" (131–33). He is quite right: it would be highly unlikely for Ruiz to seek inspiration in rabbinical literature—but the *Sefer Šaʿašūʿīm* cannot be classified as such by any stretch of the imagination. The fact that it is in Hebrew and written by a Jewish author does not qualify it as "rabbinical." On the contrary, in terms of its content it is a purely secular work.

[26] According to Edna Aizenberg, Ruiz's double portrayal of Jews (Ecclesiastical and secular) "exemplifies well the dual dicta of *spiritualitas* and *carnalitas* that structure his work, enriching its texture, but more than once confounding even the most perceptive of its readers" (159).

Medieval Christian authors tend toward stock, stereotypical references to Jews, whether considered collectively or in individual portrayals.[27] While Ruiz does open his work with a perfunctory reference to the Jews as the "pueblo de perdiçión" ('people of damnation') (st. 1b), the majority of his references to Jews lack the pointed resentment and disdain typical of his time and rather attest to familiarity with the Jewish community of Toledo and with Jewish culture in general. Lida de Malkiel (*Estudios* 25) cites several instances of Ruiz's personal knowledge of the *judería* ('Jewish quarter') of Toledo, in which city he would have passed much of his life. He demonstrates familiarity with Jewish religious customs in describing his frustration at not being able to meet with his beloved Doña Endrina. Ruiz compares the jealousy of the male relatives guarding her to that of the Jews guarding the scrolls of the Torah:[28]

> Era dueña en todo e de dueñas señora;
> non podía ser con ella una ora:
> mucho de omne se guardan allí do ella mora,
> más mucho que non guardan los jodíos la Tora. (st. 78)
>
> (She was in every way a lady and mistress of all ladies;
> I could not be with her for even an hour.
> They guard her closely against men there where she lives,
> Even more than the Jews guard the Torah.)

Although his comments may appear flippant, they reveal a sophisticated understanding of the nature of the relationship between Jews and the scrolls themselves. Traditionally, the scrolls indeed are guarded as jealously as a medieval Iberian might guard a younger female relative. They are kept in beautifully adorned cases and adorned with silver crowns. When the Torah scroll is carried through the congregation it is customary to kiss it. In the case of a synagogue fire, one is expected to enter the burning building in order to save the scroll as if it were a person.[29]

---

[27] Dwayne Carpenter ("Social") cites several such examples in works such as the *Poema de Mio Cid* (66–68), the *Loores de Nuestra Señora* (62) and *Milagros de Nuestra Señora* of Gonzalo de Berceo (64), *Cantigas de Santa María* of Alfonso X (64), and the *Libro del Caballero Zifar* (69–70).

[28] The Torah scroll contains the first five books of the Hebrew Bible (Pentateuch). It is produced according to highly exacting technical specifications that detail the preparation of the parchment, ink, and quills to be used. Consequently, it takes up to one full year for a scribe to copy the scroll and therefore is a prohibitively expensive document (*EJ*, "Torah").

[29] See *Talmud Bavli* (Shabbat 115a). Other strictures include the prohibition of having sexual relations while a Torah scroll is present in the room (Berakhot 25b) and the practice

Juan Ruiz's knowledge of Jewish law also extended to the celebration of the Passover (Sp. *pascua judía*, Heb. *pesaḥ*). In the episode of Don Carnal and Doña Cuaresma, Don Carnal flees Lenten fasting and seeks refuge in the *judería*, where he finds consolation:

> fuyó de la iglesia, fuese a la jodería:
> resçebiéronlo bien en su carneçería;
> Pascua de pan çenzeño estonçe les venía:
> plogo a ellos con él e él vido buen día. (st. 1183)
>
> (He fled the church, and went to the Jewish quarter;
> They received him well in their butchery;
> They were about to celebrate Passover then,
> He kept them entertained and had a good time of it.)

Here Ruiz demonstrates familiarity with the practice of eating unleavened bread during the Passover, as well as an awareness that Jews do not adhere to Lenten abstinence from meat. In his trip to the *judería* during Lent, he is greeted by the butchers (who are open for business in order to supply the community with the traditional paschal lamb) and rabbis (who supervise Kosher slaughter): "A Don Carnal resçiben todos los carniçeros/todos los rabís con todos sus aperos" (st. 1212a–b) ('All the butchers go out to receive Sir Carnal/all the Rabbis with all their implements').[30]

Ruiz also comments on customary practices that are not religious in nature, such as the traditionally Jewish occupation of moneylending (León Tello 107–08). However, in referring to it, he avoids derogatory language and speaks in terms of technical detail. The reference appears in his discussion of the good social habits necessary for success with women. He advises would-be Romeos to shun gambling in the interests of maintaining a healthy portfolio, thereby increasing one's desirability as a partner. In order to demonstrate the extent to which gambling can sap one's finances, he notes that even Jewish moneylenders give you a better deal than the gaming table:[31]

> Non quieras jugar dados nin seas tablejero,
> ca es mala ganançia, peor que de logrero:

---

of rending one's garment upon hearing of the desecration or burning of a Torah scroll (Mo'ed Katan 26a).

[30] Although the implication is that Don Carnal is a bad Christian by eating meat with Jews during Lent and that the Jews are incorrect for doing so themselves, "el anti-judaismo automático no era siempre anti-semitsmo" ('automatic anti-Judaism was not always anti-Semitism') (Zahareas and Pereira 331).

[31] On gambling in medieval Spain, see Carpenter ("Alea").

el judío al año da tres por quatro; pero,
el tablax de un día dobla el su mal dinero. (st. 554–556)

(Do not even think of playing dice, nor of being a backgammon player,
for it is a bad deal, worse yet than usury:
the Jew charges 25% annually; but,
the casino owner doubles his damned money in a single day!)

While this account is not technically detailed or revealing of any privileged knowledge of Jewish banking practice, it does establish the Jewish banker as a fixture in the daily life of Castile without resorting to denigrating language or imagery.[32] As such, it is representative of Ruiz's relatively enlightened representation of Castilian Jewry. This openness to, and familiarity with, Jewish culture suggests that Ruiz may also have been curious about works by Hebrew authors, if only indirectly (i.e., through an oral exposition by someone who had read Ibn Zabāra in Hebrew). The key to his interest in the Hebrew *maqāmāt* lies in the figure of the protean author/narrator/protagonist of the *LBA*, the first such example in Latin and Romance literature.

Autobiography in the LBA

One of the most characteristic features of the *LBA* is its autobiographical voice, its "yo Juan Royz, Açipreste de Fita" (st. 19b–c) ('I, Juan Ruiz, Archpriest of Hita'). Western authors have practiced autobiography since antiquity, and in Christian literature its foremost innovator and practitioner is St. Augustine (*Confessions*). It was also widely cultivated by later medieval

[32] Here I must disagree with Richard Burkard, who considers Ruiz to regard Jewish moneylending as "meager and banal" and the author's tone as having "an element of resentment." Far from positive, Burkard sees it as yet another example of the "perennial European motif of the 'shylock'" (*Archpriest* 131 n. 16). However, Ruiz uses the word "judío" just as we might use the word "bank," without any trace of resentment or malice. Anthony Zahareas and Oscar Pereira read these lines similarly, concluding that "no hay tanto aquí intención antisemita, sino simplemente dentro del terreno de un antijudaísmo cristiano, cotejo de los dos tipos de préstamos" ('here there is not so much anti-Semitic intention, but quite simply rather a comparison of the two types of loans [usury vs. gambling] within the terrain of a [generalized] Christian anti-Semitism') (164). The bankers are Jews; therefore, if you want a loan, you must go to a Jew. Since it would be unseemly for a priest to openly praise the Jewish community, we must pay attention to what Ruiz does *not* say. That is, in a medieval Christian environment, one may read the absence of *de rigeur* anti-Judaism as a form of tolerance. Compare with the portrayal of Jewish moneylenders Raquel and Vidas in (*Poema de Mio Cid* 111–14) or to the various negative portrayals of Jews brought together by Carpenter ("Social").

authors.[33] The question of Juan Ruiz's use of autobiography is still being debated by critics of the *LBA*, who ascribe a variety of sources and influences to Juan Ruiz. In 1906, Julio Puyol y Alonso wrote that while salacious behavior was hardly uncommon among Spanish clergymen in the fourteenth century, it would be foolish to assume that the *LBA* was a factual account of Ruiz's own exploits (104). Some years later, Marcelino Menéndez y Pelayo asserted that the book was indeed autobiographical, but that Ruiz may have embellished somewhat his amorous misadventures.[34] Yet even the most precursory reading of the *LBA* makes it difficult to accept it as authentic autobiography. Why would any author, let alone a member of the clergy, paint themselves such an unflattering portrait? The Juan Ruiz portrayed in the *LBA* is a lecherous buffoon, one whose every sexual advance earns him humiliation, rejection, and scorn. In his first attempt to woo a woman named Cruz, the Archpriest dispatches his go-between, Ferrand García, on his behalf. The wily García seduces Cruz for himself:

> E, porque yo non podía con ella ansí fablar,
> puse por mi mensajero, coidando recabdar,
> a un mi compañero; sópome el clavo echar:
> él comió la vïanda e a mí fazié rumiar. (st. 113)
>
> (And, as I could not speak with her thusly,
> I chose as my messenger, thinking I would profit,
> one of my friends; he really knew how to screw me:
> he ate the steak and left me the salad!)

Another time, he contracts the services of a professional go-between, *Trotaconventos* ('Convent-hopper'), who meets with little success (and much scorn) in her attempt to woo a Muslim girl on his behalf:

> Dixo Trotaconventos a la mora por mí:
> 'Ya amiga, ya amiga, quánto ha que non vos vi!
> Non es quien ver vos pueda, ¿y cómo sodes ansi?
> Salúdavos amor nuevo.' Diz la mora: 'Iznedrí.'
>
> 'Fija, mucho vos saluda uno que es de Alcalá,
> enbíavos una çodra con aqueste alvalá:

[33] See Lehmann, Zumthor, de Looze (*Pseudo-Autobiography*), and Lejeune. For an excellent overview of autobiography in Europe, see Obermeier.

[34] "Creemos que el fondo de la narración es verídico, como lo prueba su misma simplicidad y llaneza y la ausencia de orden y composición que en el libro se advierte" ('We believe that the foundation of the narrative is true, as its simplicity, plainness, and lack of order and composition evident in the book prove') (Menéndez y Pelayo xcii).

el Crïador es convusco, que d'esto tal mucho ha;
tomaldo, fija señora.' Diz la mora: 'Legualá.'

Fija, ¡sí el Crïador vos dé plazer con salud,
que non gelo desdeñedes, pues que más traher non pud!
Aducho buenos vos adugo, pues fabladme alaúd,
non vaya de vós tan muda.' Diz la mora: '¡Ascut!'[35]

Desque vido la vieja que non recabdava ý,
diz: 'Quanto vos he dicho, bien tanto me perdí;
pues que ál non me dezides, quiérome ir de aquí.'
Cabeçeó la mora, díxole: '¡Amxí, amxí!' (st. 1509–12)

(Trotaconventos said to the Moorish girl for me:
"Hey girlfriend, hey girlfriend, long time no see!
Nobody can find you, why is that?
A new lover greets you." The Moorish girl said: "Iznedrí"[36] ['I don't know'].

"Daughter, a man from Alcalá sends many greetings,
he sends a blouse with this letter,
The Creator is with you, for he has much more like this;
take it, my lady, my daughter." The Moorish girl said: "Legualá" ['No, by God'].

"Daughter, God gives you pleasure along with health,
don't disdain him for it, I couldn't do any better!
I bring you good news, speak to me, for the love of God,
that I not go away, and you so quiet!" The Moorish girl said: "¡Ascut!" ['Shut up!]

Once the old lady saw she was getting nowhere,
she said: "Everything I've said to you has been a waste of breath;
if you have nothing else to say to me, I'm getting out of here."
The Moorish girl shook her head, and said to her: "¡Amxí, amxí!" ['Go away, go away!'])

The Archpriest's other efforts to pitch woo on his own behalf garner similar results. The one time Ruiz actually has sex is when he is raped by a strapping mountain girl (Sp. *serrana*) who lures him into her hut with promises of a hot meal. Soon after lunch is over, she has her way with the Archpriest:

---

35 Here Juan Ruiz accurately reproduces the initial /a/ characteristic of the imperative singular in colloquial Andalusī (/askút/) as opposed to the initial /i/ of Classical Arabic (/ískut/) (Corriente, *Grammatical* 100 and 100 n. 154).

36 This is Ruiz's rendering of the combination of the negative marker (in the Andalusī vernacular) /iš/, with /nadrí/, a first-person singular agentive imperfective form of a *lām*- (third radical) defective verb, *darā* (Corriente, *Grammatical* 119). The classical form would be "*lástu ádrī*." This is a good example of how the Classical and vernacular registers of Arabic can differ so as to be mutually unintelligible.

La vaqueriza traviessa
diz: 'Luchemos un rato;
liévate dende apriesa,
desbuélvete de aqués hato.'
Por la muñeca me priso,
ove de fazer quanto quiso:
creet que fiz buen barato. (st. 971)

(The randy cowgirl
said: "Let's wrestle for a while:
get up from there quick,
and take off those clothes."
She took me by the wrist,
I had to do whatever she wanted:
Believe me, I struck a good deal.)

One must ask why a cleric would want to represent himself as a lecher, albeit a failed one.[37] While anticlerical literature is not unheard of in the Middle Ages (Caro Baroja; Laurence; Odber de Baubeta), its authors do not commonly claim to portray their *own* inappropriate behavior, in the tradition of Augustinian confessional autobiography (Toro-Garland).[38]

In traditional Augustinian conversion narrative, the author describes his own sins in order to contrast his pre- and post- conversion behaviors. André Michalski sees the *LBA* as a playful twist on the Augustinian narrative in which the protagonist-Archpriest is converted from Catholicism to the religion of *Buen amor* ('good love') (58, cited in Brownlee, *Status* 59). Leo Spitzer reads the Archpriest's exploits as representative of the human capacity for sin, and not necessarily his own actual or imagined sins.[39] Anthony

---

[37] Another, earlier medieval Iberian poet who chronicled his pseudoautobiographical failed amorous exploits in verse was Ibn Quzmān (Abū Bakr Muḥammad ibn ʿAbd al-Malik, d. 1160 in Cordova), most notably in his *zajal* no. 87. (ed. Corriente and Makkī 266–74; trans. García Gómez, *Mejor* 177–81). If one were subscribe to the theory of Sáez and Trenchs (later supported by Márquez-Villanueva in "Nueva") that Juan Ruiz spent the first ten years of his life in Granada, it is possible that the Archpriest might have been able to read Ibn Quzmān's work, written as it was in Andalusī vernacular, and not Classical, Arabic. Monroe has pointed out a distinction between the unreliable narrators of *maqāmāt*, whose narrators chronicle the successful deceptions they suffer at the hands of the rogue, and those of Ibn Quzmān's *zajals*, that chronicle his own failed deceptions ("Mystery" 41).

[38] Neither is Juan Ruiz the first naughty Archpriest in Castilian literature; he is preceded in the thirteenth century by the non-autobiographical *mal arçipreste* of the anonymous *Poema de Fernán González*, who pays for his lasciviousness with his life (ed. Victorio 161–63, st. 645–58).

[39] "...the Archpriest, in using this self-incriminating procedure, wished to depict that potential sinner which existed in himself, as in all human beings: he reveals himself, not as

Zahareas (40–41), Dayle Seidenspinner-Núñez (*Allegory* 55), and Marina Brownlee (*Status* 68) adopt more nuanced positions, explaining that the ambiguity of the author/narrator/protagonist reflects the didactic ambiguity of the text.

The conflation of the author, narrator, and protagonist in the *LBA* coincides with a movement in French and Italian vernacular literature toward identifiable authors and the innovation of manuscripts that represent the work of a single author (after the fashion of the *diwān* of Arabic and Hebrew poetic tradition). Thirteenth-century Europe witnessed a development in author-consciousness that was expressed in the appearance of single-author codices of vernacular literature, in particular of poetry. Eventually the single-author manuscript begins to prevail over the scattered collections of troubadour material typical of earlier periods of vernacular poetry in Europe (Huot 39–45). Laurence de Looze argues that this innovation in packaging the written lyric heralds a "new professionalism and self-consciousness on the part of fourteenth-century writers in Spain, France, and England" (*Pseudo* 6). This is evident in other Castilian authors such as Juan Manuel, whose authorial presence is quite strong in his works (Macpherson, "Don Juan Manuel" 3). De Looze (*Pseudo* 9) sees a precedent in the French *Roman de la rose* (late thirteenth century) and cites works roughly contemporary with Juan Ruiz in French, among them the *Voir-dit* (ca. 1360) of Guillaume de Machaut, and the *Espinette amoreuse* (ca. 1369) of Jean Froissart.[40] In these works, which de Looze—following Gybbon-Monypenny—designates "pseudo-autobiography," the narrative voice is constituted by an ambiguous unity of author and protagonist. The works share three characteristics: a "new exploitation of the analogy…between the author's life or 'body' and the author's book," a "new quasi-professional position for the poet," and a "crisis of truth" (*Pseudo* 8). Where Gybbon-Monypenny fell a bit short of the mark, de Looze hits it dead on. As we shall demonstrate, his "crisis of truth" in the figure of the narrator is key in relating the *LBA* to the Hebrew and Arabic *maqāmāt*. And while de Looze does not delve into the question of the *maqāmāt*, he points us in their direction.

---

having committed the sins he describes, but as capable, in his human weakness, of having committed them" (Spitzer 106).

[40] The latter two works, however, appear after the *LBA* and can hardly be models for it (Lida de Malkiel, *Estudios* 22).

The LBA *and the* Maqāmāt: *"Historia de una inseguridad"*[41]

The idea that Juan Ruiz was familiar with, and somehow drew upon, Hebrew literary sources, has been for some time a bone of contention among students of the *LBA*.[42] While it is true that there is no smoking gun that can definitively place Juan Ruiz in contact with *Šaʿašūʿīm*, the study of medieval literature and culture must take care not to restrict itself to a single methodology (i.e., Bédierian philology).[43] Medievalists are avid students of folklore and do not hesitate to attribute oral sources to authors;[44] yet the idea that a Hebrew text be transmitted orally into Castilian seems to be difficult for some critics to consider.

The story of this debate begins with a fairly innocuous, seemingly offhand comment by Francisco Fernández y González made in an 1894 lecture read to the *Real Academia Española*. He writes, innocently enough, that the *LBA* has the "forma de macama" ('form of a *maqāma*') (55). More than half a century later, Américo Castro argued that the *LBA* was structured in imitation of Ibn Hazm's amorous autobiographical treatise, *Ṭawq al-Ḥamāma* ('The Dove's Neck Ring') ("*Libro*" 195–205).[45] Gybbon-Monypenny first refutes Américo Castro's argument,[46] countering that the similarities between Ruiz and Ibn Hazm must be coincidental, for it is practically impossible that Ruiz would have had access to Ibn Hazm's work ("Autobiography" 65). María Rosa Lida de Malkiel refutes Castro's theory, but offers an alternative: that many

[41] cf. "España, o la historia de una inseguridad," ('Spain, or the history of an insecurity') the title of the first chapter of Castro's *España en su historia*.

[42] See, for example, the refutation of Lida de Malkiel's theories about the *LBA* by Sánchez-Albornoz ("Originalidad") and Menocal's critique thereof (*Arabic* 18–19 n. 5).

[43] [La filología] "es, insisto, una ciencia histórica, que no responde a una sola metología, sino que ajusta múltiples metodologías a los perfiles exactos de su objeto singular" ('[Philology] is, I insist, a historical science that does not respond to a single methodology, but rather one that adjusts multiple methodologies to the exact profiles of its singular object of study') (Funes and Tenenbaum lxix-–lx). Here Funes and Tenenbaum argue for a multiple-text approach to studying the epic cycle of the *Mocedades de Rodrigo* that includes editions of a rhymed chronicle, a prose redaction, and a conjectural reconstruction of an epic poem. That is, they combine strict positivist textual criticism with cultural analysis and a bit of speculation in order to render a fuller understanding of the subject. We would do well to follow their lead in the study of the *LBA* and other texts.

[44] See, for example, Sautman, Conchado and Di Scipio.

[45] See Castro ("*Libro*" 195–205) and the long chapter by the same title in *España* (355–446a).

[46] Abū Muḥammad ʿAlī ibn Ḥazm (994–1064), resident of Cordova and one of the most outstanding thinkers of his time and prolific author of works on poetry, theology, Islamic law, and history (*EI*, "Ibn Hazm").

of the structural and thematic oddities of the *LBA*[47] might be accounted for by Juan Ruiz's familiarity, direct or otherwise, with *Šaʿašūʿīm* (*Masterpieces* 21–25; *Dos Obras* 31–36; *Estudios* 21–30).[48] Critical responses to her arguments have been overwhelmingly negative, and in that of Sánchez-Albornoz, unabashedly vitriolic.[49]

It is interesting to note that some critics, despite their denial that the Hebrew *maqāmāt* may have influenced "European" literature such as the *LBA*, give descriptions of Ruiz's work that could be used verbatim to describe the Arabic and Hebrew *maqāmāt*. For example, Menéndez Pelayo describes it as

> un enjambre de visiones picarescas que derraman de improviso un rayo de alegría sobre la grandeza melancólica de las viejas y desoladas ciudades castellanas: Toledo, Segovia, Guadalajara, teatro de las perpetuas y non sanctas correrías del autor. El nos hace penetrar en la intimidad de truhanes y juglares, de escolares y de ciegos, [y] de astutas Celestinas... (xci)
>
> (a mishmash of picaresque visions that extemporaneously cast a ray of happiness over the melancholy grandeur of the old and desolate Castilian cities: Toledo, Segovia, Guadalajara, theater of the perpetual and profane wanderings of the author. He brings us into the inner life of ruffians and minstrels, students and blind men, [and] astute go-betweens.)

Likewise, Marina Brownlee might well be describing the atemporality of the *maqāma* when she writes that

> the protagonist does not undergo any chronological development or have any indication whatsoever of age attached to him. While not knowing his age, we similarly do not know how much time elapses between the beginning and the end of the narration. Indeed, rather than being linear, the temporal designations of this autobiography are clearly (and surprisingly) cyclical in nature (suggesting, I would argue, the limitations of human memory). ("Genre" 57)

---

[47] On exactly these, as well as other formal features of the *maqāma*, see Drory ("Maqama") and *EI*, "Maḳama." For a history of the genre, see Hämeen-Anttila.

[48] It should be noted that she first published (nearly twenty years earlier) an exhaustive study of the Latin sources of the *LBA* ("Notas").

[49] See Menocal's assessment of the argument of Sánchez-Albornoz (*Arabic*, 18–19 n. 5). Curiously, although nearly twenty years pass between Lida de Malkiel's comments and Castro's 1980 revision of his 1952 article, he does not make mention of her writing. He does, however, discuss Ibn Zabāra as an influence on Juan Ruiz, which he did not in 1952 (Castro, *España* 355–446).

In her identification of the *LBA* with the *maqāma* genre, Lida de Malkiel focuses on the importance of the autobiographical narrator and concludes that the narrator/protagonist of Ibn Zabāra,

> exactly as Juan Ruiz, is the protagonist of a single, rather loose narration, functioning as a frame-story for debates, dissertations, aphorisms, proverbs, portraits, parodies, tales and fables which, in turn, may introduce other tales and fables. The *Book of Delights* begins and ends with explanatory pieces and dedications in lyric verse at the beginning and in rhymed prose at the end, characteristics which recall the 1330 version of the *Book of Good Love*, with its initial lyrics to the Virgin and its epilogue in narrative verse. The narrator-protagonist reports that there appeared to him, a giant, his future interlocutor throughout the rest of the work, a situation which recalls the appearance of Sir Love as "a tall man" (181c), who is Juan Ruiz's interlocutor in the most important debate in his poem. The giant, with all kinds of promises, offers to conduct Yosef to his city. After a long deliberation for and against trips, comparable to Juan Ruiz's deliberation for and against love, Yosef accepts, just as after the debate with Sir Love, the Archpriest starts his longest episode. The wanderings of the two travelers bring to mind Juan Ruiz's journeys through the cities and across mountains. Finally, Yosef's displeasure with the unfamiliar city and nostalgia for his native land recall the line in which the lonely Juan Ruiz, passing through the city of Segovia, expresses the nostalgia for his home.... Such is the skeleton of the autobiographical narrative in the *Book of Delights*; to the similarities already indicated, we should add an equal taste for the reminiscences of the Scriptures, a tract on physiognomy, the caricature of an ugly woman, a humoristic portrait based on antithesis and verbal paradox, and invective against wine, a series of vilifications of the interlocutor... all of which have their exact counterparts in the *Book of Good Love*. (*Masterpieces* 21–22)

Lida de Malkiel then refutes both Gybbon-Monypenny and Castro by asserting that the *LBA* does not meet the criteria for "amorous pseudo-autobiography" set by Gybbon-Monypenny himself, arguing that such works

> narran un amor cortés llevado a formas extremas de refinamiento; el autor se identifica como protagonista, mencionando pormenores personales; se presenta favorablemente como dechado de amantes trovadorescos; inserta poemas líricos trovadorescos dirigidos a su dama. Gybbon-Monypenny no puede menos de reconocer lo evidente, a saber, que ninguno de estos rasgos figura en el *Buen amor* y, tras apurar su ingenio para explicarlo, concluye que tal ausencia se debe a que el *Buen amor* es una parodia de la autobiografía cortés. (*Estudios* 21)
>
> (narrate a courtly love carried to extreme forms of refinement; the author identifies himself as protagonist, mentioning personal details; he presents himself favorably as an example of a troubadouresque lover; he inserts troubadouresque lyric poems addressed to his lady. Gybbon-Monypenny can do no less than recognize what is evident, that is, that none of these features is present in the *LBA*, and after straining his intellect to prove it, concludes that

such an absence is owing to the fact that the *Buen amor* is a parody of the courtly autobiography.)

Lida de Malkiel concludes that there are no precedents for the narrator of the *LBA* in Christian literature, and that, although Castro is correct in seeking models in the Arabic and Hebrew literature of Iberia, they are not to be found in the work of Ibn Hazm (*Estudios* 22). Instead, she points to *Šaʿašūʿīm* as a more likely model, as we have seen. The effort of de Looze to place Juan Ruiz in a Christian tradition of pseudo-autobiography is more sophisticated, but cannot alone account for the idiosyncrasies of the narrator of the *LBA*. The answer to the question of the *LBA* and *Šaʿašūʿīm* lies in our understanding of the figure of Ruiz as narrator.

The "Crisis of Truth" and the Unreliable Narrators of the Maqāmāt

The figure of the narrator is essential in establishing authority with the audience. This authority—or lack of it—is realized by the way in which the narrator involves the audience, addressing them directly. In traditional storytelling, one assumes that the narrator desires the trust of the audience and wants the audience to regard him or her as reliable. The storyteller or narrator achieves this by addressing the audience in a sympathetic and engaging manner and by exhibiting a reliability and consistency in his storytelling. The story makes sense, is plausible within the limits of the given genre, and does not contradict itself (Rimmon-Kenan 100–03).

In the *LBA*, however, we have in Juan Ruiz an unstable narrator who contradicts the impulse to establish a consistent, reliable voice. Instead, we are presented with a voice constituted by contradictions: an Archpriest narrating his amorous exploits, a cleric writing in the vernacular. In his personality as narrator, Ruiz is much closer to the popular lyric tradition of the *juglares* than to the religious, church-sponsored works of *mester de clerecía*.[50] One of his own characters even describes him as an accomplished *juglar*.[51] Ruiz does not engage in the anti-*juglar* polemic found in works of *clerecía* such as the *Libro de Alexandre*:

---

[50] Zahareas writes that Juan Ruiz "invests [the] grossness and absurdity…with his own art and refinement, especially a subtle use of figurative language" (79).

[51] His go-between Trotaconventos ('Convent Hopper') relates to a prospective girlfriend that he "sabe los instrumentes e todas juglarías" ('he knows how to play musical instruments as well as all manner of minstrelsy') (st. 1489b).

> Mester trayo fermoso, non es de joglería;
> mester es sin peccado, qua es de clerecía:
> fablar curso rimado por la quaderna vía,
> a sílabas contadas, qua es grant maestría. (Berceo, *Alixandre* 149, st. 2)[52]
>
> (I bring a beautiful style, not that of a *juglar*;
> An impeccable style, that of the clergy:
> declaiming lines rhymed in *cuaderna vía*,
> by counted syllables, which demonstrates great mastery.)

On the contrary, Ruiz is a proud composer of "cantigas, de dança e troteras," ('dancing and walking songs') (1513a) including off-color "caçurros" (songs typical of itinerant, low-rent *juglares*) and "bulras" ('jocular ditties') (1514d). He is a moral authority preaching good behavior by gleefully detailing his own bad behavior. Instead of earning the audience's confidence, he introduces us to one contradiction after another, and instead of forging an author-audience relationship based on trust, he leads the reader into murky ambiguity and abandons him there.

It is difficult to locate an exact counterpart to the ambiguous Archpriest-narrator of the *LBA* in the European tradition of amorous pseudo-autobiography described by Gybbon-Monypenny. However, we do see analogues to this figure in narrators of Arabic and Hebrew *maqāmāt* penned in medieval Iberia. In the *LBA*, we are faced with an unstable narrator bearing the name of the author Juan Ruiz, but who is also recast in the form of other characters within the work (Don Melón and Don Carnal) without abandoning his identity as author/narrator. So, instead of the usual process by which an author creates a narrator, this almost seems to be a case of the narrator creating the author. After all, we have far more information about Juan Ruiz-narrator than about Juan Ruiz-author. In the *LBA*, the mimetic firewall between author, narrator, and protagonist breaks down. In the place of a clearly autobiographical narrator in which reality and literary representation are united, or a clear division between real author and fictional narrator where reality and literary representation are separate, we have in the curious figure of the Archpriest Juan Ruiz a continuum between possibly real author, possibly autobiographical narrator, and possibly fictional character.[53]

Juan Ruiz takes personal responsibility for this ambiguity, holding it up as a general lesson for the reader to beware of deception and to scrutinize actively

[52] See also Brian Dutton's comments on Berceo's attitude towards *juglaría* (Berceo, *San Millán* 175–84).

[53] On the question of the protean author/narrator figure, see Zahareas (*Art* 40–41), López Morales (38–50), Seidenspinner-Núñez (*Allegory* 54–55), Brownlee ("Permutations 98–101; "Autobiography" 71–82), Picard (7–16) and Santos (55–63).

the differences between appearance and reality, for things are not always as they seem.[54] In his prologue, he exhorts the reader to read between the lines, to distinguish the meaning of his words from the signs themselves:

> E ruego e consejo a quien lo leyere e lo oyere, que guarde bien las tres cosas del alma: lo primero, que quiera bien entender e bien juzgar la mi entençión por que lo fiz e la sentençia de lo que ý dize, e non al son feo de las palabras: e segund derecho,[55] las palabras sirven a la intençión e non la intençión a las palabras. (Prologue, ll. 125–31)
>
> (I beseech and advise whoever reads or hears it, that they bear in mind the three parts of the soul: the first, that they might strive to understand and judge well my intentions in writing it, and the meaning of what it says, and not the ugly sound of the words.)

In his introduction in verse, he reiterates the need to distinguish between the esoteric and the exoteric, between outer and inner meanings. He maintains that his book, although written in the vernacular and treating fairly risqué subject matter in a seemingly irreverent way, has great value for the reader:

> Non creades que es libro neçio, de devaneo,
> Nin tengades por chufa algo que en él leo:
> Ca, segund buen dinero yaze en vil correo,
> Ansí en feo libro está saber non feo.
> El axenuz, de fuera negro más que caldera,
> Es de dentro muy blanco más que la peñavera;
> Blanca farina está so negra cobertera,
> Açúcar dulçe e blanco está en vil cañavera.
> So la espina está la rosa, noble flor;
> So fea letra está saber de grand dotor;
> Como so mala capa yaze buen bevedor,[56]
> Ansí so mal tabardo está el buen amor. (16–19)
>
> (Do not take this for a simple or foolish book,
> Neither take for a joke anything I read from it:
> For, just as good money is found in a shoddy wallet,
> So in an ugly book one finds non-ugly wisdom.
> The fennel seed, black as a kettle on the outside,

[54] On the deceptiveness of appearances in the *LBA*, see Reiss and Urbina.
[55] The reference is to the *Moralia* of Saint Gregory (XXVI, ch. 7) cited by Gracian in *Decretum* (II, XXII, V, ii) (ed. Blecua 10 nn. 129–31). See also H. Kelly (13–21).
[56] This can be taken two ways: either the "bevedor" is a good one because he is able to hold his liquor (which would mean that the Archpriest is condoning heavy drinking), or he is good because he has the means to pay his tab despite his shabby cloak.

Is very white on the inside, even more so than ermine.
White flour is beneath a black husk,
Sugar sweet and white is inside a rough cane.
Beneath the spine is the rose, noble flower,
Beneath ugly lettering is the wisdom of a great doctor.
Just as beneath a cheap cape lies a good drinker,
So beneath a shoddy cover *Good Love* is found.)

Ruiz is not unique among contemporary Castilian authors in calling the reader's attention to the instability of the sign and demanding a close reading. This sentiment is echoed in the *Proverbios morales* of Santob de Carrión, who was writing in Castile at the same time as Juan Ruiz.[57] His imagery in the *Proverbios morales* is quite similar, and coincides with that of Ruiz more than once:

mucha espada
Dy [sic] fyno azero sano
Sabe de rrota vayna
Salir, e del gusano
Se faze la seda fyna.
E astroso garrote
Faze muy çiertos trechos,
E algunt rroto pellote
Cubre blancos pechos;
E muy sotil trotero
Aduze buenas nuevas,
E muy vil bozerro
Presenta çiertas pruevas.
Por nasçer en el espino,
Non val la rosa çierto
Menos, nin el buen vyno
Por nasçer en el sarmiento.
(ed. González-Llubera 14, vv. 172–85)

(Many a sword of good and fine steel comes from a torn sheath, and it is from the worm that fine silk is made.
And a miserable catapult can be most accurate, and a torn pelt can [still manage to] cover up white breasts;
And a conniving messenger can bring good news, and a lowly lawyer can introduce truthful arguments.

[57] The work exists in manuscripts in Castilian and in *aljamiado* text, Castilian written in Hebrew characters. This suggests that Santob wrote for both Jewish and Christian Castilian audiences (See the introduction of González-Llubera to his edition of Santob de Carrión, iv).

> For being born on the thornbush, the rose is certainly not worth less, nor is good wine if taken from the [grapes of the] lower branches of the vine). (trans. Perry 19–20, vv. 172–85)

Like his contemporary Santob, Juan Ruiz emphasizes the deceptiveness of appearances as a challenge to the audience to engage a critical eye. He uses ambiguity and unreliability as a means of eliciting active participation. Wolfgang Iser has written on the authorial uses of ambiguity, arguing that "it is the elements of indeterminacy that enable the text to "communicate" with the reader, in the sense that they induce him to participate both in the production and the comprehension of the work's intention" (24). In this case, the ambiguities of the text do not merely "enable" the reader to engage the text. Rather, she is under orders from an artfully deceptive author to apply her intellect in order to discern truth from falsehood. However, the author misleads the audience, undermining their ability to distinguish truth from falsehood. This stance, as we shall see, is characteristic of works of fiction in the Andalusī rationalist tradition.

The "Crisis of Truth" and the Kalām

The use of ambiguity and unreliability in the *LBA* as a technique to engage the reader has been observed by Laurence de Looze, who identifies one of the essential features of pseudo-autobiography as a "crisis of truth," in which the reader realizes he can no longer take the narrator's word at face value:

> The basic problem is as follows: what to do with an author who claims that his book is a "book of the self," who repeatedly calls upon his readers to understand the work correctly, but who also continually undermines stable meaning, beginning with his own identity? (*Pseudo* 45)

He traces this use of ambiguity to the *kalām* (rationalist philosophy) that flourished in al-Andalus in the eleventh and twelfth centuries and was exported to Christian Europe in the thirteenth and fourteenth:[58]

---

[58] The Averroism that flourished in the first half of the thirteenth century at Paris was formally renounced in 1270 and 1277 by Étienne Tempier, Archbishop of Paris. St. Albertus Magnus and his student St. Thomas Aquinas both attempted to incorporate aspects of Ibn Rushd's commentaries on Aristotle in order to reconcile the thought of the Andalusī with the tenets of Christianity (Cruz Hernández, *Ibn Rushd* 70). In Catalonia, Ramón Llull wrote several anti-Averroist treatises in the first two decades of the fourteenth century (Cruz Hernández, *Pensamiento* 283–84). On the influence of Ibn Rushd in the West, see Renan, Arnaldez, Fakhry, and *EI* ("Ibn Rushd").

> The relativity of truth which I have seen as characterizing the fourteenth century comes to the fore in the *Libro de buen amor*. We should bear in mind that the theory of "two truths" (one for philosophy, one for theology) that seemed to contradict each other—a theory in vogue in western Europe in the thirteenth century—was at base a Spanish contribution. (*Pseudo* 44)

It is this same struggle between the "two truths" of philosophy and theology that touched off the Maimonidean controversy in the Jewish communities of Spain and Southern France that raged during the first half of the thirteenth century (Silver; Septimus 61–63; Dobbs-Weinstein; Faur). In al-Andalus, a similar debate had taken place in the previous century between orthodox Sunni Muslim clerics and rationalist thinkers such as Ibn Rushd, who sought to reconcile Islamic faith with Greek philosophy. One who engaged in rationalist approaches to traditional Islamic doctrines was viewed as a *zindīq*, or intellectually dangerous heretic. The foremost practitioners of Islamic rationalism in al-Andalus were the Muʿtazilites,[59] who argued in favor of metaphorical interpretation (*taʾwīl*) of the Qurʾān. This focus on the tension between the written word and its possible interpretations, characteristic of medieval rationalist thought, is reflected in the figure of the unreliable narrator in the *maqāmāt* written in Hebrew and Arabic in the two centuries prior to the time of Juan Ruiz.

In the Arabic *maqāma*, the narrator's reliability is established by a chain of transmission leading from the fictive narrator/character to the author through two or three intermediaries. In the *maqāmāt* of al-Saraqusṭī, the chain is as follows:

> The author said:
> Al-Mundhir ibn Humām narrated and said:
> Al-Sāʾib ibn Tammām narrated to us and said:
> I was in a certain country…(trans. Monroe 114; ed. al-Warāglī 114)

This means that before the narration reaches the reader, it has to pass from al-Sāʾib ibn Tammām, to al-Mundhir ibn Humām, to al-Saraqusṭī, to whomever is transcribing al-Saraqusṭī's words. Notwithstanding this construction of narrative transmission, we are later assured that it is al-Saraqusṭī who "composed" these *maqāmāt*:

> Let it be known that the following are fifty *maqāmāt* composed by Abū-l Ṭāhir Muḥammad ibn Yūsuf al-Tamīmī al-Saraqusṭī in Córdoba, one of the cities of al-Andalus [Spain]. (trans. Monroe 113; ed. al-Warāglīl 17)

[59] For Islamic Rationalism in general, see Watt, Hourani, H. Wolfson (*Philosophy* and *Repercussions*). On Muʿtazilite theology, see Peters. On religious heterodoxy in Muslim al-Andalus, see Fiero Bello.

In Islamic tradition, such a chain of transmitters of a narrative text recalls the *isnād* cited at the beginning of a *ḥadīṯ*.[60] While in the *ḥadīṯ* tradition, the reader must rely on documented external witnesses to the soundness of the text, in narratives such as the *maqāma* and the *LBA*, the reader is dependent on the author/narrator himself to vouch for his own trustworthiness. In order for the narrator of a *ḥadīṯ* to be considered reliable, he must provide evidence of his own perceptiveness, moral fiber, and talent at verbatim memorization. Al-Saraqusṭī's narrator displays none of these. His narrator, al-Sā'ib ibn Tammām, is dim-witted, easily led astray, and extremely forgetful. He constantly contradicts himself. At the beginning of *maqāma* 30 ("The Poets"), he describes his love/hate relationship with the rogue character Abū Ḥabīb al-Sadūsī:

> Al-Sā'ib ibn Tammām said:
> In the person of the Master Abū Ḥabīb, I had been afflicted with a companion who hardly visited his injuries upon me infrequently...with a man who sent calamities my way and set snares in my path.... Despite that, I yearned to meet him, I sought to prolong my encounters with him.... In sum, I sought out his shape and form in every person who approached me. (trans. Monroe 307; ed. al-Warāglī 264)

Despite the constant abuse he suffers at al-Sadūsī's hands, ibn Tammām rejoices whenever he sees his tormentor. In the beginning of *maqāma* 32, ibn Tammām comes upon al-Sadūsī in the road: "then I scrutinized him, and lo, he was al-Sadūsī, whose like and equal are hard to find, so I kissed the toe-thong and heel-strap of his sandal" (trans. Monroe 340; ed. al-Warāglī 304–05).

There is a contradiction between the narrator's behavior and his integrity. Because his narrator al-Sā'ib ibn Tammām is repeatedly duped by the rogue al-Sadūsī, he cannot possibly be trusted to transmit a narrative intact. But is the narrator himself to blame? After all, if we follow al-Saraqusṭī's *isnād*, ibn Tammām (the narrator) recounts his exploits to al-Mundhir ibn Humām, who then narrates to al-Saraqusṭī. Yet another ambiguity enters the fray: it is possible that the weak link is not the narrator ibn Tammām, but the transmitter, al-Mundhir ibn Humām. In short, it is difficult to tell who has kidnapped the truth. Just as Juan Ruiz warns us in the prologue to the *LBA* to "bien entender e bien juzgar la mi entençión por que lo fiz e la sentençia de lo que ý dize" (10) ('understand and judge well my intention in writing it,

[60] On *hadīth* and its role in narrative literature, see the section of chapter 2 entitled "*Ḥadīth* and early prose fiction in Arabic."

and the meaning of what it says'), al-Saraqusṭī does likewise in the colophon of one of the manuscripts of his *maqāmāt*:

> We implore whoever considers and takes note of these words of ours, and strives and aspires to understand them with a critical appraisal, to be judicious and apply allegorical interpretation [*ta'wīl*] in his examination of them... and to realize that the human soul can move from one situation to another, can change its condition, and can alternate between truth and falsehood. (trans. Monroe 45; ed. al-Warāglī 467)

The author is entering into the game, and al-Saraqusṭī admits that it is difficult to know what is a lie and what is true and that this is part of the challenge of being human and part of the joy of the text. Both authors are enlisting the audience in negotiating the "crisis of truth" described by de Looze (*Pseudo* 8).

Authors of later *maqāmāt* written in Hebrew in medieval Iberia play out their own versions of the author-narrator game. Judah al-Ḥarīzī wrote his Hebrew *maqāmāt* at the beginning of the thirteenth century. Like al-Saraqusṭī, he consciously models his text on the *maqāmāt* of al-Ḥarīrī in an effort to prove the superiority of Hebrew as a vehicle for literary excellence. His *Taḥkemonī*, he admits, is an attempt to raise Hebrew to the level of a high prestige secular literary language, on a par with Arabic (trans. Reichert 1: 58; ed. Toporovsky and Zamora 29–30). He follows the classical Arabic *maqāmāt* in the figure of a luckless narrator (here named Heman the Ezrahite) persecuted by the literary rogue, Heber the Kenite. He sets up an unstable relationship between author and narrator. Instead of establishing a chain of transmission similar to the *isnād* of the Islamic *ḥadīṯ* literature (as does al-Ḥarīrī and his Andalusī imitator al-Saraqusṭī), he has the character and author speak for themselves. In a speech made to the narrator, the character Heber the Kenite gives us the idea that it is the narrator Heman the Ezrahite—and not the author—who is responsible for composing al-Ḥarīzī's *maqāmāt*:

> Know for a certainty that my name is Heber, the Kenite, and at the tree of Zaanannim is my encampment. And in many places you will meet me and in every Makama which you compose you will find me and I will answer you before you call me. (trans. Reichert 1: 58; ed. Toporovsky and Zamora 29–30)

With the phrase "in every Makama which you compose," the character Heber the Kenite seems to be speaking to the author through the narrator, Heman the Ezrahite. However, (like al-Saraqusṭī) in the prologue to the *Taḥkemonī*, al-Ḥarīzī has already taken the credit (or the blame) for composing his *maqāmāt* and creating the characters portrayed within them. In giving this disclaimer, the author is echoing a Talmudic saying used to establish the boundaries between reality and fiction: "it never was and never happened, but is only a parable."[61] The Hebrew *maqāmāt* tend to be more allegorical and less realistic than the Arabic *maqāmāt* because of this restriction: the authors wish to avoid misrepresenting reality and so make it perfectly clear that what they are writing is fiction (Drory, "Maqama" 205). With this disclaimer, the author revokes suspension of disbelief in order to effect more complex relationships between author, narrator, and character.

In the model of narrative transmission employed by al-Saraqusṭī, a narrator relates a story to an author, who then writes it down. In order to establish unequivocally that what follows is fiction and not reportage, al-Ḥarīzī inverts the mimetic relationship between narrator and author. The narrator, Heman the Ezrahite, explains to Heber the Kenite (the rogue), that he is informed by the author, and not the opposite: "Heman, the Ezrahite speaks: The author of this book told me plainly of the pearls of his thought and of the metaphors of his tongue" (trans. Reichert 1: 44; ed. Toporovsky and Zamora 19). That is, he announces the work's fictionality by directly addressing the audience, an action known in theater criticism as "breaking the fourth wall" (Pavis 154).

The way in which the authors of Arabic and Hebrew *maqāmāt* deal with the relationship between audience, narrator, and author is conditioned by the literary cultures of Islam and Judaism. While Arabic authors such as al-Saraqusṭī parodied the authority of traditional oral transmission by adhering to the traditional structure of *isnād* (chain of transmission) and *maṭn* (body of message) found in *ḥadīṯ*, Hebrew authors sought to respect rabbinical warnings against misrepresenting reality and deliberately (but artfully) drew the reader's attention to their works' fictionality.[62] Later authors of *maqāmāt* in both Hebrew and Arabic continued to experiment with the way they expressed fictionality, bringing us closer to the protean author/narrator/protagonist of the *LBA*.

The last author of *maqāmāt* we shall examine, Joseph ben Meir ibn Zabāra, brings us full circle back to our discussion of the *LBA*. Ibn Zabāra, a physician living in Barcelona, wrote his *Šaʿašūʿīm* at the end of the twelfth

---

[61] See chapter 2, n. 72.

[62] See Drory ("Maqama"). We discuss this process more thoroughly in our discussion of performance in the Hebrew and Arabic *maqāmāt* of medieval Iberia in chapter 2.

century. His text departs from the classical form of the *maqāma* represented by the work of al-Hamadhānī and al-Ḥarīrī;[63] like the *LBA*, it is a more free-ranging treatise touching on several subjects and including proverbs, short tales, debates, and poetry. Like the classical *maqāmāt*, the content is framed by a series of discussions or encounters between the protagonist and his antagonist. *Šaʿašūʿīm* brings us one step farther away from the narrator of the classical *maqāmāt* and one step closer to the narrator/protagonist of the *LBA*.[64]

One innovation of Ibn Zabāra is of particular interest: the narrator, Ibn Zabāra himself, functions as another literary character within the sometimes fantastic and openly fictional world created by the author.[65] In al-Ḥarīzī's *Taḥkemonī*, the narrator is passing along the words of the author; here, as in the *LBA*, the narrator *is* the author. His blurring of the real and the fictional is a game intended to elicit the active participation of the reader, a function fulfilled in the Arabic *maqāmāt* by the unreliability of the narrator.

Ibn Zabāra's skillful dovetailing of the real and the fictional begins in the prologue, where he performs an antithetical segue. It begins with a glowing panegyric to his real-life sponsor, Sheshet Benveniste, and moves into a scathing invective against the fictional rogue character, 'Enan Hanatas (trans. Hadas 182; ed. Davidson 2–3). In this way, he brings the real Benveniste and the fictional Hanatas into the same arena. He writes a similarly deft transition at the beginning of the first chapter, where he opens in the third person, describing himself:

> There once was a man in the County of Barcelona, whose name was Joseph ibn Zabāra. From his youth up he had dwelt at ease, in amity with his friends, and they that were his friends loved him; among them was he respected and esteemed, bound to all by ties of affection. He for his part honored and exalted them, served them and healed them. For those of them that were sick he compounded suitable remedies, in accordance with his knowledge and skill.... (trans. Hadas 47; ed. Davidson 5)

[63] Later *maqāmāt* began to display characteristics of the *risāla* genre of treatise, which was sometimes written in dialogue and was not necessarily a narrative genre. See *EI* ("Risāla") especially section six, "Risāla and maḳāma." On Ibn Zabāra's work relative to the *maqāma* genre, see Dishon (*Šaʿašūʿīm* 22–30).

[64] Roughly contemporary with the *LBA* is an Arabic *maqāma* by the Granadan Ibn al-Murābiʿ al-Azdī (d. 1350), which likewise conflates the author, narrator, and protagonist (de la Granja).

[65] On the variations of the narrator/protagonist in the Hebrew *maqāmāt*, see Dishon (*Šaʿašūʿīm* 25–26).

In the very next paragraph, he switches to the first person: "It was nighttime, and I, Joseph, was sleeping in my bed with a sweet sleep, the only recompense for my fatigue…" (ed. Davidson 5). Ibn Zabāra has come up with a new solution to the problem of fictionality. By representing himself as a character in an obviously fantastic world, and furthermore a character dreaming the narration we are about to read,[66] he avoids the problem of having to state openly that his work is one of fiction and that his narrator does not, in fact, exist. He is off the hook, and so tells the reader openly: "this is a dream that I had as a character in a book that I wrote." Here the author does not suspend disbelief, but rather encourages it. The author leaves little room for doubt, and his "I, Joseph" vividly heralds the "yo, Juan Royz" of the *LBA* over 100 years hence.

Aside from the unified author-narrator character, The *LBA* bears a number of striking similarities to *Šaʿašūʿīm*, some of which were pointed out by Lida de Malkiel.[67] Her arguments have drawn a good deal of criticism on grounds both general and specific.

Critics of the *LBA* have been dismissive of Lida de Malkiel's ideas. Anthony Zahareas has characterized her study as "general and…vague," adding that because Ibn Zabāra's work does not deal with matters amorous, it is unlikely to have served as a structural model for Ruiz (*Art* 10 n. 7).[68] Louise Haywood agrees, writing that "the narrator [in the *LBA*] does not relate any personal amorous adventures and thus the *Book of Delights* is quite different from the *Libro*" (27).[69] She also notes the absence of any surviving manuscripts of medieval vernacular or Latin *maqāmāt* and doubts that the Archpriest's social milieu would have made it possible for him to become

[66] By the thirteenth century, Aristotle's *De somno et vigilia, De somniis, and De divinatione per somnum* had been anonymously translated into Latin, and the idea that dreams were not necessarily divine in origin had taken hold in the European intellectual imagination. Petrarch (1304–1374), for example, was bluntly skeptical of divine dreams (Kruger 84 and 87). This distinction was one between divinely delivered reality (prophetic dream) and human imagination ("normal" dream) (E. Wolfson 119). On the dream in medieval Castilian literature, focusing largely on sentimental romances (and therefore quite different from portentous dreams, as in the *Cantar de Mio Cid*), see Palley (31–63), Cerghedean, and Goldberg ("Dream").

[67] See Lida de Malkiel (*Dos obras* 31–32). There are also differences in the structures of the two texts. For example, the *LBA* does not maintain the same narrator/interlocutor relationship throughout, but rather limits it to the Archpriest's dialogue with Don Amor (st. 181–88 and 388–575).

[68] Richard Burkard concurs, noting that "*The Book of Delight* contains not a single amatory or erotic episode" (*Archpriest* 127).

[69] This is akin to arguing that the filmic techniques popularized by the director of a spaghetti Western cannot possibly have influenced the director of a later political thriller, because the themes of the two films differed.

acquainted with the Hebrew *maqāmāt*.[70] Richard Burkard argues that Ruiz cannot have been influenced by Ibn Zabāra because he does not openly name any Hebrew sources as he does Latin ones (*Archpriest* 130).

Other critics seem to regard the entire matter of Hebrew and Arabic literature as an irrelevant nuisance and argue that we should stick closer to "home" in our search for Ruiz's sources and influences. Alberto Blecua flatly declares that it is simply unnecessary to take the *maqāmāt* into consideration and that we can find everything we need within "Western" tradition.[71] According to Dayle Seidenspinner-Núñez, "a more reasonable approach" is to limit our inquiry "within the context of European tradition" (*Allegory* 40).[72] We must bear in mind that the question of "influences" is hardly a zero sum game. To suggest that Ruiz was influenced in part by Ibn Zabāra or other Hebrew and Arabic works does not in any way deny that the overwhelming majority of his influences are from Latin and Romance tradition. Despite this, critics have accused proponents of Ruiz's Hebrew and Arabic heritage of exactly that, seemingly suggesting that such arguments are a stain on Ruiz's purely Latin heritage. For example, Gybbon-Monypenny has written that "it is the great weakness of his case that Castro totally, one is tempted to say deliberately, ignores the possibility of European literary influences on the structure of the *Libro de buen amor*." ("Autobiography" 64).[73]

In any event, it would be untenable to argue that the structure of the *LBA* is identical to that of *Šaʿašūʿīm* or that Ibn Zabāra was Ruiz's only model. Rather, I submit that Juan Ruiz was influenced by Ibn Zabāra—along with other of the many texts and traditions available to medieval Iberian writers—through his social interactions with learned Castilian Jews and that

[70] Haywood also admits "my conclusions are based on the best evidence available to me and must remain tentative until such time as a full study of the Arabic and, more especially, the Hispano-Hebraic *maqāmāt* has been carried out and is available to scholars working in the Western tradition" (31). One might ask why a text by an author native to a Barcelona that had been under Christian rule for centuries would not be considered part of the "Western" tradition.

[71] "La estructura del *Libro de buen amor* puede explicarse por la conjunción de tradiciones literarias occidentales sin necesidad de acudir a las *maqāmāt*" (Ruiz, ed. Blecua xxiv) ('The structure of the *Libro de buen amor* can be explained by the multiple Western literary traditions without need to resort to the *maqāmāt*').

[72] We fully agree, with the proviso that texts by medieval Iberian authors—in any language—are both European (the Iberian Peninsula is geographically part of the European continent) and Western (the Iberian Peninsula is at the Western limit of the medieval world, whether Christian or Islamic. The name *maġrib*, or the Islamic west that included al-Andalus and what is now Morocco, means 'West').

[73] Regardless one's opinion of Castro's arguments and methods, to assert that he denied the influence of Latin and Romance literature on the *LBA* is simply incorrect.

this combination of influences is an important part of the enduring appeal of the *LBA*.

Let us examine some of the coincidences between *Šaʿašūʿīm* and the *LBA* in greater detail. Both works are much more loosely organized than the classical *maqāma*. They are not divided into clearly demarcated chapters of comparable length. Both authors expound on topics in which they specialize: the Archpriest on religion and morals, and Ibn Zabāra on medicine. Their interlocutors, Don Amor and ʿEnan Hanatas, are both described as physically imposing.[74] Both contain invectives against wine.[75] Both contain proverbs drawn from antiquity on the subject of small women,[76] and both contain excerpts from treatises on physiognomy.

This last topic plays an important part in placing the Archpriest in the tradition of unreliable hapless narrators of the medieval Iberian Hebrew and Arabic *maqāmāt*, particularly in assessing the (un)reliability of the author/narrator. In the *LBA*, the Archpriest dispatches his new go-between, Trotaconventos, to woo his beloved on his behalf. In making her sales pitch, she gives a detailed description of the Archpriest's features:[77]

> "Señora" diz la vieja, "yo·l veo a menudo:
> el cuerpo ha bien largo, mienbros grandes, trefudo;
> la cabeça non chica, velloso, pescoçudo;
> el cuello non muy luengo, cabelprieto, orejudo;
> las çejas apartadas, prietas como carbón;
> el su andar enfiesto, bien como de pavón;

[74] *LBA*: "un ome grande, fermoso, mesurado, a mí vino" (st. 181c); *Šaʿašūʿīm*: "And it came to pass as I slumbered that I saw an appearance of a man before me in my dream, in the likeness of a man exceeding tall" (ed. Davidson 8; trans. Hadas 47–48). Burkard's claim that Ibn Zabāra's antagonist Enan is not a man at all, but rather a "fire breathing giant" is problematic, as Enan is only revealed as such at the work's end (*Archpriest* 128).

[75] The invectives against wine found in the *LBA* (st. 544–45) and in *Šaʿašūʿīm* (ed. Davidson 10; trans. Hadas 51) coincide in several details concerning the physical detriments of excessive wine bibbing. According to Ruiz, wine "faze perder la vista" ('makes one lose one's vision') and to Ibn Zabāra it "blindeth the eyes." The Archpriest warns that wine "tira la fuerça si·s toma sin medida" ('weakens one if taken in excess') and "faze tenblar los miembros" ('makes one's limbs shake'); Ibn Zabāra, that "it weakeneth the power of the body" and "corrupt[s] all the members of the body." Finally, Ruiz claims that the winedrinker "todo seso olvida" ('forgets all sense'); Ibn Zabāra, that he will suffer "forgetfulness" and "foolish[ness]."

[76] *LBA*: "del mal tomar lo menos, dízelo el sabidor,/ por ende de las mugeres la mejor es la menor" (st. 1617c–d); *Šaʿašūʿīm*: "I have chosen the least of the evil" (trans. Hadas 66; ed. Davidson 30). None of the editors or translators of Zabāra cites a source for the anecdote as applied to women. However, Blecua attributes the general concept to Aristotle's *Nicomachean Ethics*, as indicated by Cicero in his *De officiis* (Ruiz, ed. Blecua 419 n. 1617c).

[77] For personal description in medieval Spanish literature in general, see Goldberg ("Personal"); in the *LBA* specifically, see Kane.

el paso sosegado e de buena razón;
la su nariz es luenga: esto le descompón.
Las ençivas bermejas e la fabla tunbal;
la boca non pequeña, labros al comunal,
más gordos que delgados, bermejos como coral;
las espaldas bien grandes, las muñecas atal.
los ojos ha pequeños, es un poquillo baço;
los pechos delanteros, bien trefudo el braço;
bien conplidas las piernas; el pie, chico pedaço". (st. 1485–1488)

("Madame" said the old lady, "I see him often:
he has a large body with long, muscular limbs;
his head is not small, he's got a good head of hair and a thick neck;
his neck is not long, he's a big-eared brunette;
His eyebrows are separated, black like coal;
His gait is stately, much like that of a peacock;
his step is calm and measured;
his nose is long; this ruins his proportions.
His gums are red and his voice clarion;
his mouth is not small, his lips regular-sized,
more thick than thin, red like coral;
his back is wide and his wrists are thick.
He has small eyes and is a bit dark;
His chest is prominent, his arm quite muscular;
His legs well-formed, his foot, a little thing.")

The description seems largely positive, as might be expected from a go-between whose livelihood depends on successfully matching her clients (such as the Archpriest) with their love objects. Peter Dunn has written on the significance of this portrait of the author.[78] He surveys the Latin physiognomic literature of Medieval Europe and suggests that features of the description of Juan Ruiz given by Trotaconventos are suggestive of the Archpriest's sexual prowess ("Figuras" 84–88). However, for some reason the Archpriest cannot realize this potential and instead meets with a series of misadventures. He is a man "whose temperament promises success, but who is rendered helpless by some contrary influence. A cynical clown who stumbles over himself, and who can blame his fate for the falls" ("Figuras" 89). This clown is very reminiscent of al-Saraqusṭī's antagonist, Abū Ḥabīb al-Sadūsī, who repeatedly blames his misdeeds on "Fate" or "Time" (Ar. *dahr* or *zamān*) (trans. Monroe 124, 131, 133, 353, 361, 366, 414, 440, and 514; ed. al-Warāglī 28, 42, 44, 316, 325, 332, 380, 406, and 478). However,

[78] On literary portraiture, see also Briere.

because the narrators of the *maqāmāt* are unreliable in both word and deed, we must turn a critical eye not only to the "clowning" actions of the Archpriest, but also to the description of himself that he relates to the reader. Because it is clear that the Archpriest narrator is incompetent in his exploits as a lover and willfully deceptive as a narrator, we must watch his every move. When a man who sermonizes about the falseness of appearances sets forth a detailed description of himself, one had better apply scrutiny in reading it. To this end, let us examine Ibn Zabāra's brief discourse on physiognomy in *Šaʿašūʿīm*. It is based on material from the Arabic *Sirr al-asrār* ('Secret of Secrets'), from which the Latin *Secretum secretorum* and Aragonese *Poridat de poridades* were translated (Davidson, "Introduction" lxxxii–lxxxvi).[79] For purposes of comparison, we reproduce the relevant passage from Ibn Zabāra's text here:

> He whose eyes are sunken and quick to behold and perceive, that man is cunning and wily and of many devices.... And if his nose is in part thin, but his nostrils are full and large, he is a contentious man, full of dissension and quarrelsome.... If his lips be large and thick he is dull, evil by nature, and contentious. He whose ears are large is simple and full of folly. He whose neck is short is a deceiver, every man's adversary and enemy. He whose abdomen is large and whose ribs are well covered with flesh, his folly will neither depart nor minish.... Every tall man is a fool, sinful in speech, blind, and a follower of lustfulness. (trans. Hadas 54–55; ed. Davidson 17–20)

If we map the attributes of the Archpriest described by Trotaconventos in the *LBA* to their values as explained by Ibn Zabāra, a much different understanding of the description emerges. What now to make of the Archpriest? His small eyes give away his "cunning and wily" nature. His long body (i.e., he is tall) marks him as a "fool" who is "sinful in speech"; his not-very long neck as "every man's adversary and enemy." Would his thick lips make him an attractive suitor, despite them marking him as "dull, evil in nature, and contentious?"[80] In light of Ibn Zabāra's physiognomic lore, even the most skilled go-between would be hard put to pass off a man who was "orejudo" and therefore "simple and full of folly."[81] In short, a close analysis of the Archpriest's features according to Ibn Zabāra's physiognomy reveals what a

[79] For the corresponding section in the Aragonese translation, see Pseudo Aristotle (62–63).

[80] A man with thick lips is "loco et de gruesso entendimiento" ('crazy and of crude understanding'). Luckily this is tempered by their redness, which means that he is "tenprado en todos sos fechos" ('cautious in all his deeds') (Pseudo Aristotle 64, l. 14–16).

[81] A man with large ears is "torpe et retenedor de lo que oye" ('stupid but remembers what he hears') (Pseudo Aristotle 64, l. 25).

casual appraisal does not: far from a virile, handsome suitor, our Archpriest is but a simple villain, and the narrator (and perhaps Trotaconventos as well) a deceiver.[82] The calculated unreliability of the narrator extends even to his own description of himself, another move in Juan Ruiz's narratological fan dance of ambiguity fueled by rationalist cynicism.

The didactic ambiguity and narrative instability precipitated by the Averroist "crisis of truth" is the impulse behind the dubious self-portrait of the Archpriest that we have just seen. It is also the most consistent characteristic of the narrators of Hebrew and Arabic Iberian *maqāmāt*. Ruiz freely adapts the narrative resources used by authors of these *maqāmāt* in their treatment of the narrator figure. Like al-Saraquṣṭī, he relies on ambiguities such as the unreliability of the narrator, and the deceptiveness of exteriors, to engage the reader. Like al-Ḥarīzī, he is explicit in announcing the objectives of his text to the reader and in pointing out the contradictions therein. Like Ibn Zabāra, he combines the author and narrator into a single character who ranges across mimetic boundaries. It may not be feasible to call the *LBA* a Castilian *maqāma*;[83] however, on the strength of its structural and didactic affinities with the *maqāma*, the *LBA* easily qualifies as the Castilian first cousin of the Hebrew and Arabic *maqāmāt*. Still, this idea has encountered stiff resistance from medieval Hispanists.[84]

There is not now—and may never be—a smoking gun, concrete evidence that Juan Ruiz knew of *Šaʿašūʿīm*. There is, however, a good deal of evidence that suggests he was in some way familiar with the Hebrew *maqāmāt* of Ibn Zabāra and other Peninsular authors. The Toledo of his day was clearly a place where multilingualism and multiglossia were commonplace and had long been a center of translation from Arabic and Hebrew into Latin and Castilian. Ruiz himself is an avowed multiculturalist who peppers his poetry with Andalusī Arabic and Latin, writes of Arabic music, of his attempted seduction of a Muslim woman, and of his familiarity with the local Jewish

[82] Additionally, the Archpriest's thick head of hair as described by Trotaconventos means that one should "guardat uos del commo uos guardariedes de la biuora mortal" ('be on guard against him as against a lethal serpent') (Pseudo Aristotle 62, ll. 15–18).

[83] Nonetheless, Lida de Malkiel does not hesitate to do exactly that: "The *Book of Good Love* belongs to the literary genre of Semitic *maqāmāt*, an essentially didactic genre" (*Masterpieces* 25).

[84] As Louise Haywood suggests (31), not one of the critics of Lida de Malkiel discussed above refers to original Arabic or Hebrew texts in their studies. Even the strident Sánchez-Albornoz relied entirely on translations of Arabic historical sources. See, for example, the bibliographical notes in Sánchez-Albornoz ("Originalidad"). This fact has not eluded contemporary historians in their surveys of twentieth-century Spanish medieval historiography, especially in the case of Arabists such as Christys (5).

community. He seems quite at ease among his Jewish and Muslim neighbors, and his literary persona does not hesitate to eat, drink, dance, and fraternize with them. It is even possible that he spent his childhood in al-Andalus. Our author lived his life in a highly multicultural society, and his work clearly registers this experience.

The very genres to which the *LBA* belongs, the frametale and *maqāma*, are characterized by crossings both linguistic and religious: Petrus Alfonsi converted from Judaism to Christianity before composing his *Disciplina clericalis* based on Arabic and Hebrew sources. Judah al-Ḥarīzī translated the *maqāmāt* of al-Ḥarīrī from Arabic into Hebrew (in Toledo), in which language he then wrote his own *Taḥkemonī*. Alfonso X ordered the translation of *Kalīla wa-Dimna* into Castilian, which provides Juan Manuel (a contemporary of Juan Ruiz) with the structure for his *Conde Lucanor*. Juan Ruiz lived in the same Toledo of al-Ḥarīzī and the Alfonsine translators, in the same Castile as Juan Manuel. He was heir to a fledgling Castilian literary tradition that was practically a by-product of translations from Arabic made by Jews.[85]

Remarkably, despite all of this, some Hispanists persist in denying that Hebrew literature may have somehow had an impact on the *LBA*, arguing instead that there is "no need" to go beyond Latin and Romance in order to understand Juan Ruiz's work. Notwithstanding the scholarly shortcomings of such an approach, it is curious that in today's dizzyingly multicultural world, where the free interchange of people and information across borders has become the norm, and where digital technology has brought even the most isolated into intimate communication, that one would want to project onto Juan Ruiz a narrowness and parochialism that rang just as false in the fourteenth century as it does in the twenty-first.

[85] In Girón Negrón's words, "Arabic enabled Castilian literary prose to be born" ("Translations" 234).

CHAPTER SIX

SOCIAL CHANGE, MISOGYNY, AND THE *MAQĀMA* IN JAUME ROIG'S *SPILL*

Juan Ruiz, as a Christian cleric living in Castile-León, lived in a world whose social paradigms were still largely defined by feudalism and by the division of the estates into nobility, clergy, and commoner. While the Christian conquests of al-Andalus, as we have seen, created significant wealth and opportunity for non-nobles, the sophistication and volume of commercial activity had yet to produce a significant population of what moderns would describe as bourgeois: lawyers, traders, and other specialized professionals whose income afforded them a standard of living previously known only to nobles. However, in the fifteenth century, bourgeois culture was very much a part of life in Valencia, where physician Jaume Roig practiced medicine and wrote. More than some 100-odd years separate Ruiz from Roig: the former was a Castilian cleric who lived in a socio-political atmosphere that was as yet (relatively) tolerant of Jews, while Roig's Valencia was home to some of the worst violence in 1391 (the crucial tipping point for Christian-Jewish relations in Christian Iberia) and 1413–1414 (during the Disputation of Tortosa). Ruiz's Toledo had been an imperial city and important intellectual center for centuries; Roig's Valencia was just coming into its own as an important literary town during his lifetime.

The literary boom in Valencia during the late fifteenth and early sixteenth centuries was fueled by a mercantile economy that no longer adhered to the values of medieval feudalism. Because many writers no longer depended upon or aspired to courtly patronage, some of them (with Roig leading the way) produced works that reflected their middle-class experience and distanced themselves from courtly genres and conventions. In our discussion of the Arabic *maqāmāt*, we have seen that innovation in narrative fiction often accompanies significant socio-political upheaval. The Arabic *maqāma* genre was a product of the shift between (Arab) ʿAbassid and (Persian) Sasānid dynasties in Iraq. In al-Andalus, al-Saraqusṭī wrote his own *maqāmāt* during a time when the courtly patronage of the *mulūk at-ṭawāʾif* (Sp. *Reyes de Taifas*, 'Party Kings') gave way to that of the far more socially conservative Almohads (Ar. *al-muwaḥiddūn*). Critics of the Spanish picaresque novel have long associated its emergence with the changing social and economic conditions of sixteenth-century Castile. Some of these same conditions obtained in fifteenth- century Valencia, where Jaume Roig wrote his long and curious narrative poem, the *Spill* (ca. 1455).[1] The *Spill* is a fiercely misogynous first-person narrative relating the misadventures of the narrator at the hands of four consecutive wives. In the *Spill*, Roig adapts the narrative resources of the Hebrew *maqāma* to reflect the angst generated by a powerful emergent Valencian bourgeoisie (including a large population of *conversos*) that edged out the nobility on the political stage.[2] His work portrays a world of self-made knights, merchants, physicians and lawyers, whose moral cynicism and material indulgence reflect the angst of a new class defined by personal and professional success rather than by hereditary title and property.[3] As in the *maqāma*, Roig's itinerant first-person narrator relates his repeated misadventures in an effort to educate the reader. As with the *maqāmāt*, Roig writes in a highly restrictive rhymed prose in a display of rhetorical virtuosity, and we read his story through the eyes of an author/narrator/protagonist. However, while narrators of *maqāmāt* tend to blame their repeated misfortune on "Time" or "Fate" (although it is clearly a result of their own stupidity), Roig's narrator blames women, who in his view are responsible for (or at the very least represent) the worst excesses of bourgeois materialism and moral decrepitude. In this way, Roig unites the narrative and stylistic conventions of the Arabic and Hebrew *maqāmāt* with the Iberian tradition of misogynist literature and prefigures the picaresque

[1] Although the *Spill* circulated in several manuscripts, only one survives. (Ms. Vat. Lat. 4806), which Chabàs dates between 1490 and 1492, and Carré i Pons between 1479 and 1505. The early printed editions are as follows: (Valencia: Francesc Diaz Romano, 1531), (Barcelona: Jaume Cortey, 1561), (Valencia: Joan de Arcos, 1561), (Valencia: Carles Ros, 1735), (Barcelona: Francesch Pelay Briz, 1865). See the modern editions of Carré i Pons, Miquel i Planas, and Chabás i Llorente, the Castilian translation of Miquel i Planas, and the English translation of Delgado-Librero. The latter includes a detailed textual history in pages 38–49. In the present study I cite the original Valencian (by verse number) and the English translation (by page number), both from the edition/translation of Delgado-Librero.

[2] According to Martín de Riquer, the *Spill* is "profundament burguesa" ('profoundly bourgeois') as a work of literature in that the sole objective of the protagonist is to live in Valencia "ben considerat, amb una muller bona i fidel i voltat de fills" ('well thought of, with a good, faithful wife, and surrounded by children') (3: 240–41).

[3] "L'*Espill* és una obra molt il·lustrativa i simptomàtica de les tensions culturals viscudes per tot arreu d'una Europa que, des de la cosmovisió medieval, s'obrí cap a les expectatives del nou ordre burgés" ('The *Spill* is a work very illustrative and symptomatic of the cultural tensions experienced all over a Europe that, from the medieval worldview, was opening itself up to the expectations of the new bourgeois order') (Vellón i Lahoz 20).

novel in the episodic tale of the unfortunate exploits of a self-made man in constant conflict with characters representing the worst of a society in which traditional values are being displaced by a new social order.

In this chapter, I will address the formal and thematic similarities between the *Spill* and the *maqāma*, paying particular attention to the possibility that (as in the case of the *LBA*) Roig may have been exposed to Hebrew *maqāmāt* through social contact with numerous Jewish and/or *converso* physicians in Valencia with whom he was acquainted. I then discuss the question of the social angst generated by the rise of the Valencian bourgeois, in which the local *converso* population played no small part. I argue that in the *Spill* this angst takes the shape of a relentless misogyny, a trope well familiar to fifteenth-century Iberian readers and authors. Thus, Roig contributed to Peninsular traditions of frametale and misogynist literature expressed first in Hebrew and Latin, and later in Castilian and (Valencian) Catalan.

Social Change and Literary Innovation

Changes in literary values such as genre and poetic style are precipitated by social change. Shifts in economic systems, government, social organization, and demography often have an impact on contemporary literature. The new literature seeks to affirm these changes by undermining the values of the old establishment and asserting those of the new. Peter Dronke has written that in such moments, "truth emerges from testing—but this testing often takes the form of undermining the sureness of authorities, institutions and points of view, just as, linguistically, of undermining an established decorum of genres and diction" (5–6, cited in Young, *Rogues* 15). Thus, genre and conventional aesthetics are linked to institutional power and patronage.[4]

The *Spill* appears at a historical midpoint between the innovation of the Arabic *maqāma* and the Castilian picaresque novel, both of which appeared during periods of decline in courtly literary patronage. The Arabic *maqāma* was the product of a shift away from courtly patrons, who favored the *qaṣīda* genre (ode) of Classical Arabic poetry. Because authors of *maqāmāt* functioned outside of a courtly environment, they were at liberty to innovate, to experiment, and to challenge conventional values of the literary

[4] For example, in twenty-first-century North America, the popular novel is supported by the mainstream publishing industry, while poetry is largely the purview of the academic press.

establishment.[5] Their preference for rhymed prose (*sajʿ*) over verse (*šiʿr*) was rooted in questions of political power and social change. Authors of the *maqāmāt* parodied traditional narrative genres such as *ḥadīth* (and, one might argue, the rhymed prose of the Qurʾān itself), and their protagonists presented the reader with an ironic, cynical point of view. While practitioners of the classical *qaṣīda* had long lampooned their enemies in works of satirical invective (*hijāʾ*), authors of the *maqāmāt* lampooned the very institutions that had produced such genres. Their criticism was not directed against prominent individuals, but rather, against society itself.[6]

The ironic narrator as outsider is also a key feature of the Castilian picaresque novel, likewise the result of a shift away from courtly and ecclesiastical patronage when middle-class writers were carving out a space for themselves on the literary scene.[7] At a time when the medieval feudal court had long since ceased to be a reality, the picaresque mocked those writers who still clung to pretensions of courtly culture.[8]

Some of the social and economic factors that gave rise to *Lazarillo* and *Guzmán de Alfarache* in Castile in the sixteenth century already obtained in Valencia in the fifteenth. These correspond in part to the conditions of tenth-century Baghdad where al-Hamad̲ānī wrote the first *maqāmāt*. These societies were past their peak of imperial expansion and boasted a growing middle class whose experience and values pit them against the landed nobility, who favored the outmoded values of courtly genres.[9] The picaresque can then be conceived as a middle-class genre giving voice to professionals, merchants, downwardly-mobile petty nobility, *conversos*, and other members of the growing ranks of the *mijantes* (middle class).

---

[5] The position of James Monroe is that "if the *qaṣīdah* is a genre for the consumption of insiders privy to royal courts, the *maqāma* may be viewed as the literature of outsiders no longer welcome at those courts" ("Preliminary Study" 12).

[6] On the shift from personal to institutional satire in the *maqāma* and in *Don Quijote*, see Monroe ("Preliminary" 13–17). On *hijāʾ* poetry, see *EI*, "Hid̲j̲āʾ."

[7] Anne Cruz writes that "Spain's feudal disintegration [during the fifteenth and sixteenth centuries], ruthlessly brought to bear on those whose disenfranchisement would be its end result, conforms with the ironized and distanced position manifested by the picaresque narrator" (7).

[8] "Since the compulsion to fashion one's self as a socially individuated being corresponds to an acute awareness of social alienation, the picaresque genre cannot fail to parody the autobiographical mode or mimic the canonical discourses that invariably aimed to anchor their authors in increasingly evanescent realms, whether as courtiers, intellectuals, or explorers of new worlds" (Cruz 7).

[9] In the case of the Castilian picaresque, the rigorous adulation of the beloved typical of the courtly poetry favored by the nobility was replaced with a misogynist, conflictive vision of male-female relations (Maravall, *Picaresca* 651).

The protagonists of the *maqāmāt* succeed or fail not by virtue of high or low birth, but rather by their wits. And while audiences of courtly genres such as the chivalric romance identify with idealized heroes hailing from the upper ranks of nobility, those of the *maqāmāt* and picaresque identified with the alienation and struggles of the middle class, whose prosperity depended upon their own industriousness. The *maqāma*-esque narrator claims to edify the reader by providing his life as a negative example, and the picaresque narrator finds moderate success at the end of his own career by learning from his own failures. In the case of the *Spill*, the narrator offers his own miserable life as one long cautionary tale. The basic elements of the *maqāmāt* shared by the picaresque are also present in the *Spill*: a middle-class, first-person narrator who recounts a series of misadventures in anti-heroic, comic mode. However, the *Spill* also shares with the *maqāmāt* liberal measures of learned interjection and highly restrictive formal requirements; rhyming prose in the *maqāmāt* and tetrasyllabic verse in the *Spill*.

Therefore, while the general socio-economic conditions of Roig's Valencia would have set the stage for the production and success of a *maqāma*-esque work, the specific literary values espoused by Roig would have to speak to his audience, who would have no reason to appreciate the rhetorical style, *topoi*, or discursive particulars of *maqāmāt* by (for example) al-Ḥarīzī or Ibn Shabbetay. This is why it is still possible to speak of the *Spill* as a Valencian *maqāma*, despite its lack of rhymed prose, a trickster antagonist, and other features of the classical *maqāmāt*. Indeed, authors of Hebrew *maqāmāt* such as Ibn Zabāra and Ibn Shabbetay strayed considerably from the generic conventions introduced by al-Hamaḏānī and canonized by al-Ḥarīrī, and yet critics do not hesitate to refer to their work as *maqāmāt*.[10]

Social change in Fifteenth-Century Valencia

As in Castile, the fifteenth century in the Kingdom of Aragon saw the decline of the feudal system and the rise of a robust middle class consisting of lawyers, notaries, physicians, merchants, artisans, and friars. Although Barcelona would dominate international trade in the Kingdom of Aragon until nearly the end of the fifteenth century, Valencia was an important hub, particularly for the agricultural products of the region, but also in bringing goods from Mediterranean trade into Castile.

[10] See, for example, Schirmann (*Hebrew Poetry* 2: 11 and 67).

By the middle of the fifteenth century, Valencia rose to challenge Barcelona's supremacy as a commercial center (Giménez Soler, *Edad media* 336), attracting merchants from all over the Mediterranean.[11] In addition to the exports of the agricultural products of its rich countryside, Valencia was port of entry for much of the Mediterranean trade with Castile. In this environment, the middle classes eventually dominated the local economy, edging out even royal interests in municipal affairs (Giménez Soler, *Edad media* 288). In Valencia, the mass conversions of Jews in 1391 and 1413–1414 accelerated the process. Thousands of new *conversos* became active in local trade and politics (Meyerson, *Jewish* 109). This, in addition to the fact that the political life of the local nobility had been quite fractious since the Christian conquest (Narbona Vizcaíno 142–50), meant that Valencia was a decidedly bourgeois city. By the mid-fifteenth century, the Valencian municipal government was overwhelmingly dominated by non-nobles. In the upper chamber, the *consell secret* or *cambra alta*, sat only lawyers and professional elected officials. The lower chamber (*cambra baixa* or *consell de cent*) admitted only six nobles and over 100 non-nobles, among them barristers, notaries, elected officials and appointees of the upper chamber (Belenguer Cebrià 42). Only until the reign of Ferdinand the Catholic did the municipality come to be dominated by royal official power (Belenguer Cebrià 82–85). The efforts of Alfonso V "The Magnanimous" of Aragon (1416–1458) to expand his Mediterranean holdings and to establish a court at Naples during this time may also have contributed to a decreased focus on the affairs of Valencia itself.[12]

These changes brought about a divide in Valencian literary circles between the poets of the nobility, who favored courtly lyric styles such as are found in the medieval *cancioneros* of Castile-León and Aragon, and middle-class poets, who favored the type of innovative and satirical verse Roig writes in the *Spill*.[13] In particular, Roig and his successors rebelled against Provençal-influenced, heavily formulaic language of the medieval troubadours, turning

[11] See the essays edited by Furió on the presence in Valencia of merchants from Italy, North Africa, Languedoc, and the Netherlands.

[12] On Aragonese expansion in the Mediterranean, see Giménez Soler (*Edad* 200–06). On Naples in particular, see Del Treppo (160–88).

[13] "Aristocratic writers like Roís de Corella, Guillem Ramon de Vila·rasa, Lluís de Castellví, and Joan de Proixità attended the tertulia of Berenguer Mercader, whereas a more bourgeois group (Joan Moreno, Jaume Gassull, Narcís de Vinyoles, Baltasar Portell, etc) formed around Bernat Fenollar (c. 1438–1516), a canon of the cathedral. While the former preferred a more erudite, classical type of literature, the latter were more inclined to satire and bourgeois humor of the type we encounter in the *Spill*" (Delgado-Librero 29–30). Gassull (a nobleman) in particular enjoyed lampooning the language of lawyers and notaries (Riquer 3: 345).

instead to the language of Valencian peasants and burghers for inspiration (Fuster 354).

Conversos *in Early Fifteenth-Century Valencia*

Valencia's Jews, and especially her *conversos*, played an important role in the rise of the middle class and the changes in literary tastes that resulted from it. For the Jewish community, the general environment in the second half of the fourteenth century was one of relative economic prosperity and political stability, punctuated by episodes and periods of violent anti-Semitism (Baer 2: 30–50). Starting with the plague of 1348, the Jewish communities of the Crown of Aragon were beset by an increasing level of internal strife. Such was the state of affairs leading up to the devastating pogroms of 1391. Originating in Seville in June of that year, the violence reached Valencia on July 9, when its *aljama* or Jewish quarter was decimated. Hundreds perished at the hands of an anti-Semitic mob, and scores of Valencian Jewish notables were forcibly converted to Christianity (Baer 2: 100). These conversions debilitated the Jewish communities of Valencia, leaving their numbers greatly reduced and the ranks of their leadership thin at best (Baer 2: 130). At the same time, the already growing ranks of the Christian middle class were instantly expanded by the addition of thousands of new *conversos*.

In the second decade of the fifteenth century, the Dominican Vincent Ferrer conducted a well-organized, virulent campaign to convert the Jews of Castile and Aragon.[14] His efforts undid much of the healing and restoration of Spain's Jewish communities that had been accomplished since the pogroms of 1391. He successfully lobbied for harsher legal restrictions on nearly all aspects of Jewish life, including dress, hairstyles, the use of Christian names, and even that of the honorific title "Don" (Baer 2: 166–68). His plan to debilitate the Jewish communities featured measures both economic and social, the ultimate goal being the physical and social alienation of the Jews from their Christian neighbors. These laws presented an ultimatum: either convert or cease to associate with Christians, effectively ending Jewish involvement in public life and bringing about a new level of social marginalization for Jews.

---

[14] On the anti-Semitic preaching of Vincent Ferrer, see Millás Vallicrosa ("San Vicente"), Vendrell Gallostra, and Ambrosio Sánchez. For a study of anti-Semitism in Ferrer's sermons, see Viera.

Faced with such a choice, hundreds of Valencian Jews converted. Many such *conversos* took very common Valencian names, such as Soler, Fuster, and Pujol, which makes it extremely difficult for modern historians to identify them from archival sources.[15]

Jewish and Converso *Physicians in Fifteenth-Century Aragon and Valencia*

The role of Jews and *conversos* in the medical community of Valencia is of particular interest in evaluating the social environment of Jaume Roig, particularly as regards the possibility of his familiarity with Hebrew *maqāmāt*. Had Roig been familiar with Hebrew *maqāmāt* such as Ibn Shabbetay's *Minḥat Yehudah* and/or al-Ḥarīzī's *Taḥkemonī*, it would have been through his Jewish and/or *converso* colleagues.

The medical profession in Aragon was dominated by Jewish practitioners and authors up until the fifteenth century. Among the first Jews known to practice medicine in the Ebro Valley during the tenth and eleventh centuries are Marwān Ibn Chanah (ca. 985–1040) and Menaḥem Ibn al-Fawwal. The rulers of the Banū Hūd dynasty (ca. 1039–1110) continued to employ Jews such as Ibn Biklarish as court physicians (Martínez Loscos 35–42). The trend continued under Christian rulers in the twelfth and thirteenth centuries; Archbishop Vidal de Canellas of Huesca employed Abrayme Abanale as his personal physician, and Sheshet Benveniste (d. ca. 1209) served at the courts of Alfonso II (r. 1162–1196) and Pedro II (r. 1196–1213) of Aragon.[16]

The fourteenth century witnessed the heyday of Jewish physicians in Christian society; during this period several Christian monarchs retained their services and granted them liberal economic concessions as well. Over ten Jewish physicians from Zaragoza, Valencia, Barcelona and Lérida appear as having been granted privileges by the crown prince Pedro IV of Aragon in the years following 1330. Perhaps the most famous Jewish figure of fourteenth- century Aragon was Ibn Shaprut Shem Tob Ben Isaac of Tudela, who practiced medicine by royal authorization given in Valencia in 1382. These are but a few among scores of examples of Jewish physicians rendering services to influential Jews and Christians alike, including several examples of service to royals and high nobility (Rubió i Lluch, "Notes"). By the end

[15] Angelina Garcia also lists Vives, Font, Moliner, de Piera, Flores, Rodríguez, Bou, Ballester, and Miró (216–18).

[16] On Jewish physicians at the courts of Catholic monarchs in the thirteenth and fourteenth centuries, see also Castro (*Realidad* 443–92).

of the fourteenth century, however, Jewish physicians began to suffer more professional restrictions. During this time, Jewish practitioners had to be certified not by the King himself, but by a team of two examiners, one Jewish (Jucef Abenardut) and one Christian (Pere Ros de Ursins).[17]

If the nearly complete destruction of the Jewish communities in the pogroms of 1391 did not put an end to the Jewish medical profession in Aragon, it did everything but that. We must assume that many physicians were counted among the thousands of Jewish notables of Barcelona, Zaragoza and Valencia who were converted in that year.[18] The increasing restrictions upon their profession in the years to follow would have been enough to tilt the balance in favor of abandoning the Jewish religion in order to be able to practice freely. Those who did not convert would unlikely be able to continue to treat—legally—those of their patients who did. *Conversos* were under a great amount of social pressure to avoid associating with Jews, which would include a family doctor who had been treating you since childhood. Eventually, such pressures were compounded by increasing institutional inspection and regulation. In 1400, Martí I commissioned Maestre Domingo Polo to inspect all the physicians in the Crown of Aragon and to fine those not in compliance with regulation. While the order was written to inspect all physicians regardless of religion, Polo issued fines disproportionately to Jewish practitioners (Martínez Loscos 57).

By the reign of Ferdinand I (1412–1416), Jewish medicine in Aragon was in a state of total decadence. However, little scholarly attention seems to have been paid to *converso* physicians during this period. As inspector of physicians beginning in 1434, Roig personally would have known dozens, if not hundreds of doctors in the area. A great number of these would have been *conversos* who had perhaps received their medical training as Jews, including many more second-generation *conversos* whose parents had

---

[17] Even in the earlier part of the century we see one extreme case in which the Valencian physician Aron Vidal was, for the first three years of his licensure, prohibited from visiting Christian clients without being accompanied by a Christian physician (Martínez Loscos 56).

[18] One of the bugbears of studying the *converso* phenomenon is that converts did not typically publicize the fact of their Jewish past—they suffered enough social stigma without contributing to it themselves. As a result, from where the modern scholar stands, once a Jew converted to Christianity, he effectively disappeared from the horizon. There were, of course, several notable exceptions, among them *converso* poets who either boasted of their own lineage or satirized that of others and the very high-profile polemicists who sought to validate their new religion by denigrating their former one. On the poets, see Kaplan (*Evolution*). On the polemicists, see, for example, Berger and Chazan (*Barcelona* and *Daggers*). On an author both poet and polemicist, see Kramer-Hellinx.

converted in 1391. Moving in social circles populated by such people, he would have been well familiar with the angst and alienation experienced by his *converso* colleagues.

Jaume Roig and the Spill

Roig was a successful physician and public servant representative of the emerging *mijantes*,[19] or Valencian middle class. He served as examiner of physicians of Valencia and was the director of the prestigious hospital, En Clappers. His father, uncles, and grandfather had held similar positions before him, which suggests that he was from a very solidly upper-middle class background and we can hardly consider him an *arriviste* striver.[20]

The *Spill*, or *Llibre de les dones* of Valencian physician Jaume Roig (d. 1478) is a unique work of episodic verse narrative that has received relatively little critical attention outside of Valencia and Catalonia. In vivid (sometimes nauseating) detail, and with a darkly ironic tone, the autobiographical narrator tells his audience of the wiles of women, the pitfalls of marriage, and the specific misadventures he has suffered at the hands of four consecutive wives. In Book 3, he is visited in a nocturnal vision by King Solomon, who upbraids him for repeatedly walking into the same trap and corroborates his misogynist rant by adding one of his own based mostly on biblical example. All this, maintains the author, so that younger men will not make the same mistakes as him.

As a work of frametale literature, the *Spill* falls between the Castilian *Libro de buen amor* (1335) and the first picaresque novel, *Lazarillo de Tormes* (1554). It has in common with these two works (and with the *maqāmāt*) an autobiographical author/narrator/protagonist who relates his travels and encounters with various agents of his misfortune, an explicit didactic purpose, and a tendency toward social satire.

---

[19] We follow Francesc Eiximenis' use of the term: "la cosa publica es composta sumariament de tres estaments de persones, ço és, de menors, *mijantes* e majors" ('the public is composed primarily of three classes of persons, that is, of the lower, middle, and upper classes,' emphasis mine). See Eiximenis (41), cited in Maravall (*Estudios* 376).

[20] On the biography of Jaume Roig, see the sources brought together by Chabás i Llorente appended to his edition of Roig (413–41).

Style and Language

Like the authors of Hebrew and Arabic *maqāmāt*, Roig chose to write his work in a highly restrictive verse form. While *maqāmāt* are written in rhyming prose interspersed with verse, Roig wrote the *Spill* in the equivalent of a poetic straight jacket, a tetrasyllabic verse he refers to as "Noves rimades comediades" (681–82) ('rhymed, halved *noves*').[21] Roig most likely adapted his tetrasyllable from the *codolada*, a verse form alternating lines of 7/8 and 4/5 syllables used for invective poetry in fourteenth- and fifteenth-century Catalan literature, and from the *letovaris* verse (4/5 syllables), used to describe lovesickness and its remedies.[22]

Just as al-Saraqustī chose to write *luzūmīyya* rhymed prose, which required a rhyme twice as frequently as conventional *saj*ʿ, Roig imposed upon himself more stringent versification in an effort to showcase his talents and one-up his predecessors and contemporaries. In this he seems to have been successful, at least in the short term, for in fifteenth- and sixteenth- century Valencian literary circles, the tetrasyllable verse came to be known as "*La codolada de Jaume Roig*." ('the *codolada* verse style of Jaume Roig').[23] Again, as in the *maqāmāt*, this terse, restrictive style forces the author to use rare words, coin neologisms (which abound in the *Spill*), and resort to poetic license in syntactical and other grammatical matters. In a society that values technical mastery, such a choice can catapult a work to wide popularity (as was very much the case with the *maqāmāt* of al-Ḥarīrī in eleventh- century Iraq). However, as Castilian began to upstage Catalan as a prestige literary dialect, and the prose novel displaced verse as the premier vehicle for narra-

[21] "The term *noves rimades* referred to a sequence of octosyllabic rhyming couplets used in narrative poetry by 13th- to 15th-century Catalan writers. The meter in which most of the *Spill* is written is tetrasyllabic (according to Catalan scansion) or pentasyllabic (according to Castilian scansion) couplets, that is, halved *noves rimades*. This meter would later become very popular and was also known as the *vers de Jaume Roig*" (Delgado-Librero 515 n. 35). See also the introduction of Chabás i Llorente to his edition of Roig (xi). On the *codolada* and *noves rimades* forms, see Millá y Fontanals (*Estudios* 3: 361–440).

[22] The *letovaris* genre described the symptoms of lovesickness (*amor hereos*) composed in verses of four syllables (Martín Pascual 237). On *amor hereos* in medieval Catalan literature, see Cantavella ("Terapèutiques"). On *letovaris* poetry, see Riquer (1: 554, 638, and 643–46). On the "Mal de amors" of Pere March as first example of *letovaris*, see the introduction of Cabré to his edition of March (54). On an obscene variety of *letovaris*, see Pérez-Cors (8–9). For a *letovaris* by Joan Basset (fifteenth century) in tetrasyllable, see Bohigas (65–72).

[23] Miquel i Planas maintains that the work was known to Roig's contemporaries as "*La codolada de Jaume Roig*," until printed editions gave it the titles by which it is known to modern scholars, *Llibre de consells, Llibre de les dones*, and *Spill* ("Noticia preliminaria" xxxvii n. 1).

tive, Roig's masterpiece fell by the wayside, doubly marginalized by stylistic and socio-linguistic factors.[24]

The *Spill* may also count linguistic register among its formal idiosyncrasies, at least according to its author. In his prologue, Roig mentions that he has written his work in "l'algemia/he parleria/dels de Paterna/Torrent Soterna" ('the plain language and speech of the people from Paterna, Torrent, and Soterna') (686–90; 2: 323). These three villages were populated primarily by agricultural laborers, and Roig's use of the word *algemia* ('non-Arabic' or 'Romance') suggests that he wrote his work in imitation of the speech of the Muslim peasantry of the Valencian countryside.[25] Why would Roig choose to write the story of a self-made mercenary turned failed family man in (an approximation of) the dialect of a religious and socio-economic minority?[26]

Jaume Roig, Converso?

There is no known documentary evidence that suggests Roig was himself a *converso*. Delgado-Librero suggests that the professions pursued by the male members of the Roig family (lawyer, notary, doctor), along with "the family name, and Jaume Roig's vast knowledge of the Old Testament . . . indicate a

[24] Martí de Riquer views (with some measure of bitterness) Roig's choice of verse over prose as a serious tactical error, accusing him of hobbling the success of the *Spill* through his choice of a hopelessly outdated verse form: "Al meu entendre, el gran error de Jacme Roig fou escriure el *Spill* en vers, i precisament en aquest vers tan curt, amb la qual cosa, a mitjan del segle XV, seguia fidel a una tradició narrativa del XII. Si hagués escrit la seva obra en prosa, avui la llegiríem amb molt més gust i tindria un nombre de lectores que difícilment pot assolir, i la nostra literatura comptaria amb una peça essencial en la història de la novel·la moderna" ('To my understanding, the great error of Jaime Roig was to write the *Spill* in verse, and precisely in such a short verse form, by means of which, in the middle of the fifteenth century, he remained loyal to a narrative tradition of the twelfth. If he had written his work in prose, we would read it today with much more enjoyment and it would have a number of readers that would be difficult to assess, and our [i.e., Catalan] literature would include an essential part of the history of the modern novel') (3: 242). Prof. Riquer might have pushed back the Catalan claim to the proto-novel 250 years had he considered that Joseph Ibn Zabāra, a Catalan Jew from Barcelona, had already written a proto-novel, the *Sefer Šaʿašūʿīm* in (rhyming) prose at the beginning of the thirteenth century—in Hebrew.

[25] In the fifteenth century, Muslims (largely farmers and laborers) accounted for a significant minority of the population of the kingdom of Valencia. Scholarly estimates range from 30 to 50 of the total population of the kingdom. See Hinojosa Montalvo (1: 42), Guiral-Hadziiossif (337–38), and Harvey (*Islamic* 6).

[26] As we shall address below, Victorio Agüera erroneously equates *algemia* with Arabic, specifically the Classical Arabic of the *maqāmāt*.

possible Jewish origin, a matter that has not been suggested or studied and that deserves investigation" (1: 150). Because his family had long been active in the public life of the Christian community, it is extremely doubtful that he was raised as an openly practicing Jew. His great-grandfather had held several public service positions in Valencia already at the beginning of the fourteenth century. His grandfather was a notary, and his father was a doctor of both medicine and law and preceded Jaume as examiner of physicians of Valencia (Carré i Pons, "Medicina" 13).

In light of the fact that the great majority of Valencian *conversos* became Christian in the wake of the pogroms of 1391, it is unlikely that Roig was a second- or even third-generation *converso*. However, given the total lack of information about the women in Roig's family, it is not improbable that one or more of his female relatives might have been born Jewish. In any event, as examiner of physicians, Roig would have been surrounded with medical professionals who had converted after 1391 and would have been active in social circles heavily populated by *conversos*. We have one such example in the Valencian physician Magister Astruc Rimoch, who converted to Christianity in 1414 and took the name Magister Francesc de Sant Jordi. By the time Roig returned from his studies in Paris and assumed the post of examiner of physicians, Magister Francesc would have been practicing medicine in Valencia (Baer 2: 218).

Because it is so difficult to ascertain one's *converso* status through family history, it is often more productive to examine cultural and textual practices of populations and individuals thought to be *conversos* or crypto-Jews. It has been demonstrated that the women of a *converso* or crypto-Jewish family are most active in transmitting the identity and practices of the community (Janet Jacobs 42–66 and Gitlitz 39–40). Let us suppose that Roig was a second- or third- generation *converso* and that his mother or grandmother either herself converted in the wake of the Disputation of Tortosa or was born into a *converso* family. Members of such *converso* and crypto-Jewish communities tend to demonstrate an interest in, and affinity for, typically Jewish practices, whether religious (liturgical, ritual) or customary (culinary, ludic). One of the salient features of *converso* and crypto-Jewish religious practice is a disproportionate focus on the Old Testament and minimization (or outright rejection) of the New.[27] Roig's use of biblical material is decidedly non-canonical, based on comparison with several contemporary

---

[27] See Gitlitz (429).

para-scriptural sources.[28] Antònia Carré i Pons argues that the *Tanakh* (Hebrew OT), and not the Latin Vulgate, is the base for Roig's references, and most likely via a Catalan or Judeo-Catalan translation. The variations in Roig's citations of biblical texts brought to light by Carré i Pons more likely result from the demands of the rhyme scheme, and given his self-professed comedic mode, Roig's narrator did not necessarily take scriptural authority very seriously. Furthermore, if we accept the argument that Roig is working in the tradition of unreliable *maqāma*-esque storytellers, preachers, and the like, Solomon could be deliberately represented as misquoting the Bible, in a conscious effort to undermine his authority.

Another feature of the *Spill* that suggests Roig's *converso* heritage is his noted preference for Old Testament sources. Other authors of misogynous treatises and narratives in Romance also make allusions to Old Testament stories (the OT contains a tremendous amount of narrative material in comparison with the New Testament), but their reliance on OT narrative pales in comparison to that of Roig. For example, the Venetian *Proverbia quae dicuntur super natura feminarum* (late thirteenth century), the French *Livre de lamentations de Mathéolus* (early fifteenth century), the Boccaccio's *Corbaccio*, and the Alfonso Martínez de Toledo's *Libro del Arçipreste de Talavera* (mid-fifteenth century) all contain far more allusions to Christian saints, historical figures, and characters from classical mythology than to OT characters.

Throughout the four chapters, but especially in chapter three during Solomon's lecture, Roig presents one after another example of women's behavior (both positive and negative, it should be noted) drawn from the

[28] "Roig recull algunes variantes d'antigues versions de la Bíblia derivades de la traducció dels Setanta, que consta que van sobreviure a Europa occidental fins al segle XIV, al costat de la Vulgata" ('Roig compiles some variants of old versions of the Bible derived from the Septuagint, which proves their survival in Western Europe until the fourteenth century, alongside the Vulgate') (Carré i Pons, "L'estil" 205–06). Bonifatius Ferrer translated the whole of the Vulgate into Valencian Catalan (published posthumously in 1478) shortly before his death in 1417. There is also a complete translation into Catalan extant in manuscript form (Paris Bibliothèque Nationale MS esp 2–2), a 1465 translation of most of the Old Testament (London, Egerton 1526), and a 1461 translation of Genesis 2: 21 through Psalms (Paris, Bibliothèque Nationale MS esp 5) (Morreale "Apuntes" and "Vernacular"). There is no major study of which I am aware that assesses the extent to which these might be based on the Masoretic texts of the *Tanakh* (Hebrew OT).

NT,[29] OT, [30] Christian hagiography,[31] and history.[32] Delgado-Librero notes that the overwhelming majority of Roig's allusions are to the Old Testament as opposed to the new (4 n 4) and that his intimate familiarity with the Old Testament suggests a religious upbringing privileging the Old Testament. This *converso* and crypto-Jewish preference for Old Testament stories persisted for centuries. For example, in 1603, a witness in the trial of Mexican crypto-Jew Antonio Méndez claimed that the accused "no alaua sino los passos del Testamento Viejo y se enternesçe con ellos, alaua mucho al predicador que trae muchos" ('only praised the passages from the Old Testament and was fond of them, [and] highly praised the preacher who used many of them').[33] Another Mexican crypto-Jew, Manuel de Sosa y Prado, was denounced to the Inquisition in 1694 because he and his brother used to talk about "La Historia de Esther, y los dos se lastimauan de ella, mostrandose mui contritos, y aficionados al testamiento Viejo" ('the story of Esther, and the two felt her pain, showing themselves to be very contrite, and fond of the Old Testament').[34] In some instances, certain Old Testament figures took on Christian significance. A Portuguese *converso*, Paulo Rodrigues, (Coimbra, 1573) compares the Christian devotion to Saint Catherine of Siena to *converso* devotion to Queen Esther.[35]

While many of the characters and Old Testament stories to which Roig refers would have been widely known by any Aragonese, Christian, Jewish or Muslim, with a basic religious education, a significant number of Roig's

---

[29] See the references to Mary Magdalene (v. 11065), Mary (Martha's sister) (v. 14618), and Holy Mary (v. 3396).

[30] See the references to Abigail (vv. 11883, 11891, 15236, and 15238), Bathsheba (v. 11700), Deborah (v. 15239), Dinah (v. 15738), Esther (vv. 15224–5), Hagar (vv. 8718 and 15232), Judith (vv. 15222–23), Leah (v. 15234), Lot's wife (v. 15727), Michal (v. 11073), Naomi (vv. 8747 and 14620), Rachel (v. 15244), Rahab (v. 15241), Rebecca (v. 15227), Ruth (v. 15227), Sarah (v. 15228) and also by her former name, Sarai (v. 15229), Tamar (v. 10164), Tobit (vv. 11095 and 15313), Vashti (vv. 13131, 13146, 14619, 14821, and 15737) and Yael (vv. 12809 and 15243). These do not include references to men or places from the OT, which are also numerous.

[31] See the references to Saints Agnes (v. 15260), Anastasia (v. 15259), Anne (v. 6159), Catherine (v. 15257), Elizabeth of Portugal (v. 15254), Lucia (v. 15260), Marina (v. 15158), Monica (v. 3829), Sophia (v. 12513), and Veronica (v. 3830).

[32] See the references to Cava (v. 7203), Leonor (granddaughter of Jaume I of Aragon) (v. 9472), Sibilia de Fortià (the second wife of Peter IV the Ceremonious of Aragon) (v. 1343), and Violant de Bar (v. 3837).

[33] Archivo Nacional de la Nación, (Mexico City: Sección de Inquisición), Vol. 276 doc 14, 4230b, cited in Gitlitz (438–39 n. 26).

[34] See (AGN Vol 529 doc 11, 269a), quoted in Gitlitz (439 n. 29).

[35] See Cunha de Azevedo Mea (308), cited in Gitlitz (470). See also Perry and Cruz (106). This belief has seemingly persisted in the New World for centuries and in New Mexico, the "Festival of Saint Esther" is still celebrated (Janet Jacobs 62–63).

Old Testament allusions are to stories that figure prominently in the Jewish tradition and are largely ignored by the Christian. For example, Esther and Vashti are both mentioned five times.[36] It is also noteworthy that the Book of Esther (recited publicly in Jewish communities during the festival of Purim) centers on the persecution of the Jews and that its eponymous heroine is a secular Jew who reveals her identity only after she has been married to the king. Such a story would naturally resonate with the experience of the *conversos* (Walfish 125). The popularity of the Esther story extended even to the Valencian biblical theatre of Roig's time. Within this dramatic tradition, all performances drawn from the NT are closely associated with significant dates in the Catholic liturgical calendar and interpreted according to traditional Christology. Those drawn from the OT, however, are not (Huerta Viñas 9).

The Maqāmāt *and the* Spill

Like the *LBA*, Jaume Roig's *Spill* displays several formal and thematic traits that set it apart from other Romance language verse narratives of its time. It is, in many ways, a unique work, and much of what makes it so cannot be accounted for in the Latin and Romance literatures of the High Middle Ages. In particular, the author-narrator-character complex in the *Spill* (like that of the *LBA*, with the exception that Roig's narrator is not pseudo-autobiographical) lacks any exact analogue in medieval Romance literature.

While modern critics are in agreement that the *Spill* is a unique work in medieval Romance, it remains a curiosity, a bit of a literary platypus, and according to Delgado-Librero, "no consensus has been reached as to what the *Spill* is and what it means" (60). Victorio Agüera is alone in venturing to background the narrative innovation of the *Spill* against non-Latin sources.[37] His thesis is that Roig was familiar with the Arabic *maqāma* genre

---

[36] Compare to frequency of references to other morally suspect or recalcitrant biblical women: Mary Magdalene (4), Leah (3), Rahab (1), Jezebel (1), and Tamar (1).

[37] It should be noted that Agüera's argument (*Pícaro* 87–90) for the influence of the *maqāma* was made in the context of an argument positing the *Spill* as the first picaresque narrative in a Romance language, a connection first made by Millá y Fontanals (*Estudios* 402). In addition to these comments, Sirera makes an oblique reference to a possible connection between the structure of the *Spill* and "Eastern" literature: "no podem oblidar que—la pràctica totalitat d'aquests elements podem trobar-los tant a la narrativa occidental com a l'oriental anterior al segle XV" ('we cannot forget that—we can also find these [picaresque] elements brought together in Western as well as Eastern narrative before the fifteenth century') (141).

of rhymed prose narrative, from which Roig was inspired to give the *Spill* its episodic structure, ironic, proto-picaresque narrator, and tetrasyllabic rhyme ("Jaume Roig" 150).[38] This argument has met with some resistance, especially from Catalan-speaking scholars (Delgado-Librero 1: 74). However, while Agüera argues that Roig was directly influenced by contact with readers of Arabic *maqāmāt*, it is far more likely that Roig was influenced by readers of Hebrew *maqāmāt* such as those of al-Ḥarīzī, Ibn Zabāra, and especially Ibn Shabbetay. It is through these authors that certain narrative resources of the Hebrew *maqāmāt* were transmitted to authors of Romance verse narratives.[39] The authors of these Hebrew texts introduce into Peninsular literature the conflated author/narrator/protagonist, ironic voice, and explicit didactic tone that inform later, Christian authors such as Ruiz and Roig. What set the *Spill* apart from other Romance texts is the didactic stance of its narrator and its episodic structure.[40] Roig clearly intends for his work to serve as an example to his readers, that they avoid making the same mistakes he made and thereby be spared from a lifetime of suffering. He frames his autobiography from the perspective of an old man, broken and embittered:

Yo com absent
del mon vivint
aquell iaquint
aconortat
d'ell apartat
dant hi del peu
vel ihubileu
mort çivilment
ja per la gent

[38] Monroe (*Art* 74) and Hämeen-Anttila (298–99) have also discussed the possible role of the Arabic *maqāma* in the development of the picaresque novel, but both conclude that an argument for direct influence is untenable.

[39] See Ibn Shabbetay's description of his (fictional?) recitation of *Minḥat Yehuda* at court (ed. Huss 2: 33, ll. 779–93), perhaps that of Alfonso VIII, whose Arabic eulogy was composed by Ibn Shabbetay's sponsor, Abraham al-Fakhar (*EJ*, "Ibn Alfakhar"). While this event has not been substantiated by archival sources, it is certainly plausible and serves as an example of how Christian audiences learned about the Hebrew works of their Jewish neighbors, leaving no paper trail in the process.

[40] Victorio Agüera has noted that "la peculiaridad del Spill se reduce, en último análisis, al uso de una estructura que, con la posible excepción del *Libro de buen amor*, aparece por primera vez en la literatura hispánica. Ella es el uso de la forma autobiográfica con una finalidad didáctica y que da unidad al material episódico de la obra" ('the peculiarity of the *Spill* can be reduced, in the final analysis, to the use of a structure that, with the possible exception of the *Libro de buen amor*, appears for the first time in Hispanic literature. It is the use of the autobiographical form for didactic ends that gives unity to the episodic material of the work') ("Jaume Roig" 150).

desconegut
per tots tengut
com hom saluatie
tenint hostatie
en lo meu llit
prou enuellit
antich de dies
per malalties
molt afligit
uell enllegit
per molt greus mals
yres y tals
ja consumit
ab poch delit...(160–82)

(I live as if absent from the world, consoled by having left it, separated from it, having kicked it. Old and retired, I am dead to the law, already unknown to people, considered by all as a wild man. Living in my bed, quite aged and many days old, I am much afflicted by illness. Old and ugly, I am already consumed by very grave ailments, fits of ire and the like. With little joy, I am uneasy.) (2: 317)

This unfortunate narrator claims to be writing his book for the benefit of those younger than he, specifically, for those "iouents verts/ he inesperts/ del toch del foch/ polls del bech groch" (293–96) ('Green young men, [who have not yet been burned], chickens of yellow beak') (2: 318), who still have a chance at a life of happiness. Roig explains that those who read this book will be forewarned and will certainly avoid the errors the author details within:

be sap de maça
qui'n es ferit
lo meu sperit
n'a portat pena
sobre la[ ]squena
mals huytant'anys
treballs afanys
he greu turment
vellant durment
no çessant may
de cridar ay
he sospirat
ben informat
publicament
tot scasament
qui se'n uol pexer

vull fer conexer
ben auisar
he diuisar
exordi fent
succintament
la llur costuma
narrant en suma (382–404)

(He who is injured by the mallet knows it well: for eighty years, my spirit has borne [women's] punishment on its back: ills, hardships, exertions, and a grave torment. Awake or asleep, I have sighed, never ceasing to scream *ouch*. Well informed, I want to warn, publicly and in complete detail, whoever wants to feed from it. I want to admonish him well and make him discern, succinctly making an exordium and summarily narrating the ways of women.) (2: 319)

Agüera rejects the idea that this explicit exemplarity descends from the medieval *exempla* tradition (*Pícaro* 14). In his estimation, Roig adapted this structure and didactic stance from the example of the Arabic and Hebrew *maqāmāt*, and these works informed not only the didactic, episodic, pseudo-autobiographical form of the *Spill*, but also other traits of the *maqāma* genre such as the use of rhymed prose and the division of the autobiographical narrator into two characters (Jaume Roig and Solomon). However, his argument for the influence on the *Spill* of the Arabic *maqāmāt* is difficult to support.

The first problem with Agüera's hypothesis is that he does not test it by attempting to place Roig in contact with readers of Arabic or Hebrew *maqāmāt*. It is enough for him that Roig "pudo haberse familiarizado [con la *maqāma*] mediante el trato y convivencia con los judíos y moriscos[41] de [Valencia]." ('could have familiarized himself [with the *maqāma*] through interaction and *convivencia* with the Jews and Moriscos of [Valencia]') (*Pícaro* 90). While it would be futile to attempt to present documentary evidence of Roig's familiarity with any given *maqāma* text, it is worthwhile to attempt to constitute the social circumstances that would have made such familiarity possible.

It is highly unlikely that Roig would have had contact with any readers of Arabic *maqāmāt* and even more so that he himself would have known Arabic. By the fifteenth century, the state of Arabic and Islamic learning

[41] The use of the term *morisco* here is an anachronism. The term for a Muslim living under Christian rule is *mudéjar*. After Islam was outlawed in 1501 and Valencian Muslims were forcibly converted to Christianity (Granada 1501, Castile 1502), they became known as *moriscos*, a derogatory term for a new Christian of Muslim background (Chejne 7; *EI*, "Mudejar").

in all the Christian territories of the Iberian Peninsula was in such decline that Classical Arabic was used only for the most pedestrian documents, and there was no Arabic literary scene to speak of.[42] After the conquest of much of the Iberian Peninsula by Christian rulers in the twelfth and thirteenth centuries, Islamic education was nearly entirely debilitated (López-Morillas, "Language" 54–55). When a Muslim city was conquered, its governing elite and nearly all educated Muslims left for Granada or North Africa. Even in cities such as Valencia where the original terms of surrender had included provisions for the preservation of Islamic institutions,[43] over time the ruling Christians undermined them.[44] However, a large population of Muslims living under Christian rule, known as *mudéjares*, remained (*EI*, "Mudéjar"). In a matter of years, the Muslim population was almost entirely stripped of its educated elite.[45] Eventually the situation deteriorated to the point where the community became almost entirely ignorant of Classical Arabic, which gave rise to *aljamiado* literature—Castilian or Aragonese language written in Arabic characters (López-Morillas, "Language" 54–57). Aljamiado texts

[42] L.P. Harvey notes that "the Valencians continued to speak Arabic, and to write it for administrative purposes, but they do not seem to have participated in the exchange of intellectual life of the Islamic world as a whole, and they produce no writers of any note after the conquest. The explanation for this is presumably that Muslims with any talent emigrated to Granada, if not further afield" (*Islamic* 7). Boswell maintains that already by the fourteenth century, "it is quite likely that most northern Mudéjares read little if any Arabic" (382). Catlos (whose study of the construction of *mudéjar* identity in the Crown of Aragon is otherwise outstanding) argues for *mudéjar* Romance/Arabic vernacular bilingualism: "there can be no doubt that Aragonese and Catalan *mudéjares* continued to speak and write in Arabic through the 13th century, both on a popular and educated level" (*Victors* 239). However, he conflates evidence of learned and vernacular practice by offering written documents in Classical Arabic as proof of the "*mudéjars*' native language" (*Victors* 241), thus failing to distinguish between two registers that are mutually unintelligible. There is no inherent contradiction in a *mudéjar* who is Romance monolingual, yet highly literate in Classical Arabic, while relatively ignorant of vernacular Andalusī Arabic. A modern analogue might be an Anglophone North American Muslim, highly trained in Classical Arabic, yet unable to conduct even the most rudimentary discussion in Colloquial Moroccan or Egyptian Arabic.

[43] For example, the charter granted to the Muslims of the Uxó valley by James I in 1250 allows for the continuation of Islamic practice in prayer, marriage, legal proceedings, and social autonomy (Harvey, *Islamic* 125).

[44] For example, while "in the thirteenth-century accusations against Muslims by Christians were heard in Islamic courts," the Islamic legal system was eventually co-opted, so that "between 1355 and 1369 89 percent of all cases involving only Muslims were heard by Christian judges, and often were decided according to Christian and not Islamic law" (Meyerson, *Muslims* 189).

[45] Consider the difficulty encountered by Juan de Segovia in locating a Muslim scholar able to translate the Qur'ān for him in his priory in Savoy in 1455. Finally, the Castilian King Juan II had to order Yça Gidelli, the *faqīh* of Segovia to go to Savoy to work on the project (Wiegers 69–71).

were largely (but not entirely) religious:[46] translations of the Qurʾān, legal compendia, and prayer books, intended for an audience whose formal Islamic education was limited to knowledge of the Arabic alphabet. Given the Islamic injunction against translating the Qurʾān directly into a language other than Arabic, the existence of an *aljamiado* Qurʾān demonstrates the sad state of Islamic education in the fifteenth century.[47] It is therefore unlikely that Roig would have known any readers of Arabic *maqāmāt*.

The second problem with Agüera's thesis is his assertion that Roig adopted his unique tetrasyllable verse in imitation of the rhyming prose (Ar. *sajʿ*) of the Arabic and Hebrew *maqāmāt*.[48] He notes that Roig claims to have written his work using the rustic *algemia* of the Muslim peasantry of the Valencian countryside (ed. vv. 686–90; trans. 2: 323). It is significant that Roig uses the word *algemia* (Castilian *aljamía*), which clearly refers to Romance (and not Arabic) spoken or written by Muslims.[49] Agüera, however, understands *algemia* quite differently, maintaining that "Jaume Roig, al usar las palabras 'aljamía' y 'jerga' se está refiriendo a algo relacionado con lo árabe" ('Jaume Roig, in using the words "aljamía" and "jerga," is referring to something related to the Arabic') (*Pícaro* 75). He then takes this as proof that Roig's choice of the tetrasyllable verse was done in imitation of the rhymed Classical Arabic prose of the *maqāmāt*.[50] On the contrary, it is highly improbable that Roig's tetrasyllable is an imitation of the rhyming Arabic prose. First,

[46] For *aljamiado* texts of a secular literary nature, see Galmés de Fuentes (*Historia*; *Batallas*) and *La leyenda de la Doncella Carcayona* (ed. Valero Cuadra).

[47] It is prohibited in traditional Islam to produce a translation of the Qurʾān that is independent of the original Arabic text. Therefore, the earliest translations,into languages such as Persian (tenth c.) and Turkish (twelfth c.), were interlinear, quasi-translations, more properly referred to as 'interpretations' (Ar. *tafsīr*, pl. *tafāsīr*). In modern editions, the translated text normally appears facing the original. See *EI*, "al-Ḳurʾān." On the *aljamiado* Qurʾāns of *mudéjares* and *moriscos*, see López-Morillas (*Corán*, "Genealogy," and *Qurʾān*).

[48] On the use of rhyming prose in Arabic *maqāmāt*, see Young (*Rogues* 21–43).

[49] The Classical Arabic *ʿajamīyya* means barbaric or non-Arab. It was a term applied to the languages spoken by non-Arab Muslims, originally Persians. In al-Andalus, it was used by Muslims to describe the Romance dialects spoken in the Iberian Peninsula, where in Andalusī Arabic the verb *yaʿjam* meant simply 'to speak Romance' (Corriente, *Dictionary* 345) and *EI* ("Aljamía"). For an example of *ʿajamīyya* used to describe Andalusī Romance, see Monroe ("Maimonides").

[50] "No hay motivo para sorprenderse de que Roig usase una forma métrica que existía en la tradición de las *maqamat* hispanas a partir del siglo XI. Si Roig había tejido su obra en la 'aljamía' de los de Paterna, se refería con ello a la forma y al fondo del *Spill*, es decir, a la tradición de las *maqamat*"('There is no reason to be surprised that Roig used a metric form that was already in use in the Hispanic *maqāma* tradition that dates to the eleventh century. If Roig had woven his work in the 'vernacular' of the inhabitants of Paterna, he used it to refer to the form and content of the *Spill*, that is, in the tradition of the *maqāmāt*') (Agüera, "Jaume Roig" 175).

as noted above, *algemia* always refers to a non-Arabic language—even Roig himself declares that his language is "romanç" ('Romance') (v. 680)—so that Roig could not possibly have been referring to the Classical Arabic language of the *maqāmāt*. Although Agüera maintains that *algemia* indicates Arabic (*Pícaro* 75–76), it is clear that the word, derived from the Arabic *ʿajamiyya*, is always used to refer to a non-Arabic language, here Valencian.[51] Let us assume, for argument's sake, that Roig was attempting to approximate the style of *colloquial* Valencian Arabic which was still widely spoken during the mid-fifteenth century.[52] Even so, he would be imitating a dialect as far removed from the ultra-refined Classical Arabic of the *maqāmāt* as colloquial Valencian Romance is from the Latin poetry of Ovid or Horace.

The language of the *maqāmāt* of al-Ḥarīrī and al-Saraqusṭī,[53] two of the best-known and oft-referenced authors of the genre in al-Andalus, was an extremely rarefied, artificially obscure brand of Classical Arabic, particular to high-level administrators and literati of the medieval Arab world.[54] In fact, it is believed that al-Ḥarīrī's primary objective in writing his *maqāmāt* was to preserve and showcase the usages of extremely rare words (*EI*, "Maḳama"). Given the sorry state of Arabic letters in fifteenth-century Valencia, it is nearly impossible that Roig could have counted among his intimates anyone with the education necessary to read and understand Arabic *maqāmāt*.

If we cannot establish a venue of transmission of the style of the Arabic *maqāmāt* to Roig's pen in his social environment, we must turn our attention to the internal textual evidence. I have mentioned that Agüera cites the episodic structure and didactic stance of the narrator as the two traits that identify the *Spill* with the Arabic *maqāma* tradition. This idea needs to be nuanced, as there is a difference between authors of Arabic and Hebrew *maqāmāt* in the way they express their didactic intentions. The Arabic authors al-Ḥarīrī (whose Arabic *maqāmāt* are examined by Agüera) and al-Saraqusṭī are not explicit in their didactic purpose. That is, they do not specifically present the behavior of their characters as a negative example. At no point

---

[51] On this distinction, see Ciscar Pallares and Epalza (111–14). On morisco dialect, see Galmés de Fuentes ("Lengua").

[52] In fact, Meyerson argues that Valencian Muslims were bilingual and spoke colloquial Arabic even into the seventeenth century (*Muslims* 228). While he suggests that Valencian Muslims still read Classical Arabic into the sixteenth century, the total absence of literary production after the thirteenth century suggests that most literate Muslims would have had a limited reading proficiency (with limited comprehension) of Classical Arabic for purposes of prayer. On Valencian Arabic, see Barceló Torres.

[53] For full bibliography on the Arabic *maqāmāt*, see the references in chapter 2.

[54] On the style of the Arabic *maqāma* as interpreted by authors of Hebrew and Syriac *maqāmāt*, see Katsumata.

do they say "do not do what I have done." Rather, they rely on the educated reader's active critical capacity to deduce the work's exemplarity by discerning the intellectual and moral flaws of the narrator evident in his words and deeds. Al-Ḥarīrī invokes the didactic purpose of his work only secondarily, as a way to excuse his use of fictional events for purposes of instructing the reader in rhetoric and rare vocabulary. He claims that although the tales he relates are as false as the animal fables (i.e., those found in *Kalīla wa-Dimna*), his intention in writing them is to educate, and therefore he is justified:

> Since deeds depend on intentions, and in these lies the effectiveness of religious obligations,—What fault is there in one who composes stories for instruction not for display, and whose purpose in them is the education and not the fablings?—Nay, is he not in the position of one who assents to doctrine, and "guides to the right path"? (trans. Chenery 1: 107; ed. Saba 14–15)[55]

Al-Saraqusṭī, whose *Maqāmāt al-Luzūmīyya* are not included in Agüera's study,[56] is only slightly more forthright in discussing the didactic purpose in the colophon of his work. He contends that his *maqāmāt* are an opportunity for the reader to develop his or her critical skills in interpreting the language of the author and the behavior of the characters he has invented:

> These *maqāmāt* have issued from a mind exhausted by its effort, and from a goal neither wished for nor desired by me, but rather, from the darkening of horizons and the concern and apprehension over the passing of life; from the vain departure of words, from the failure of truth to praise those words from the moment it first goes to drink from them to the time it leaves, even if they have only issued—as God be my witness—from a soul that hovers over truth, grazes and freely pastures on the meadow of hope, consistently offers guidance toward righteousness, and constantly proceeds in the direction of repentance while, at the same time, it aims at seriousness in its jesting, and follows the path of earnestness in its joking. In the name of God—may he be exalted—we implore whoever considers and takes note of these words of ours, and strives and aspires to understand them with a critical appraisal, to be judicious and apply allegorical interpretation in his examination of them, and to make it his practice and conclusion to judge them favorably, and to realize that the human soul can move from one state to another, can change its condition, and can alternate between truth and falsehood, whereas God, in His excellence, erases its sin, hastens its return to Him, and accepts its repentance. (trans. Monroe 502–03; ed. al-Warāglī 467)

[55] On the problem of fictionality in medieval Arabic literature and especially the development of the *maqāmāt* in light of the Aesopic tradition, see Drory (*Models* 22–27).

[56] Al-Saraqusṭī's work was not translated into Spanish until 1999 (trans. Ferrando Frutos) and into English in 2002 (trans. Monroe), nearly twenty years after the appearance of Agüera's dissertation and subsequent monograph ("Jaume Roig"; *Pícaro*).

While al-Saraqusṭī clearly expresses didactic concern here, his is not an exemplary didacticism. That is, he is not explicitly offering his work (nor the blunders of the narrator) as a negative example for others to avoid. Rather, he excuses himself for the vanity of his undertaking, for the seeming frivolity of his writing, and somewhat obliquely suggests that readers should understand that even those who behave as poorly as the rogue al-Sadūsī or as foolishly as the narrator al-Sā'ib ibn Tammām can earn redemption if they turn to God. His apology is more of a reflection on the flawed character of humankind and the unwavering mercy of God than an attempt to directly influence the behavior of the reader. In fact, his recommendation that readers "apply allegorical interpretation" in their reading of his *maqāmāt* suggests that he encourages critical and interpretative readings of his work, and not simple obedience or adhesion to any specific doctrine. While Roig frames the *Spill* as an exemplary tale, al-Saraqusṭī sees his work more as a textbook for critical thought.[57] Therefore, it seems unlikely that Roig would have adopted his explicit exemplary didactic stance from the Arabic *maqāmāt*, be they of al-Ḥarīrī, or al-Saraqusṭī.[58]

From where, then, might Roig have adopted his unique didactic stance? We have seen that the near-total demise of Arabic letters in Valencia in the thirteenth century and the poor state of Islamic education in the fifteenth make it virtually impossible that Roig would have been influenced by Arabic *maqāmāt*. However, as Agüera also suggests (if only in passing), Roig might have had exposure to Hebrew *maqāmāt* written in the thirteenth century in Castile and Catalonia.[59] Of the Hebrew *maqāmāt*, al-Ḥarīzī's *Taḥkemonī* is strictest (and most unapologetic) in his adherence to the Arabic example of al-Ḥarīrī. [60] Other Hebrew *maqāmāt*, such as the *Minḥat Yehudah, soneh hanašīm* ('Offering of Yehudah, the Woman-hater') of Ibn Shabbetay or the *Sefer Šaʿašūʿīm* ('Book of Delights') of Ibn Zabāra more freely interpret the structural and stylistic exigencies of the genre. Such Hebrew *maqamat* were widely read in the Jewish communities of medieval Iberia and were likely to

57 On the didactic nature of the *Spill*, see Carré i Pons ("L'estil" 186–91).

58 The difficulty of transmission from Arabic to European languages of the genre is supported by Hämeen-Anttila, based on the difficulty of the Arabic, although he is more inclined to admit the possibility of transmission via the Hebrew *maqāmāt*. Ultimately, though, he rejects the idea that the Spanish picaresque was influenced by the *maqāmāt* (298–99).

59 On the Arabic and Hebrew *maqāmāt* in al-Andalus, see Drory ("Maqama").

60 "Now the thing that has stirred up my spirit to compose this book was that a wise man among the sages of the Arabs and one of the choicest of the enlightened whose tongue is powerful in Arabic poetry and through whose mouth the vision of song is spread abroad—he is the famous Al-Hariri, all the authors of poetry except him are barren" (trans. Reichert 34–35; ed. Toporovsky and Zamorah 11).

have been familiar to some of Roig's peers, specifically the Hebrew-educated *converso* physicians who had converted in the wake of the Disputation of Tortosa.[61]

The question of influence is further complicated by the existence of a medieval French text that most likely provided Roig with a model for the exemplary misogamous narrative. Delgado-Librero has established that Roig was influenced in large part by Jean Le Fèvre's Old French translation of the *Lamentations of Mathéolus*.[62] In the introduction to the second book, Mathéolus explains that his book is a warning to all those who have not yet had to suffer his fate, that of marriage. Even though it may be too late to save himself, he might still be able to help those who have not yet fallen into the trap:

> Par moy, qui muir a grief martire,
> Doit on a tous les autres dire
> Que euls de marier se gardent
> Et qu'a cest exemple regardent
> Pour eschever femme et son art.
> Quant la prochaine maison art
> Ou l'en i voit le feu boubter,
> On doit de la sienne douter. (vv. 19–26)
>
> (Since I am dying a terrible death, I should serve as a warning to all other men not to get married and to learn from my mistakes, thereby escaping woman and her wiles. If one's neighbour's house is on fire and one sees the flames leaping higher, one ought to fear for one's own house.)[63]

The didactic tone is identical to that of Roig: the author puts forth his own experience as a warning to the younger, less experienced reader. So, while Le Fèvre's text may well have served as a model for Roig's didactic, autobiographical stance,[64] its existence alone is not sufficient to discount the

---

[61] The popularity of the Hebrew *maqāmāt* is attested by several sixteenth-century editions published in the Sephardic communities of Constantinople and Venice (Habermann 118–19). On the Disputation of Tortosa and its effect on the Jewish community, see Baer (2: 170–234).

[62] This is an Old French translation of the Latin *Liber Lamentationum Matheoluli* (ca. 1290) dating from the early fourteenth century. For English translations of several sections, see Blamires (177–97). God appears to Mathéolus in book 3 of the *Lamentations*, just as Solomon appears to Roig's narrator in book 3 of the *Spill*. See Morel-Fatio (630–54), cited in Delgado-Librero (1: 81).

[63] English translation of excerpt by Karen Pratt in Blamires (182).

[64] Other works of autobiography have also been held to influence the structure and moral stance of the *Spill*, including St. Augustine's *Speculum peccatoris* and Vicent of Beauvais' various *Specula* (Carré i Pons, "L'estil" 192).

possible influence of texts such as Ibn Shabbetay's *Minḥat Yehuda*, which predates Le Fèvre's Latin source and may well have influenced it. Neither does it account for the narrator's cynicism nor for the episodic structure of the *Spill*, perhaps the two proto-picaresque features of the *Spill* that can best be explained by the influence of the *maqāma* genre.

The Cynical Narrator

As in the case of the *LBA*, the argument for the influence of the Hebrew *maqāma* on the *Spill* is most compelling with regard to Roig's narrator, in whom several of the features and behaviors of the narrators of Hebrew *maqāmāt* converge. Like the narrators of the *maqāmāt*, Roig's seems to be incapable or unwilling to act in order to change his fate. He characterizes himself as a man with poor judgment and weak resolve. As a young man, he readily eats up the lies of a professional go-between (much like *Trotaconventos* in the *LBA*) who offers to find him a wife, only to have the marriage end in disgrace. Later, and with the benefit of hindsight, he bemoans his gullibility to the reader:

> Ffalsa parlera
> vella uelera
> m'en babuxa
> hi'm tabuxa
> de tot mentia
> de sa falsia
> *yo la'n cregui* (2029–35, emphasis mine)

> (The deceitful prattler, the old matchmaker tricked me and confounded me. She lied about everything, and *I believed her lies*) (2: 339).

The anxiety of the suitor who blames unmet marital expectations on the go-between is also attested in more than one case in Hebrew *maqāmāt*. Zeraḥ, the protagonist of Ibn Shabbetay's *Minḥat Yehuda*, is outraged when the wily go-between Kozbī tricks him into marrying a beautiful young woman, who at the last moment is replaced with a hideous hag:

> Zerah was left naked and bare with Rizpah bat Aiah. At length the sun rose and found him limping on his thigh with Rizpah [the hag] instead of Ayala Sheluha [the promised bride]...He tore his clothes, strewed ashes on his head, and cried, "A plot! Deceit! A pack of lies! For this I mourn and wail and raise bitter lament. The money is gone, the shame remains! No gold and no beauty! The plot was thick, it took me in—a fool believes whatever he is told...." (trans. Scheindlin 285; ed. Huss 1: 25–26, vv. 590–607)

Al-Ḥarīzī, perhaps following the example of Ibn Shabbetay, writes of how Heman the Ezrahite was lured by a deceitful go-between into marrying a horrible old hag. Thoroughly disgusted by her appearance and enraged by the deception, Heman delivers a withering anti-palinode, describing in detail the horrific appearance of his fraudulent bride, whom he then savagely beats to death, fleeing the scene by mule (ed. Toporovsky and Zamorah 79; trans. Reichert 2: 127). Most likely both of these examples, but certainly that of Ibn Shabbetay, precede the version in the second book of *De Vetula*, in which Pseudo-Ovid describes a similar deception. Just before the poet enters his beloved's room for a much-anticipated tryst, the go-between swaps the poet's beloved, a young and beautiful virgin, for a withered elderly woman.[65] Like their counterparts in the Arabic *maqāmāt*, these hapless narrators repeatedly fall victim to such tricks, traps into which, it seems, they must ever fall.

Roig's narrator also displays a total inability to fend for himself, or to limit the indulgences of his wives. He buys his first wife a luxurious wardrobe of furs, velvet, and precious stones, which she rejects in a dramatic display of ingratitude and insouciance:

> arunça'l nas
> caboteiant
> he morreiant
> ab gran menyspreu
> dona-y del peu
> vestir no[ ]u uol (2072–77)

> (she wrinkled her nose, shaking her head and making faces, with great contempt. She kicked it all and refused to wear it) (2: 339).

Roig's response to this and other displays of such abuse is totally passive. He merely punctuates the accounts of his bride's behavior with utter resignation, admitting: "[vaig] sofir l'enpastre/ no li dich res" (2088–90) ('I suffered the ranting and said nothing to her [in my defense]') (2: 339). Again, when he discovers that his wife had lied to him about her dowry and that her property was all mortgaged, he lamely says:

> hagui'm begut
> ja les adiues
> a mi noçiues
> al cos e bossa (2126–29)

---

[65] See *Pseudo-Ovid* (ed. Robathan 98–100, vv. 486–549) and the English translation in Burkard (*Archpriest* 180–81). For the medieval French version by Jean Le Fèvre, see Pseudo-Ovid (ed. Cocheris 151–58, vv. 3113–296).

(I swalllowed up my irritation, which was harmful to me, to my body and to my purse) (2: 340).

He suffers one indignation after another without a word in his defense. Even the most basic of household functions is an opportunity for his wife to abuse him and for him to lamely put up with it:

quant mal dinar
pijor sopar
n'agui *callant*
he soportant
hi quant mal dia
res no'm valia (2577–82)

(How many bad dinners and worse suppers I endured *in silence*! And how many bad days! Nothing helped.) (2: 345, emphasis mine.)

This narrator willingly suffers abuse from which he makes no move to free himself. His is a deliberately unsympathetic voice meant to ironize his misogynist rant. His complaints of his wife's abusive behavior (and therefore his credibility as a narrator) are undercut by his unwillingness to lift a finger in order to improve his lot. In this, he very much resembles the gullible heroes of the Arabic and Hebrew *maqāmāt*. To wit, David Segal has written that "more than half the fun... [of reading al-Ḥarīzī's *Tahkemonī*] is the savouring of an account whose teller is deliberately laying out his own cupidity, naiveté, and comeuppance for entertainment's sake,"[66] which could be equally applied to Roig's narrator. His foolishness and gullibility are so extreme that Solomon himself is moved to intervene. In book three of the *Spill*, the Wise King visits Roig-narrator in a nocturnal vision, berating him for his passivity and insistence on repeatedly exposing himself to the abuse of women:

E tu uell corp
com alquimista
auent ia uista
llur art frustrada
altra uegada
esperimenta
no se'n absenta
ni se'n aparta
mi may se farta
bufar al foch

[66] See the notes to his English translation of al-Ḥarīzī (456).

> he com en ioch
> lo perdedor
> gran iugador
> ab mala sort
> para pus fort
> he mil iochs muda
> ffins que perduda
> ha sa moneda
> may se'n refreda
> ven tot quant te
> quant no y ha que
> per iugar furta
> a mort s'a hurta
> per tornar tost
> ffins que desbost
> guanye qui's uulla
> alli's despulla
> en lo taulell (9956–80)

> (And you, old and curved man, are like an alchemist who, having seen his art frustrated, does the experiment again, does not leave or go away from it, and doesn't ever tire of blowing into the fire. And like the great player who loses in a game with bad luck and tries further and changes one thousand strategies, until he has lost his money. He never cools down. He sells all he has and when he has nothing he steals so he can play. He hurls himself to death so that he can return soon, until destitute, no matter who wins, he takes off his clothes at the [gaming] table.) (2: 434)

Here we have a narrator who complains incessantly about his circumstances but does not lift a finger to change them. This disposition of the narrator calls the exemplarity of his work into question. His tacit consent of the abuse he suffers is a choice for which he may be held responsible; he is an accomplice to his own suffering, and once we realize this we can hardly take his complaints seriously. Like the Archpriest of Hita, Roig's narrator is another "cynical clown" whose misogynist diatribe is clearly ironized by his behavior: he complains incessantly yet takes no action. He inherits this discrepancy between intention and deed from the narrators of the Hebrew *maqāmāt* of al-Ḥarīzī, Ibn Zabāra, and Ibn Shabbetay.

This intentionally unreliable narrator helps to carry out the didactic programs of the *maqāmāt*, the *LBA*, and the *Spill*. Roig, like Ruiz, is explicit in his didactic purpose. Both authors purport to set forth a negative example for the reader. Ruiz explains that he shows us the wrong way to love:

> Conpuse este nuevo libro en que son escriptas algunas maneras e maestrías e sotilezas engañosas del loco amor del mundo, que usan algunos para pecar. Las

quales, leyéndolas e oyéndolas omne o muger de buen entendimiento se quiera salvar, descogerá e obrarlo ha—.E Dios sabe que la mi intençión non fue de lo fazer por dar manera de pecar ni por maldezir, mas fue por reduçir a toda persona a memoria buena de bien obrar e dar ensienplo de buenas costumbres e castigos de salvaçión. (Prologue, lines 95–101 and 31–35)

(I wrote this new book in which are written some deceptive manners, techniques, and subtleties of crazy, worldly love, which some practice in order to sin. In reading these techniques, a man or woman of sound understanding who might wish to save him or her self, might select them and put into practice.... And God knows that my intention was not to do it in order to sin or to speak ill, but rather in order to distill [it] into easily remembered form for every person of good works, and to give an example of good behavior and advice leading to salvation.)

Roig, for his part, shows the wrong way to marry, the lesson being that one should not marry at all:

Si[ ]y llegireu
conexereu
ab prou claror
tan manifesta
la desonesta
he uiciosa
tant perillosa
amor inica
que huy's practica
mes pecoral
que humanal
sols per delit
la per profit
mes auariçia
que amiçiçia
no cur tractar
De mon parlar
tots si'm creureu
elegireu
no may amar
ans desamar (323–44)

(If you read it [my book], you will know, with enough clarity, the great and manifest error, the indecent and depraved, dangerous and iniquitous love that is practiced today, which is more bestial than human, and only for pleasure. The love that is motivated by profit is avarice rather than friendship, and I do not care to deal with it. From my speech, if you believe me, you will all choose never to love but rather to loathe.) (2: 318–319)

In both cases, the purported didactic stance of the narrator is undermined by his own behavior, which contradicts the lessons he claims to teach us. Like Juan Ruiz, Roig's narrator sets forth his personal experience as a negative example for his readers, lest they suffer the same fate he did. Similarly, in the introductory poem to *Minḥat Yehudah*, Ibn Shabbetay claims that he wrote his work in order to guide his audience away from the errors of marriage and family life, to serve as a warning to them:

> So that they not fall from what has been advised to them,
> I have written this book to bear witness to them.
> I will warn them with the best response of my mouth,
> reproach them with a pleasant rebuke.
> Take the instruction of a man who brings a voluntary offering,
> pearls of poetry, not rubies and sapphires.
> Listen to this offering, the fruits of his wisdom, and from all
> the offerings, the sweetest is the Offering of Yehudah. (ed. Huss 1: vv. 6–9)[67]

From the above examples, we see that the stated didactic purpose of the Hebrew *maqāmāt* of Ibn Zabāra (Barcelona, ca. 1200) and Ibn Shabbetay (Toledo, ca. 1200) most resemble that of the *LBA* and the *Spill*: they seek to teach by explicit pseudo-autobiographical negative example. This position is absent from Latin and previous Romance sources with the sole exception of the narrator of *Liber Lamentationum Matheoluli* and its French translation, *Les Lamentations de Mathéolus*. None of the Latin and Romance sources unites an unreliable narrator, an explicit didactic stance and an episodic structure. The more specific coincidences of the narrator's outrage at his own gullibility in *Minḥat Yehudah* and the *Spill* further suggest that Roig had at his disposal the narrative resources of medieval Iberian Hebrew *maqāmāt*.

The Voice of Difference?

However one understands Roig's choice of a narrator who is described as speaking *algemia*, it is clear that his intent was to lend his narrator a voice that would distinguish him from the dialect of prestige of his time. In the context of fifteenth-century Valencia, Roig's narrator is a geographic, socio-economic, and linguistic minority. He is a peasant turned burgher, perhaps a Muslim, and tells his tale in an uncommon rhyme style that makes his story

---

[67] On misogyny in *Minhhat Yehudah*, see I. Davidson (*Parody* 8–11), Hamilton ("Transformation" 195–252), and Fishman.

difficult to understand. Seen from any angle, his is a voice of difference. How, then, do we account for Roig's choice of this voice?

As discussed above, the identification of non-courtly writers with a middle-class identity is reflected in the formal aspects of their work, including versification, theme, and linguistic register. These are often conscious choices made by the authors in order to actively undermine the literary values of the courtly environments from which they are excluded (or which they purposefully shun). Just as the misogyny of the *Spill* (and of other non-courtly literature) is a reaction to the cult of the beloved that dominated courtly poetics, Roig's use of rustic dialect is an act of defiance to courtly poets' adherence to high-register vernacular.

If we can take Roig's reference to *algemia* as an inference that his narrator is a *mudéjar*, it is then possible that his narrator's voice of difference is something more than a reaction to courtly poetic values. Let us suppose that Roig was a crypto-Jew, a descendent of *conversos* whose family had long since abandoned the practice of Judaism and had severed all ties with what remained of the Valencian Jewish community, yet secretly still identified as Jewish.[68] Feeling that they were not completely legitimate Christians, such people would have lived in constant fear that their true identity would be revealed.[69] Such an author may well search (whether consciously or not) for a poetic voice that expresses this anxiety. What (or who) would this voice sound like?[70] As a highly educated urban professional, Roig's daily speech would not have differed significantly from that of the nobility. Therefore, his use of the *algemia* of the *mudéjar* peasantry would be an attempt to appropriate a register readily identifiable as belonging to a marginalized group, a group with every reason to feel the anxiety that a crypto-Jewish Roig would have felt secretly. We can thus read his use of their dialect as evidence of a personal affinity and empathy with the underdog, rather than a simple exercise in popular philology. While it seems counterintuitive to choose this voice in composing a highly erudite work of rhymed prose fiction, the literary appropriation of colloquial speech is well attested in medieval Iberian literature from centuries before Roig. From the tenth century, Andalusī authors mined colloquial verse and popular sayings and

[68] The definitive study on crypto-Jewish culture is that of Gitlitz.

[69] This fear is one of the key components of modern crypto-Jewish identity discussed by Janet Jacobs (21–41).

[70] The still-open question of an identifiable "*converso* voice" has been the subject of recent debate. See Aronson-Friedman, Edwards et al., Hutcheson ("Inflecting"), Hutcheson and Seidenspinner-Núñez, ("Responses"), and Seidenspinner-Núñez ("Commentary").

proverbs.[71] This interest is also evident in Castilian authors such as Juan Ruiz, who reproduces snatches of colloquial Andalusī Arabic in the *LBA* (Martínez Ruiz). Ruiz's contemporary Don Juan Manuel likewise made use of Andalusī proverbs (Nykl, "Arabic"; Hoyos Hoyos), and both the *LBA* and the *Celestina* of Fernando de Rojas (which appears after the *Spill*) contain numerous *refranes* (proverbs and sayings) (Gella Iturriaga; Cantalapiedra; López Catro). The late fifteenth century also witnessed the appearance of two collections of such *refranes* in Castilian (López de Mendoza Santillana; Doctor Castro).[72] Later Valencian poets followed Roig's lead in showcasing popular speech, most notably Jaume Gassull (d. ca. 1515), author of "La brama dels llauradors de la horta de València" ('The Braying of the Workers of the Countryside of Valencia') (1490).[73]

Bourgeois Misogyny

Along with the increased attention to common speech and other realities of daily life, the fifteenth-century shift away from courtly values and toward a more bourgeois literary sensibility brought changes in the way authors expressed traditional medieval misogyny. While Roig stands on the shoulders of a very well represented tradition of misogynous writers in medieval Iberia, his narrator's hatred of women breaks with the style of misogyny evident in works by medieval clerics and nobles and offers the reader a distinctly bourgeois brand of misogyny. Roig's misogyny gives voice to the growing pains of an adolescent middle class. He projects his own social anxieties onto women, blaming them for the excesses of bourgeois life.

As a misogynous writer, Roig is in good company among medieval Iberian authors. The misogynist treatise or diatribe was a well-worn genre in medieval Iberian literature when Jaume Roig appeared on the scene. In the thirteenth and fourteenth centuries, there are several examples of misogynous tales in

---

[71] See López-Morillas ("Language" 38), Hanlon ("Sociolinguistic"), and Abu-Haidar (46). See also al-Zajjālī's collection of popular proverbs from thirteenth-century Granada (ed. Ould Mohamed Baba; trans. Bencherifa).

[72] On such collections in Catalan, see Conca, Guia and Romeu i Figueras.

[73] The modern edition of Gassull's poem is by Miquel i Planas (*Cançoner* 225–34). See also Riquer (3: 345–53) and Sirera (194–96). On the satirical poetry of fifteenth-century Valencia, see Palacios, and Pitarch and Gimeno. Josep Guia suggests that these authors may have acquired a fondness for the speech of the Valencian peasantry while spending extended periods of time in the countryside fleeing the plague in the year 1489 (222–42). His theory calls into question the authorship of Roig, who is known to have died in 1478.

works such as *Disciplina clericalis, Calila e Dimna, Sendebar*, and the *LBA*.[74] Roughly contemporary with the *Spill*, and equally strident in its misogyny is the *Libro del Arcipreste de Talavera* or *Corbacho* (ca. 1468).[75] Both the latter and the Catalan *Somni* of Bernat Metge (1399) find inspiration in Boccaccio's highly popular and widely circulated misogynous opus, *Il Corbaccio*.[76]

Part of Roig's accomplishment in the *Spill* is his adaptation of the *maqāma* to the changing realities and literary values of mid-fifteenth-century Valencia. His treatment of women is part of this adaptation. In the Arabic and Hebrew *maqāmāt*, the cynical narrator habitually blames his misfortune on "Fate" or "Time" (though it is clear to the audience that he is the sole author of his own troubles). In the *Spill*, he blames women, including his mother, his four wives, and the various women he encounters in the course of his travels throughout Aragon and France.[77] Roig's misogyny is rooted in an emergent bourgeois culture and framed in terms of first-person experience. His narrator blames the negative qualities of the bourgeois world on women.[78] For him, they embody the excesses of Valencian bourgeois culture: crude materialism, frivolous litigation, vanity, spite, and selfishness.[79] In the Castilian picaresque, particularly in *Lazarillo de Tormes*, we find many of these same faults personified in the series of Lázaro's masters: the Blind Man is spiteful, the Priest selfish and grasping, the Squire vain and materialistic. However, in *Lazarillo*, the author blames the institutions that traditionally upheld a feudal system, above all the Nobility and the Church. The picaresque narrator must struggle against those who cling to the outmoded feudal system in order to achieve even modest material success. In the *Spill*, the narrator's

---

[74] These examples, along with those from other works, are studied by Goldberg ("Sexual").

[75] On misogyny in the *Corbacho*, see Sims, Seidenspinner-Núñez ("Guay"), and Solomon (67–146).

[76] In his introduction to his edition of the *Spill*, Miquel i Planas writes that the *Spill* and the *Somni* "adoptan el pretexto de una visión o sueño, y ponen en boca de un personaje extrahumano lo más violento de los improperios con que gratifican al otro sexo" ('adopt the pretext of a vision or dream, and put in the mouth of a superhuman character the most violent indiscretions with which they grace the other sex') (lxix).

[77] On misogyny in the *Spill*, see Cantavella (*Cards*), Carré i Pons ("Lletra"), Vellón i Lahoz, Solomon, and Archer (108–20).

[78] By way of comparison with the picaresque novel in Castile, Anne Cruz writes that the protagonist of *Lazarillo de Tormes* is a "carrier of collective guilt" who "shouldered the blame for the numerous ills that plagued sixteenth-century Spain" (10). In the *Spill*, it is women who shoulder the blame for the ills of bourgeois Valencia.

[79] See, for example, the detailed descriptions of the narrator's wives' conspicuous consumption of clothing, home furnishings, and delicacies in verses 2060–2089 and 4066–4111. See also the comments of Solomon (78–79). For an excellent analysis of the bourgeois aspects of Roig's misogyny, see Vellón i Lahoz. On the material culture depicted by Roig, see Querol Faus (41–56).

struggle for bourgeois survival is against women. According to him, women are the ones responsible for his difficulty establishing and maintaining his middle-class status.

The first woman to mistreat Roig's narrator is his own mother, who thrusts him, penniless, into the world to find his own way. After his father's death, his mother sends him away and legally repudiates him, seeking to keep his inheritance for herself and increase her prospects for remarriage. The narrator recounts how she literally hustles him out of the door of his late father's house, providing several suggestions as to how he might go about making a living. Her advice is very explicit on the value of success based on one's labor, going into the specifics of several trades:

> Com m'abexa
> tantost de casa
> que'm donas brasa
> ben adreçat
> hun peu calçat
> altre descalç
> gipo al falç
> tot esquinçat
> ben desayrat
> hi sens camisa
> dix a[ ]ta guisa
> ves hon te uulles
> cerca hon mulles
> d'uy[ ]mes ta sopa
> esta[ ]nit sopa
> dema camina
> a[ ]la brogina
> he si no't plau
> berguant al Grau
> te poras fer
> ho llantener
> de cap de guaytes
> ho si t'afaytes
> ser bon barber
> a[ ]ton plaer
> cantant cançons
> ballant als sons
> de les tisores
> tots iorns dos ores
> prou guanyaras
> ho si uolras
> esser obrer
> de tintorer

dos sous he nou
auras per sou
o si troter
puys escuder
esser uolies
tant be uiuries
pensa sta[ ]nit
ton bon partit
no't puch tenir
ves a[ ]sseguir
taula ni llit
ti't'o per[ ]dit
comte no'n fasses
que'n mi trob[a]sses
peus e mans tens
guanya't prou bens
cerca uentura (862–911)

(So that I would get a move on, she immediately threw me out of her house well equipped: one shoe on and the other off, my jacket on in any which way and completely torn, totally snubbed and without a shirt. As she was throwing me out, she said: "Go at your pleasure wherever you want. Look for a place where you can dunk your bread from now on. Tonight, have supper, tomorrow, use a drift net. And if you don't like it, you'll be able to become a brigantine sailor at the Grau, or the lantern-bearer of a police corporal. Or if you shave you can be a good barber: singing songs at your pleasure, dancing to the sounds of the scissors, and working two hours a day, you will earn enough. Or if you want to be a worker in a dye shop, you will have a salary of two sous and nine diners. Or if you'd want to be an apprentice and then a squire, you'd live just as well. Think tonight about your best benefit. I can't have you: go on out. Bear this in mind: don't think that you'll find a table or a bed at my house. You have feet and hands: earn enough riches, seek your fortune.") (2: 325–6)

This callous, even sarcastic rejection at the hands of his own mother furnishes the narrator with a drive to succeed that is rooted in the most classically self-hating type of misogyny: that of one's own mother.[80] From his earliest days, the protagonist learns that the war for bourgeois survival is fought on

[80] Psychoanalysis offers at least two explanations for male misogyny that are based on the mother-son relationship. One is that misogyny is a displacement of unresolved anger harbored against the mother because of her rejection of the son during his Oedipal phase. Alternatively, a man with an unhealthy attachment to his mother may regard sex with women as filthy and disgusting because he is unable to separate his erotic impulse from his maternal bond. Finally, the process of disidentifying with the mother in the passage from boyhood to adulthood may result in a general vilification of women (Gilmore 155–59).

two fronts. The external threat is a world where success depends on one's own efforts and the fortunes of the market, but the internal threat—and the one most easily targeted—is woman.

The example set by his mother is repeated by every other woman he encounters. All the wrongs he suffers are at the hands of women. After he is forced from his mother's house, his aunt likewise rejects him (916–17). When he becomes ill, the attendant at the hospital where he admits himself is a "ffalsa ronçera" ('false flattering woman') (926). Following his illness, he is employed by a Catalan knight, whose wife plots against the narrator and conspires to have him driven away (996–1067). In his next job, as a merchant's agent, he is cheated by a female innkeeper (1393–1412). Later, during his travels in Paris, he champions a local bourgeois woman in a tournament, after which she then poisons her husband (1512–1603). Finally, he stays at an inn run by a woman who serves her guests human flesh (presumably that of other, deceased guests) (1647–1741). His hatred of women, it seems, is the lens through which he views the world, to the extent that his entire experience in France is summed up by his poor opinion of French women:

> Molt agui grat
> d'aquell pays
> may uiu diuis
> bandoleiar
> ni bregueiar
> homens prou richs
> e paçifichs
> suaus benignes
> dones malignes
> moltes vegades
> viu condempnades
> mil bandeiauen
> mes ne peniauen
> que de rayms
> per uaris crims (1742–56)
>
> (I was very pleased by that country. I never saw discord, banditry or fighting. The men were quite rich and peaceful, affable and benign. The women were evil, and many times I saw them condemned: they exiled one thousand and there were more hanged women than grapes for different crimes.) (2: 335)

In fact, his favorable impression of the French seems to be based on their willingness to punish their women. This differs considerably from his experiences in Valencia, where women were allowed to ruin his life, albeit with his tacit consent. This bit of francophilia only reinforces the narrator's social pretensions—he models his bourgeois values by endorsing a distinctly French brand of misogyny, much in the way one might conspicuously consume French wine or cheese as a display of bourgeois taste.

Materialism and Misogyny in the Hebrew Maqāma

While Roig's particular brand of bourgeois misogyny owes much to Latin and Romance tradition, it also shares some very specific features with Hebrew *maqāmāt* written in Castile and Aragon. Women's materialism is a natural *topos* of bourgeois misogyny, yet it also belongs to the Hebrew *maqāmāt* of Christian Iberia.[81] Though studies of late medieval society do not typically include Jews in discussions of the growing middle class, authors such as Ibn Shabbetay and al-Ḥarīzī were indeed members of the bourgeoisie, earning their living as physicians, secretaries, and the like. Therefore it should not be surprising that their literary expression of misogyny coincides with that of their Christian counterparts in the middle classes, to which the physician Roig most certainly belonged.

There are two compelling examples of complaints of women's materialism in late twelfth- and early thirteenth-century Hebrew *maqāmāt* that anticipate Roig's text. The first is found in Ibn Shabbetay's *Minḥat Yehudah*. The protagonist Zeraḥ is a young man who renounces women entirely in order to dedicate his life to studying the Torah (an oxymoron, since there is no ascetic tradition within Judaism, and it is considered transgressive for an able-bodied man to turn one's back on family life).[82] Despite his resolve, a resourceful go-between sells him on a beautiful young woman, but substitutes an ugly old hag for her at the last minute. Instead of a night of inaugural conjugal passion, Zeraḥ instead is treated to a lengthy list of household items that he must buy for his wife in order to placate her:

---

[81] On misogyny in the medieval Iberian Hebrew *maqāmāt*, see Roth ("Wiles"), Dishon (*Šaʿašūʿīm* 53–91; "Images"), Fishman, T. Rosen ("Tongues"; "Sexual"; *Unveiling*), and Jill Jacobs. For a comprehensive bibliography on misogyny in medieval Hebrew literature, see Yassif (529 n. 89).

[82] Tova Rosen notes the following two problems that precipitate misogyny in Hebrew literature: "one is the discord between the negativity of woman and the positive postulate of marriage; the other is the contrariety between the philosopher's spiritual path and the indulgence in matter which is caused by family life. In the male philosopher's view, these were practical and indeed most excruciating problems" (*Unveiling* 103). That is, misogyny is an immature response to the discrepancy between the ideal and the reality of marriage, which is a requirement even for the most studious of Jewish men, who did not have the option of an officially celibate way of life such as the Catholic priesthood.

> Go and fetch me vessels of silver and vessels of gold, dresses and chains, bracelets and mufflers, a house and a flat, a chair and a lamp, a table and spoons, a pestle and groats, a blanket and spindle-weight, a mat and a tub, a basket and spindle, a cauldron and bottle, a basin and clothespress, a broom and a kerchief; a pan, furnace, barrel, and shovel; a pot, vessels, goblets, and charms; gowns, veils, turbans, and robes; linen, nose rings, purses and lace; crescents, amulets, sashes, embroidery, headdresses, rings, checkered cloth, armlets, and anklets; and besides these, special clothes to wear on Sabbaths and festivals. This is by no means all you shall have to provide. But if this is beyond your means, what you will see befall you will drive you mad. (trans. Scheindlin 285; ed. Huss 2: 26, ll. 609–18)

The message is quite clear: marriage is about money, not love, and all the romantic ideals and literary aspirations of Zeraḥ's youth must now take a back seat to providing a richly extravagant living for his wife.

Judah al-Ḥarīzī, perhaps following the lead of Ibn Shabbetay, describes a similar scene in *maqāma* 8 of his *Taḥkemonī*. In this case, Heman the Ezrahite is also promised a beautiful young bride, who brings a healthy dowry to the marriage—or so he was led to believe. As in Ibn Shabbetay's version, the promised bride is revealed to be a hideous old woman, and poor to boot. After coming to grips with her unconventional looks, Heman asks her:

> "My daughter, although your face is like briers and thorns, tell me, what have you in the house? And where are your dresses and your mantles, your signets and your cords, your crescents and your bracelets, your luxurious perfumes, your anointing pots?"
>
> She said:
>
> "I lack for nothing because God has favored me and I have plenty. But I left all my clothes tied up in the house of my lord, my father, at home."
>
> I said to her:
>
> "And what is the deposit that you left in your lord's house?"
>
> She said to me:
>
> "I left two old sacks, and broken pots, and a dish, and a caldron and a cloak and a veil—and a staff and a sack, and torn clothes, and spotted vessels, and two platters, and three pots." Now when I heard her words, I fell upon my face, and my thoughts perished and they found no vision from the Lord. (trans. Reichert 1: 124–25; ed. Toporovsky and Zamorah 79)

As in the *Spill*, the narrator's ideals are clear-cut: he wants to have a wife and children and continue to lead a peaceful life (and perhaps continue his literary pursuits). But the demands of a bourgeois lifestyle allow him no such peace. His first wife demands all manner of luxuries in order to be happy. Roig recalls how just shortly after the wedding he rushed out to buy her what she wanted:

De[ ] fet pensi
que li daria
yo prouehi
he l'arehi
perles robins
velluts çetins
conduyts marts uays
veruins duays
per cots guonelles
angles bruxelles
e bell domas (2060–2069)

(I immediately thought about what I would give her and what I would do. I provided and decked her with pearls, rubies, velvet, satins, *conduyts*, marten furs, squirrel furs, fabrics from Vervins and Douay for coats and gowns, fabrics from England and Brussels, and beautiful Damask.) (2: 339)

Naturally, this indulgence does not pacify her and the marriage is eventually dissolved. For his second wife, Roig thinks to take a widow, hoping for a more mature and less materialistic partner. But what he gets instead is a woman who is openly pious, but secretly vain. She makes a great show of modesty and plain appearance, but inwardly she is just as materialistic as the first wife:

Que desus uist
cot e mantell
de gros burell
roba iusana
de fina llana
prima llistada
vert blau pintada
duy'almexia

Ella texia
de son ofiçi
algun seliçi
tots los uenia
may se'n uestia
algu'n[ ]la[ ]squena
Dijous de Çena
d'abit uestida
he prim çenyida
la creu portaua
may se tocaua
de diçiplina

Al coll iustina
duya e mostres
de patenostres
he agnus d'or
en dret del cor
lo llit uolia
lla hon dormia
fflux moll e bla
egual e pla
ab flos e rama
ab timiama
lo perfumaua

Acostumaua
taula bastida
he ben fassida
no quaresmal
mas de carnal
may deiunaua
ni pex meniaua
gran mal li feya
o axi[ ]u deya
quant se leuaua
aconsolaua
lo seu uentrell
ab hun guobell
de maluesia (4066–111)

> (Although on top she wore a gown and a cloak made out of burail, she wore undergarments made out of delicate wool and a fine small cloak painted with green and blue stripes. As her own enterprise, she occasionally wove some hair shirts, but she sold them all and never put one on her back. On Maundy Thursday, wearing her habit quite tightly, she carried the cross, but she never scourged herself. Around her neck she wore a corset and samples of paternosters, and a gold lamb over her heart. The bed where she slept she wanted soft, delicate and smooth, even and flat. She perfumed it with flowers, twigs, and thymiama. She was accustomed to a well-provided and stocked table, not to a Lenten table, but to one that included meats. She never tasted nor ate fish: it made her sick, or so she said. When she got up, she consoled her stomach with a glass of Malmsey wine.) (2: 363)

All three of the narrators of Ibn Shabbetay, al-Ḥarīzī, and Roig see the worst excesses of their bourgeois surroundings in the behavior of their own wives and blame them for it. Their misogyny is a displacement of the angst one experiences in having to earn a living as a member of the middle class. Such angst would come naturally to a writer, who would just as soon spend his days composing verses as attending to patients or drafting correspondence for the king. Their particular brand of bourgeois misogyny is a result of their abandonment of courtly literary values and engagement with the daily realities of making a living.

In conclusion, Jaume Roig's Valencia was a society in the throes of a social transformation in which the feudal system was being replaced with a new bourgeois order. During his lifetime, thousands of Valencian Jews were converted to Christianity and swelled the ranks of the middle class to which Roig belonged. In his professional life Roig dealt with scores of *converso* and Jewish physicians on a daily basis. The language and style of the *Spill* are clearly rooted in a bourgeois rejection of medieval poetic values, and Roig's idiosyncratic use of a predominately Muslim dialect of rural Valencian Catalan suggests an identification with (or at the very least an interest in) an experience of social marginalization typical of *converso* and crypto-Jewish writers. In addition, several of Roig's literary innovations in the *Spill* point toward a familiarity with the Hebrew *maqāmāt* of authors from Castile and Aragon, including its episodic structure, its hapless narrator who offers his experience as a negative example for the reader, and a misogyny that centers on female materialism.

As in the case of the *LBA*, it may be difficult to prove that Roig was personally familiar with the work of Ibn Shabbetay, al-Ḥarīzī, or Ibn Zabāra. But absent any feasible precedents in Latin or Romance literatures for some of the *Spill*'s idiosyncrasies, it is quite difficult to dismiss the possibility out of hand. From our modern-day perspective, formal institutional study of literary texts may seem to be divided neatly into Romance and Hebrew, and even further divided into Castilian and Catalan and so forth. These are walls we have constructed for various political and economic reasons over the centuries and serve their purposes. However, it bears repeating that the social reality in which Hebrew *maqāmāt* and works such as the *Spill* were written, read, heard, copied, and otherwise transmitted or discussed was not similarly compartmentalized. In Roig's Valencia, readers and writers of Hebrew regularly became readers and writers of Latin and Romance. Jewish and formerly Jewish readers of Hebrew were friends, colleagues, and lovers of people who were active in Catalan and Latin literary activities. Jaume Roig the author was also Jaume Roig the person, who worked, prayed, dined, drank, and socialized in a city whose social—and literary—life was constituted by adherents of Islam and Judaism, as well as Christianity.

WORKS CITED

Abbou, I.D. *Musulmans andalous et judéo-espagnols*. Casablanca: Éditions Antar, 1953.

Abu-Haidar, Jareer A. *Hispano-Arabic Literature and the Early Provençal Lyrics*. Richmond: Curzon, 2001.

Abulafia, David. *Frederick II: A Medieval Emperor*. London: Allen Lane, 1988.

Abulafia, Ṭodros Ha-Levi ben Yehudah. *The Garden of Parables and Saws, a Collection of Poems* [Hebrew]. Ed. David Yellin. Jerusalem, 1932.

ADMYTE: Archivo digital de manuscritos y textos españoles. Ed. Francisco Marcos Marín, Charles B. Faulhaber, Ángel Gómez Moreno, and Antonio Cortijo Ocaña. Madrid: Micronet, 1992.

Agüera, Victorio. "Jaume Roig y la tradición picaresca." Diss. The Catholic U. of America, 1972.

——. *Un pícaro catalan del siglo XV: El* Spill *de Jaume Roig y la tradición picaresca*. Barcelona: Ediciones Hispam, 1975.

Aguilar, María D., Ignacio L. Henares Cuéllar, and Rafael J. López Guzmán. *Mudéjar iberoamericano: Una expresión cultural de dos mundos*. Granada: Universidad de Granada, 1993.

Aizenberg, Edna. "The People of the Book and the Ambiguity of the *Book of Good Love*." *Romance Notes* 26.2 (1985): 155–63.

Alain of Lille. *The Art of Preaching*. Trans. Gillian R. Evans. Kalamazoo, Mich.: Cistercian Publications, 1981.

Alemany Bolufer, Jose. *La antigua versión castellana del* Calila y Dimna. Madrid: Suc. de Hernando, 1915.

Alfonso X. *Lapidario*. Ed. Sagrario Rodríguez M. Montalvo. Madrid: Gredos, 1981.

——. *Libro de ajedrez, dados y tablas* (1283). MS El Escorial: Monasterio, T.I.6. Transcr. Lloyd A. Kasten and John Nitti. *ADMYTE*.

al-Ġazzālī, Imām Abū Ḥāmid Muḥammad. *Kimiyā-yi Saʿadat*. Ed. Aḥmad Amram. Tehran: Markazī, 1974.

——. *The Alchemy of Happiness*. Trans. Claud Field. Armonk, NY: M.E. Sharpe, 1991.

al-Ḥarīrī, Abū Muḥammad al-Qāsim ibn ʿAlī. *Maqāmāt al-Ḥarīrī*. Ed. ʿIsa Saba. Beirut: Dār Sadr; Dār Beirūt, 1970.

——. *The Assemblies of Al Ḥarīri*. Trans. Thomas Chenery. 2 vols. London: Willams and Norgate, 1867.

al-Ḥarīzī, Judah. *Las asambleas de los sabios (Tahkemoni)*. Trans. Carlos Del Valle Rodríguez. Murcia: Universidad de Murcia, 1986.

——. *The Book of Tahkemoni: Jewish Tales from Medieval Spain*. Trans. David Simha Segal. London: The Littman Library of Jewish Civilization, 2001.

——. *The Tahkemoni*. Trans. Victor Emanuel Reichert. 2 vols. Jerusalem: Raphael Haim Cohen, 1965–1973.

——. *Taḥkemonī* [Hebrew]. Eds. Yisrael Toporovsky and Yisrael Zamorah. Tel Aviv: Meḥaberot Lesifrūt, 1952.

ʿAlī, Muḥammad, and Muḥammad ibn Ismāʾil al-Bukhārī. *A Manual of Hadith*. 2nd ed. Lahore: Ahmadiyya Anjuman Ishaat Islam, 1951.

al-Jāḥiẓ, Abū ʿUthmān ʿAmr ibn Baḥr al-Fuqaymī al-Baṣrī. *Kitāb al-ḥayawān*. Ed. Muḥammad Harūn ʿAbd al-Salām. 8 vols. Cairo: Mustafà al-Baʾbī al-Halabī, 1965.

Allen, Roger. *An Introduction to Arabic Literature*. New York: Cambridge University Press, 2000.

al-Maqqarī, Aḥmad ibn Muḥammad. *The History of the Mohammedan Dynasties in Spain.* Trans. Pascual de Gayangos. 2 vols. New York: Johnson Reprint, 1843.
al-Saraqusṭī, Abū l-Ṭāhir Muḥammad ibn Yūsuf. *Al-Maqāmāt Al-Luzūmīyya.* Ed. Ḥasan al-Warāglī. Tetuan: Manšūrāt ʿŪkāz, 1995.
——. *Al-Maqāmāt Al-Luzūmiyya.* Trans. James T. Monroe. Leiden: Brill, 2002.
——. *Las sesiones del Zaragocí: Relatos picarescos (maqamat).* Trans. Ignacio Ferrando Frutos. Saragossa: Universidad de Zaragoza, 1999.
al-Shāfiʿī, al-Imām Muḥammad ibn Idris. *Jumāʿ al-ʿIlm.* Ed. Aḥmad Muḥammad Shākir. Cairo: Ṭabaʿāt Halabī, 1940.
——. *Treatise on the Foundations of Islamic Jurisprudence.* Trans. Majid Khadduri. 2nd ed. Cambridge: The Islamic Texts Society, 1987.
Alvar, Carlos. *La poesía trovadoresca en España y Portugal.* Madrid: Editorial Planeta; Real Academia de Buenas Letras, 1977.
Alvárez, Lourdes María. "Beastly Colloquies: Of Plagiarism and Pluralism in Two Medieval Disputations between Animals and Men." *Comparative Literature Studies* 39.3 (2002): 170–200.
——. "Petrus Alfonsi." Menocal et al. 282–91.
al-Zajjālī, Abū Yaḥyā ʿUbaid Allāh. *Proverbes Andalous de Abu Yahya Ubaid Allah Az-Zaggali (1220–1294).* Trans. Mohamed Bencherifa: Ministere d'Etat Charge des Affaires Culturelles et de L'Enseignement Originel, 1971.
al-Zawzānī, Abī ʿAbd al-Sakuyn ibn Aḥmad. *Sharḥ al-muʿallaqāt al-sabʿ al-Ṭiwāl.* Ed. ʿUmar Farūq al-Tibāʿ. Beirut: Tawziʿ dār al-qalam al-tibāʿa wa-l-našr, 1990.
Ambrosio Sánchez, M. "Predicaciones y antisemitismo: el caso de San Vicente Ferrer." *Proyección histórica de España en sus tres culturas: Castilla y León, América y el Mediterráneo.* Ed. Eufemio Lorenzo Sanz. Valladolid: Junta de Castilla y León, Consejería de Cultura y Turismo, 1993. 195–204.
Anderson, George K. *The Literature of the Anglo-Saxons.* Princeton: Princeton University Press, 1949.
Anzaldúa, Gloria. *Borderlands = La frontera: The New Mestiza.* 2nd ed. San Francisco: Spinsters/Aunt Lute Books, 1987.
Archer, Robert. *The Problem of Woman in Late-Medieval Hispanic Literature.* Woodbridge, UK. London: Tamesis, 2004.
Arie, R. "Notes sur la maqama andalouse." *Hesperis-Tamuda* 9.2 (1968): 204–05.
Armistead, Samuel G. "A Brief History of *Kharja* Studies." *Hispania* 70.1 (1987): 8–15.
——. "*Kharjas* and *Villancicos.*" *Journal of Arabic Literature* 34.1–2 (2003): 3–19.
Arnaldez, Roger. *Averroes: A Rationalist in Islam.* Trans. David Streight. Notre Dame: University of Notre Dame Press, 2000.
Aronson-Friedman, Amy. "Identifying the *Converso* Voice." Diss. Temple University, 2000.
Arrom, José Juan. "Las primeras imágenes opuestas y el debate sobre la dignidad del indio." *De palabra y obra en el Nuevo Mundo.* Eds. Miguel León-Portilla, Manuel Gutiérrez Estévez, Gary H. Gossen and J. Jorge Klor de Alva. Mexico City: Siglo Veintiuno Editores, 1992. 63–86.
Arteaga, Alfred. *An Other Tongue: Nation and Ethnicity in the Linguistic Borderlands.* Durham: Duke University Press, 1994.
Ashtor, Eliyahu. *The Jews of Moslem Spain.* Trans. Aaron Klein and Jenny Machlowitz Klein. 3 vols. Philadelphia: Jewish Publication Society of America, 1973.
Asín Palacios, Miguel. *El original árabe de la Disputa del asno contra Fr. Anselmo Turmeda.* 2nd ed. Madrid: Centro de Estudios Históricos, 1914.
Assis, Yom Tov. *The Jews of Spain: From Settlement to Expulsion.* Jerusalem: Hebrew University Press, 1988.
Avalle-Arce, Juan Bautista. "Una tradición literaria: el cuento de los dos amigos." *Nueva Revista de Filología Hispánica* 11 (1957): 1–35.
Ayerbe-Chaux, Reinaldo. El Conde Lucanor: *Materia tradicional y originalidad creadora.* Madrid: J. Porrúa Turanzas, 1975.

Aznar, José María. "Seven Theses on Today's Terrorism." Inaugural University Lecture. Sep. 24, 2004. Georgetown University Office of the President. 11 Nov. 2004. <http://data.georgetown.edu/president/aznar/inauguraladdress.html>.

Bach, Kent. "Speech Acts." *Routledge Encyclopedia of Philosophy*. Ed. Edward Craig. London: Routledge, 1998. 81–86.

Baer, Yitzhak. *A History of the Jews in Christian Spain*. Trans. Louis Schoffman. 2 vols. Philadelphia: Jewish Publication Society, 1978.

Bakhtin, M.M. *The Dialogic Imagination: Four Essays*. Trans. Michael Holquist. Austin: University of Texas Press, 1981.

Balard, Michel, and Alain Ducellier, eds. *Le partage du monde: Échanges et colonisation dans la méditerranée*. Paris: Publications de la Sorbonne, 1998.

Baldwin, Spurgeon. Introduction. *The Medieval Castilian Bestiary*. By Giacomo Lentini. Ed. Spurgeon Baldwin. Exeter: University of Exeter Press, 1982. i–xxiii.

Ballesteros Beretta, Antonio, and Miguel Rodríguez Llopis. *Alfonso X el Sabio*. Barcelona: El Albir, 1984.

Barceló Torres, María del Carmen. *Minorías islámicas en el País Valenciano: historia y dialecto*. Valencia: Universidad de Valencia Secretariado de Publicaciones Facultad de Filología Instituto Hispano-Arabe de Cultura, 1984.

Barkai, Ron. *Cristianos y musulmanes en la España medieval: El enemigo en el espejo*. Madrid: Rialp, 1984.

Barlaam e Josafat. Eds. John E. Keller and Robert W. Linker. Madrid: Consejo Superior de Investigaciones Científicas, Instituto "Miguel de Cervantes", 1979.

Barletta, Vincent. *Covert Gestures: Crypto-Islamic Literature as Cultural Practice in Early Modern Spain*. Minneapolis: University of Minnesota Press, 2005.

Barroso, Graciela. "Alfonso X y la escuela de traductores de Toledo." *Actas Academia Luventicus* 5 (2003): 1–10.

Barrucand, Marianne, and Achim Bednorz. *Moorish architecture in Andalusia*. 2nd ed. Köln: New York Taschen, 2002.

Bartlett, Robert. *The Making of Europe: Conquest, Colonization, and Cultural Change, 950–1350*. London: Allen Lane, 1993.

Bartosik-Vélez, Elise. "The Three Rhetorical Strategies of Christopher Columbus." *Colonial Latin American Review* 11, no. 1 (2002): 33–46.

Basso, Keith H. *Western Apache Language and Culture: Essays in Linguistic Anthropology*. Tucson: University of Arizona Press, 1990.

Bataillon, Louis J. *La prédication au XIIIe siècle en France et Italie*. Aldershot-Brookfield: Variorum, 1993.

Bauman, Richard. "Performance." *Folklore, Cultural Performances, and Popular Entertainments*. Ed. Richard Bauman. New York: Oxford University Press, 1992. 41–49.

——. *Story, Performance, and Event*. Cambridge: Cambridge University Press, 1986.

——. "Verbal Art as Performance." *Linguistic Anthropology: A Reader*. Malden, MA: Blackwell, 2001. 165–88.

——, and Barbara A. Babcock. *Verbal Art as Performance*. Prospect Heights, Ill.: Waveland Press, 1984.

——, and Donald Braid. "The Ethnography of Performance in the Study of Oral Traditions." *Teaching Oral Traditions*. Ed. John Miles Foley. New York: Modern Language Association, 1998. 106–22.

——, and Charles Briggs. "Poetics and Performance as Critical Perspectives on Language and Social Life." *Annual Review of Anthropology* 19 (1990): 59–88.

Baxter, Ron. *Bestiaries and Their Users in the Middle Ages*. Stroud, Gloucestershire: Sutton; Courtauld Institute, 1998.

Belenguer Cebrià, Ernest. *València en la crisi del segle XV*. Barcelona: Edicions 62, 1976.

Benallou, Lamine. "En cuanto a la transcripción de las frases árabes en *El Conde Lucanor* de don Juan Manuel. Presentación y crítica." *La traducción y la crítica literaria. Actas de las Jornadas de Hispanismo Arabe. Madrid, 24–27 de mayo de 1988*. Ed. Fernando De Greda.

Madrid: Agencia Española de Cooperación Internacional—Instituto de Cooperación con el Mundo Árabe, 1990. 227–33.

Ben-Shammai, Haggai. "Kalām in medieval Jewish philosophy." *History of Jewish Philosophy*. Ed. Daniel H. Frank and Oliver Leaman. London: Routledge, 1997. 115–48

Berceo, Gonzalo de. *El Libro de Alixandre*. Ed. Dana Arthur Nelson. Madrid: Gredos, 1979.

——. *Obras Completas*. Ed. Brian Dutton. 2nd ed. London: Tamesis Books, 1984.

——. *La Vida de San Millán de La Cogolla de Gonzalo de Berceo*. Ed. Brian Dutton. 2nd ed. London: Tamesis Books, 1967.

Berger, David. *The Jewish-Christian Debate in the High Middle Ages*. Philadelphia: Jewish Publication Society, 1979.

Berkey, Jonathan Porter. *Popular Preaching and Religious Authority in the Medieval Islamic Near East*. Seattle: University of Washington Press, 2001.

Berlioz, Jacques. "L'*exemplum* homilétique." *Comprendre le XIIIe siècle: Etudes offertes à Marie-Thérèse Lorcin*. Eds. Pierre Guichard and Daniele Alexandre-Bidon. Lyon: Presses Universitaires, 1995. 270–99.

——, and Marie-Anne Polo. "Les prologues des recueils d'*exempla* (XIIIe–XIVe siècles). Une grille d'analyse." *La predicazione dei frati dalla metà del '200 alla fine del '300. Atti del XXII Convegno internazionale. Assisi, 13–15 ottobre 1994*. Spoleto: Centro Italiano di Studi Sull'alto Medioevo, 1994. 269–99.

Bhaba, Homi. *The Location of Culture*. London: Routledge, 1994.

Biblia Sacra Iuxta Vulgatam Clementinam. Eds. Alberto Colunga and Lorenzo Turrado. 4th ed. Madrid: Biblioteca de Autores Cristianos, 1965.

Biglieri, Aníbal A. "*El Conde Lucanor*, Ejemplo 36: (El Autor), (La Realidad), El Texto." *Revista Canadiense de Estudios Hispánicos* 113 (1987): 461–75.

Bin Gorion, Micha Joseph. *Mimekor Yisrael*. Trans. I.M. Lask. Ed. Emmanuel Bin Gorion. 3 vols. Bloomington: Indiana University Press, 1976.

Blamires, Alcuin, ed. *Woman Defamed and Woman Defended: An Anthology of Medieval Texts*. Oxford: Clarendon, 1992.

Blachère, Régis. "Étude sémantique sur le nom maqama." *Al-Mashriq* 47 (1953): 646–52.

Blamires, Alcuin, ed. *Woman Defamed and Woman Defended: An Anthology of Medieval Texts*. Oxford: Clarendon, 1992.

Blau, Joshua, and Joseph Yahalom. *Mas'e Yehuda*. Jerusalem: Mekhon Ben Tzvi; Hebrew University, 2002.

Bohigas, Pere. *Lírica trobadoresca del segle XV*. Valencia: Institut de Filologia Valenciana; Publicacions de l'Abadia de Montserrat, 1988.

Bonebakker, S.A. "*Adab* and the Concept of *Belles-Lettres*." *'Abbasid Belles-Lettres*. Ed. Julia Ashtiany, T.M. Johnstone, J.D. Latham, R.B. Serjeant and G. Rex Smith. Cambridge: Cambridge University Press, 1989. 16–30.

Borrás Gualis, Gonzalo M., Federico Mayor, Manuel Pizarro Moreno, and Juan Benavides Courtois. *El Arte mudéjar*. Zaragoza: Ediciones UNESCO: Ibercaja, 1995.

Bossong, Georg. "Science in the Vernacular Languages: The Case of Alfonso X El Sabio." *De Astronomia Alphonsi Regis: Actas del simposio sobre astronomía alfonsí celebrado en Berkeley (Agosto 1985)*. Barcelona: Universidad de Barcelona, 1987. 13–22.

Boswell, John. *The Royal Treasure: Muslim Communities under the Crown of Aragon in the Fourteenth Century*. New Haven: Yale University Press, 1977.

Bosworth, C.E. *The Medieval Islamic Underworld*. 2 vols. Leiden: E.J. Brill, 1976.

Botterill, Steven. Introduction. *De Vulgari Eloquentia*. By Dante Alighieri. Ed. Steven Botterill. Cambridge: Cambridge University Press, 1996. ix–xxvi.

Bourdieu, Pierre. "The Berber House." *Rules and Meanings: The Anthropology of Everyday Knowledge*. Ed. Mary Douglas. New York: Penguin, 1977. 98–110.

——. "La maison Kabyle ou le monde renversé." *Échanges et communications: Mélanges offerts à Claude Lévi-Strauss à l'occasion de son 60ème anniversaire*. Eds. Jean Pouillon and Pierre Maranda. The Hague: Mouton, 1971. 739–58.

Boyarin, Daniel. "Placing Reading: Ancient Israel and Medieval Europe." J. Boyarin, *Ethnography*. 10–37.
Boyarin, Jonathan, ed. *The Ethnography of Reading*. Berkeley: University of California Press, 1993.
——. "Voices around the Text: The Ethnography of Reading at Mesivta Tifereth Jerusalem." J. Boyarin, *Ethnography*. 212–37.
Brann, Ross. "The Arabized Jews." Menocal et al. 435–54.
——. *The Compunctious Poet: Cultural Ambiguity and Hebrew Poetry in Medieval Spain*. Baltimore: Johns Hopkins University, 1991.
Briere, Daniel H. "Physiognomy and the *Libro de buen amor*." *Medieval Perspectives* 2.1 (1987): 129–36.
Brown, Peter. *A Companion to Chaucer*. Oxford: Blackwell Publishers, 2000.
Brownlee, Marina S. "Autobiography as Self-(Re)Presentation: The Augustinian Paradigm and Juan Ruiz's Theory of Reading." *Mimesis: From Mirror to Method, Augustine to Descartes*. Eds. John D. Lyons and Stephen G. Nichols, Jr. Hanover: University Press of New England for Dartmouth Coll., 1982. 71–82.
——. "Genre as Meaning in the *Libro de buen amor*." *Poetics of Love in the Middle Ages*. Eds. Moshe Lazar and Norris J. Lacy. Fairfax, VA: George Mason University, 1989. 53–65.
——. "Permutations of the Narrator-Protagonist: The Serrana Episodes of the *Libro de buen amor* in Light of the Doña Endrina Sequence." *Romance Notes* 22.1 (1981): 98–101.
——. *The Status of the Reading Subject in the* Libro De Buen Amor. Chapel Hill: University of North Carolina Dept. of Romance Languages: Distributed by University of North Carolina Press, 1985.
Bulliet, Richard. *Conversion to Islam in the Medieval Period: An Essay in Quantitative History*. Cambridge: Harvard University, 1979.
Burkard, Richard W. *The Archpriest of Hita and the Imitators of Ovid: A Study in the Ovidian Background of the* Libro de buen amor. Newark, DE: Juan de la Cuesta, 1999.
——. "*Pseudo Ars Amatoria*: A Medieval Source for the Don Amor Lecture in the *Libro de buen amor*." *Kentucky Romance Quarterly* 25 (1978): 385–98.
Burnett, Charles. "Arabic into Latin: the Reception of Arabic Philosophy into Western Europe." *The Cambridge Companion to Arabic Philosophy*. Ed. Peter Adamson and Richard Taylor. Cambridge, 2005. 370–404.
——. "The Institutional Context of Arabic–Latin Translations of the Middle Ages: A Reassessment of the 'School of Toledo'." *Vocabulary of Teaching and Research between the Middle Ages and Renaissance*. Ed. O. Weijers. Turnhout: Brepols, 1995. 214–35.
——. "The Translating Activity in Medieval Spain." *The Legacy of Muslim Spain*. Ed. Salma K. Jayyusi. Leiden: E.J. Brill, 1994. 1036–58.
——. "The Works of Petrus Alfonsi: Questions of Authenticity." *Medium Ævum* 66.1 (1997): 42–79.
Burns, Robert I. *Islam under the Crusaders, Colonial Survival in the Thirteenth-century Kingdom of Valencia*. Princeton: Princeton University Press, 1973.
——. *Medieval colonialism: Postcrusade exploitation of Islamic Valencia*. Princeton: Princeton University Press, 1975.
——, Paul E. Chevedden, and Mikel de Epalza. *Negotiating Cultures: Bilingual Surrender Treaties in Muslim-Crusader Spain under James the Conqueror*. Leiden: E.J. Brill, 1999.
Burton, John. *An Introduction to the Hadith*. Edinburgh: Edinburgh University Press, 1994.
Cabré, Lluís, ed. *Obra completa*. Pere March. Barcelona: Barcino, 1993.
Cabrillana Ciézar, Nicolás. *Santiago Matamoros, Historia e Imagen*. Málaga: Centro de Ediciones de la Diputación de Málaga, 1999.
Caldera, Ermanno. "Arabes y judíos en la perspectiva cristiana de Juan Manuel." *Salina: Revista de Lletres* 13 (1999): 37–40.
Cantalapiedra, Fernando. "Los refranes en *Celestina* y el problema de su autoría." *Celestinesca* 8.1 (1984): 49–53.

Cantavella, Rosanna. *Els cards i el llir: Una lectura de l'Espill de Jaume Roig*. Barcelona: Quaderns Crema, 1992.
——. "Terapèutiques de l''amor hereos' a la literatura catalana mediveal." *Actes del Novè Col·loqui Internacional de Llengua i Literatura Catalanes*. Ed. Rafael Alemany, Antoni Ferrando and Lluís B. Meseguer. Alicante; Valencia: Publicacions de l'Abadia de Montserrat; Universitat d'Alacant; Universitat de València; Universitat Jaume I, 1993. 191–207.
Caro Baroja, Julio. *Introducción a una historia contemporánea del anticlericalismo español*. Madrid: Istmo, 1980.
Carpenter, Dwayne E. "'Alea Jacta Est': At the Gaming Table with Alfonso the Learned." *Journal of Medieval History* 24.4 (1998): 333–45.
——. *Alfonso X and the Jews: An Edition of and Commentary on* Siete Partidas *7.24 "De los judíos"*. Berkeley: University of California Press, 1986.
——. "Social Perception and Literary Portrayal: Jews and Muslims in Medieval Spanish Literature." *Convivencia: Jews, Muslims, and Christians in Medieval Spain*. Eds. Vivian B. Mann, Thomas F. Glick and Jerrilyn D. Dodds. New York: George Braziller and The Jewish Museum, 1992. 61–81.
Carré i Pons, Anotònia. "L'estil de Jaume Roig: les propostes ètica y estètica de l'*Espill*." *Intel·lectuals i escriptors a la baixa Edat Mitjana*. Eds. Lola Badia and Albert Soler. Barcelona: Publicacions de l'Abadia de Montserrat, 1994. 185–219.
——. "Lletra de batalla per l'*Espill* de Jaume Roig." *Antipodas* 5 (1993): 143–54.
——. "La medicina com a referons cultural a l'*Espill* de Jaume Roig." *Jaume Roig i Crostòfor Despuig: Dos assaigs sobre cultura i literatura dels segles XV i XVI*. Ed. Anotònia Carré i Pons and Josep Solervicens. Barcelona: Eumo, 1996. 7–71.
Castro, Américo. *España en su historia: Cristianos, moros y judíos*. 2nd ed. Barcelona: Crítica, 1983.
——. "El *Libro De Buen Amor* Del Arcipreste De Hita." *Comparative Literature* 4.3 (1952): 193–213.
——. *La realidad histórica de España*. Mexico City: Porrúa, 1954.
——. *Santiago de España*. Buenos Aires: Emecé, 1958.
Castro, Doctor. *Seniloquium, Refranes que dizen los viejos*. Ed. Fernando Cantalapiedra and Juan Moreno. Valencia: Anexos de la Revista *Lemir*, 2004. *LEMIR: Revista Electrónica sobre Literatura Española Medieval y Renacimiento*. Universitat de Valencia. 1996. 21 March 2006. <http://parnaseo.uv.es/Lemir/Textos/Seniloquium/Index.htm>.
Catechism of the Catholic Church. Vatican City: Libreria Editrice Vaticana, 1994.
Catlos, Brian A. "Contexto y conveniencia en la Corona de Aragón: Propuesta de un modelo de interacción entre grupos etno-religiosos minoritarios y mayoritarios." *Revista d'Història Medieval* 12 (2001–2002): 259–68.
——. "Cristians, musulmans i jueus a la corona d'Aragó: Un cas de conveniència." *L'Avenç* 263 (2001): 8–16.
——. *The Victors and the Vanquished: Christians and Muslims of Catalonia and Aragon, 1050–1300*. Cambridge: Cambridge University Press, 2004.
Caton, Steven. *"Peaks of Yemen I Summon": Poetry as Cultural Practice in a North Yemeni Tribe*. Berkeley: University of California Press, 1990.
Cattrysse, Patrick. "The Polysystem Theory and Cultural Studies." *Canadian Review of Comparative Literature/Revue Canadienne de Littérature Comparée* 24.1 (1997): 49–55.
Cerghedean, Gabriela. "Dreams in Medieval Spanish Literature: Roles, Traditions, and Theories." Diss. University of Wisconsin, Madison, 2002.
Chabás i Llorente, Roc. Introduction. *Spill o Libre de les dones per Mestre Jacme Roig*. By Jaume Roig. Ed. Roc Chabás i Llorente. i–xix.
Charland, Thomas Marie. *Artes praedicandi; Contribution à l'histoire de la rhétorique au moyen âge*. Paris: J. Vrin, 1936.
Chattopadhyay, Swati. "A Critical History of Architecture in a Post-Colonial World: A View from Indian History." *Architronic* 6.1 (1997): 1–3.
Chauvin, Victor. *Bibliographie des ouvrages arabes ou relatifs aux Arabes*. 12 vols. Liège: H. Vaillant-Carmanne, 1892–1922.

Chazan, Robert. "The Anti-Jewish Violence of 1096: Perpetrators and Dynamics." *Religious Violence between Christians and Jews: Medieval Roots, Modern Perspectives.* Ed. Anna Sapir Abulafia. Hampshire: Palgrave, 2002. 21–43.
——. *Barcelona and Beyond: The Disputation of 1263 and its Aftermath.* Berkeley: University of California, 1992.
——. *Daggers of Faith: Thirteenth-Century Christian Missionizing and Jewish Response.* Berkeley: University of California, 1989.
——. *Fashioning Jewish Identity in Medieval Western Christendom.* Cambridge: Cambridge University Press, 2004.
Chejne, Anwar G. *Islam and the West: The Moriscos.* Albany: SUNY, 1983.
Christys, Ann. *Christians in Al-Andalus: (711–1000).* Richmond: Curzon, 2002.
Ciscar Pallares, Eugenio. "'Algaravia' y 'Algemia': Precisiones sobre la lengua de los moriscos en el Reino de Valencia." *Al-Qantara* 15.1 (1994): 131–62.
Clanchy, M. T. *From Memory to Written Record, England, 1066–1307.* 2nd ed. Oxford: Blackwell, 1993.
Clements, Robert John, and Joseph Gibaldi. *Anatomy of the Novella: The European Tale Collection from Boccaccio and Chaucer to Cervantes.* New York: New York University Press, 1977.
Codde, Philippe. "Polysystem Theory Revisited: A New Comparative Introduction." *Poetics Today* 24.1 (2003): 91–126.
Cohen, Jeffrey Jerome, ed. *The Postcolonial Middle Ages.* New York: St. Martin's Press, 2000.
Cohen, Jeremy. "Christian Theology and Anti-Jewish Violence in the Middle Ages: Connections and Disjunctions." *Religious Violence between Christians and Jews: Medieval Roots, Modern Perspectives.* Ed. Anna Sapir Abulafia. Hampshire: Palgrave, 2002. 44–60.
——. "The Mentality of the Medieval Jewish Apostate: Peter Alfonsi, Hermann of Cologne, and Pablo Christiani." *Jewish Apostasy in the Modern World.* Ed. Todd M. Endelman. New York: Homes and Meier, 1987. 20–47.
Coleman, Joyce. *Public Reading and the Reading Public in Late Medieval England and France.* New York: Cambridge University Press, 1996.
Conca, Maria, Josep Guia, and Josep Romeu i Figueras. *Els primers reculls de proverbis catalans.* Barcelona: Publicacions de l'Abadia de Montserrat, 1996.
Cooper, Helen. *The Structure of the Canterbury Tales.* Athens, GA: University of Georgia Press, 1984.
Corominas, Joan. Introduction. *Libro de buen amor.* By Juan Ruiz. Ed. Joan Corominas.
Corriente, Federico. "By No Means *Jarchas Mozárabes.*" *Romance Philology* 50.1 (1996): 46–61.
——. *A Dictionary of Andalusī Arabic.* Leiden: E.J. Brill, 1997.
——. *A Grammatical Sketch of the Spanish Arabic Dialect Bundle.* Madrid: Instituto Hispano-Árabe de Cultura, 1977.
——. *Las Muʿallaqat: Antología y panorama de Arabia preislámica.* Madrid: Instituto Hispano-Arabe de Cultura, 1974.
Criado de Val, Manuel, ed. *El Arcipreste de Hita: El libro, el autor, la tierra, la época.* Barcelona: SERESA, 1973.
Cruz, Anne J. *Discourses of Poverty: Social Reform and the Picaresque Novel in Early Modern Spain.* Toronto: University of Toronto Press, 1999.
Cruz Hernández, Miguel. *Abu-l Walid Ibn Rushd: Vida, obra, pensamiento, influencia.* Cordova: Monte de Piedad y Caja de Ahorros de Córdoba, 1986.
——. *El pensamiento de Ramon Llull.* Madrid: Fundación Juan March; Editorial Castalia, 1977.
Cunha de Azevedo Mea, Elvira. *Sentenças de Inquisição de Coimbra em metropolitanos de D. Frei Bartolomeu dos Mártires (1567–1582).* Oporto: Arquivo Histórico Dominicano Português, 1982.
de Capua, Giovanni. *Fábulas Latinas Medievales.* Trans. Eustaquio Sánchez Salor. Torrejón de Ardoz: Akal, 1992.

——. *Johannis De Capua Directorium Vitae Humanae; Alias, Parabola Antiquorum Sapientum*. Ed. Joseph Derenbourg. Paris: F. Vieweg, 1887.
——. *Texto y concordancias del* Exemplario contra los engaños y peligros del mundo *(1493) I-1994, Biblioteca Nacional, Madrid*. Ed. Francisco Gago Jover. Madison: Hispanic Seminary of Medieval Studies, 1989.
Dagenais, John. *The Ethics of Reading in Manuscript Culture: Glossing the* Libro De Buen Amor. Princeton: Princeton University Press, 1994.
——. "Medieval Spanish literature in the twenty-first century." *The Cambridge History of Spanish Literature*. Ed. David T. Gies. Cambridge: Cambridge University Press, 2004. 39–57.
——, and Margaret Greer. "Decolonizing the Middle Ages: Introduction." *Journal of Medieval and Early Modern Studies* 30.3 (2000): 431–48.
Dahan, Gilbert. *The Christian Polemic against the Jews in the Middle Ages*. Trans. Jody Gladding. Notre Dame: University of Notre Dame Press, 1998.
Davidson, Herbert A. *Moses Maimonides: The Man and His Works*. New York: Oxford University Press, 2005.
Davidson, Israel. "Introduction." *Sefer Shaashuim*. By Joseph Ibn Zabāra. Ed. Israel Davidson. New York: Jewish Theological Seminary, 1914. xv–ci.
——. *Parody in Jewish Literature*. New York: AMS Press, 1966.
Dawūd, Muḥammad. *Al-amthāl al-ʿamīyya fī Tiṭwān wa-l bilād al-ʿarabīyya*. Tetouan: Al-majmūʿa al-ḥadarīyya, 1999.
De Haan, F. "Barlaam and Joasaph in Spain." *Modern Language Notes* 10.1 (1895): 11–17.
——. "Barlaam and Joasaph in Spain, II." *Modern Language Notes* 10.3 (1895): 69–73.
de la Granja, F. "La *Maqama de la fiesta* de Ibn Al-Murabi Al-Azdi." *Études d'orientalisme dedieés a la mémoire de Lévi-Provencal*. Vol. 2. Paris: Maisonneuve et Larose, 1962. 591–603.
Delgado-Librero, María Celeste. "Jaume Roig's *Spill*: A Diplomatic Edition and an English Translation of Ms. Vat. Lat. 4806." Diss. University of Virginia, 2003.
de Looze, Laurence. *Pseudo-Autobiography in the Fourteenth Century*. Gainesville, FL: University of Florida Press, 1997.
——. "Subversion of Meaning in Part I of *El Conde Lucanor*." *Revista Canadiense de Estudios Hispánicos* 19.2 (1995): 341–55.
Del Treppo, Mario. Els mercaders catalans i l'expansió de la Corona catalano-aragonesa al segle XV. Trans. Jaume Riera i Sans. Barcelona: Curial, 1976.
De Stefano, Antonino. *L'idea imperiale di Federico II*. Parma: All'insegna del Veltro, 1978.
Devoto, Daniel. *Introducción al estudio de don Juan Manuel y en particular de El Conde Lucanor: Una bibliografía*. Paris: Ediciones hispano-americanas, 1972.
Deyermond, Alan. *Historia de la literatura española 1: La edad media*. Barcelona: Ariel, 1973.
——. *La literatura perdida de la Edad Media castellana: catálogo y estudio.*: Universidad de Salamanca, 1995.
——, and Roger M. Walker. "A Further Vernacular Source for the *Libro de Buen Amor*." *Bulletin of Hispanic Studies* 46 (1969): 193–200.
Díaz-Férnandez, José María. *Santiago y América*. Galicia: Xunta de Galicia, Consellería de Cultura e Xuventude; Arcebispado de Santiago de Compostela, 1993.
Dishon, Judith. "Images of Women in Hebrew Literature." *Women of the Word: Jewish Women and Jewish Writing*. Ed. Judith R. Baskin. Detroit: Wayne State University Press, 1994. 35–47.
——. Sefer Šaʿašūʿīm *of Joseph ben Meir Ibn Zabāra* [Hebrew]. Jerusalem: R. Mas, 1985.
Dobbs-Weinstein, Idit. "The Maimonidean Controversy." *History of Jewish Philosophy*. Eds. Daniel H. Frank and Oliver Leaman. London: Routledge, 1997. 331–49.
Dodds, Jerrilynn. *Al-Andalus: The Art of Islamic Spain*. New York: Metropolitan Museum of Art, 1992.

——. "The Arts of al-Andalus." *The Legacy of Muslim Spain*. Ed. Salma K. Jayyusi. Leiden: Brill, 1992. 599–620.

——. "Mudejar Tradition and the Synagogues of Medieval Spain: Cultural Identity and Cultural Hegemony." *Convivencia: Jews, Muslims, and Christians in Medieval Spain*. Eds. Vivian Mann, Thomas Glick and Jerrilynn Dodds. New York: George Braziller; The Jewish Museum, 1991. 113–31.

Doron, Aviva. "'Dios, haz que el Rey se apiade de mí.' Entrelazamiento de lo sacro y lo profano en la poesia hebrea-toledana en el trasfondo de la poesía cristiana-española." *Sefarad* 46 (1986): 151–60.

——. *A Poet in the King's Court: Ṭodros Halevi Abulafia, Hebrew Poetry in Christian Spain* [Hebrew]. Tel Aviv: Dvir, 1989.

Dronke, Peter. *Verse with Prose From Petronius to Dante: The Art and Scope of the Mixed Form*. Cambridge: Harvard University Press, 1994.

Drory, Rina. "The maqama." Menocal et al. 190–210.

——. *Models and Contacts: Arabic Literature and Its Impact on Medieval Jewish Culture*. Leiden: E.J. Brill, 2000.

Duby, Georges. "The Culture of the Knightly Class." *Renaissance and Renewal in the Twelfth Century*. Eds. Robert L. Benson and Giles Constable. Cambridge: Harvard University Press, 1982. 248–62.

Duggan, Christopher. *A Concise History of Italy*. Cambridge: Cambridge University Press, 1994.

Duggan, Joseph J. *The* Cantar De Mio Cid*: Poetic Creation in its Economic and Social Contexts*. Cambridge: Cambridge University Press, 1989.

Dundes, Alan. "Texture, Text, and Context." *Southern Folklore Quarterly* 28 (1968): 251–65.

Dunn, Peter N. "'De las figuras del Arcipreste'." Libro de buen amor *Studies*. Ed. G.B. Gybbon-Monypenny. London: Tamesis, 1970. 79–93.

——. "Framing the Story, Framing the Reader: Two Spanish Masters." *The Modern Language Review* 91 (1996): 94–106.

Easthope, Antony. "Bhaba, hybridity and identity." *Textual Practice* 12.2 (1998): 341–48.

Ecker, Heather L. *Caliphs and Kings: The Art and Influence of Islamic Spain*. Seattle: University of Washington Press, 2004.

——. "From Masjid to Casa-Mezquita: Neighbourhood Mosques in Seville after the Castilian Conquest (1248–1634)." Diss. University of Oxford, 2000.

——. "How to Administer a Conquered City in Al-Andalus: Mosques, Parish Churches and Parishes." Robinson and Rouhi 45–66.

Eco, Umberto. *Art and Beauty in the Middle Ages*. New Haven: Yale University Press, 1986.

Edwards, John, David M. Gitlitz, Martha Krow-Lucal, Francisco Márquez Villanueva, Mark D. Meyerson, David Nirenberg, Angel Sáenz-Badillos, Judit Targarona Borrás, and John Zemke. "Forum: Inflecting the Converso Voice." *La corónica* 25.2 (1997): 159–205.

Einbinder, Susan. *Beautiful Death: Jewish Poetry and Martyrdom in Medieval France*. Princeton: Princeton University Press, 2002.

Eiximenis, Francesc. *Regiment de la cosa pùblica*. Ed. Daniel de Molins de Rei. Barcelona: Varias, 1927.

El Fuero de Teruel. Ed. Max Gorosch. Uppsala: Almqvist & Wiksells, 1950.

Eliade, Mircea. "Transmigration." *The Encyclopedia of Religion*. Ed. Mircea Eliade. New York: MacMillan, 1986. 21–26.

Elman, Yaakov, and Israel Gershoni, eds. *Transmitting Jewish Traditions: Orality, Textuality, and Cultural Diffusion*. New Haven: Yale University Press, 2000.

El-Shamy, Hasan M. *Types of the Folktale in the Arab World: A Demographically Oriented Tale-Type Index*. Bloomington, IN: Indiana University Press, 2004.

Encyclopedia Judaica CD-ROM Edition (Version 1.0). Ed. Geoffrey Wigoder. Jerusalem: Keter; Judaica Multimedia, 1997 (= *EJ*).

Encyclopedia of Islam CD-ROM Edition. Leiden: E.J. Brill, 2004 (= *EI*).

England, John. "'Los que son muy cuerdos entienden la cosa por algunas sennales': Learning the Lessons of *El Conde Lucanor*." *Bulletin of Hispanic Studies* 76.3 (1999): 345–64.

Epalza, Mikel. "Sociolingüística de mudéjares y moriscos." *Las lenguas prevalencianas*. Ed. Federico Corriente. Valencia: Universitat de València, 1987. 111–14.

Escribà, Gemma. *The Jews in the Crown of Aragon: Regesta of the Cartas Reales in the Archivo de la Corona De Aragón. Part II: 1328–1493*. Ed. Yom Tov Assis. Vol. 3. Jerusalem: Ginzei Am Olam and Hispania Judaica, Dinur Institute, Hebrew University, 1995.

Espinosa Durán, Angel. *Almanzor: Al-Mansur, el victorioso por Allah*. Madrid: Alderabán, 1998.

Even-Zohar, Itamar. "Factors and Dependencies in Culture: A Revised Outline for Polysystem Culture Research." *Canadian Review of Comparative Literature* 24.1 (1997): 15–34.

——. "Israeli Hebrew Literature: A Historical Model." *Ha-Sifrut/Literature* 4 (1973): 427–40.

——. "The 'Literary System'." *Poetics Today* 11.1 (1990): 27–44.

——. "The Making of Culture Repertoire and the Role of Transfer." *Target: International Journal of Translation Studies* 9.2 (1997): 355–63.

——. "The Position of Translated Literature within the Literary Polysystem." *Poetics Today* 11.1 (1990): 45–51.

Fakhry, Majid. *Averroës (Ibn Rushd): His Life, Works and Influence*. Oxford: Oneworld, 2001.

Faulhaber, Charles B. "Semitica Iberica: translations from Hebrew and Arabic into the medieval Romance vernaculars of the Iberian Peninsula." *Bulletin of Spanish Studies* 81.7–8 (2004): 873–96.

Faur, José. "Anti-Maimonidean Demons." *Review of Rabbinic Judaism* 6.1 (2001): 3–52.

Feliciano, María Judith. "Muslim Shrouds for Christian Kings? A Reassessment of Andalusi Textiles in Thirteenth-Century Castilian Life and Ritual." Robinson and Rouhi 101–32.

Fernández y González, Francisco. *Discursos leídos ante al Real Academia Española*. Madrid: El Progreso Editorial, 1894.

Fiero Bello, María Isabel. *La heterodoxia en al-Andalus durante el periodo omeya*. Madrid: Instituto Hispano-Arabe de Cultura, 1987.

Fine, Elizabeth C. *The Folklore Text: From Performance to Print*. Bloomington: Indiana University Press, 1984.

Fishman, Talya. "A Medieval Parody of Misogyny: Judah Ibn Shabbetai's Minhat Yehudah, Soneh Hanashim." *Prooftexts: A Journal of Jewish Literary History* 8.1 (1988): 89–111.

Fletcher, Richard. "The Early Middle Ages." *Spain, A History*. Ed. Raymond Carr. Oxford: Oxford University Press, 2000.

Foz, Clara. "Bibliografía sobre la escuela de traductores de Toledo." *Quaderns* 4 (1999): 85–91.

Funes, Leonardo. "La leyenda de Barlaam y Josafat en el *Libro de los estados* de Don Juan Manuel." *Letras* 15–16 (1986): 84–91.

——, and Felipe Tenenbaum. *Mocedades De Rodrigo: Estudio y edición de los tres estados del texto*. London: Tamesis, 2004.

Furió, Antoni, ed. *València, un mercat medieval*. Valencia: Diputació Provincial de Valencia, 1985.

Fuster, Joan. "Poetes, moriscos i capellans." *Obres completes*. Ed. Joan Fuster. Barcelona: Edicions 62, 1968. 317–508.

Galmés de Fuentes, Álvaro. "La lengua de los moriscos." *Manual de dialectología hispánica*, Ed. Manuel Alvar. Barcelona: Ariel, 1996. 111–18.

——. *El Libro de las batallas: narraciones épico-caballerescas*. 2 vols. Madrid: Gredos, 1975.

——. *Historia de los amores de París y Viana*. Madrid: Gredos, 1970.

——. *Influencias sintácticas y estilísticas del árabe en la prosa medieval castellana*. Madrid: Gredos, 1996.

——. *Las jarchas mozárabes: Forma y significado, filología*. Barcelona: Crítica, 1994.

Garcia, Angelina. *Els Vives: Una família de jueus valencians*. València: E. Climent, 1987.
García Canclini, Néstor. *Hybrid Cultures: Strategies for Entering and Leaving Modernity*. Minneapolis: University of Minnesota Press, 1995.
García-Serrano, Francisco. *Preachers of the City: The Expansion of the Dominican Order in Castile (1217–1348)*. New Orleans: University Press of the South, 1997.
Garulo, Teresa. *La literatura árabe de al-Andalus durante el siglo XI*. Madrid: Hiperión, 1998.
Gaster, Moses. *Exempla of the Rabbis*. New York: Ktav, 1968.
Gella Iturriaga, Jose. "444 refranes de *La Celestina*." La Celestina *y su contorno social: Actas del I Congreso Internacional sobre* La Celestina. Ed. Manuel Criado de Val. Barcelona: Hispam, 1977. 245–68
Gensini, Sergio. *Politica e cultura nell'italia di Federico II*. Pisa: Pacini, 1986.
Geoffrey of Vinsauf. *Documentum de Modo et Arte Dictandi et Versificandi*. Trans. Roger P. Parr. Milwaukee: Marquette University Press, 1968.
George, Wilma, and Brundson Yapp. *The Naming of the Beasts: Natural History in the Medieval Bestiary*. London: Duckworth, 1991.
Georges, Robert A. "Toward an Understanding of Storytelling Events." *Journal of American Folklore* 82 (1969): 313–28.
——, and Michael Owen Jones. *People Studying People: The Human Element in Fieldwork*. Berkeley: University of California Press, 1980.
Gerli, E. Michael. "Textualidad y autoridad: hacia una teoría de los orígenes de la escritura señorial (el caso de *El libro del Conde Lucanor*)." *Propuestas teórico-metodológicas para el estudio de la literatura hispánica medieval*. Ed. Lillian von Der Walde Moheno. Mexico City: Universidad Nacional Autónoma de México-Universidad Autónoma Metropolitana, 2003. 335–49.
Gil, José S. *La escuela de traductores de Toledo y los colaboradores judíos*. Toledo: Diputación Provincial de Toledo, 1985.
Gil y Gil, Pablo, Julián Ribera, and Mariano Sánchez, eds. *Colección de textos aljamiados*. Zaragoza: Litografía de Guerra y Bacque; Tipografía de Comas Hermanos, 1888.
Gilmore, David D. *Misogyny: The Male Malady*. Philadelphia: University of Pennsylvania Press, 2001.
Giménez Soler, Andrés. *Don Juan Manuel. Biografía y estudio crítico*. Zaragoza: F. Martínez, 1932.
——. *La edad media en la Corona de Aragón*. Barcelona: Editorial Labor, 1930.
Girón Negrón, Luis. "How the Go-between Cut Her Nose: Two Ibero-Medieval Translations of a *Kalilah wa Dimnah* Story." Robinson and Rouhi 230–59.
Gitlitz, David M. *Secrecy and Deceit: The Religion of the Crypto-Jews*. Albuquerque, N.M.: University of New Mexico Press, 2002.
Gittes, Katharine S. *Framing the* Canterbury Tales*: Chaucer and the Medieval Frame Narrative Tradition*. New York: Greenwood, 1984.
Glick, Thomas F. *From Muslim Fortress to Christian Castle: Social and Cultural Change in Medieval Spain*. Manchester, England: Manchester University Press, 1995.
——. *Islamic and Christian Spain in the Early Middle Ages*. Princeton, N.J.: Princeton University Press, 1979.
——, and Oriol Pi Sunyer. "Acculturation as an Explanatory Concept in Spanish History." *Comparative Studies in Society and History* 11.2 (1969): 136–54.
Goldberg, Harriet. "The Dream Report as Literary Device in Medieval Hispanic Literature." *Hispania* 66 (1986): 21–31.
——. *Motif-index of Medieval Spanish Folk Narratives*. Tempe, Ariz.: Medieval & Renaissance Texts & Studies, 1998.
——. "Personal Descriptions in Medieval Texts: Decorative or Functional?" *Hispanófila* 87 (1986): 1–12.
——. "Sexual Humor in Misogynist Medieval Exempla." *Women in Hispanic Literature*. Ed. Beth Miller. Berkeley: University of California Press, 1983. 67–83.

Gómez-Peña, Guillermo. *Codex Espangliensis: From Columbus to the Border Patrol.* San Francisco: City Lights, 2000.
Gómez Redondo, Fernando. *Historia de la prosa medieval castellana*. Madrid: Cátedra, 1998.
González-Casanovas, Roberto J. "Alfonso X's Rhetoric of Humanist Education: Professional Literacy in the Scientific Prologues." *RLA: Romance Languages Annual* 2 (1990): 434–41.
González Llubera, Ignasi. "Un aspecte de la novel·lística oriental a la literatura medieval europea." *Estudis Universitaris Catalans* 22 (1936): 463–73.
——. Introduction. *Llibre d'ensenyaments delectables: Sèfer Xaaixuïm*. Joseph Ibn Zabāra. Barcelona: Editorial Alpha, 1931.
González Palencia, Ángel. *El Arzobispo Don Raimundo de Toledo*. Barcelona: Editorial Labor, 1942.
——. Introduction. *Disciplina Clericalis.* By Petrus Alfonsi. Ed. and Trans. Ángel González Palencia. vii–xl.
——. *Los mozárabes de Toledo en los siglos XII y XIII.* 3 vols. Madrid: Instituto de Valencia de Don Juan, 1926–1930.
Goñí Gaztambide, José. *Historia de la bula de la cruzada en España*. Vitoria: Editorial del Seminario, 1958.
Goytisolo, Juan. "El Legado Andalusí: Una Perspectiva Occidental". 1997. Ministerio de Educación y Cultura: Centro Nacional de Información y Comunicación Educativa. 8 February 2006. <http://www.cnice.mecd.es/tematicas/juangoytisolo/1997_12/1997_12_andalus.htm>.
Grabar, Oleg. *The Mediation of Ornament*. Princeton: Princeton University Press, 1992.
Guedemann, Moritz. *Das Jüdische Unterrichtswesen Während Der Spanisch-Arabischen Periode: Nebst Handschriftlichen Arabischen Und Hebräischen Beilagen*. Wien: Gerold, 1873.
Guia, Josep. *Fraseologia i estil: enigmes literaris a la València del segle XV*. València: E. Climent, 1999.
Guillaume, Alfred. *The Traditions of Islam: An Introduction to the Study of the Hadith Literature*. Beirut: Khayats, 1966.
Guiral-Hadziiossif, Jacqueline. *Valence, port méditerranéen au XVe siècle*. Paris: Publications de la Sorbonne, 1986.
Gutwirth, Eleazar. "Actitudes judías hacia los cristianos en la España del siglo XV: Ideario de los traductores de latín." *Actas del II Congreso Internacional "Encuentro de las tres culturas."* Toledo: Ayuntamiento de Toledo, 1985. 189–96.
——. "On the Hispanicity of Sephardi Jewry." *Révue des Études Juives* 145.3–4 (1986): 347–57.
Gybbon-Monypenny, C.B. "Autobiography in the *Libro De Buen Amor* in Light of Some Literary Comparisons." *Bulletin of Hispanic Studies* 34.2 (1957): 63–78.
Habermann, Abraham Meir. "The *Book of Taḥkemonī* and its Editions" [Hebrew]. *Essays in Poetry and Piyyūt* [Hebrew]. Jerusalem: Reuven Mas, 1972. 115–36.
Halawah, Hidyāwī. *Luqmān al-Ḥākim*. Cairo: Maktabāt Madbūlī al-Saġīr, 1993.
Hämeen-Anttila, Jaakko. *Maqama: A History of a Genre*. Wiesbaden: Harrassowitz, 2002.
Hamesse, Jacqueline. "The Scholastic Model of Reading." *A History of Reading in the West*. Ed. Guglielmo Cavallo and Roger Chartier. Amherst, MA: University of Massachusetts Press, 1999. 103–19.
Hamilton, Michelle M. "Transformation and Desire: The Go-between in Medieval Iberian Literature." Diss. University of California at Berkeley, 2001.
——, Sarah J. Portnoy, and David A. Wacks, eds. *Wine, Women and Song: Hebrew and Arabic Literature of Medieval Iberia*. Newark, DE: Juan de la Cuesta Hispanic Monographs, 2004.
Hammer, Michael Floyd. "Framing the Reader: Exemplarity and Ethics in the Manuscripts of the *Conde Lucanor*." Diss. University of California at Los Angeles, 2004.
Hanagid, Samuel. *Poemas*. Trans. Angel Sáenz-Badillos and Judit Targarona Borrás. Córdoba: Ediciones El Almendro, 1988.

———. *Poemas II: en la corte de Granada*. Trans. Ángel Sáenz-Badillos and Judit Targarona Borrás. Cordoba: El Almendro, 1998.
Hanlon, David. "Islam and Stereotypical Discourse in Medieval Castile and León." *Journal of Medieval and Early Modern Studies* 30.3 (2000): 479–504.
———. "A sociolinguistic view of *hazl* in the Andalusian Arabic *muwashshah*." *Bulletin of the School of Oriental and African Studies* 60.1 (1997): 35–46.
Harney, Michael. *Kinship and Polity in the* Poema de Mío Cid. West Lafayette, IN: Purdue University Press, 1993.
Harvey, L.P. "The Alfonsine School of Translators: Translations from Arabic into Castilian Produced under the Patronage of Alfonso the Wise of Castile." *Journal of the Royal Asiatic Society* (1977): 109–17.
———. *Islamic Spain 1250–1500*. Chicago: University of Chicago, 1990.
Ḥaṣan, Mustafà Ḥaṣan. *Animals in Arabic Poetry* [Arabic]. Riyadh: Dār al-muʿrāj al-dawlīyya lil-našr, 1998.
Hasan, Suhaib. *An Introduction to the Science of Hadith*. Riyadh: Darussalam, 1996.
Haskins, Charles Homer. *Studies in the History of Medieval Science*. Cambridge: Harvard University Press, 1927.
Haywood, Louise M. "Juan Ruiz and the *Libro de Buen Amor*: Contexts and Milieu." *A Companion to the* Libro de Buen Amor. Eds. Louise M. Haywood and Louise O. Vasvári. Woodbridge, UK: Tamesis, 2004. 21–38.
Hearder, Harry, and Jonathan Morris. *Italy: A short history*. 2nd ed. Cambridge: Cambridge University Press, 2001.
Heliodoro Valle, Rafael. *Santiago en América*. Querétaro: Gobierno del Estado de Querétaro, 1996.
Henderson, Arnold Clayton. "Medieval Beasts and Modern Cages: The Making of Meaning in Fables and Bestiaries." *PMLA* 97.1 (1982): 40–49.
Hermes, Eberhard. "The Author and His Times." *The Disciplina Clericalis of Petrus Alfonsi*. Berkeley: University of California Press, 1977. 3–102.
Hernández, Francisco J. "The Venerable Juan Ruiz, Archpriest of Hita." *La corónica* 13 (1984): 10–22.
Hernández Morejón, Antonio, ed. *Historia bibliográfica de la medicina española*. Vol. 1. 1842–45. New York: Johnson Reprint Corporation, 1967.
Hernández Valcárcel, Carmen. "Algunos aspectos del cuento en el *Libro del caballero Zifar*: Estructuras de la narrativa breve." *Actas del III Congreso de la Asociación Hispánica de Literatura Medieval*. Ed. María Isabel Toro Pascua. Vol. 1. Salamanca: Biblioteca Española del Siglo XV, Departamento de Literatura Española e Hispanoamericana, 1994. 469–78.
Herskovits, Melville. *Acculturation: The Study of Culture Contact*. New York: J.J. Augustin, 1938.
Hillgarth, Jocelyn N. "Spanish Historiography and Iberian Reality." *History and Theory* 24 (1985): 23–43.
———. *The Spanish Kingdoms, 1250–1516*. Oxford: Clarendon Press, 1976.
Hinojosa Montalvo, José. *Los mudéjares: la voz del Islam en la España cristiana*.? vols. Teruel: Centro de Estudios Mudéjares, Instituto de Estudios Turolenses, 2002.
Hitchcock, Richard. "Don Juan Manuel's Knowledge of Arabic." *Modern Language Review* 80 (1985): 594–603.
Holloway, Julia Bolton. "The Road through Roncesvalles: Alfonsine Formation of Brunetto Latini and Dante-Diplomacy and Literature." *Emperor of Culture: Alfonso X the Learned and His Thirteenth-Century Renaissance*. Ed. Robert I. Burns. Philadelphia: University of Pennsylvania Press, 1990. 109–23.
Holsinger, Bruce W. "Medieval Studies, Postcolonial Studies, and the Genealogies of Critique." *Speculum* 77 (2002): 1195–227.
The Holy Qur'an: English Translation of the Meanings and Commentary. Presidency of Islamic Researches, IFTA, Call and Guidance, ed. Medina: The Custodian of the Two Holy Mosques King Fahd Complex for the Printing of the Holy Qurʾān, 1988.
Hourani, George. *Islamic Rationalism*. Oxford: Clarendon, 1971.

Housley, N. "Frontier societies and crusading in the later Middle Ages." *Intercultural Contacts in the Medieval Mediterranean*. Ed. B. Arbel. London and Portland, OR: Frank Cass, 1996. 104–19.

Hoyos Hoyos, Carmen. "El elemento árabe en *El Conde Lucanor* de D. Juan Manuel." *Proyección histórica de España en sus tres culturas: Castilla y León, América y el mediterráneo*. Ed. Eufemio Lorenzo Sanz. Madrid: Junta de Castilla y León, 1993. 117–28.

Hudson, Deal W. "A Catholic View of Conversion." *Handbook of Religious Conversion*. Ed. H. Newton Malony and Samuel Southard. Birmingham, Ala.: Religious Education Press, 1992. 108–22.

Huerta Viñas, Ferran. *Teatre bíblic: Antic Testament*. Barcelona: Editorial Barcino, 1976.

Humbert of Romans. *Treatise on Preaching*. Trans. The Dominican Students. Ed. O.P. Walter M. Conlon. London: Blackfriars, 1955.

Huot, Sylvia. *From Song to Book: The Poetics of Writing in Old French Lyric and Lyrical Narrative Poetry*. Ithaca: Cornell University Press, 1987.

Hurwitz, Barbara. "Ambivalence in Medieval Religious Polemic: The Influence of Multiculturalism on the *Dialogues* of Petrus Alphonsi." *Languages of Power in Islamic Spain*. Ed. Ross Brann. Bethesda, MD: CDL Press, 1997. 156–77.

Hutcheson, Gregory. "Inflecting the *Converso* Voice." *La corónica* 25.1 (1996): 3–5.

——, and Dayle Seidenspinner-Núñez. "'Inflecting the *Converso* Voice': Responses." *La corónica* 25.2 (1997): 195–205.

Ibn ʿAbd al-Rabbihi, Ibn ʿUmar Aḥmad ibn Muḥammad. *al-ʿIqd al-farīd*. Ed. Aḥmad Amīn, Aḥmad al-Zayn and Ibrāhīm al-Ibyārī. 7 vols. Beirut: Dār al-Kitāb al-ʿArabī, 1982.

Ibn Abī al-Rijāl, Abū'l ḥasan ʿAlī. *Judizios de las estrellas* (1254). Madrid Nacional ms. 3065. Trans. Alfonso X and Yehuda ben Mošé ha-Kohén. Transcr. Lloyd A. Kasten and John Nitti. *ADMYTE*.

Ibn al-Jawzī, Abū al-Faraj ʿAbd al-Raḥmān ibn ʿAlī. *Kitāb al-Quṣṣāṣ wal-Muḏakkirīn*. Beirut: Institut de Lettres Orientales, 1971.

Ibn al-Muqaffaʿ, ʿAbdallāh. *Calila e Dimna*. Ed. Juan Manuel Cacho Blecua and María Jesus Lacarra. Madrid: Editorial Castalia, 1984.

——. *Deux versions hébraïques du livre de Kalîlâh et Dimnâh*. Trans. Jacob ben Eleazar (13th c.). Ed. J. Derenbourg. Paris: Bibliothèque de l'École des Hautes Études, 1881.

——. *Kalilah et Dimnah*. Edited by P. Louis Cheikho. 3rd ed. Beirut: Imprimerie Catholique, 1947.

Ibn Bakhtīšūʿ, ʿUbayd Allāh ibn Jibrāʾil. *El Libro de las utilidades de los animales*. Trans. Carmen Ruiz Bravo-Villasante. Madrid: Fundación Universitaria Española, 1980.

Ibn Buṭlān. *The Physicians' Dinner Party*. Ed. Felix Klein-Franke. Wiesbaden: Otto Harrassowitz, 1985.

Ibn Gabirol, Shelomo. *El Alma lastimada: Ibn Gabirol*. Trans. Angel Sáenz-Badillos. Cordova: Ediciones El Almendro, 1992.

Ibn Manẓur, Muḥammad ibn Mukarram. *Lisān al-ʿarab*. Cairo: al-dār al-miṣrīiyya lil-taʾlif wa-al-tarjam, 1966.

Ibn Quzmān, Muḥammad ibn ʿAbd al-Malik. *Diwān Ibn Quzmān al-Qurṭūbī*. Eds. Federico Corriente and Maḥmūd ʿAlī Makkī. Cairo: al-Majlis al-ʿAlā lil-Ṯaqāfat al-Maktabah al-ʿArabīyah, 1995.

——. *Ibn Quzman, Poète Hispano-Arabe Bilingue*. Trans. O.J. Tuulio. Helsinki: Societas Orientalis Fennica, 1941.

——. *El mejor Ben Quzmán en 40 zéjeles*. Trans. Emilio García Gómez. Madrid: Alianza, 1981.

——. *Todo Ben Quzman*. Trans. Emilio Garcia Gomez. Madrid: Gredos, 1972.

Ibn Rušd, Abū-l Walīd. *Averroes' Middle Commentary on Aristotle's Poetics*. Trans. Charles E. Butterworth. Princeton, Princeton University Press, 1986.

——. *Ṭalkhīs kitāb al-šiʿr*. Ed. Charles E. Butterworth and Aḥmad ʿAbd al-Majīd Harīdī. Cairo: al-ḥayʾah al-miṣrīyah al-ʿamma lil-kitāb: bi-al-taʾawūn maʿa Markaz al-Buḥūṯ al-Amrīkī bi-Miṣr, 1986.

Ibn Shabbetay, Judah ben Isaac. *'Minhat Yehudah', ''Ezrat ha-nashim' ve-'En mishpat'*. Ed. Matti Huss. 2 vols. Jerusalem: Hebrew University, 1991.
——. "The Misogynist." Trans. Raymond P. Scheindlin. *Rabbinic Fantasies: Imaginative Narratives from Classical Hebrew Literature*. Ed. David Stern and Mark J. Mirsky. New Haven: Yale University Press, 1990. 269–94.
Ibn Shāhīn, Nissim ben Yaʿqob. *The Arabic Original of Ibn Shāhīn's Book of Comfort, Known as the Hibbur Yaphê of R. Nissīm B. Yaʿqobh*. Ed. Julian Obermann. New Haven: Yale University Press, 1933.
——. *An Elegant Composition Concerning Relief After Adversity*. Trans. William M. Brinner. New Haven: Yale University Press, 1977.
Ibn Zabāra, Joseph ben Meir. *The Book of Delight*. Trans. Moses Hadas. New York: Columbia University Press, 1960.
——. *Libro de los entretenimientos*. Trans. Marta Forteza-Rey. Madrid: Editoral Nacional, 1983.
——. *Llibre d'ensenyaments delectables: Sèfer Xaaixuïm*. Trans. Ignasi González-Llubera. Barcelona: Editorial Alpha, 1931.
——. *Reis met de Duivel: Sefer Sjaʿasjuʿim*. Trans. R. Fontaine, Arie Schippers and Irene E. Zwiep. 2nd ed. Kampen, Netherlands: Kok, 1999.
——. *Sefer Shaashuim*. Ed. Israel Davidson. Berlin: Eshkol, 1925.
Iglesias Santos, Montserrat, ed. *Teoría de los polisistemas*. Madrid: Arco/Libros, 1999.
Ikhwān al-Ṣafā'. *The Case of the Animals versus Man before the King of the Jinn: A Tenth-Century Ecological Fable of the Pure Brethren of Basra*. Trans. Lenn E. Goodman. Boston: Twayne, 1978.
Iser, Wolfgang. *The Act of Reading: A Theory of Aesthetic Response*. Baltimore: Johns Hopkins University Press, 1978.
Jacob of Voragine. *Legenda aurea*. Ed. Arrigo Levasti. Florence: Le lettere; Diane de Selliers, 2000.
Jacobs, Janet Liebman. *Hidden Heritage: the Legacy of the Crypto-Jews*. Berkeley: University of California Press, 2002.
Jacobs, Jill. "'The Defense Has Become the Prosecution:' *Ezrat HaNashim*, a Thirteenth-century Response to Misogyny." *Women in Judaism: A Multidisciplinary Journal* 3.2 (2003): 1–9.
Jacobs, Melville. *The Content and Style of an Oral Literature: Clackamas Chinook Myths and Tales*. New York: Wenner-Gran Foundation for Anthropological Research, 1959.
Jacquart, D. "L'école des traducteurs." *Tolède, XIIᵉ–XIIIᵉ siècles*. Ed. Louis Cardaillac. Paris: Editions Autrement, 1991. 177–91.
Jauss, Hans Robert. "Theory of Genres and Medieval Literature." *Modern Genre Theory*. Ed. David Duff. Longman: Harlow, England, 2000. 127–47.
——. *Toward an Aesthetic of Reception*. Minneapolis: University of Minnesota Press, 1982.
Jayyusi, Salma K. "Andalusi Poetry: The Golden Period." *The Legacy of Muslim Spain*. Ed. Salma K. Jayyusi. Leiden: E.J. Brill, 1992. 317–66.
Jenaro MacLennan, Luis. "Sobre los orígenes folklóricos de la Serrana Gadea de Ríofrío (*Libro De Buen Amor*)." *Vox Románica* 47 (1988): 180–83.
Johnston, Mark D. "Do *Exempla* Illustrate Everyday Life?" Paper given at 1994 MLA Convention, Medieval Studies Section. Chicago: 13 Nov 1994. *The Labyrinth: Resources for Medieval Studies*. 2001. 19 February 2006. <http://www.georgetown.edu/labyrinth/e-center/johnston.html>.
Jones, Alan, Richard Hitchcock, and L.P. Harvey, eds. *Studies on the Muwassah and the Kharja*. Reading, England: Ithaca, 1991.
Jones, Joseph R., and John E. Keller. Introduction. *Scholar's Guide*. By Petrus Alfonsi. Trans. Jones and Keller 13–30.
Jones, Michael. "The Crown and the Provinces in the 14th century." *France in the later Middle Ages, 1200–1500*. Ed. David Potter. Oxford: Oxford University Press, 2003.
Juan Manuel. *El libro de los estados*. Eds. Ian Richard Macpherson and Robert Brian Tate. Madrid: Castalia, 1991.

——. *Obras completas*. Ed. José Manuel Blecua. 2 vols. Madrid: Gredos, 1982.

Jumʿah, Ḥuṣayn. *Animals in Pre-Islamic Poetry* [Arabic]. Damascus: Dānīya lil-ṭibāʿa wa-l-našr, 1989.

Just, Felix, S.J. "Symbols of the Four Evangelists." *Catholic Resources*. 20 March 2006. <http://catholic-resources.org/Art/Evangelists_Symbols.htm>.

Juynboll, G.H.A. *Muslim Tradition: Studies in Chronology, Provenance and Authorship of Early Hadīth*. Cambridge: Cambridge University Press, 1983.

Kabir, Ananya Jahanara, and Deanne Williams, eds. *Postcolonial Approaches to the Middle Ages: Translating Cultures*. Cambridge: Cambridge University Press, 2005.

Kafumah, ʿAbdallāh. *Majallāt Luqmān*. Tetouan: al-Maṭbaʿa al-maḥdīyah, 1960.

Kane, Elisha K. "The Personal Appearance of Juan Ruiz." *Modern Language Notes* 45.2 (1930): 103–09.

Kantorowicz, Ernst Hartwig. *Frederick the Second, 1194–1250*. Trans. E.O. Lorimer. New York: Ungar, 1967.

Kaplan, Gregory B. *The Evolution of* Converso *Literature*. Gainesville, FL: University Press of Florida, 2002.

Katsumata, Naoya. "The Style of the Maqama: Arabic, Persian, Hebrew, Syriac." *Arabic and Middle Eastern Literatures* 5.2 (2002): 117–37.

Keen, Benjamin. *The Aztec Image in Western Thought*. New Brunswick: Rutgers University Press, 1971.

Keith, A. Berriedale. *A History of Sanskrit Literature*. Oxford: Oxford University Press, 1920.

Keller, John E. "The Literature of Recreation: *El Libro de los engaños*." *Hispanic Medieval Studies in Honor of Samuel G. Armistead*. Ed. E. Michael Gerli and Harvey Sharrer. Madison: Hispanic Seminary of Medieval Studies, 1992. 193–200.

Kelly, Douglas. *Medieval French Romance*. New York: Twayne, 1993.

Kelly, Henry Ansgar. *Canon Law and the Archpriest of Hita*. Binghamton: Center for Medieval & Early Renaissance Studies, State University of New York, 1984.

Khidr, Hāzim ʿAbdallāh. *The Description of Animals in Andalusī Poetry: The Age of the Taifas and the Almoravides* [Arabic]. Baghdad: Dār al-Šuʾūn al-ṯaqāfiyya al-ʿĀmmah "Afāq ʿArabīya", 1987.

Kramer-Hellinx, Nechama. "Polemical Disputation and Jewish Theology in the Poetry of the Spanish Converso Ferrant Sánchez De Talavera." *Queens College Journal of Jewish Studies* 6 (2004): 21–36.

Kruger, Steven F. *Dreaming in the Middle Ages*. Cambridge: Cambridge University Press, 1992.

Lacarra, María Jesús. *Cuentística medieval en España: Los orígenes*. Zaragoza: Departamento de Literatura Española, Universidad de Zaragoza, 1979.

——. Introduction. *Calila e Dimna*. By ʿAbdallāh Ibn al-Muqaffa. Eds. Cacho Blecua and Lacarra. 9–70.

——. Introduction. *Sendebar*. Ed. María Jesús Lacarra. 11–53.

——. *Pedro Alfonso*. Zaragoza: Diputación General de Aragón, Departamento de Educación y Cultura, 1991.

Lapidus, Ira M. "Review of *Conversion to Islam in the Medieval Period: An Essay in Quantitative History*, by Richard W. Bulliet." *The American Historical Review* 86.1 (1981): 187–88.

Larner, John. *Italy in the Age of Dante and Petrarch, 1216–1380*. London: Longman, 1980.

La Tabula Exemplorum Secundum Ordinem Alphabeti. Ed. J.T. Welter. Paris: E.H. Guitard, 1926.

Latham, J.D. "Ibn al-Muqaffaʿ and Early ʿAbbasid Prose." *ʿAbbasid Belles-Lettres*. Ed. Julia Ashtiany, T.M. Johnstone, J.D. Latham, R.B. Serjeant and G. Rex Smith. Cambridge: Cambridge University Press, 1989. 48–77.

Laurence, Kemlin M. "The Medieval Controversy Concerning Burial Privileges: An Aspect of Anticlerical Satire in the *Libro De Buen Amor*." *Bulletin of Hispanic Studies* 49 (1972): 1–6.

Lawless, Elaine J. "Narrative in the Pulpit: Persistent Use of *Exempla* in Vernacular Religious Contexts." *The Journal of the Midwest Modern Language Association* 21 (1988): 48–64.
Lawrence, C.H. *The Friars: The Impact of the Early Mendicant Movement on Western Society*. The Medieval World. Ed. David Bates. London: Longman, 1994.
Lecoy, Félix. *Recherches sur le* Libro De Buen Amor*, de Juan Ruiz, Archiprêtre De Hita*. Paris: E. Droz, 1938.
Leder, Stefan, ed. *Story-Telling in the Framework of Non-Fictional Arabic Literature*. Wiesbaden: Harrassowitz, 1998.
Le Fèvre, Jehan. *Les Lamentations de Mathéolus et le Livre de Leesce*. Ed. A.G. Van Hamel. *Bibliothèque de l'École Des Hautes Études*. Fasc. 95–97. Paris: Émile Bouillon, 1892.
Le Goff, Jacques. *Saint Louis*. Paris: Gallimard, 1996.
Lehmann, Paul. "Autobiographies of the Middle Ages." *Transactions of the Royal Historical Society* 5.3 (1953): 41–52.
Lejeune, Philippe. *L'autobiographie en France*. Paris: Colin, 1972.
León Tello, Pilar. *Judíos de Toledo*. 2 vols. Madrid: CSIC, Instituto "B. Arias Montano", 1979.
Levine Melammed, Renée. *A Question of Identity: Iberian Conversos in Historical Perspective*. New York: Oxford University Press, 2004.
Levinson, Joshua. "Dialogical Reading in the Rabbinic Exegetical Narrative." *Poetics Today* 25.3 (2004): 497–528.
Lévi-Provençal, Evariste. *España musulmana hasta la caída del Califato de Córdoba*. Trans. Emilio García Gómez and Leopoldo Torres Balbás. Historia de España. Ed. Ramón Menéndez Pidal. Vol. 5. Madrid: Espasa-Calpe, 1957.
La leyenda de la Doncella Carcayona. Ed. Pino Valero Cuadra. Alicante: Universidad de Alicante, 2000.
Libro de Alexandre. MS Madrid: Nacional, Vitrina 5–10. Transcr. Francisco A. Marcos Marín. *ADMYTE*.
Lida de Malkiel, María Rosa. *Dos obras maestras españolas: El* Libro de buen amor *y* La Celestina. Teoría e Investigación. Buenos Aires: Editorial Universitaria de Buenos Aires, 1966.
——. *Estudios de literatura española y comparada*. Buenos Aires: Editorial Universitaria de Buenos Aires, 1969.
——. *La idea de la fama en la edad media castellana*. México: Fondo de Cultura Económica, 1952.
——. "Notas para la interpretación, influencia, fuentes y texto del *Libro de buen amor*." *Revista de filología hispánica* 2 (1940): 105–50.
——. "Tres notas sobre Don Juan Manuel." *Romance Philology* 4.2–3 (1950): 155–94.
——. *Two Spanish Masterpieces: The* Book of Good Love *and the* Celestina. Urbana: University of Illinois Press, 1961.
Limor, Ora, and Gedaliahu A. G. Stroumsa, eds. *Contra Iudaeos: Ancient and Medieval Polemics Between Christians and Jews*. Tübingen: J.C.B. Mohr (Paul Siebeck), 1996.
Linehan, Peter. "At the Spanish Frontier." *The Medieval World*. Eds. Peter Linehan and Janet Nelson. London: Routledge, 2001. 37–59.
——. *History and the Historians of Medieval Spain*. Oxford: Clarendon Press, 1993.
Llull, Ramon. *Llibre de les bèsties*. Ed. Pere Bohigas. Barcelona: Edicions 62, 1965.
Loewe, Raphael. Introduction. *Meshal Haqadmoni: Fables from the Distant Past*. By Isaac ibn Sahula. Ed. and trans. Raphael Loewe. Portland: Littman Library of Jewish Civilization, 2004. xv–cxxxi.
Lomax, Derek W. *The Reconquest of Spain*. London: Longman, 1978.
Lomba Fuentes, Joaquín. "El marco cultural de Pedro Alfonso." *Estudios sobre Pedro Alfonso de Huesca*. Ed. María Jesús Lacarra. Huesca: Instituto de Estudios Altoaragoneses, 1996. 147–75.
López Catro, Armando. "Refranes y cantares en *La Celestina*." *Voz y Letra: Revista de Literatura* 11.1 (2000): 27–38.

López Guzmán, Rafael J. *Arquitectura mudéjar: Del sincretismo medieval a las alternativas hispanoamericanas*. Manuales Arte Cátedra. Madrid: Cátedra, 2000.
López Morales, Humberto. "La estructura del narrador en *El Libro de buen amor*." Criado de Val. 38–50.
López-Morillas, Consuelo. "A Broad View of *Calila e Digna* Studies on the Occasion of a New Edition." *Romance Philology* 25.1 (1971): 85–96.
——. *El Corán de Toledo: Edición y estudio del manuscrito 235 de la Biblioteca de Castilla-La Mancha*. Oviedo: Biblioteca Árabo-Románica, Forthcoming.
——. "The Genealogy of the Spanish Qur'ān." *Journal of Islamic Studies* (Forthcoming).
——. "Language." Menocal et al. 33–59.
——. *The Qur'ān in Sixteenth-century Spain: Six morisco versions of Sūra 79*. London: Tamesis, 1982.
——. *Textos aljamiados sobre la vida de Mahoma: el profeta de los moriscos*. Salamanca: CSIC: Agencia Española de Cooperación Internacional, 1994.
Lourie, Elena. *Crusade and Colonisation: Muslims, Christians, and Jews in Medieval Aragon*. Aldershot, Hampshire, UK: Variorum, 1990.
Mabardi, Sabine. "Encounters of a Heterogeneous Kind: Hybridity in Cultural Theory." *Critical Studies* 13.1 (2000): 1–20.
Maccoby, Hyam. *Judaism on Trial: Jewish-Christian Disputations in the Middle Ages*. Portland: Vallentine Mitchell, 1996.
MacDonald, Elizabeth Drayson. "Translation or Re-Creation? A Textual Comparison between Two Sections of Juan Ruiz's *Libro De Buen Amor* and Their Latin and French Counterparts." *Forum for Modern Language Studies* 35.4 (1999): 372–85.
MacKay, Angus. *Spain in the Middle Ages: From frontier to empire, 1000–1500*. New York: St. Martin's Press, 1977.
Macpherson, Ian Richard. "Don Juan Manuel: The Literary Process." *Studies in Philology* 70 (1973): 1–18.
——, and Robert B. Tate. Introduction. Juan Manuel, *Estados* 7–48.
Magaletta, Giuseppe. *Musica e poesia alla corte di Federico II di Svevia*. Foggia: Bastogi, 1989.
Mallette, Karla. *The Kingdom of Sicily, 1100–1250: A Literary History*. Philadelphia: University of Pennsylvania Press, 2005.
Manrique, Nelson. *Vinieron los sarracenos—: El universo mental de la conquista de América*. Lima: Desco, 1993.
Maravall, José Antonio. *El Concepto de España en la Edad Media*. Madrid: Instituto de Estudios Políticos, 1954.
——. *Estudios de historia del pensamiento español*. Madrid: Ediciones Cultura Hispánica, 1983.
——. "La idea de la Reconquista en España durante la Edad Media." *Arbor* 101.27 (1954): 1–37.
——. *La literatura picaresca desde la historia social: (siglos XVI y XVII)*. Madrid: Taurus, 1986.
Marín, Diego. "El elemento oriental en Don Juan Manuel: síntesis y revaluación." *Comparative Literature* 7 (1955): 1–14.
Marmo, Vittorio. *Dalle fonti alle forme: Studi sul* Libro de buen amor. Naples: Liguori, 1983.
Márquez-Villanueva, F. *El concepto cultural alfonsí*. Madrid: Mapfre, 1994.
——. "Hispano-Jewish Cultural Interactions: A Conceptual Framework." *Encuentros and Desencuentros: Spanish-Jewish Cultural Interaction Throughout History*. Ed. Carlos Carrete Parrondo and Avivah Doron. Tel Aviv: University Publication Projects, 2000. 13–25.
——. "La nueva biografía de Juan Ruiz." *Morada de la palabra: Homenaje a Luce y Mercedes López-Baralt*. Ed. William Mejías López. Vol. 1. Arecibo: University of Puerto Rico, 2002. 33–51.
——. "Nuevos Arabismos en un pasaje del *Libro de buen amor* (941 Ab)." Criado de Val. 202–07.

——. *Santiago: Trayectoria de un mito*. Barcelona: Edicions Bellaterra, 2004.
Marsan, Rameline E. *Itinéraire espagnol du conte médiéval, VIIe–XVe siècles*. Paris: Klincksieck, 1974.
Martin, Hervé. *Le métier de prédicateur a la fin du moyen age (1350–5320)*. Paris: Les Editions du Cerf, 1988.
Martín Pascual, Llúcia. *La tradició animalística en la literatura catalana medieval*. Valencia: Generalitat Valenciana, 1996.
Martinez, Manuel Luis. "Telling the Difference between the Border and the Borderlands: Materiality and Theoretical Practice." *Globalization on the Line: Culture, Capital, and Citizenship at U.S. Borders*. Ed. Claudia Sadowski-Smith. New York, NY: Palgrave, 2002. 53–68.
Martínez Loscos, Carmen. *Orígenes de la medicina en Aragón: los médicos árabes y judíos*. Saragossa: Institución "Fernando el Católico" (CSIC), 1958.
Martínez Ruiz, Juan. "La tradición hispano-árabe en el *Libro de buen amor*." Criado de Val. 187–201.
Marzūq, ʿAbdallāh. *The Wisdom of Luqmān* [Arabic]. Riyadh: Dār al-Muslīm, 1998.
McDonald, M.V. "Animal-Books as a Genre in Arabic Literature." *Bulletin of the British Society for Middle Eastern Studies* 15.1–2 (1988): 3–10.
Memmi, Albert. *The Colonizer and the Colonized*. Trans. Howard Greenfeld. Boston: Beacon Press, 1967.
——. *Portrait du colonisé*. Paris: Gallimard, 1985.
——. *Portrait of a Jew*. Trans. Judy Hyun. New York: Orion Press, 1962.
Menéndez y Pelayo, Marcelino. *Orígenes de la novela*. Vol. 1. Buenos Aires: Espasa-Calpe, 1946.
Menéndez Pidal, Gonzalo. "Como trabajaron las escuelas alfonsíes." *Nueva Revista de Filología Hispánica* 5.4 (1951): 363–80.
Menéndez Pidal, Ramón. *La España del Cid*. 2 vols. Madrid: Editorial Plutarco, 1929.
Menocal, María Rosa. *The Arabic Role in Medieval Literary History: A Forgotten Heritage*. Philadelphia: University of Pennsylvania Press, 1987.
——. "Beginnings." *The Cambridge History of Spanish Literature*. Ed. David T. Gies. Cambridge: Cambridge University Press, 2004. 58–74.
——. "Bottom of the Ninth: Bases Loaded." *La corónica* 17.1 (1988): 32–40.
——. "Life Itself: Storytelling as the Tradition of Openness in the *Conde Lucanor*." *Oral Tradition and Hispanic Literature: Essays in Honor of Samuel M. Armistead*. Ed. Michael M. Caspi. New York: Garland, 1995. 469–95.
——. *The Ornament of the World*. Boston: Little Brown, 2002.
——. *Shards of Love: Exile and the Origins of the Lyric*. Durham: Duke University Press, 1994.
——, Raymond P. Scheindlin, and Michael Anthony Sells. *The Literature of Al-Andalus, The Cambridge History of Arabic Literature*. Cambridge: Cambridge University Press, 2000.
Meyerson, Mark D. *A Jewish Renaissance in Fifteenth-century Spain*. Princeton: Princeton University Press, 2004.
——. The Muslims of Valencia in the Age of Fernando and Isabel: Between Coexistence and Crusade. Berkeley: University of California, 1991.
Michael, Ian. "The Function of the Popular Tale in the *Libro de Buen Amor*." *Libro de Buen Amor Studies*. Ed. G.B. Gybbon-Monypenny. A. London: Támesis, 1970. 177–218.
Michaelsen, Scott, and David E. Johnson. *Border Theory: The Limits of Cultural Politics*. Minneapolis: University of Minnesota Press, 1997.
Michalski, André. "La parodia hagiográfica y el dualismo Eros-Thanatos en el *Libro de Buen Amor*." Criado de Val. 57–77.
Mignolo, Walter D. *Local Histories/Global Designs: Coloniality, Subaltern Knowledges, and Border Thinking*. Princeton, NJ: Princeton University Press, 2000.
Millá y Fontanals, Manuel. *De los trovadores en España*. Barcelona: Consejo Superior de Investigación Científica (CSIC), 1966.

——. *Estudios sobre historia, lengua y literatura de Cataluña*. Ed. Marcelino Menéndez Pelayo. Vol. 3. *Obras completas*. 8 vols. Barcelona: A. Verdaguer, 1890.

Millás Vallicrosa, José María. "La aportación astronómica de Pedro Alfonso." *Sefarad* 3 (1943): 65–105.

——. "Moshé Sefaradí's Works on Astronomy." [Hebrew] *Tarbiz* 9 (1937): 55–64.

——. "Review of 'The Polemic of Shelomo Bonafed and the Notables of Zaragoza' [Hebrew], by Ḥayim Schirmann. *Qobets ʿal yad* 14.4 (1947–48): 8–72." *Sefarad* 9.1 (1949): 241–43.

——. "San Vicente Ferrer y el Antisemitismo." *Sefarad* 10 (1950): 182–84.

Miller, Elaine. *Jewish Multiglossia: Hebrew, Arabic and Castilian in Medieval Spain*. Newark, DE: Juan de la Cuesta, 2000.

Miquel i Planas, Ramón. *Cançoner satírich valenciá*. Barcelona: Biblioteca Catalana, 1911.

——. "Noticia preliminaria." *Spill o Libre de consells de Jaume Roig: Poema satírich del segle XV*. Ed. Ramon Miquel i Planas. 2 vols. Barcelona: Biblioteca Catalana, 1929–1950. ix–lxxi.

Moffitt, John F. *The Islamic Design Module in Latin America: Proportionality and the Techniques of Neo-Mudéjar Architecture*. Jefferson, N.C.: McFarland & Co., 2004.

Monroe, James T. *The Art of Badīʿ az-Zamān al-Hamadhānī as Picaresque Narrative*. Beirut: Center for Arab and Middle East Studies, American University of Beirut, 1983.

——. "Maimonides on the Mozarabic Lyric." *La corónica* 17.2 (1988–89): 18–32.

——. "The Mystery of the Missing Mantle: The Poet as Wittol? (Ibn Quzmān's *Zajal* 20)." *Journal of Arabic Literature* 37.1 (2006): 1–45.

——. Preliminary Study. *Al-Maqāmāt al-Luzūmīyya*. By Abū l-Ṭāhir Muḥammad ibn Yūsuf al-Saraqusṭī. Trans. Monroe. 1–79.

——. "Salmà, el toro abigarrado, la doncella medrosa, Ka'b Al Ahbar y el conocimiento del árabe de Don Juan Manuel: Prolegómenos al 'Zejel num. 148' de Ibn Quzman." *Nueva Revista de Filología Hispánica* 36 (1988): 853–78.

Montêquin, François-Auguste de. *Muslim Architecture of the Iberian Peninsula: Eastern and Western sources for Hispano-Islamic Building Arts*. West Cornwall, CT: Locust Hill Press, 1987.

Montiel, Isidoro. *Historia y bibliografía del "Libro de Calila y Dimma"*. Madrid: Editora Nacional, 1975.

Morag, Shelomo. "The Jewish Communities of Spain and the Living Traditions of the Hebrew Language." *Moreshet Sepharad: The Sephardi Legacy*. Ed. Haim Beinart. Jerusalem: Magnes, 1992. 103–14.

Morel-Fatio, Alfred. "Rapport sur une mission philologique à Valencie suivi d'une étude sur le *Livre des femmes*, poème du XVᵉ siècle, de Maître Jaume Roig." *Bibliothèque de l'École de Chartres* 45 (1884 and 1885): 630–54; 108–29.

Morón Arroyo, Ciriaco. "Practical Intelligence: Don Juan Manuel." *Languages of Power in Islamic Spain*. Ed. Ross Brann. Bethesda, MD: CDL, 1997. 197–210.

Morreale, Margherita. "Apuntes bibliográficos para la iniciación al estudio de las traducciones bíblicas medievales en catalán." *Analecta Sacra Tarraconensia* 31–32 (1958): 271–90.

——. "Vernacular scriptures in Spain." *The Cambridge History of the Bible*. Ed. G.W.H. Lampe. Cambridge: Cambridge University Press, 1969. 465–91.

Morrison, Karl Frederick. *Conversion and Text: The Cases of Augustine of Hippo, Herman-Judah, and Constantine Tsatsos*. Charlottesville: University Press of Virginia, 1992.

——. *Understanding Conversion*. Charlottesville: University Press of Virginia, 1992.

Muhawi, Ibrahim, and Sharīf Kanaana. *Speak, Bird, Speak Again: Palestinian Arab Folktales*. Berkeley: University of California Press, 1989.

Murfin, Ross, and Supriya M. Ray. *The Bedford Glossary of Critical and Literary Terms*. Boston: Bedford/St. Martin's, 2003.

Naḥmanides. *The Writings of Our Teacher Moshe ben Naḥman* [Hebrew]. Ed. H.D. Chavel. Vol. 1. Jerusalem: Rav Kūk, 1963.

Narbona Vizcaíno, Rafael. *Valencia, municipio medieval. Poder político y luchas ciudadanas. 1239–1418.* Valencia: Ajuntament de Valencia, 1995.
Navarro Peiro, Ángeles. *Narrativa hispanohebrea: siglos XII–XV: introducción y selección de relatos y cuentos.* Córdoba: El Almendro, 1988.
——. "La versión hebrea de *Calila y Dimna* de Yaʿaqob ben Elʿazar." Targarona Borrás and Sáenz-Badillos 468–75.
Niederehe, Hans J. "Alfonso el Sabio y la fisonomía lingüística de la Península Ibérica de su época." *La lengua y la literatura en tiempos de Alfonso X. Actas del Congreso Internacional. Murcia, 5–10 Marzo 1984.* Ed. Fernando Cremona and Francisco J. Flores. Murcia: Universidad de Murcia, 1985. 415–32.
Nirenberg, David. *Communities of Violence: Persecution of Minorities in the Middle Ages.* Princeton: Princeton University Press, 1996.
——. "Enmity and Assimilation: Jews, Christians, and Converts in Medieval Spain." *Common Knowledge* 9.1 (2003): 137–55.
Norris, H.T. "Review of *Conversion to Islam in the Medieval Period: An Essay in Quantitative History*, by Richard W. Bulliet." *Bulletin of the School of Oriental and African Studies* 44.1 (1981): 162–63.
Nykl, A. R. "Arabic Phrases in *El Conde Lucanor.*" *Hispanic Review* 10.1 (1942): 12–17.
Obermeier, Anita. *The History and Anatomy of Auctorial Self-Criticism in the European Middle Ages.* Amsterdam: Rodopi, 1999.
O'Callaghan, Joseph F. *A History of Medieval Spain.* Ithaca: Cornell University Press, 1983.
——. *The Learned King: The Reign of Alfonso X of Castile.* Philadelphia: University of Pennsylvania Press, 1993.
——. *Reconquest and crusade in medieval Spain.* Philadelphia: University of Pennsylvania Press, 2003.
Odber de Baubeta, Patricia Anne. *Anticlerical Satire in Medieval Portuguese Literature.* Lewiston, NY: Mellen, 1992.
O'Grady, Desmond. *The Golden Odes of Love: al-Mu'allaqat.* Cairo: American University in Cairo Press, 1997.
Olivelle, Patrick. Introduction. *Pañcatantra: The Book of India's Folk Wisdom.* New York: Oxford University Press, 1997. ix–xlv.
Omidsalar, Maḥmoud. "Storytellers in Classical Persian Texts." *Journal of American Folklore* 97 (1984): 204–12.
Ortiz, Fernando. *Contrapunteo cubano del tabaco y el azúcar.* Ed. Enrico Mario Santí. Madrid: Cátedra: Música Mundana Maqueda, 2002.
Ould Mohamed Baba, Ahmed-Salem. *Estudio dialectológico y lexicológico del refranero andalusí de Abū Yahyā Azzajjālī.* Zaragoza: Universidad de Zaragoza, 1999.
Pagis, Dan. *Hebrew Poetry of the Middle Ages and the Renaissance.* Berkeley: University of California Press, 1991.
Pakter, Walter. *Medieval Canon Law and the Jews.* Ebelsbach: Gremler, 1988.
Palacios, Josep. *Poemes satírics del segle XV.* Valencia, 1974.
Palley, Julian. *The Ambiguous Mirror: Dreams in Spanish Literature.* Valencia: Albatros, 1983.
Panvini, Bruno. *Poeti italiani della corte di Federico II.* 2nd ed. Napoli: Liguori, 1994.
Pañcatantra: The Book of India's Folk Wisdom. Trans. Patrick Olivelle. New York: Oxford University Press, 1997.
Paredes, Américo. *A Texas-Mexican Cancionero: Folksongs of the Lower Border.* Urbana, Ill.: University of Illinois Press, 1976.
Parker, Margaret. *The Didactic Structure and Content of* El Libro de Calila e Digna. Miami: Ediciones Universal, 1978.
Patai, Raphael. *Arab Folktales from Palestine and Israel.* Detroit: Wayne State University Press, 1998.

Pavis, Patrice. *Dictionary of the Theatre: Terms, Concepts, and Analysis*. Trans. Christine Shantz. Toronto: University of Toronto Press, 1998.
Payne, Stanley G. *A History of Spain and Portugal*. Madison: University of Wisconsin Press, 1973.
Penzol, Pedro. *Las traducciones del "Calila e Dimna"*. Madrid: Imprenta de Ramona Velasco, viuda de P. Perez, 1931.
Pérès, Henri. *La poésie andalouse en arabe classique au XIe siècle*. 2nd ed. Paris: Librairie d'Amérique et d'Orient, 1937.
Pérez Castro, Federico. *Poesía secular hispano-hebrea*. Madrid: Consejo Superior de Investigaciones Científicas (CSIC), 1989.
Pérez-Cors, Empar. *Versos bruts: pomell de poesies escatològics*. Barcelona: Quaderns Crema, 1989.
Pérez Firmat, Gustavo. *Life on the Hyphen: the Cuban-American Way*. Austin: University of Texas Press, 1994.
Perry, Mary E., and Anne J. Cruz. *Cultural Encounters: the Impact of the Inquisition in Spain and the New World*. Berkeley: University of California Press, 1991.
Peters, J.T.R.M. *God's Created Speech*. Leiden: E.J. Brill, 1976.
Petrus Alfonsi. *Diálogo contra los judíos*. Trans. Esperanza Ducay. Ed. Klaus-Peter Miethe. Huesca: Instituto de Estudios Altoaragoneses, 1996.
——. *Die Kunst, vernüftig zu Leben (Disciplina clericalis)*. Trans. and ed. Eberhard Hermes. Zurich: Atemis Verlags, 1970.
——. "Disciplina clericalis." *Patrilogia latina cursus completus*. Ed. Jacques-Paul Migne. Cols. 671–706. Paris: Garnier, 1899.
——. *Disciplina clericalis*. Eds. Alfons Hilka and Werner Söderhjelm. Vol. 28, *Acta Societatis Scientiarum Fennicæ*. Helsinki, 1911.
——. *Disciplina clericalis*. Ed. and trans. Ángel González Palencia. Madrid: Consejo Superior de Investigaciones Científicas (CSIC), 1948.
——. *Disciplina clericalis*. Ed. and trans. María Jesús Lacarra. Zaragoza: Guara Editorial, 1980.
——. *The Disciplina Clericalis of Petrus Alfonsi*. Ed. Eberhard Hermes. Trans. P.R. Quarrie. Berkeley: University of California Press, 1977.
——. *The Scholar's Guide*. Trans. Joseph R. Jones and John E. Keller. Toronto: The Pontifical Institute of Medieval Studies, 1969.
PhiloBiblon: Electronic Bibliographies of Medieval Catalan, Galician, Portuguese, and Spanish Texts. Eds. Charles B. Faulhaber, Arthur Askins, Harvey Sharrer, and John May. Berkeley: Bancroft Library; Regents of the University of California, 1999. 19 Feb 2006. <http://sunsite.berkeley.edu/Philobiblon/phhm.html>.
Picard, Hans Rudolf. "Constitution et fonction du moi narrateur dans el *Libro De Buen Amor* de Juan Ruiz." *L'autoportrait en Espagne: Litterature et Peinture*. Ed. Guy Mercadier. Aix-en-Provence: Univ. de Provence, 1992. 7–16.
Pitarch, Vicent, and Lluís Gimeno. *Poesia eròtica i burlesca dels segles XV i XVI*. Valencia: E. Climent, 1982.
Poema De Fernán González. Ed. Juan Victorio. Madrid: Cátedra, 1998.
——. MS El Escorial: Monasterio, b.IV.21. Transcr. John S. Geary. *ADMYTE*.
Poema de Mio Cid. Ed. Ramón Menéndez Pidal. Madrid: Espasa-Calpe, 1975.
Powers, James F. *A Society Organized for War: The Iberian Municipal Militias in the Central Middle Ages, 1000–1284*. Berkeley: University of California Press, 1987.
Pratt, Mary Louise. *Imperial Eyes: Travel Writing and Transculturation*. London: Routledge, 1992.
Procter, Evelyn. *Alfonso X of Castile: Patron of Literature and Learning*. Oxford: Oxford University Press, 1951.
Pseudo-Aristotle. *Poridat de las Poridades*. Ed. Lloyd A. Kasten. Madrid: Hispanic Seminary of Medieval Studies, University of Wisconsin, 1957.

Pseudo-Ovid. *The Pseudo-Ovidian De Vetula*. Ed. Dorothy M. Robathan. Amsterdam: Adolf M. Hakkert, 1968.
——. *La Vieille*. Trans. Jehan Le Fèvre. Ed. Hippolyte Cocheris. Paris: Auguste Aubry, 1861.
Puyol y Alonso, Julio. *El Arcipreste de Hita*. Madrid: Sucesora de M. Minuesa de los Ríos, 1906.
Querol Faus, Fina. *La vida valenciana en el siglo XV: Un eco de Jaume Roig*. Valencia: Instituto de Estudios Ibéricos y Etnología, 1963.
Racconti esemplari di predicatori del due e trecento. Eds. Giorgio Varanini and Guido Baldassari. 3 vols. Rome: Salerno Editrice, 1993.
Rama, Angel. *Transculturación narrativa en América Latina*. Mexico City: Siglo Veintiuno, 1982.
Rambaldo, Ana. "La paradójica Aldara y la Maqamat Hispano-Hebrea." *Cuadernos Hispanoamericanos* 374 (1981): 450–53.
Ray, Jonathan. "Beyond Tolerance and Persecution: Reassessing Our Approach to Medieval Convivencia." *Jewish Social Studies* 11.2 (2005): 1–18.
——. *The Sephardic Frontier: The Reconquista and the Jewish Community in Medieval Iberia*. Ithaca: Cornell University Press, 2005.
Real Academia Española. *Diccionario de la lengua española*. 21st. ed. Madrid: Real Academia Española, 1992.
Recull de eximplis e miracles, gestes e faules e altres ligendes ordenades per A-B-C. Ed. Mariano Aguiló y Fuster. Barcelona: Verdaguer, 1881.
Reiss, Edmund. "Ambiguous Signs and Authorial Deceptions in Fourteenth-Century Fictions." *Sign, Sentence, Discourse: Language in Medieval Thought and Literature*. Eds. Julian N. Wasserman and Lois Roney. Syracuse: Syracuse University Press, 1989. 113–37.
Renan, Ernest. *Averroès et l'averoïsme*. 1852. Paris: Callman-Lévy, 1903.
Ribera y Tarragó, Julián. *Orígenes del justicia de Aragón*. Zaragoza: Comas Hermanos, 1897.
Riera i Sans, Jaume, and Eduard Feliu. *Disputa de Barcelona de 1263 entre mestre Mosse de Girona i fra Pau Cristià*. Barcelona: Columna, 1985.
Rimmon-Kenan, Shlomith. *Narrative Fiction: Contemporary Poetics*. London: Methuen, 1983.
Riquer, Martí de. *Història de la literatura catalana*. 10 vols. Barcelona: Edicions Ariel, 1964.
Robinson, Cynthia. "Mudéjar revisited." *Res* 43 (2003): 51–77.
——, and Leyla Rouhi, eds. *Under the Influence: Questioning the Comparative in Medieval Castile*. Leiden: E.J. Brill, 2005.
——, and Leyla Rouhi. Introduction. Robinson and Rouhi 1–18.
Rodríguez Adrados, Francisco, and Gert-Jan van Dijk. *History of the Graeco-Latin Fable*. 3 vols. Leiden: E.J. Brill, 1999.
Roig, Jaume. *Espill*. Ed. Anotònia Carré i Pons. Barcelona: Teide, 1994.
——. *Spill o Libre de consells de Jaume Roig: Poema satírich del segle XV*. Ed. Ramon Miquel i Planas. 2 vols. Barcelona: Biblioteca Catalana, 1929–1950.
——. *Spill o Libre de les dones per Mestre Jacme Roig*. Ed. Roc Chabás i Llorente. Barcelona: L'avenç, 1905.
Romano Ventura, David. *La ciencia hispanojudía*. Madrid: Mapfre, 1992.
——. "El papel judío en la transmisión de la cultura." *De historia judía hispánica*. Barcelona: Universitat de Barcelona, 1991. 431–54.
Rosen, Jonathan. *The Talmud and the Internet: A Journey between Worlds*. New York: Farrar, Straus, 2000.
Rosen, Tova. "On Tongues Being Bound and Let Loose: Women in Medieval Hebrew Literature." *Prooftexts: A Journal of Jewish Literary History* 8.1 (1988): 67–87.
——. "Sexual Politics in a Medieval Marriage Debate." *Exemplaria* 12.1 (2000): 157–84.

——. *Unveiling Eve: Reading Gender in Medieval Hebrew Literature*. Philadelphia: University of Pennsylvannia Press, 2003.
Roth, Norman. "Jewish Collaborators in Alfonso's Scientific Work." *Emperor of Culture: Alfonso X the Learned of Castile and His Thirteenth-Century Renaissance*. Ed. Robert I. Burns. Philadelphia: University of Pennsylvannia, 1990. 58–71.
——. "The 'Wiles of Women' Motif in the Medieval Hebrew Literature of Spain." *Hebrew Annual Review* 2 (1978): 145–66.
Rouse, Mary A., and Richard H. Rouse. *Authentic Witnesses: Approaches to Medieval Texts and Manuscripts*. Notre Dame, Ind.: University of Notre Dame Press, 1991.
Rubió i Lluch, Antoni. "Notes sobre la ciència Oriental a Catalunya." *Estudis Universitaris Catalans* 3 (1999): 485–88.
Rubió Vela, Agustín. *Epistolari de la València medieval*. Valencia: Institut Interuniversitari de Filologia Valenciana; Barcelona: Publicacions de l'Abadia de Montserrat, 1998.
Ruiz, Juan. *El libro de buen amor*. Ed. Alberto Blecua. Madrid: Cátedra, 1992.
——. *Libro de buen amor*. Ed. Joan Corominas. Madrid: Gredos, 1967.
Sadan, Joseph. "Un intellectuel juif au confluent de deux cultures: Yehūda al-Ḥarīzī et sa biographie arabe. " *Judíos y musulmanes en al-Andalus y el Magreb. Contactos intelectuales*. Ed. Maribel Fierro. Madrid: Casa de Velázquez, 2002. 105–51.
Saenger, Paul. "Reading in the Later Middle Ages." *A History of Reading in the West*. Ed. Guglielmo Cavallo and Roger Chartier. Amherst, MA: University of Massachusetts Press, 1999. 120–48.
Sáenz-Badillos, Ángel. "Participación de judíos en las traducciones de Toledo." *La escuela de traductores de Toledo*. Toledo: Diputación Provincial de Toledo, 1996. 65–70.
——. "Ṭodros frente a Ṭodros: Dos escritores hebreos de Toledo en el siglo XIII." *Jewish Studies at the Turn of the Century: Proceedings of the 6th EAJS Congress. Toledo, July 1998*. Eds. Judit Targarona Borrás and Angel Sáenz-Badillos. Vol. 1. Leiden: E.J. Brill, 1999. 504–12.
——, and Judit Targarona Borrás. *Diccionario de autores judíos: (Sefarad, siglos X–XV)*. Córdoba: Ediciones El Almendro, 1988.
Sáez, Emilio, and José Tranchs. "Juan Ruiz De Cisneros (1295/96–1351/53) autor del *Buen Amor*." Criado de Val. 365–70.
Sáez-Arance, Antonio. "Constructing Iberia: National Traditions and the Problem(s) of a Peninsular History." *European Review of History* 10.2 (2003): 189–202.
Saldívar, José David. *Border Matters: Remapping American Cultural Studies*. Berkeley: University of California Press, 1997.
Salisbury, Joyce E. *The Beast Within: Animals in the Middle Ages*. New York: Routledge, 1984.
Sánchez-Albornoz, Claudio. *España, Un Enigma Histórico*. Buenos Aires: Editorial Sudamericana, 1956.
——. "Originalidad creadora del Arcipreste frente a la última teoría sobre el *Buen amor*." *Estudios Polémicos*. Madrid: Espasa-Calpe, 1979. 258–75.
Santillana, Iñigo López de Mendoza. *Refranes que dizen las viejas tras el fuego*. Ed. Hugo O. Bizzarri. Kassel: Edition Reichenberger, 1995.
Santob de Carrión. *The Moral Proverbs of Santob De Carrión: Jewish Wisdom in Christian Spain*. Trans. T. Anthony Perry. Princeton: Princeton University Press, 1987.
——. *Proverbios Morales*. Ed. Ignacio González Llubera. Cambridge: Cambridge University Press, 1947.
——. *Proverbios Morales*. Ed. T. Anthony Perry. Madison: Hispanic Seminary of Medieval Studies, 1986.
Santos, José. "La disolución del 'yo' en el *Libro de buen amor*: La puesta en práctica de los límites de la expresión." *Romance Review* 5.1 (1995): 55–63.
Saperstein, Marc. *Decoding the Rabbis: A Thirteenth-century Commentary on the Aggadah*. Cambridge: Harvard University Press, 1980.
Sapir Abulafia, Anna. *Christians and Jews in Dispute: Disputational Literature and the Rise of Anti-Judaism in the West (c. 1000–1150)*. Aldershot, Hampshire: Ashgate, 1998.

Sautman, Francesca Canadé, Diana Conchado, and Giuseppe Carlo Di Scipio, eds. *Telling Tales: Medieval Narratives and the Folk Tradition*. New York: St. Martin's Press, 1998.
Scheindlin, Raymond P. *The Gazelle: Medieval Hebrew Poems on God, Israel, and the Soul*. Philadelphia: Jewish Publication Society, 1991.
——. *Wine, Women, & Death: Medieval Hebrew Poems on the Good Life*. Philadelphia: Jewish Publication Society, 1986.
Schippers, Arie. "Ibn Zabāra's *Book of Delight* (Barcelona, 1170) and the Transmission of Wisdom from East to West." *Frankfurter Judaistische Beiträge* 26 (1999): 149–61.
——. *Spanish Hebrew Poetry and the Arabic Literary Tradition: Arabic Themes in Hebrew Andalusian Poetry*. Leiden: E.J. Brill, 1994.
Schirmann, Jefim [Ḥayim]. *Hebrew Poetry in Spain and Provence* [Hebrew] 2 vols. Jerusalem; Tev Aviv: Mossad Bialik; Dvir, 1956.
——, and E. Fleischer. *Studies on Hebrew Poetry in Christian Spain and Southern France* [Hebrew]. Jerusalem: Y.L. Magnes, 1997.
Schreckenberg, Heinz. *Die Christliche Adversus-Judaeos Texte (11.–13. Jh.) mit einer Ikonographie des Judenthemas bis zum 4 Laterankonzil*. Frankfurt am Main: Peter Lang, 1991.
——. *Die Christlichen Adversus-Judaeos Texte und ihr literarisches und historisches Umfeld (1.–11. Jh.)*. Frankfurt am Main: Peter Lang, 1982.
Schwartzbaum, Hayim. "International Folkore motifs in Petrus Alfonsi's *Disciplina clericalis*." *Sefarad* 21 (1961): 267–99.
——. "International Folkore motifs in Petrus Alfonsi's *Disciplina clericalis*." *Sefarad* 22 (1962): 17–58 and 321–44.
——. "International Folkore motifs in Petrus Alfonsi's *Disciplina clericalis*." *Sefarad* 23 (1963): 54–73.
Scott Meisami, Julie. *Structure and Meaning in Medieval Arabic and Persian poetry: Orient Pearls*. London: RoutledgeCurzon, 2003.
——, and Paul Starkey, eds. *Encyclopedia of Arabic Literature*. 2 vols. London: Routledge, 1998.
Searle, John R. *Speech Acts: An Essay in the Philosophy of Language*. London: Cambridge University Press, 1969.
Seidenspinner-Núñez, Dayle. *The Allegory of Good Love: Parodic Perspectivism in the Libro De Buen Amor*. Berkeley: University of California Press, 1981.
——. "'¡Guay del que duerme solo!': The Discourse of Antifeminism and the Collapse of the Narrator in Arçipreste de Talavera." *Anclajes: Revista del Instituto de Análisis Semiótico del Discurso* 1.1 (1997): 159–77.
——. "Inflecting the *Converso* Voice: A Commentary on Recent Theories." *La corónica* 25.1 (1996): 6–18.
Sela, Shlomo. *Abraham Ibn Ezra and the Rise of Medieval Hebrew Science*. Leiden: E.J. Brill, 2003.
Sells, Michael Anthony. *Approaching the Qur'án: The Early Revelations*. Ashland, Ore.: White Cloud Press, 1999.
Sendebar. Ed. María Jesús Lacarra. Madrid: Cátedra, 1996.
Seniff, Dennis P. "'Así fiz yo de lo que oý': Orality, Authority, and Experience in Juan Manuel's *Libro de la caza, Libro infinido* and *Libro de las armas*." *Josep Maria Solà-Solé: Homage, homenaje, homenatge: Miscelánea de estudios de amigos y discípulos*. Eds. Antonio Torres-Alcalá, Victorio Agüera and Nathaniel B. Smith. Barcelona: Puvill Libros, 1984. 1: 91–109.
——. "Orality and Textuality in Medieval Castilian Prose." *Oral Tradition* 2.1 (1987): 150–71.
Septimus, Bernard. *Hispano-Jewish Culture in Transition: The Career and Controversies of Ramah*. Cambridge: Harvard University, 1982.
Shatzmiller, Joseph. *Jews, Medicine, and Medieval Society*. Berkeley: University of California Press, 1994.
Sherwood, Merriam. Introduction. *The Book of Delight*. Ibn Zabāra, trans. Hadas 3–43.
Šukr, Šakir Hādī. *Animals in Arabic Literature* [Arabic]. Beirut: Maktabat al-Nahda al-ʿarabīyya: ʿAlām al-kutub, 1985.

Siddiqi, Muhammad Zubair, and Abdal Hakim Murad. *Hadith Literature: Its Origin, Development and Special Features*. 2nd ed. Cambridge: The Islamic Texts Society, 1993.
Silver, Daniel. *Maimonidean Criticism and the Maimonidean Controversy*. Leiden: E.J. Brill, 1965.
Sims, Edna N. "Towards a More Complete Portrayal of Womankind." *Círculo: Revista de Cultura* 19 (1990): 165–72.
Sirera, Josep Lluís. *Història de la literatura valenciana*. Valencia: Edicions Alfons el Magnànim; Institució Valenciana d'Estudis i Investigació, 1995.
Slyomovics, Susan. *The Merchant of Art: An Egyptian Hilali Oral Epic Poet in Performance*. Berkeley: University of California Press, 1987.
Soellner, Rolf. *Shakespeare's Patterns of Self-Knowledge*. Columbus, OH: Ohio State University Press, 1972.
Solomon, Michael. *The Literature of Misogyny in Medieval Spain: the Arcipreste de Talavera and the* Spill. New York: Cambridge University Press, 1997.
Soto i Company, Ricard. "Repartiment i 'repartiments': l'ordenació d'un espai de colonització feudal a la Mallorca del segle XIII." *De al-Andalus a la sociedad feudal: los repartimientos bajomedievales*. Barcelona: CSIC Institución Milá y Fontanals, 1990. 1–51.
Le Speculum Laicorum. Ed. J.T. Welter. Paris: A. Picard, 1914.
Spitzer, Leo. "Note on the Poetic and the Empirical 'I' in Medieval Authors." *Romanische Literaturstudien 1936–1956*. Tubingen: Max Niemeyer Verlag, 1959. 100–112.
Stalls, Clay. *Possessing the Land: Aragon's Expansion into Islam's Ebro Frontier under Alfonso the Battler 1104–1134*. Leiden: E.J. Brill, 1995.
Steiger, Arnold. "El Conde Lucanor." *Clavileño* 4.23 (1953): 1–8.
Steiner, George. *After Babel: Aspects of Language and Translation*. 2nd ed. Oxford: Oxford University Press, 1992.
Steinsaltz, Adin. *The Essential Talmud*. Trans. Chaya Galai. New York: Basic Books, 1976.
Stock, Brian. *The Implications of Literacy*. Princeton: Princeton University Press, 1983.
Stross, Brian. "The Hybrid Metaphor: From Biology to Culture." *Journal of American Folklore* 112.445 (1999): 254–67.
Subirats, Eduardo, ed. *Américo Castro y la revisión de la memoria: El Islám en España*. Madrid: Ediciones Libertarias, 2003.
Taboada, Hernán G.H. *La sombra del Islam en la conquista de América*. Mexico City: Universidad Nacional Autónoma de México, 2004.
Tales of Sendebar. Mishle Sendabar. Trans. and Ed. Morris Epstein. Philadelphia: Jewish Publication Society of America, 1967.
Talmud Bavlī. Jerusalem: H. Vagshal, 1992.
Targarona Borrás, Judit, and Ángel Sáenz-Badillos, eds. *Jewish Studies at the Turn of the Twentieth Century: Proceedings of the 6th EASJ Congress. Toledo, July 1998*. Vol. 1. Leiden: E.J. Brill, 1999.
Taylor, Archer. *The Proverb*. Cambridge: Harvard University Press, 1931.
Taylor, Barry. "Raimundus De Biterris's *Liber Kalile et Dimne*: Notes on the Western Reception of an Eastern *Exemplum*-Book." *Cultures in Contact in Medieval Spain: Historical and Literary Essays Presented to L.P. Harvey*. Eds. David Hook and Barry Taylor. London: King's College London Medieval Studies, 1990. 183–203.
Thompson, Stith. *Motif-Index of Folk-Literature*. Bloomington: Indiana UP, 1955–58.
Tolan, John. "Los diálogos contra los Judíos." *Estudios sobre Pedro Alfonso de Huesca*. Ed. María Jesús Lacarra. Huesca: Instituto de Estudios Altoaragoneses, 1996. 181–230.
——. "Pedro Alfonso, precursor de la literatura apologética." *Diálogo contra los judíos*. Ed. María Jesús Lacarra. Huesca: Instituto de Estudios Altoaragoneses, 1996. ix–lvii.
——. *Petrus Alfonsi and His Medieval Readers*. Gainesville, FL: University of Florida, 1993.
Toro-Garland, Fernando de. "El Arcipreste protagonista literario del medievo español, el caso del 'Mal Arcipreste' del *Fernán González*." Criado de Val. 327–26.

Toubert, Pierre, and Agostino Paravicini Bagliani. *Federico II e le scienze*. Palermo: Selerio, 1994.
Toussaint, Manuel. *Arte mudéjar en América*. Mexico City: Porrúa, 1946.
Tronzo, William. *Intellectual Life at the Court of Frederick II Hohenstaufen*. Washington, D.C.: National Gallery of Art; University Press of New England, 1994.
Turmeda, Anselm de. *Disputa de L'ase*. Ed. Marcal Olivar. Barcelona: Barcino, 1993.
——. *Dispute de l'âne*. Ed. Armand Llinarès. Paris: J. Vrin, 1984.
Urbina, Eduardo. "Now You See It, Now You Don't: The Antithesis Corteza/Meollo in the *Libro De Buen Amor*." *Florilegium Hispanicum: Medieval and Golden Age Studies Presented to Dorothy Clotelle Clarke*. Eds. John S. Geary and Charles B. Faulhaber. Madison, WI: Hispanic Seminary of Medieval Studies, 1983. 139–50.
Valdeón Baruque, Julio, Josep M. Salrach i Marés, and Javier Zabalo Zabalegui. *Feudalismo y consolidación de los pueblos hispánicos (siglos XI–XV)*. Barcelona: Labor, 1980.
Vansina, Jan. *Oral Tradition as History*. Madison: University of Wisconsin Press, 1985.
Vellón i Lahoz, Xavier. "Literatura misògina i moral burguesa: la corporalitat com a espai de la sàtira a l'*Espill*." *Zeitschrift für Katalanistik: Revista d'Estudis Catalans* 9 (1996): 20–32.
Vendrell Gallostra, Francisca. "La actividad proselitista de Vicente Ferrer durante el reinado de Fernando I de Aragón." *Sefarad* 13 (1953): 87–104.
Vicente García, Luis Miguel. "La astrología en *El Libro de buen amor*: Fuentes y problemas sobre el uso de conceptos astrológicos en la literatura medieval española." *Revista de Literatura* 61.122 (1999): 333–47.
Viera, David J. "The Treatment of the Jews in Vincent Ferrer's Vernacular Sermons." *Fifteenth-Century Studies* 26 (2000): 215–24.
Vincent of Beauvais. *Speculum historiale*. Vol. 3. Graz: Akademische Druck, 1964–65.
Walfish, Barry. Esther in Medieval Garb: Jewish Interpretation of the Book of Esther in the Middle Ages. Albany: State University of New York Press, 1993.
Wallhead Munuera, Celia. "Three Tales from *El Conde Lucanor* and their Arabic Counterparts." *Juan Manuel Studies*. Ed. Ian Macpherson. London: Tamesis, 1977. 101–17.
Walsh, John K. *El libro de los doze sabios, o Tractado de la nobleza y lealtad (ca. 1237): Estudio y edicion*. Madrid: Real Academia Española, 1975.
Walter of Châtillon. *Alexandreis*. Ed. Marvin L. Colker. Patavii: In Aedibus Antenoreis, 1978.
——. *The Alexandreis of Walter of Châtillon: A Twelfth-Century Epic. A Verse Translation*. Trans. David Townsend. Philadelphia: University of Pennsylvania Press, 1996.
Wasserstein, David. *The Rise and Fall of the Party-Kings: Politics and Society in Islamic Spain 1002–1086*. Princeton: Princeton University Press, 1985.
Watt, W. Montgomery. *Free Will and Predestination in Early Islam*. London: Luzac, 1948.
Welter, J.T. *L'exemplum dans la littérature religieuse et didactique du moyen age*. Paris: Occitania, 1927.
——. Introduction. *La Tabula Exemplorum Secundum Ordinem Alphabeti*. i–lvi.
Westra, Haijo. "Medieval Worldviews and Cultural Policies." *Reflections on Cultural Policy: Past, Present and Future*. Eds. Evan Alderson et al. Calgary: Wilfrid Laurier, 1993.
Wiegers, Gerard Albert. *Islamic Literature in Spanish and Aljamiado: Yça of Segovia (fl. 1450), his antecedents and successors*. Leiden: E.J. Brill, 1994.
Williams, A. Lukyn. *Adversus Judaeos; A bird's-eye view of Christian apologiae until the Renaissance*. Cambridge: Cambridge University Press, 1935.
Williams, Mike. "The 'Speech Act Method': Studying Power and Influence in Conversation Interaction and a Critique of Conversation Analysis." *Sheffield Online Papers in Social Research* 6 (2002). 19 Feb. 2006. <http://www.shef.ac.uk/socst/Shop/mike2.pdf>.
Wolfson, Elliot R. *Through a Speculum That Shines: Vision and Imagination in Medieval Jewish Mysticism*. Princeton: Princeton University Press, 1994.
Wolfson, Harry Austryn. *Repercussions of the Kalam in Jewish Philosophy*. Cambridge: Harvard University Press, 1979.

——. *The Philosophy of the Kalam*. Cambridge: Harvard University Press, 1976.
Wright, Gwendolyn. *The Politics of Design in French Colonial Urbanism*. Chicago: University of Chicago Press, 1991.
Yahalom, Yoseph. "The Function of the Frame-Story in Hebrew Adaptations of the Maqamat" [Hebrew]. *Israel Levin Jubilee Volume: Studies in Hebrew Literature*. Ed. Reuven Tsur et al. Vol. 1. Tel Aviv: Katz Research Institute for Hebrew Literature, Faculty of Humanities, Tel-Aviv Univ, 1994. 135–54.
Yassif, Eli. *The Hebrew Folktale: History, Genre, Meaning*. Bloomington: Indiana University Press, 1999.
Young, Douglas C. "Wine and Genre: *Khamriyya* in the Andalusi *Maqama*." Hamilton et al. 87–99.
——. *Rogues and Genres: Generic Transformation in the Spanish Picaresque and Arabic Maqāma*. Newark, DE: Juan de la Cuesta, 2004.
Yūsuf, Muḥammad Khayr Ramaḍān. *Luqmān the Wise and His Wisdom* [Arabic]. 2nd ed. Damascus: Dār al-qalam, 1994.
Zahareas, Anthony N. *The Art of Juan Ruiz, Archpriest of Hita*. Madrid: Estudios de Literatura Española, 1965.
——, and Oscar Pereira. *Itinerario del Libro del Arcipreste: Glosas críticas al* Libro de buen amor. Madison: Hispanic Seminary of Medieval Studies, 1990.
Zink, Michel. *La prédication en langue romane avant 1300*. Paris: Champion, 1976.
Zubaidi, A.M. "The impact of the Qur'an and Hadith on Medieval Arabic Literature." *Arabic Literature to the End of the Umayyad Period*. Eds. A.F. Beeston, et al. Cambridge: Cambridge University Press, 1983. 322–43.
Zumthor, Paul. "Autobiographie au Moyen Age?" *Langue, Texte, Énigme*. Ed. Paul Zumthor. Paris: Seuil, 1975. 165–80.
Zwartjes, Otto. *Love Songs from al-Andalus: History, Structure and Meaning of the Kharja*. Leiden: E.J. Brill, 1998.

INDEX

Abanale, Abrayme, 201
ʿAbbāsid era, 14, 50; cultural florescence, 32; foundation of Caliphate in Baghdad, 91; literature of, 41; storytellers, 70
ʿAbd al-Jalīl ʿAlī, ʿAwadallah, 62 n. 33
See also poetry, oral epic, Egyptian
ʿAbd al-Raḥmān III, ʿUmayyad Caliph of Cordova, 160
Abenabad. *See* al-Muʿtamid ibn ʿAbbād of Seville
Abenardut, Jucef, 202; family, service to Alfonso XI, 163, 165. *See also* Ibn Ardut
Abū Dulaf, 69 n. 52, 72–73, 76
Abulafia, Ṭodros ben Judah Halevi, 88 n. 6, 162–63, 165; among Galician-Portuguese and Provençal poets, 162; at court of Alfonso X, 165 n. 22
Abulafia, Todros ben Joseph Halevi, 165 n. 22
acculturation, 3, 6–8; Andalusī-Castilian, 90
adab, 31, 32 n. 35, 33, 39, 65 n. 44; sayings attributed to Idrīs and Luqmān, 37 n. 40; versions of "The Two Townsfolk and the Countryman," 38
Adāb kabīr, 106
Adelantado de la frontera de Murcia, title held by Don Juan Manuel, 13, 15, 141, 151
adīb, 31, 39
Adversus judaeos, 26
Aesopic fable tradition. *See* fables, Aesopic
aesthetic sensibility, Christian, Jewish, Muslim, 10
Agazzari, Filippo degli. *See* Filippo degli Agazzari
aggadah, 76–85 *passim*; compared to *hadīṯ*, 78; invalid basis for legal argumentation, 78
ahl al-ḏimma, 7. *See also ḏimmī*
Airas de Santiago, João, 88 n. 6
ʿajamīyya, 214 n. 49, 224
al-Andalus, 2; center of convergence of narrative traditions, 41; Christian conquest of. *See* conquest of al-Andalus by Christians; prestige of in modern Arab world, 10 n. 23
Albertus Magnus, Saint, 181 n. 58
albuhera, 152, 152 n. 43
Alcocer, conquest of by Cid, 134
Alcoraz, battle of, 23
Alexandreis, 89 n. 8
Alexandrine verse, 89 n. 8, 157
al-Fakhar, Abraham, 210 n. 39
alfaquim, 161
al-Farabī, 94
Alf layla wa-layla. See Thousand and One Nights
Alfonso I 'the Battler', King of Aragon, 13; bilingual surrender treaties of, 19 n. 6; godfather of Petrus Alfonsi, 24
Alfonso II, King of Aragon, 161, 164, 201
Alfonso V 'the Magnanimous', King of Aragon, court at Naples, 199
Alfonso VII, King of Castile-Leon, 161
Alfonso VIII, King of Castile-Leon, 210 n. 39
Alfonso X 'the Learned', King of Castile-Leon, 13, 40, 85; author of *Cantigas de Santa Maria*, 99; as Infante or Crown Prince, 14, 85; patron of translation 25, 26, 94–100 *passim*, model for nephew Don Jon Manuel, 148; school of Arabic and Latin studies, 96; status of Jewish courtiers under, 161; translator of *Kalīla wa-Dimna*, 14, 32 n. 35, 131
Alfonso XI, King of Castile-Leon, 163, 165
al-Ghazālī, Abū Ḥāmid Muḥammad, 70, 72–73
algemia. See ʿajamīyya
al-Ḥakam II of Cordova, 150, 150 n. 37, 154
al-Hamaḏānī, Badīʿ al-Zamān, 42, 68, 186, 197–98
Alhambra, 135
Alhaquem. *See* al-Ḥakam II of Cordova
al-Ḥarīrī, Qāsim ibn ʿAlī, 12, 42, 51 n. 15, 184, 186, 193, 198, 204, 215–17
al-Ḥarīzī, Judah, 10, 12, 43, 43 n. 5, 47, 50, 158, 184–85, 193, 198, 201, 210, 217, 220, 232, 234; as canonical author, 12;